Praise for *Development with the Force.com Platform,* Third Edition

"The third edition of *Development with the Force.com Platform* is a must-read for anyone building enterprise applications in the cloud. Whether you're a CEO or a code ninja, Jason's insight into the Force.com platform is priceless. Why waste time learning from your own mistakes when you can learn from a master."

—**Howard Brown**, CEO and Founder, RingDNA

"I absolutely love this book. Jason has organized and written it in a simplified manner which makes the concepts easy to grasp for all audiences. I recommend it for any developer, consultant, or manager new to or currently working with the Force.com platform."

—**Stephanie Buchenberger**, Salesforce.com Delivery Manager, Appirio

"Solid evolution of an already well-written book! The layout, format and content make it a great tutorial for developers new to Apex as well as an informative and thorough reference for the most experienced architect. Very up to date to the platform with practical examples that will undoubtedly be used again and again."

—**Tom Hedgecoth**, Vice President, Global Consulting – sakonent

"This is still the best, most comprehensive book on the Force.com platform written. If you are new to Force.com, then this is the place to start. If you're an experienced developer, then this is the book you'll return to, over and over again. It's an essential companion for all Force.com developers."

—**Kevin Ott**, Senior Director, Engineering, Cisco Systems

"Jason touches on all the core elements of Force.com with a balanced blend of configuration and code. If you're new to the platform, this book will save you countless hours as you come up to speed—and if you're a seasoned expert you probably already own it. In either case, consider it required reading."

—**Adam Purkiss**, Principal Architect, MondayCall Solutions, and Organizer of the Bay Area Salesforce Developer User Group

"As a Salesforce system administrator and business analyst making the transition to Force.com developer, this book helps me daily. It's at the perfect level to cut through the vast amount of information available for developing on Force.com on the one hand, and get to the details needed to make my programs work on the other. I keep this book open perpetually, and it's the first place I go when I get stuck. The sample coding is strong and very reusable; it's the #1 tool in my box. I'd highly recommend *Development with the Force.com Platform* to anyone making the transition from Salesforce system administrator or business analyst to developer."

—**Gene Teglovic**, PSA Consultant, Financialforce.com

Development with the Force.com Platform

Building Business Applications in the Cloud

Third Edition

Jason Ouellette

✦✦Addison-Wesley

Upper Saddle River, NJ • Boston • Indianapolis • San Francisco
New York • Toronto • Montreal • London • Munich • Paris • Madrid
Cape Town • Sydney • Tokyo • Singapore • Mexico City

The publisher offers excellent discounts on this book when ordered in quantity for bulk purchases or special sales, which may include electronic versions and/or custom covers and content particular to your business, training goals, marketing focus, and branding interests. For more information, please contact:

U.S. Corporate and Government Sales
(800) 382-3419
corpsales@pearsontechgroup.com

For sales outside the United States, please contact:

International Sales
international@pearsoned.com

Library of Congress Control Number: 2013950238

Visit us on the Web: informit.com/aw

ISBN-13: 978-0-321-94916-5
ISBN-10: 0-321-94916-1

Text printed in the United States on recycled paper at Courier in Westford, Massachusetts.

First printing: December 2013

Editor-in-Chief
Mark Taub

Executive Editor
Laura Lewin

Development Editor
Songlin Qiu

Managing Editor
Kristy Hart

Project Editor
Andy Beaster

Copy Editor
Karen Annett

Indexer
Heather McNeill

Proofreader
Chuck Hutchinson

Technical Reviewers
Adam Purkiss
Gene Teglovic

Publishing Coordinator
Olivia Basegio

Cover Designer
Chuti Prasertsith

Compositor
Nonie Ratcliff

For Landon

Contents at a Glance

1 Introducing Force.com   1

2 Database Essentials   21

3 Database Security   71

4 Business Logic   99

5 Advanced Business Logic   143

6 User Interfaces   185

7 Advanced User Interfaces   233

8 Mobile User Interfaces   263

9 Batch Processing   281

10 Integration with Force.com   301

11 Advanced Integration   339

12 Social Applications   369

Index   387

Table of Contents

1 Introducing Force.com   1

Force.com in the Cloud Computing Landscape   1

Platform as a Service (PaaS)   2

Force.com as a Platform   4

Force.com Services   7

Inside a Force.com Project   9

Project Selection   9

Team Selection   11

Lifecycle   12

Tools and Resources   15

Sample Application: Services Manager   17

Background   17

User Roles   18

Development Plan   19

Summary   19

2 Database Essentials   21

Overview of Force.com's Database   21

Objects   22

Fields   23

Relationships   25

Query Language   26

Data Integration   29

Working with Custom Objects   32

Force.com Developer Edition   32

Tools for Custom Objects   33

Object Creation   35

Field Creation   38

Entering and Browsing Data   41

Additional Database Features   43

Sample Application: Data Model   49

Data Model Design Goals   49

Data Model Specification   50

Implementing the Data Model   58

Importing Data   64

Summary   69

3   **Database Security   71**

Overview of Database Security   71

Object-Level Security   74

Profiles   74

Permission Sets   76

Field-Level Security   77

Record-Level Security   79

Record Ownership   79

User Groups   80

Sharing Model   80

Sample Application: Securing Data   84

Designing the Security Model   85

Implementing the Security Model   88

Testing the Security Model   94

Summary   98

4   **Business Logic   99**

Introduction to Apex   100

Introducing the Force.com IDE   101

Installation   101

Force.com Perspective   101

Force.com Projects   103

Problems View   103

Schema Explorer   103

Apex Test Runner View   103

Execute Anonymous View   104

Apex Language Basics   105

Variables   105

Operators   109

Arrays and Collections   110

Control Logic   113

Object-Oriented Apex   117

Understanding Governor Limits   120

Database Integration in Apex   120

   Database Records as Objects   121

   Database Queries   122

   Persisting Database Records   128

   Database Triggers   130

   Database Security in Apex   133

Debugging Apex Using Developer Console   133

   Checkpoints   133

   Execution Logs   134

Unit Tests in Apex   136

   Test Methods   136

   Test Data   136

   Running Tests   137

Sample Application: Validating Timecards   138

   Force.com IDE Setup   138

   Creating the Trigger   138

   Unit Testing   140

Summary   142

5 Advanced Business Logic   143

Aggregate SOQL Queries   144

   Aggregate Functions   144

   Grouping Records   145

   Grouping Records with Subtotals   146

Additional SOQL Features   148

   Inner Join and Outer Join   148

   Semi-Join and Anti-Join   150

   Multi-Select Picklists   154

Salesforce Object Search Language (SOSL)   154

   SOSL Basics   155

   SOSL in Apex   155

Transaction Processing   156

   Data Manipulation Language (DML) Database Methods   157

   Savepoints   159

   Record Locking   161

Apex Managed Sharing   162

Sharing Objects   162

Creating Sharing Rules in Apex   163

Sending and Receiving Email   168

Sending Email   168

Receiving Email   172

Dynamic Apex   174

Dynamic Database Queries   175

Schema Metadata   177

Dynamic Instance Creation   179

Custom Settings in Apex   180

Sample Application: Adding Email Notifications   181

Summary   183

6 User Interfaces   185

Introduction to Visualforce   186

Overview of Visualforce   186

Getting Started with Visualforce   188

Visualforce Controllers   191

Standard Controllers   191

Custom Controllers   193

Controller Extensions   197

View Components   198

View Component Basics   198

Data Components   200

Action Components   203

Primitive Components   204

Force.com-Styled Components   205

Force.com User Interface Components   208

Visualforce and the Native User Interface   209

Standard Pages   210

Standard Buttons   213

Page Layouts   213

Custom Buttons and Links   215

Custom Tabs   215

Visualforce in Production   215

   Debugging and Tuning   215

   Security   218

   Error Handling   220

   Governor Limits   221

   Unit Tests   222

Sample Application: Skills Matrix   222

   Basic Implementation   224

   Full Implementation   224

   Implementation Walk-Through   225

Summary   232

7   Advanced User Interfaces   233

Asynchronous Actions   233

   Partial Page Refresh   234

   Action as JavaScript Function   235

   Action as Timed Event   237

   Action as JavaScript Event   237

   Indicating Action Status   238

Modular Visualforce   240

   Static Resources   241

   Inclusion   242

   Composition   242

   Custom Visualforce Components   244

Dynamic Visualforce   246

   Dynamic Field References   246

   Component Generation   248

Single-Page Applications in Force.com   250

   JavaScript Remoting   250

   Force.com with AngularJS   251

Introduction to Force.com Sites   254

   Enabling and Creating a Site   254

   Security Configuration   255

   Adding Pages to a Site   256

   Authenticating Users   257

Sample Application: Enhanced Skills Matrix   258

Summary   262

8 Mobile User Interfaces   263

Overview of Salesforce Mobile Technology   263

Salesforce Applications   264

Custom Applications   265

Getting Started with Mobile Web Applications   267

Frameworks   268

Data Access   269

Deployment   270

Sample Application: Mobile Timecard Entry   272

Summary   279

9 Batch Processing   281

Introduction to Batch Apex   282

Batch Apex Concepts   282

Understanding the `Batchable` Interface   283

Applications of Batch Apex   284

Getting Started with Batch Apex   285

Developing a Batch Apex Class   285

Working with Batch Apex Jobs   286

Using Stateful Batch Apex   289

Using an Iterable Batch Scope   290

Limits of Batch Apex   292

Testing Batch Apex   293

Scheduling Batch Apex   293

Developing Schedulable Code   293

Scheduling Batch Apex Jobs   294

Sample Application: Missing Timecard Report   296

Creating the Custom Object   297

Developing the Batch Apex Class   298

Testing the Missing Timecard Feature   299

Summary   300

10 Integration with Force.com   301

Apex Callouts   301

Calling RESTful Services from Apex   302

Calling SOAP Services from Apex   304

Calling into Force.com Using REST   306

Getting Started with Force.com REST API   306

Force.com REST API Walk-Through   308

Creating Custom Apex REST Web Services   312

Calling into Force.com Using SOAP   314

Understanding Force.com SOAP API   314

Using the Enterprise API   322

Creating Custom Apex SOAP Web Services   326

Sample Application: Anonymous Benchmarking   329

Visualforce Page Design   330

Visualforce Controller Design   331

Integrating the SOAP Web Service   333

Sample Implementation   335

Summary   338

11 Advanced Integration   339

Introduction to the Force.com Streaming API   340

Overview   340

Getting Started with Force.com Streaming API   341

Working with the Force.com Bulk API   344

Overview   345

Importing Records   346

Exporting Records   347

Getting Started with Force.com Canvas   349

Overview   349

Getting Started with Force.com Canvas   350

Introduction to the Force.com Tooling API   354

Overview   355

Getting Started with Force.com Tooling API   355

Understanding the Force.com Metadata API   360

Overview   360

Getting Started with the Metadata API   361

Sample Application: Database Integration   363

Integration Scenario   363

Implementation Strategy   363

Sample Implementation   364

Summary   366

12 Social Applications   369

Overview of the Chatter Data Model   370

  Chatter Posts   370

  Chatter Comments   374

  Feed-Tracked Changes   376

  Followed Records   376

Using Chatter in Apex   378

Introduction to the Chatter REST API   379

Working with Chatter Visualforce Components   380

Sample Application: Follow Project Team   382

Summary   386

Index   387

Acknowledgments

There are many people to thank for this book.

- **Laura Lewin:** Laura is an Executive Editor at Pearson. She's the person I email when I'm late on a chapter to apologize and offer unique excuses. No matter how friendly her response, which is always extremely friendly, the exchange helps pressure and shame me into working harder to meet the deadlines.

- **Adam Purkiss, Gene Teglovic:** The technical reviewers for this edition have really impressed me with what they caught in the draft. They verified all of the code listings and made countless suggestions for improvement throughout.

- **Songlin Qiu:** Songlin is a Development Editor at Pearson. There are no figure/listing numbering, styling, grammatical, or consistency problems that go unnoticed when she's on the job.

- **Olivia Basegio:** Olivia is an Editorial Assistant at Pearson. She's a big part of making the publishing process fairly painless.

- **Kavindra Patel, Nick Tran:** These two work at Salesforce.com and have been longtime supporters of the book, especially this third edition. I can't thank them enough.

- **Jay Gauthier:** Jay is the VP of R&D at Software AG. His detailed feedback on the second edition of this book drove some of the improvements found in this edition.

- **Gretchen, Mark, Tom, and Nate:** Writing this book made me true to my panda name, so +1,000 for your associated pain and suffering. Now that it's done, I need a new name, like Well-Tempered Panda.

- **Tracey:** Thank you for supporting me as always, checking on me to see if I'm still alive in my writing chair, and making "rocket fuel" (iced coffee), which lost its kick somewhere around Chapter 6.

About the Author

Jason Ouellette is a SaaS entrepreneur and independent technology consultant with 17 years of experience in the enterprise software industry, including 9 years of hands-on work with Salesforce.com. He is currently CTO and Co-Founder of SocialPandas, a SaaS product company focused on converting social data into actionable intelligence for salespeople. In his prior role as Chief Architect of Appirio, a leading Salesforce.com consultancy, he led the development of popular Salesforce AppExchange applications such as Cloud Sync, Cloud Factor, and Professional Services Enterprise. He was recognized by Salesforce as a Force.com MVP in 2011–2013, and Force.com Developer Hero in 2009. He has a B.S. in Information and Decision Systems from Carnegie Mellon University.

Preface

I wrote this book to help developers discover Force.com as a viable, even superior tool for building business applications.

I'm always surprised at how many developers I meet who aren't aware of Force.com as a platform. They know of Salesforce, but only that it's a CRM. Even those who have heard of Force.com are amazed when I describe what Appirio and other companies are building with it. "I didn't know you could do that with Force.com" is a common reaction, even to the simplest of things such as creating custom database tables.

Since the second edition of this book, Salesforce has delivered more than six major releases. This third edition refocuses the book on custom application development and away from "clicks not code"-style, configuration-driven features. It contains updates throughout to cover new capabilities such as Developer Console, JSON support, Streaming and Tooling APIs, REST integration, and support for MVC frameworks like AngularJS in Visualforce. It also features a new chapter: Chapter 8, "Mobile User Interfaces."

Although there are more cloud-based application development platforms than ever before, Force.com continues to offer unique and outstanding value for business applications. With its core strength in customer data management, deep set of thoughtfully integrated features, and support for open standards, Force.com can save you significant time and effort throughout the software development lifecycle.

Key Features of This Book

This book covers areas of Force.com relevant to developing applications in a corporate environment. It takes a hands-on approach, providing code examples and encouraging experimentation. It includes sections on the Force.com database, Apex programming language, Visualforce user interface technology, integration to other systems, and supporting features such as workflow and analytics. SFA, CRM, customer support, and other prebuilt applications from Salesforce are not discussed, but general Force.com platform skills are helpful for working in these areas as well. The book does not cover cloud computing in general terms. It also avoids comparing Force.com with other technologies, platforms, or languages. Emphasis is placed on understanding Force.com on its own unique terms rather than as a database, application server, or cloud computing platform.

Although Force.com is a commercial service sold by Salesforce, all the material in this book was developed using a free Force.com Developer Edition account. Additionally, every feature described in this book is available in the free edition.

Throughout the text, you will see sidebar boxes labeled Note, Tip, or Caution. Notes explain interesting or important points that can help you understand key concepts and techniques. Tips are little pieces of information that will help you in real-world situations, and often offer shortcuts to make a task easier or faster. Cautions provide information about detrimental performance issues or dangerous errors. Pay careful attention to Cautions.

Target Audience for This Book

This book is intended for application developers who use Java, Ruby, or other high-level languages to build Web and rich client applications for end users. It assumes knowledge of relational database design and queries, Web application development using HTML and JavaScript, and exposure to Web services.

Code Examples for This Book

The code listings in this book are available on Github: http://goo.gl/fjRqMX. They are also available as a Force.com IDE project, also freely available on Github: https://github.com/jmouel/dev-with-force-3e.

Editor's Note: We Want to Hear from You!

As the reader of this book, you are our most important critic and commentator. We value your opinion and want to know what we're doing right, what we could do better, what areas you'd like to see us publish in, and any other words of wisdom you're willing to pass our way.

You can email or write me directly to let me know what you did or didn't like about this book—as well as what we can do to make our books stronger.

Please note that I cannot help you with technical problems related to the topic of this book, and that due to the high volume of mail I receive, I might not be able to reply to every message.

When you write, please be sure to include this book's title and author as well as your name and phone number or email address. I will carefully review your comments and share them with the author and editors who worked on the book.

Email: laura.lewin@pearson.com

Mail: Laura Lewin
          Executive Editor
          Addison-Wesley/Pearson Education, Inc.
          75 Arlington St., Ste. 300
          Boston, MA 02116

1

Introducing Force.com

This chapter introduces the concepts, terminology, and technology components of the Force.com plat-form and its context in the broader Platform as a Service (PaaS) landscape. The goal is to provide context for exploring Force.com within a corporate software development organization. If any of the following sentences describe you, this chapter is intended to help:

- *You have read about cloud computing or PaaS and want to learn how Force.com compares with other technologies.*

- *You want to get started with Force.com but need to select a suitable first project.*

- *You have a project in mind to build on Force.com and want to learn how you can leverage existing development skills and processes.*

This chapter consists of three sections:

- ***Force.com in the cloud computing landscape**—Learn about PaaS and Force.com's unique features as a PaaS solution.*

- ***Inside a Force.com project**—Examine how application development with Force.com differs from other technologies in terms of project selection, technical roles, and tools.*

- ***Sample application**—A sample business application is referenced throughout this book to provide a concrete basis for discussing technical problems and their solutions. In this chapter, the sample application's requirements and use cases are outlined, as well as a development plan, mapped to chapters of the book.*

Force.com in the Cloud Computing Landscape

Phrases like *cloud computing* and *Platform as a Service* have many meanings put forth by many vendors. This section provides definitions of the terms to serve as a basis for understanding Force.com and comparing it with other products on the market. With this background, you can make the best choice for your projects, whether that is Force.com, another PaaS product, or your own in-house infrastructure.

Platform as a Service (PaaS)

The platform is infrastructure for the development and deployment of software applications. The functionality of a platform's infrastructure differs widely across platform vendors, so this section focuses on a handful of the most well-known vendors, those who have helped to pioneer the concept of PaaS itself. The suffix "as a Service" (aaS) means that the platform exists "in the cloud," accessible to customers via the Internet. Many variations exist on this acronym, most notably SaaS (Software as a Service) and IaaS (Infrastructure as a Service). PaaS sits in the middle of these two, a multiplying force for developers to leverage the cloud itself to build and run the next generation of cloud-enabled services.

PaaS is a category within the umbrella of cloud computing. *Cloud computing* is a phrase to describe the movement of computing resources away from physical data centers or servers in a closet in your company and into the network, where they can be provisioned, accessed, and deprovisioned instantly. You plug a lamp into an electrical socket to use the electrons in your region's power grid. Running a diesel generator in your basement is usually not necessary. You trust that the power company is going to provide that service, and you pay the company as you use the service. Likewise with the wide availability of high-speed Internet connectivity, cloud computing has become as practical as centralized power generation.

Cloud computing as a general concept spans every conceivable configuration of infrastructure, well outside the scope of this book. The potential benefits are reduced complexity and cost versus a traditional approach. The traditional approach is to invest in infrastructure by acquiring new infrastructure assets and staff or redeploying or optimizing existing investments. Cloud computing provides an alternative, and PaaS in particular strives to lower the cost of developing and deploying applications through the simplification and centralization of commodity hardware and software infrastructure. The following subsections introduce the mainstream PaaS products, those focused on application developers rather than bloggers or other users, and include brief descriptions of their functionality. Consult the Web sites of each product for further information.

Amazon Web Services

Amazon Web Services refers to a family of cloud computing products. The most relevant to PaaS is Elastic Beanstalk, a platform for running Java applications that provides load balancing, auto-scaling, and health monitoring. The platform is actually built on several other Amazon Web Services products that can be independently configured by advanced users, with the most significant being Elastic Compute Cloud (EC2). EC2 is a general-purpose computing platform, not limited to running Java programs. You can provision virtual instances of Windows or Linux machines at will, loading them with your own custom operating-system image or one prebuilt by Amazon or the community. These instances run until you shut them down, and you are billed for usage of resources such as the central processing unit (CPU), disk, and network.

A raw machine with an operating system (OS) on it is a great start, but to build a business application requires you to install, manage access to, maintain, monitor, patch and upgrade, back up, plan to scale, and generally care and feed in perpetuity an application platform on the EC2 instance. Many of these tasks are still required of Amazon's higher-level Elastic Beanstalk offering. If your organization has the skills to build on .NET, Java 2 Platform Enterprise Edition (J2EE), a LAMP stack (for example, Linux, Apache, MySQL, and PHP), or other application stacks, plus the OS, database administration, and information technology (IT) operations experience, Amazon's virtual servers in the cloud could be a strong alternative to running your own servers in-house.

Amazon provides various other products that complement Elastic Beanstalk and EC2. These include Simple Queue Service for publish-and-subscribe-style integration between applications, Simple DB for managing schemaless data, and Simple Storage Service, a content repository.

Google Cloud Platform

Google Cloud Platform is the name for a family of cloud services from Google. Of all of them, App Engine is the closest to a PaaS. It's designed to host Web applications. App Engine is like having an unlimited number of servers in the cloud working for you, preconfigured with a distributed data store and Python, Java, Go, or PHP-based application server. It's much like Amazon's Elastic Beanstalk but focused on providing a higher-level application platform. App Engine includes tools for managing the data store, monitoring your site and its resource consumption, and debugging and logging. Like Amazon, Google also offers access to raw computing resources via Google Compute Engine, their answer to EC2.

App Engine is free for a set amount of storage and page views per month. Developers requiring more storage or bandwidth for their applications can purchase it by setting a maximum daily dollar amount they're willing to spend, divided into five buckets: CPU time, bandwidth in, bandwidth out, storage, and outbound email.

Windows Azure

Windows Azure is Microsoft's cloud computing initiative. It provides a wide variety of IaaS products such as virtual machines, storage, SQL database, identity, cache, service bus, and a content delivery network. Windows Azure is much lower level than Google App Engine or Amazon Elastic Beanstalk. It includes services that would be useful in building an application, but hosting the application itself is a manual process. For example, you would need to provision a virtual machine to run Windows, place your .NET-based application there, and leverage a Windows Azure SQL Database for structured storage.

Force.com

Force.com is targeted toward corporate application developers and independent software vendors. Unlike the other PaaS offerings, it does not expose developers directly to its own infrastructure. Developers do not provision CPU time, disk, or instances of running operating systems. Instead, Force.com provides a custom application platform centered around the relational database, one resembling an application server stack you might be familiar with from working with .NET, J2EE, or LAMP.

Although it integrates with other technologies using open standards such as Simple Object Access Protocol (SOAP) and Representational State Transfer (REST), the programming languages and metadata representations used to build applications are proprietary to Force.com. This is unique among the PaaS products and comes with a learning curve. The payoff for learning Force.com is a significantly higher level of abstraction than other PaaS products, ideally resulting in higher productivity for developers.

To extend the reach of Force.com to a larger developer community, Salesforce provides a subset of Force.com called Database.com. Database.com includes much of Force.com but without the user interface (UI) technologies and CRM-oriented data model. It's priced per user, record, and transaction. Along the same lines, Salesforce offers Heroku to developers who want to work directly with standard databases and development languages but still benefit from the time-saving abstractions of PaaS.

Force.com is free for developers. Production applications are priced primarily by storage used and number of unique users.

Force.com as a Platform

Force.com is different from other PaaS solutions in its focus on business applications. Force.com is a part of Salesforce.com, which started as a SaaS customer relationship management (CRM) vendor. But Force.com is not CRM. It provides the infrastructure commonly needed for any business application, customizable for the unique requirements of each business through a combination of code and configuration. This infrastructure is delivered to you as a service on the Internet.

Because you are reading this book, you have probably developed a few business applications in your time. Consider the features you implemented and reimplemented in multiple applications, the unglamorous plumbing, wiring, and foundation work. Some examples are security, user identity, logging, profiling, integration, data storage, transactions, workflow, collaboration, and reporting. This infrastructure is essential to your applications but expensive to develop and maintain. Business application developers do not code their own relational database kernels, windowing systems, or operating systems. This is basic infrastructure, acquired from software vendors or the open source community and then configured to meet user requirements. What if you could do the same for your application infrastructure? This is the premise of Force.com.

The following subsections list differentiating architectural features of Force.com with brief descriptions.

Multitenancy

Multitenancy is an abstract concept, an implementation detail of Force.com, but one with tangible benefits for developers. Figure 1.1 shows a conceptual view of multitenancy. Customers access shared infrastructure, with metadata and data stored in the same logical database.

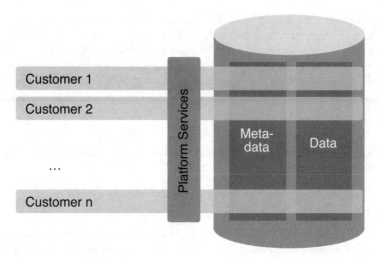

Figure 1.1   Multitenant architecture

The multitenant architecture of Force.com consists of the following features:

- **Shared infrastructure**—All customers (or tenants) of Force.com share the same infrastructure. They are assigned an independent logical environment within the Force.com platform.

  At first, some might be uncomfortable with the thought of handing their data to a third party where it is comingled with that of competitors. Salesforce's whitepaper on its multitenant technology includes the technical details of how it works and why your data is safe from loss or spontaneous appearance to unauthorized parties.

> **Note**
>
> The whitepaper is available at http://wiki.developerforce.com/page/Multi_Tenant_Architecture.

- **Single version**—Only one version of the Force.com platform is in production. The same platform is used to deliver applications of all sizes and shapes, used by 1 to 100,000 users, running everything from dog-grooming businesses to the Japanese national post office.
- **Continuous, zero-cost improvements**—When Force.com is upgraded to include new features or bug fixes, the upgrade is enabled in every customer's logical environment with zero to minimal effort required.

Salesforce can roll out new releases with confidence because it maintains a single version of its infrastructure and can achieve broad test coverage by leveraging tests, code, and configurations from its production environment. Salesforce's internal process for regression testing the platform using its customers has a name fitting its aggressive role: The Hammer. You, the customer, are helping maintain and improve Force.com in a systematic, measurable way as a side effect of simply using it. This deep feedback loop between Force.com and its users is something impractical to achieve with on-premises software. Additionally, detailed communication of release schedules and contents, opt-in features, and the critical update system for backward-incompatible changes help keep customers and developers well informed and applications stable.

> **Note**
>
> Find more details on "The Hammer" at http://blogs.developerforce.com/engineering/2013/05/here-comes-the-hammer.html.

Relational Database

The heart of Force.com is the relational database provided as a service. The relational database is the most well understood and widely used way to store and manage business data. Business applications typically require reporting, transactional integrity, summarization, and structured search, and implementing those on nonrelational data stores requires significant effort. Force.com provides a relational database to each tenant, one that is tightly integrated with every other feature of the platform. There are no Oracle licenses to purchase, no tablespaces to configure, no Java Database Connectivity (JDBC) drivers to install, no Object-Relational Mapping (ORM) to wrangle, no Data Definition Language (DDL) to write, no queries to optimize, and no replication and backup strategies to implement. Force.com takes care of all these tasks.

Application Services

Force.com provides many of the common services needed for modern business application development. These are the services you might have built or integrated repeatedly in your past development projects. They include logging, transaction processing, validation, workflow, email, integration, testing, reporting, and user interface.

These services are highly customizable with and without writing code. Although each service can be valued as an individual unit of functionality, their unification offers tremendous value. All the features of Force.com are designed, built, and maintained by a single responsible party, Salesforce. Salesforce provides documentation for these features as well as support staff on call, training and certification classes, and accountability to its customers for keeping things running smoothly. This is in contrast to many software projects that end up as a patchwork of open source, best-of-breed tools and libraries glued together by you, the developer, asked to do more with fewer people, shorter timelines, and cheaper, often unsupported tools.

Declarative Metadata

Almost every customization configured or coded within Force.com is readily available as simple Extensible Markup Language (XML) with a documented schema. At any point in time, you can ask Force.com for this metadata via a set of Web services. The metadata can be used to configure an identical environment or managed with your corporate standard source control system. It is also helpful for troubleshooting, allowing you to visually compare the state of two environments. Although a few features of Force.com are not available in this declarative metadata form, Salesforce's stated product direction is to provide full coverage.

Programming Language

Force.com has its own programming language, called Apex. It allows developers to script interactions with other platform features, including the user interface. Its syntax is a blend of Java and database-stored procedure languages like Transact-SQL (T-SQL) and can be written using a Web browser or a plug-in to the Eclipse Integrated Development Environment (IDE).

Other platforms take a different approach. Google's App Engine simultaneously restricts and extends existing languages such as Python so that they play nicely in Google's PaaS environment. This offers obvious benefits, such as leveraging the development community, ease of migration, and skills preservation. One way to understand Apex is as a domain-specific language. Force.com is not a general-purpose computing platform to run any Java or C# program you want to run. Apex is kept intentionally minimalistic, designed with only the needs of Force.com developers in mind, built within the controlled environment of Salesforce Research and Development. Although it won't solve every programming problem, Apex's specialized nature leads to some advantages in learning curve, code conciseness, ease of refactoring, and ongoing maintenance costs.

Force.com Services

Force.com can be divided into four major services: database, business logic, user interface, and integration. Technically, many more services are provided by Force.com, but these are the high-level categories that are most relevant to new Force.com developers.

Database

Force.com is built around a relational database. It allows the definition of custom tables containing up to 800 fields each. Fields contain strongly typed data using any of the standard relational database data types, plus rich types such as currency values, picklists, formatted text, and phone numbers. Fields can contain validation rules to ensure data is clean before being committed and formulas to derive values, like cells in a spreadsheet. Field history tracking provides an audit log of changes to chosen fields.

Custom tables can be related to each other, allowing the definition of complex data schemas. Tables, rows, and columns can be configured with security constraints. Data and metadata are protected against accidental deletion through a "recycling bin" metaphor. The database schema is often modifiable instantly, without manual migration. Data is imported from files or other sources with free tools, and application programming interfaces (APIs) are provided for custom data-loading solutions.

Data is queried via a SQL-like language called Salesforce Object Query Language (SOQL). Full-text search is available through Salesforce Object Search Language (SOSL).

Business Logic

Apex is the language used to implement business logic on Force.com. It allows code to be structured into classes and interfaces, and it supports object-oriented behaviors. It has strongly typed collection objects and arrays modeled after Java.

Data binding is a first-class concept in Apex, with the database schema automatically imported as language constructs. Data manipulation statements, trigger semantics, batch processing, and transaction boundaries are also part of the language.

The philosophy of test-driven development is hardwired into the Force.com platform. Methods are annotated as tests and run from a provided test harness or test API calls. Test methods are automatically instrumented by Force.com and output timing information for performance tuning. Force.com prevents code from being deployed into production that does not have adequate unit test coverage.

User Interface

Force.com provides two approaches for the development of user interfaces: page layouts and Visualforce. Page layouts are inferred from the data model, including validation rules, and then customized using a What You See Is What You Get (WYSIWYG) editor. Page layouts feature the standard Salesforce look and feel. For many applications, Page layouts can deliver some or all of the user interface with no development effort.

Visualforce allows developers to build custom user interfaces. It consists of a series of XML markup tags called components with their own namespace. As with Java Server Pages (JSP), ASP. NET, Velocity, and other template-processing technologies, the components serve as containers to structure data returned by the Controller, a class written in Apex. To the user, the resulting Web pages might look nothing like Salesforce, or adopt its standard look and feel. Visualforce components can express the many types and styles of UIs, including basic entry forms, lists, multistep wizards, Ajax, mobile applications, and content management systems. Developers can create their own components to reuse across applications.

User interfaces in Visualforce are public, private, or some blend of the two. Private user interfaces require a user to log in before gaining access. Public user interfaces, called Force.com Sites, can be made available to anonymous users on the Internet.

Integration

In the world of integration, more options are usually better, and standards support is essential. Force.com supports a wide array of integration technologies, almost all of them based on industry-standard protocols and message formats. You can integrate other technologies with Force.com using an approach of configuration plus code. Here are some examples:

- **Web services**—Apex Web Services allows control of data, metadata, and process from any platform supporting SOAP over Hypertext Transfer Protocol (HTTP), including JavaScript. This makes writing composite applications that combine Force.com with technology from other vendors in many interesting and powerful ways possible. Force.com's Web services API has evolved over many years, spanning more than 20 versions with full backward compatibility.

- **REST**—The Force.com database is accessible via REST calls. This integration method is much lighter weight than Web services, allowing Web applications to query and modify data in Force.com with simple calls accessible to any development language.

- **Business logic**—Business logic developed in Apex can be exposed as a SOAP or REST service, accessible with or without a Force.com user identity. For SOAP services, Force.com generates the Web Service Definition Language (WSDL) from your Apex code. Additionally, Force.com converts WSDL to Apex bindings to allow access to external Web services from within the platform.

- **Inbound and outbound email**—You can create virtual email inboxes on Force.com and write code to process the incoming email. Sending email from Force.com is also supported.

- **Mashups**—Force.com provides an API for making HTTP requests, including support for client-side certificates, Secure Sockets Layer (SSL), proxies, and HTTP authentication. With this, you can integrate with Web-based resources, everything from static Web pages to REST services returning JavaScript Object Notation (JSON).

- **Across Salesforce customers**—Salesforce-to-Salesforce (S2S) is a publish-and-subscribe model of data sharing between multiple Force.com environments. If the company you need to integrate with already uses Force.com and the data is supported by S2S, integration becomes a relatively simple configuration exercise. There is no code or message formats to maintain. Your data is transported within the Force.com environment from one tenant to another.

If your requirements dictate a higher-level approach to integration, software vendors like IBM's Cast Iron Systems, Informatica, MuleSoft, SnapLogic, and Jitterbit offer adapters to Force.com to read and write data and orchestrate complex transactions spanning disparate systems.

Inside a Force.com Project

This section discusses what makes a Force.com project different from a typical corporate in-house software development effort, starting with project selection. Learn some tips for selecting a project in Force.com's sweet spot. Then examine how traditional technical roles translate to development activities in a Force.com project and how technologies within Force.com impact your product development lifecycle. Lastly, get acquainted with the tools and resources available to make your project a success.

Project Selection

Some projects are better suited to implementation on Force.com than others. Running into natural limits of the PaaS approach or battling against the abstraction provided by the platform is possible. Always strive to pursue projects that play into Force.com strengths. No absolute rules exist for determining this, but projects with the following characteristics tend to work well with Force.com:

- **The project is data centered, requiring the storage and retrieval of structured data.**

  Structured data is the most important point. Implementing a YouTube-like application on Force.com is not the best idea because it primarily works with unstructured data in the form of video streams. Force.com supports binary data, so a video-sharing Web site is certainly possible to build. But handling large amounts of binary data is not a focus or core competency of Force.com. A hotel reservation system is an example of a more natural fit.

- **The user interface is composed primarily of wizards, grids, forms, and reports.**

  Force.com does not restrict you to these user interface patterns. You can implement any type of user interface, including "rich" clients that run using Flash in the browser, and even full desktop applications that integrate with Force.com via its Apex Web Services API. But to capture the most benefit from the platform, stick with structured, data-driven user interfaces that use standard Web technologies such as Hypertext Markup Language (HTML), Cascading Style Sheets (CSS), and JavaScript.

- **The underlying business processes involve email, spreadsheets, threaded discussions, and hierarchies of people who participate in a distributed, asynchronous workflow.**

  Standard Force.com features such as Chatter, workflow, approvals, and email services add a lot of value to these applications. They can be configured by business analysts or controlled in depth by developers.

- **The rules around data sharing and security are fine-grained and based on organizational roles and user identity.**

  User identity management and security are deep subjects and typically require high effort to implement in a custom system. With Force.com, they are standard, highly configurable components that you can leverage without coding. You can then spend more time thinking through the "who can see what" scenarios rather than coding the infrastructure to make them possible.

- **The project requires integration with other systems.**

  Force.com is built from the ground up to interoperate with other systems at all its layers: data, business logic, and user interface. The infrastructure is taken care of, so you can focus on the integration design. Exchange a million rows of data between your SQL Server database and Force.com. Call your Apex services from a legacy J2EE application or vice versa. Add an event to a Google calendar from within your Visualforce user interface. These scenarios and more are fully supported by the platform.

- **The project manipulates data incrementally, driven by user actions rather than a calendar.**

  Force.com is a shared resource. Simultaneously, other customers of varying sizes are using the same infrastructure. This requires Force.com to carefully monitor and fairly distribute the computing resources so that all customers can accomplish their goals with a high quality of service. If one customer's application on Force.com was allowed to consume a disproportionate share of resources, other customers' applications would suffer resource starvation. The limitations in place, called governors, prevent too much memory, CPU, disk, or network bandwidth from being concentrated in the hands of any one customer. The platform strongly enforces these governor limits, so the best Force.com applications involve computing tasks that can be split into small units of work.

- **The data volume is limited, below a few million records per table.**

  Data volume is important to think about with any system: How large is my data going to grow and at what rate? Force.com consists of a logical single transactional database. No analytical data store exists. Applications that require access to large volumes of data, such as data warehousing and analytics, cannot be built on Force.com. Other software vendors such as GoodData provide solutions in this area, but all involve copying data from Force.com to their own products.

Force.com is not an all-or-nothing proposition. If your project does not fit within these guidelines, you might still want to explore Force.com but in conjunction with other PaaS solutions such as Heroku. Thanks to Force.com's integration capabilities, Heroku and Force.com can be used together as a composite solution, with Heroku augmenting Force.com where general-purpose computing is needed.

Team Selection

The best people to staff on Force.com projects might already work at your company. Projects do not require brand-new teams staffed with Force.com experts. With the majority of the platform based in mature technology, such as relational databases and Web development, adapting existing teams can be a straightforward task.

Here are some examples of traditional software development roles and how they can contribute to a Force.com project:

- **Business analyst**—Substantial Force.com applications can be built entirely by configuration, no computer science background or coding skills required. Salesforce refers to this as "clicks, not code." Business analysts who are proficient with Microsoft Excel and its macro language, or small-scale databases like Microsoft Access and FileMaker Pro, can get hands-on with the Force.com data model, validation rules, workflows, approval rules, security models, and page layouts.

- **Data modeler**—A data model forms the core of a Force.com application. Data modelers can use their existing entity-relationship tools and techniques to design the data layer, with some deltas to account for Force.com-specific idiosyncrasies. Rather than scripts of DDL statements, their work output is Force.com's metadata XML or manual configuration of the data objects. Data modelers can also design reports and report types, which define data domains available to business users to build their own reports.

- **Database administrator**—Many traditional DBA tasks are obsolete in Force.com because there is no physical database to build, monitor, and tune. But a DBA still has plenty of work to do in planning and implementing the Force.com object model. There are objects to define or permissions to configure, and the challenges of data transformation and migration are still as relevant in Force.com as in any database-backed system.

- **Database developer**—The design of Force.com's programming language, Apex, has clearly been inspired by stored procedure languages like T-SQL. Existing database developers can adapt their skills to writing Apex code, particularly when it requires detailed work on the datalike triggers.

- **Object-oriented analysis and design specialist**—Force.com includes an object-oriented language, and persistent data is represented as objects. With all of these objects floating around, people with skills in traditional techniques like Unified Modeling Language (UML) are valuable to have on your project team. Larger applications benefit from a well-designed object model, and as in any language, designing before writing Apex code can be a real time-saver.

- **User interface designer**—Force.com supports modern Web standards for creating usable, flexible, and maintainable UIs. UI designers can help by building screen mock-ups, page layouts, and the static portions of Visualforce pages to serve as templates and assets for developers.

- **Web developer**—Developers who have built Web applications can quickly learn enough Apex and Visualforce and build similar applications on Force.com, typically with much less effort. Skills in HTML, CSS, JavaScript, or Adobe Flex are needed to build custom Force.com user interfaces.

- **4GL developer**—Developers proficient in fourth-generation languages such as Java, C#.NET, and PHP usually have no problem picking up Apex code. It has the same core syntax as Java, without the Java-specific libraries and frameworks.

- **Integration specialist**—Force.com is a producer and consumer of Web services and supports REST as well as any integration strategy based on HTTP. An integration expert can design the interaction between systems, define the remote operations, and implement them using Force.com or a specialized integration product.

- **Quality assurance (QA) engineer**—Testing is a critical part of any software project, and on Force.com testing is mandatory before code is deployed to production. A QA engineer can write automated unit tests in Apex and test plans for security and integration testing. Standard tools like Selenium can be used to automate UI testing.

- **Operations specialist**—Although there are no servers or operating systems to manage, larger deployments of Force.com can involve integration with on-premises systems. Single Sign-On (SSO) integration and data migration are two common examples. Operations experts can help in this area, as well as with application deployment and Force.com administration tasks such as user maintenance.

Lifecycle

The software development lifecycle of a Force.com project is much like an on-premises Web application development project, but with less toil. Many moving parts exist in J2EE, .NET, or LAMP projects. Most require a jumble of frameworks to be integrated and configured properly before one line of code relevant to your project is written.

This section describes areas of Force.com functionality designed to streamline the development lifecycle and focus your time on the value-added activities related to your application. Each of these areas has implicit costs and benefits. On the cost side, there is usually a loss of control and flexibility versus technologies with less abstraction. Evaluating these features and judging whether they constitute costs or benefits for your project is up to you.

Integrated Logical Database

Relational databases are still the default choice for business applications, despite the availability of alternatives like NoSQL, XML, and object-oriented databases. The relational model maps well onto business entities, data integrity is easily enforceable, and implementations scale to hold large data sets while providing efficient retrieval, composition, and transactional modification.

For business applications coded in an object-oriented language, accessing relational databases introduces an impedance mismatch. Databases organize data in terms of schemas, tables, and columns. Programs organize data and logic into objects, methods, and fields. Many ways exist to juggle data between the two, none of them ideal. To make matters more complicated, many layers of protocol are needed to transport queries, resultsets, and transactions between the program and the database.

In Force.com, the database tables are called objects. They are somewhat confusingly named because they do not exhibit object-oriented behavior. The name comes from the fact that they are logical entities that act as tables when being defined, loaded with data, queried, updated, and reported on, but are surfaced to programs as typed data structures. No mismatch exists between the way data is represented in code and the way it's represented in the database. Your code remains consistent and concise whether you are working with in-memory instances of your custom-defined Apex classes or objects from the database. This enables compile-time validation of programs, including queries and data manipulation statements, to ensure that they adhere to the database schema. This one seemingly simple feature eliminates a whole category of defects that were previously discovered only through unit tests or in production by unfortunate users.

The logical aspect of the database is also significant. Developers have no direct access to the physical databases running in Salesforce's data centers. The physical data model is a metamodel designed for multitenant applications, with layers of caches and fault tolerance, spanning servers in multiple data centers. When you create an object in Force.com, no corresponding Oracle database table is created. The metadata describing your new table is stored and indexed by a series of physical tables, becoming a unified, tenant-specific vocabulary baked into the platform's higher-level features. The synergy of integrated, metadata-aware functionality makes Force.com more than the sum of its individual features.

Metadata-Derived User Interface

As described previously, the definition of your objects becomes the vocabulary for other features. Nowhere is this more evident than in the standard Force.com user interface, commonly referred to as the "native" UI. This is the style pioneered by the Salesforce Sales and

Service Cloud products: lots of tabular displays of data, topped with fat bars of color with icons of dollar signs and telescopes, and a row of tabs for navigation.

It is worth getting to know the capabilities of the native UI even if you have reservations about its appearance or usability. To some, it is an artifact of an earlier era of Web applications. To others, it is a clean-cut business application, consistent and safe. Either way, as a developer, you cannot afford to ignore it. The native UI is where many configuration tasks are performed, often for features not yet visible to Eclipse and other tools.

If your project's user interface design is amenable to the native UI, you can build screens almost as fast as users can describe their requirements. Rapid application prototyping is an excellent addition or alternative to static screen mock-ups. Page layouts are descriptions of which fields appear on a page in the native UI. They are automatically created when you define an object and configured with a simple drag-and-drop layout tool.

Simplified Configuration Management

Configuration management is very different from what you might be accustomed to from on-premises development. Setting up a development environment is trivial with Force.com. You can provision a new development environment in a few clicks and deploy your code to it using the familiar Eclipse IDE.

When added to your Eclipse IDE or file system, Force.com code and metadata are ready to be committed to an existing source control system. Custom Apache Ant build tasks are available to automate your deployments. Sandboxes can be provisioned for testing against real-world volumes of data and users. They are automatically refreshed from snapshots of production data per your request. Force.com's packaging feature allows you to partition your code into logical units of functionality, making it easier to manage and share with others at your company or in the larger community.

Integrated Unit Testing

The ability to write and execute unit tests is a native part of the Apex language and Force.com development environment. Typically, a test framework is an optional component that you need to integrate into your development and build process. With the facility to test aligned closely with code, writing and executing tests becomes a natural part of the development life-cycle rather than an afterthought.

In fact, unit tests are required by Force.com to deploy code into production. This applies to all Apex code in the system: user interface logic, triggers, and general business logic. To achieve the necessary 75% test coverage often requires as much if not more code than the actual Apex classes.

To make sure you don't code yourself into a corner without test coverage, a great time to write tests is while you code. Many development methodologies advocate test-driven development, and writing tests as you code has benefits well beyond simply meeting the minimum require-ments for production deployment in Force.com. For example, a comprehensive library of tests adds guardrails to refactoring and maintenance tasks, steering you away from destabilizing changes.

Integrated Model-View-Controller (MVC) Pattern

The goal of the MVC pattern is maintainable user interface code. It dictates the separation of data, visual elements that represent data and actions to the user, and logic that mediates between the two. If these three areas are allowed to collide and the codebase grows large enough, the cost to fix bugs and add features becomes prohibitive.

Visualforce adopts MVC by design. For example, its view components do not allow the expression of business logic and vice versa. Like other best practices made mandatory by the platform, this can be inconvenient when you just want to do something quick and dirty. But it is there to help. After all, quick-and-dirty demos have an uncanny tendency to morph into production applications.

Integrated Interoperability

Force.com provides Web services support to your applications without code. You can designate an Apex method as a Web service. WSDL is automatically generated to reflect the method signature. Your logic is now accessible to any program that is capable of calling a Web service, given valid credentials for an authorized user in your organization. You can also restrict access by Internet Protocol (IP) address or open up your service to guests.

As in other languages, Apex provides you with a WSDL-to-Apex tool. This tool generates Apex stubs from WSDL, enabling you to integrate with SOAP-enabled business processes existing outside of Force.com. Lower-level Apex libraries are also available for raw HTTP and XML processing.

End of Life

Retiring a production application requires a few clicks from the system administrator. Users can also be quickly removed or repurposed for other applications. Applications can be readily consolidated because they share the same infrastructure. For example, you might keep an old user interface online while a new one is being run in parallel, both writing to the same set of objects. Although these things are possible with other technologies, Force.com removes a sizable chunk of infrastructure complexity, preserving more intellectual bandwidth to devote to tackling the hard problems specific to your business.

Tools and Resources

Force.com has a rich developer ecosystem, including discussion groups for reaching out to the development community on specific subjects, a source-code repository for open source projects, a Web site called AppExchange where you can browse for free and paid extensions to the platform, services companies to help you plan and implement your larger projects, and Ideas, a site for posting your ideas for enhancing the platform.

The following subsections list some tools and resources that exist to make your Force.com projects successful.

Developer Force (http://developer.force.com)

Developer Force is a rich source of information on Force.com. It contains documentation, tutorials, e-books written by Salesforce, a blog, and a wiki with links to many more resources inside and outside of Salesforce.

Developer Discussion Boards (http://community.salesforce.com)

The developer discussion boards are a public discussion forum for the Force.com development community, divided into a dozen separate boards by technology area. Users post their questions and problems, gripes, and kudos. Other users in the community contribute answers and solutions, including Salesforce employees. The boards are a great way to build a reputation as a Force.com expert and keep current on the latest activity around the platform.

Ideas (http://ideas.salesforce.com)

If you have a suggestion for improving Force.com or any Salesforce product, visit the Ideas site and post it. Other users in the community can vote for it. If your idea is popular enough, it might be added to the next release of Force.com. Incidentally, Ideas is a reusable component of Force.com, so you can build your own customized idea-sharing sites for your company.

Code Share (http://developer.force.com/codeshare)

Code Share is a directory of open source code contributions from the Force.com community, with links to the source code hosted on Google Code. Salesforce employees have contributed many projects here. Code Share projects include the Facebook Toolkit, a library for integrating with Facebook, and the Toolkit for PayPal X Payments platform, to leverage PayPal's Adaptive Payments API in Force.com applications.

Platform Documentation

Salesforce provides documentation through online, context-sensitive help within the Web user interface, as well as HTML and Portable Document Format (PDF) versions of its reference manuals. You can find all documentation at Developer Force.

AppExchange (http://www.appexchange.com)

AppExchange is a directory of ready-to-install applications developed on Force.com. The applications consist of metadata, such as Visualforce pages and Apex code, deployable into your Force.com environment. Users can rate applications from one to five stars and write reviews. Many free applications are written by Salesforce employees to illustrate new platform features. Commercial applications are also available for trial and purchase. AppExchange is how independent software vendors distribute their Force.com applications to Salesforce customers.

Dreamforce and Cloudforce

Salesforce has a series of user conferences every year called Dreamforce and Cloudforce. San Francisco hosts the largest Dreamforce venue, with thousands attending to participate in training sessions, booths, product demos, keynote speeches, breakout sessions, executive briefings, and, of course, the parties. Dreamforce and Cloudforce are fun ways to stay up to date with the technology. Refer to http://www.salesforce.com/events for more information.

Systems Integrators

For deployments including significant numbers of users, integration with other enterprise systems, or complex data migrations, consider contracting the services of a systems integrator. You can find systems integrators who have competency with Force.com, Sales Cloud, Service Cloud, and other Salesforce products. For more information, view the Salesforce consulting partners page at https://appexchange.salesforce.com/consulting.

Technical Support

When you encounter undocumented or incorrect behavior in the system, submit a defect report. If the issue can be described simply, like a cryptic error message, search for it in the discussion groups. In many cases, someone else has already run into the same problem before you, posted about it, and attracted the attention of Salesforce employees. If not, the ability to log and track Force.com platform support cases is available in Force.com's Web user interface.

Sample Application: Services Manager

Every following chapter in this book contributes to the construction of a sample application called Services Manager. Services Manager is designed for businesses that bill for their employees' time. These businesses need accurate accounting of when and where employees are staffed, numbers of hours worked, skills of the employees, project expenses, amounts billed to customers, and so forth. This section describes these features in preparation for later discussions of their design and implementation.

The goal is not to build a fully functional application for operating a professional services business, but to provide a logically related set of working code samples to accompany the technical concepts covered in this book.

Background

Imagine you own a professional services business. The services your company provides could be architecture, graphic design, software, law, or anything with the following characteristics:

- High cost, highly skilled employees
- Complex projects lasting a week or more
- Resources billed out at an hourly rate
- High cost of acquiring new customers

Your profit comes from the difference between the billing rate and the internal cost of resources. This is typically small, so your process must be streamlined, repeatable, and scalable. To increase profit, you must hire more resources and win more customer projects.

User Roles

The users of the Services Manager application span many roles in the organization. The roles are covered in the following subsections, with a summary of their responsibilities and how they use Services Manager.

Services Sales Representative

Sales reps work with customers to identify project needs and manage the relationship with the customer. Reps use the Sales Cloud product from Salesforce to manage their sales process. In general, they do not use Services Manager directly, but start the process by winning the contract.

Staffing Coordinator

Staffing coordinators manage and schedule resources for projects. When the opportunity is closed, they are notified via email. They then create a project using Services Manager and staff it by matching the availability and skills of resources against the scheduling and skill requirements of the project.

Project Manager

Project managers are responsible for success of projects on a daily basis. They direct and prioritize project activities for resources and customers. They use Services Manager to manage the detailed weekly schedules of their consultants and monitor the health and progress of their projects.

Consultant

The consultant is engaged directly with the customer and is responsible for the project deliverables. In Service Manager, he or she logs time spent on the project, indicates the completion of project milestones, and submits expenses.

Accounts Receivable

Accounts receivable is responsible for invoicing and collecting customers based on work that has been delivered. At the end of each billing cycle, they use Services Manager to generate invoices for customers.

Services Vice President

The VP is responsible for the services profit and loss and success of the team. Services Manager provides the VP with reports on utilization and other metrics for assessing the team's overall performance.

Development Plan

The Services Manager sample application is developed incrementally throughout this book, each chapter building on the previous. Every chapter covers a set of technical concepts followed by the relevant Services Manager requirements, design, and implementation. The goal is to expose you to the abstract technology and then make it practical by getting your hands dirty on the sample application.

The following list names the remaining chapters in this book, with brief descriptions of the features of Services Manager to be covered:

- Chapter 2, "Database Essentials"—Design and create the database and import data.
- Chapter 3, "Database Security"—Define users, roles, and profiles. Configure sharing rules.
- Chapter 4, "Business Logic"—Build triggers to validate data and unit test them.
- Chapter 5, "Advanced Business Logic"—Write services to generate email notifications based on user activity.
- Chapter 6, "User Interfaces"—Construct a custom user interface for tracking the skills of consultants.
- Chapter 7, "Advanced User Interfaces"—Enhance the skills-tracking user interface with Ajax.
- Chapter 8, "Mobile User Interfaces"—Create a mobile user interface for entering timecards.
- Chapter 9, "Batch Processing"—Locate missing timecards using a batch process.
- Chapter 10, "Integration with Force.com"—Calculate and transmit corporate performance metrics to a fictional industry-benchmarking organization.
- Chapter 11, "Advanced Integration"—Develop a Java program to update Force.com with information from a human resources database.
- Chapter 12, "Social Applications"—Automate built-in platform collaboration features to help project teams communicate.

Summary

This chapter has introduced you to Force.com, explained how it differs from other PaaS technologies and what infrastructure it's designed to replace, and given guidelines for its use on your projects. Here are a few thoughts to take away from this chapter:

- Force.com is a PaaS uniquely designed to make business applications easy to build, maintain, and deliver. It consists of database, business logic, user interface, and integration services, all of them interoperable and interdependent, accessible through configuration or code.

- The most suitable applications for implementation on Force.com operate primarily on structured data. Traditional software development roles are still relevant in the Force.com world, particularly Web and client/server developers. Data modeling takes on a new importance with the platform, as data objects are tightly integrated with the rest of the technology stack, and unit testing is mandatory.

- Services Manager is the sample application built on throughout this book. It's designed to serve companies in the professional services space, those selling projects to customers and billing them for the time of its skilled employees.

2

Database Essentials

In Force.com, the database provides the framework for the rest of your application. Decisions you make on how to represent data have significant consequences for flexibility and maintainability. Understanding the unique behaviors of the Force.com database is critical for successful applications. Force.com operates at a higher level of abstraction than a relational database, so although existing relational database skills are helpful, the Force.com database is a completely different animal.

This chapter covers topics in Force.com database design and development:

- **Overview of Force.com's database**—Get an overview of the Force.com database and how it's different from standard relational databases.

- **Working with custom objects**—Custom objects are components within the Force.com database that store your data. Learn how they are created and then test them by entering and browsing their data.

- **Additional database features**—The Force.com database has a few features that are less frequently used but powerful. They include fields defined as aggregates of other fields, fields that limit the valid values of another field, the ability to display the same object differently in multiple user interfaces, and objects that store frequently accessed settings for optimal performance.

- **Sample application**—Design a Force.com data model for the Services Manager, implement the objects using Schema Builder, and import sample data.

> **Note**
>
> The code listings in this chapter are available in a GitHub Gist at http://goo.gl/D0y91g.

Overview of Force.com's Database

This section provides background on the database functionality within Force.com. It covers objects, fields, relationships, queries, and how data is integrated with your application logic.

Each Force.com-specific database feature is described and contrasted with its equivalent in a standard relational database.

Objects

Strictly speaking, Force.com does not store objects in its database. Force.com's objects are more closely related to database tables than they are to anything in object-oriented programming. Objects contain fields, which are equivalent to the columns of a database table. Data is stored in objects in the form of records, like rows in a database table.

Objects belong to one of two categories: standard and custom. Standard objects provide data for Salesforce applications like Sales Cloud or core platform functionality such as user identity. They are built in to Force.com and cannot be removed, although you can extend them by adding your own fields. Custom objects are defined by you, the developer, and you'll be spending most of your time with them as you build your own applications. Custom objects include custom settings, a close relative of the custom object intended for small amounts of frequently accessed data, like user preferences.

Beyond the name, custom objects differ from their relational table counterparts in some significant ways.

Logical, Not Physical Objects

Unlike relational database tables, custom objects have no physical representation accessible to the Force.com developer. There are no physical storage parameters to tune, no tablespace files to create and manage. The Force.com platform decides how best to represent, index, back up, migrate, scale, and tune your database.

Delegated Operations

For the most part, operational concerns such as performance and reliability are managed entirely by the platform. This means you can design and build an application without worrying how to support it in production.

When you run your own database software and hardware, you inevitably face operational tasks such as backup, recovery, and replication for scalability. Although nothing prevents you from exporting the data from your Force.com instance and backing it up to your own servers, there is normally no reason to do so.

> **Note**
>
> Force.com applications that involve tens of thousands of users, tens of millions of records, or hundreds of gigabytes of total record storage belong to a category called Large Data Volume (LDV) deployments. Such deployments require special architectural considerations to maintain favorable performance. For more information, refer to the whitepaper titled "Best Practices for Deployments with Large Data Volumes" at http://wiki.developerforce.com/page/Best_Practices_for_Deployments_with_Large_Data_Volumes.

Undelete Support

Normally, when a row is deleted in a standard relational database and you need to recover it after a commit, you're out of luck unless you have backups of the database or are using a database that provides some proprietary technology like Oracle's Flashback. To avoid this situation, you could implement your own support for undeleting rows, like triggers to copy data to an audit table or a "deleted" column to accomplish a "soft" delete.

In contrast, Force.com provides undelete functionality on every object. When records are deleted, they go into the Recycle Bin, where they stay until they expire (15 days after deletion) and are gone for good or an administrator undeletes them. Deleted records can be queried and programmatically undeleted as well.

Accidentally dropping a table or another database object can also lead to a lot of unpleasant work for a system administrator. If your database vendor doesn't offer specialized recovery features, you are stuck recovering data from backups. In Force.com, deleting objects sends them to the Recycle Bin. They stay there until they expire or are explicitly erased or undeleted by an administrator. If an object is undeleted, its definition and all its data are restored.

Fields

Fields are like columns in a database. They belong to an object and have a name, label for display purposes, and constraints such as data type and uniqueness.

In Force.com, there are two categories of fields: standard and custom. Standard fields are fields that are created by Force.com for its own internal use, but are also available to users. They can be hidden from view and unused, but not completely removed or redefined. They are a part of the Force.com data model that is static, relied on to exist by other layers of Force.com technology. Examples of standard fields are Id (unique identifier) and Created By (the user who created the record). Custom fields are created by you, the developer, to store data specific to your applications.

Some important differences between Force.com database fields and relational database columns are described in the subsections that follow.

Logical, Not Physical Fields

When you define a new field for your custom object, Force.com does not create a corresponding field in its physical database. Instead, it associates your new field with an existing "Flex" field, a VARCHAR column of its generic data table. This provides Force.com with the flexibility to redefine data types, add richer data types, and perform other processing on the data outside of a database's typically rigid rules. Although this implementation detail of Force.com is not relevant to learning how to use Force.com's database, it does help explain some of its underlying behavior.

Unique Identifiers

Typical database tables include one or more columns to contain the primary key, the unique identifier for each row. In Force.com, every object has a standard field called Id. This field is automatically populated with an 18-character, case-insensitive, alphanumeric string to uniquely identify your records. Unique identifiers can also be expressed as 15-character, case-sensitive strings, and this is how they appear in the Salesforce user interface. In most cases, the two styles of unique identifiers can be used interchangeably. So when you are designing your Force.com database, there is no need to add a field to contain a unique identifier.

Validation Rules

Validation rules place restrictions on the values of a new or updated record. They prevent users and programs from inserting data that your application defines as invalid. Rules are defined in an expression language similar to the function language found in the cells of a Microsoft Excel worksheet. The validation rule in Listing 2.1 prevents a record from containing a Start Date greater than its End Date.

Listing 2.1   **Sample Validation Rule**

```
AND(
  NOT(
    ISNULL(Start_Date__c)
  ),
  NOT(
    ISNULL(End_Date__c)
  ),
  (Start_Date__c > End_Date__c)
)
```

When the expression evaluates to true, it is treated as a validation failure. For the rule to evaluate as true, the value in the fields Start_Date__c and End_Date__c must be non-null, and the value of Start_Date__c must be greater than End_Date__c.

Formula Fields

Formula fields contain values that are automatically calculated by Force.com, derived from other fields in the same object or in different objects. They use the same expression language as validation rules.

For example, Listing 2.2 shows a formula for a field called Billable_Revenue__c.

Listing 2.2   **Sample Formula Field**

```
Billable_Revenue__c = Week_Total_Hrs__c * Rate_Per_Hour__c
```

`Week_Total_Hrs__c` and `Rate_Per_Hour__c` are custom fields. When a new record is inserted or one of the two fields is updated, the two fields are multiplied, and the result is stored in the `Billable_Revenue__c` field.

Rich Data Types

Force.com supports a few flavors of the typical string, number, date/time, and Boolean data types. It also supports richer data types that lend themselves to direct usage in user interfaces with prebuilt validation, input masks, and output formatting. The rich types are phone, picklist, multi-select picklist, email, URL, geolocation, and rich text area.

Picklists are particularly valuable, as they address the clutter of "lookup tables" dangling off most relational data models. These lookup tables often contain only a key and description and can be readily replaced with picklist fields. Internally, picklists maintain their own identifiers for values, allowing their labels to be modified without updating the records that reference them.

History Tracking

Most databases do not provide developers a way to track every change made to records in a table. Typically, this is something that is implemented using another table and some code. In Force.com, any object can have History Tracking enabled on it. Every field with History Tracking enabled that is changed gets a new record inserted in a corresponding History object containing the old and new values.

> **Note**
>
> Field history data can be subject to automatic deletion. Organizations created on or after June 2, 2011, retain their history data for 18 months. You can log a case with Salesforce to request a longer retention period. Organizations created before this date retain field history data indefinitely.

Relationships

The capability to define and manage relationships between data entities is the basis for much of the value of relational databases. Relationships allow data from one entity to be logically separated from others. With this separation, data can be modified without integrity loss and combined with other entities for analysis.

Data relationships in Force.com resemble those found in standard relational databases. You can express one-to-one, one-to-many, and many-to-many relationships. But relationships in Force.com are closely controlled and managed by the platform and also integrated with many platform features. Some important points are listed in the subsections that follow.

Integrity Enforced

When you define a relationship in Force.com, a relationship field is created to contain the foreign key. Force.com prevents you from using a foreign key to a different object. It enforces that the foreign key points to an object of the correct type.

This is basic foreign key constraint checking, like in a relational database. The difference in Force.com is that you can never elect to turn it off. It is a mandatory, always-on feature, protecting your data from inconsistency.

There is one minor exception to this rule. Many standard objects contain special fields that can be related to multiple object types. For example, a support case can be assigned to an individual user or a group representing a collection of users. In the Case object, the OwnerId field can contain the ID of a record in the User object or the Group object. Both types of foreign keys are valid. Note that polymorphic foreign key fields are defined by Salesforce and cannot be created by developers.

Explicitly Defined

In Force.com, all relationships are predefined, established when objects and fields are created. With the exception of semi- and anti-joins, you do not specify join conditions when you write queries. Instead, you specify the fields you want, and Force.com takes care of traversing the necessary relationships to retrieve the data.

Query Language

Force.com has two query languages. One is called Salesforce Object Query Language (SOQL) and is used for structured queries. The other language, Salesforce Object Search Language (SOSL), is used for searching the full text of one or more objects.

SOQL

Don't let the name confuse you. Despite some similarities in syntax, SOQL is very different from SQL. It has more in common with a reporting or object-traversal language than its more mathematically grounded ancestor.

Listing 2.3 shows a sample SOQL query on a custom object. It returns the names, statuses, and expected revenue amounts for the top-ten largest uninvoiced projects started in the last quarter, in descending order by pending revenue.

Listing 2.3 **Sample SOQL Query**

```
SELECT Name, Total_Billable_Revenue_Pending_Invoice__c, Project_Status__c
  FROM Proj__c
  WHERE Invoiced__c = FALSE and Start_Date__c = LAST_QUARTER
  ORDER BY Total_Billable_Revenue_Pending_Invoice__c DESC LIMIT 10
```

The query specifies a list of columns to be returned (SELECT), the object to query (FROM), filter conditions (WHERE), sorting results (ORDER BY) in descending (DESC) order, and a hard limit on the maximum number of rows to return (LIMIT).

Selecting a single object is the simplest type of SOQL query. More advanced queries select fields from multiple related objects, nested resultsets from child objects using subqueries, and perform semi-joins and anti-joins using IN and NOT IN.

The following subsections describe the four most significant differences between SQL and SOQL.

Implicit Join

In SQL, you can join any table with any other table, typically with one or more Boolean expressions involving pairs of columns. Assuming that the data types of the columns in the join expression are comparable, the join query returns the corresponding rows of both tables as specified in your join expression.

In Force.com, data from multiple standard and custom objects can be combined, but only in ways predetermined by you when you designed your database. SOQL itself does not support any concept of joins, other than semi-join and anti-join. Using SOQL, you tell the Force.com platform which fields of which objects to retrieve, and the platform does the work of traversing the data, maintaining the integrity between objects in accordance with the relationships you defined.

This behavior has its pros and cons. You cannot perform truly ad hoc queries, in which data from multiple objects is combined in ways possibly unanticipated by the database designer. But it results in much simpler, more concise queries that can be optimized entirely by the platform.

Nested Resultsets

In SQL, querying two tables in a one-to-many relationship without aggregate functions and GROUP BY results in a cross product of the rows. For example, assume you have a table containing orders and another table with their line items, and issue the query in Listing 2.4.

Listing 2.4 **Relationship Query in SQL**

```
SELECT Orders.OrderId, OrderLineItems.LineItemId
  FROM Orders, OrderLineItems
  WHERE Orders.OrderId = OrderLineItems.OrderId
```

Assume that there are two orders (1 and 2), each with three line items (1–3 and 4–6). Table 2.1 shows the results of executing the query.

Table 2.1   **Results of SQL Join Query**

Orders.OrderId	OrderLineItems.LineItemId
1	1
1	2
1	3
2	4
2	5
2	6

To begin comparing this with Force.com, Listing 2.5 shows an equivalent query in SOQL.

Listing 2.5   **Relationship Query in SOQL**

```
SELECT OrderId, (SELECT LineItemId FROM OrderLineItems)
   FROM Orders
```

Note the lack of a WHERE clause to perform the join and the use of a subquery to nest the line items. Force.com is aware of the parent-child relationship between Orders and OrderLineItems, so it performs the join automatically. The result can be visualized as arrays of nested records, as shown in Figure 2.1. The outer record is the order, and each order contains an array of line items.

No Functions in Column List

You might have included functions like LEFT, RIGHT, MID, LEN, and IFF along with your columns in a SQL SELECT statement. SOQL does not permit functions in the SELECT list. The only exceptions are built-in aggregate functions such as COUNT, which returns the number of records in the query. But aggregate functions can't be used in a query containing any other fields in the SELECT list.

Governor Limits

Force.com prevents a single user from consuming more than its fair share of system resources. This ensures a consistent level of system performance for all tenants. Limitations placed on resource consumption are called governor limits. A few examples of governor limits are the number of records that can be queried at one time, the amount of memory used by your code, and the size of messages sent between Force.com and external hosts. Some governor limits vary based on the type of licensing agreement you have in place with Salesforce.

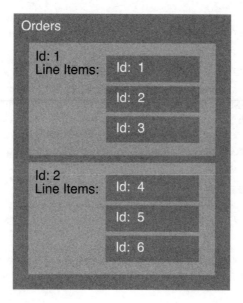

Figure 2.1   Nested results of SOQL query

SOSL

SOSL provides full-text search capabilities across many objects and fields simultaneously. This is an always inefficient and often impossible task in SOQL. SOSL statements can perform a search over all records, or incorporate SOQL to narrow the search scope and achieve the best of both worlds: structured and unstructured search. The SOSL expression in Listing 2.6 returns the IDs of records in four custom objects that begin with the word *java* in any of their fields.

Listing 2.6   **Query in SOSL**

```
FIND 'java*' IN ALL FIELDS
  RETURNING Project__c, Resource__c, Assignment__c, Skill__c
```

Data Integration

Integration refers to the incorporation of the database into the rest of your application, the business logic, and the user interface. If your application consists solely of stored procedures, there is no integration; your code runs inside the database process and hits database objects directly. More commonly, there are application servers that need to communicate with the database.

With Force.com, either you are coding "on the platform," which is akin to writing stored procedures, or you are developing a "composite application," which executes somewhere else but integrates with Force.com data and logic. The following subsections describe how integrating data in Force.com differs from traditional Web application development.

Object-Relational Mapping

In traditional Web application development, one of the most important integration technologies is Object-Relational Mapping (ORM). This layer of infrastructure maps data objects from the database to and from the data structures in your program. Any ORM technology must be well integrated into your development process, efficient at runtime, and flexible in order to accommodate all data access patterns required by your application and allow for future schema changes. Java developers might use Hibernate, Ruby has ActiveRecord, and so forth.

With Force.com, the ORM layer is built in to the platform. Data objects, metadata objects, and queries have direct representation in Apex code. When you create a new custom object, it's immediately accessible by name in Apex code. If you accidentally mistype the name of a field in your new object, your code will not compile.

For example, the snippet of Apex code in Listing 2.7 selects a single record from the Resource object, updates the value of its Hourly Cost Rate field, and commits the updated record to the database.

Listing 2.7   **Apex Code Snippet**

```
public void grantRaise(String resourceName, Decimal newRate) {
  Resource__c r = [ select Id, Hourly_Cost_Rate__c
      from Resource__c
      where Name = :resourceName limit 1 ];
  if (r != null) {
    r.Hourly_Cost_Rate__c = newRate;
    update r;
  }
}
```

Note the use of an in-line SOQL query (in square brackets), the custom object as a first-class object in code (Resource__c), and in-line data manipulation (update statement).

Metadata in XML

Metadata in Force.com is created using one of the platform's Web-based user interfaces, the Force.com IDE, or the Metadata API. Unlike SQL databases, Force.com does not use Data Definition Language (DDL) but has its own XML schema for metadata. Listing 2.8 shows a simple example of Force.com's XML metadata.

Listing 2.8   **Metadata XML for a Custom Object**

```xml
<?xml version="1.0" encoding="UTF-8"?>
<CustomObject xmlns="http://soap.sforce.com/2006/04/metadata">
    <deploymentStatus>Deployed</deploymentStatus>
    <fields>
        <fullName>Start_Date__c</fullName>
        <label>Start Date</label>
        <type>Date</type>
    </fields>
    <label>Project</label>
    <nameField>
        <label>Project Name</label>
        <type>Text</type>
    </nameField>
    <pluralLabel>Projects</pluralLabel>
    <searchLayouts/>
    <sharingModel>ReadWrite</sharingModel>
</CustomObject>
```

This XML describes an object with a human-readable name of Project. It contains a single custom field called Start Date, of type Date. The Sharing Model of ReadWrite means that all users in the organization can edit the records in the Project object. Force.com provides a Metadata API for importing metadata XML into the platform. This is how development tools such as the Force.com IDE operate.

Generated User Interfaces

In the process of defining a custom object, described in the next section, you will see a number of settings related to the visual appearance of your object. These settings help Force.com generate a user interface for manipulating the data in your object. From here on, this is referred to as the "native" user interface, native meaning that it is built in to Force.com.

Force.com's native user interface is tightly integrated with your data model. The definitions of your objects, fields, and relationships are combined with additional configuration settings to create full-featured user interfaces that can perform create, read, update, delete (CRUD) operations on your data. Note that the concept of CRUD is also referred to as read, create, edit, delete (RCED) in the Salesforce world.

SOAP and REST APIs

Force.com provides SOAP and REST APIs for accessing data from outside of its platform. Using these APIs, you can run SOQL and SOSL queries, import millions of records at a time, modify records individually or in batches, and query metadata.

Working with Custom Objects

This section describes how to create and manage custom objects in Force.com. This is an introduction to the process, so you can experiment with your own objects and data. It starts with instructions for getting your own Force.com Developer Edition account and gives a brief introduction to the tools available for working with custom objects. The rest of the section covers object creation and customization, field creation, entering and viewing data using the native user interface, and additional database features.

Force.com Developer Edition

To get hands-on with Force.com development, you need a development environment. Environments are known as organizations, or "orgs" for short. Orgs come in different shapes and sizes based on the licensing agreement with Salesforce. Salesforce gives its Developer Edition (DE) away free. DE orgs are full featured but have hard limits on the amount of storage (5MB of data, 20MB of files) and number of users (two full users and three platform-only users). When you are ready to test your application with production data and user volumes, license a Force.com Sandbox or Force.com Enterprise Edition (EE).

> **Tip**
>
> Contact a Salesforce sales representative for more information about the different licensing options for Force.com.

Registration

Visit http://developer.force.com with your Web browser. From this page, there is a link or button to create a free DE account. Complete the sign-up form. Within a few minutes, two emails are sent to the address you provide. The first email is a login confirmation containing a temporary password and a link to log in. The second email is a welcome message to Force.com, with links to resources for developers.

Logging In

Click the login link in the first email. Your browser is directed to a page that forces you to change your password. If there is maintenance scheduled for your organization, you may need to acknowledge it prior to the password change page. Passwords must be at least eight characters long and alphanumeric. Here, you also choose a security question and answer, as shown in Figure 2.2. The security challenge is used in the event that you forget your password.

At this point, you are logged in to your own Force.com organization.

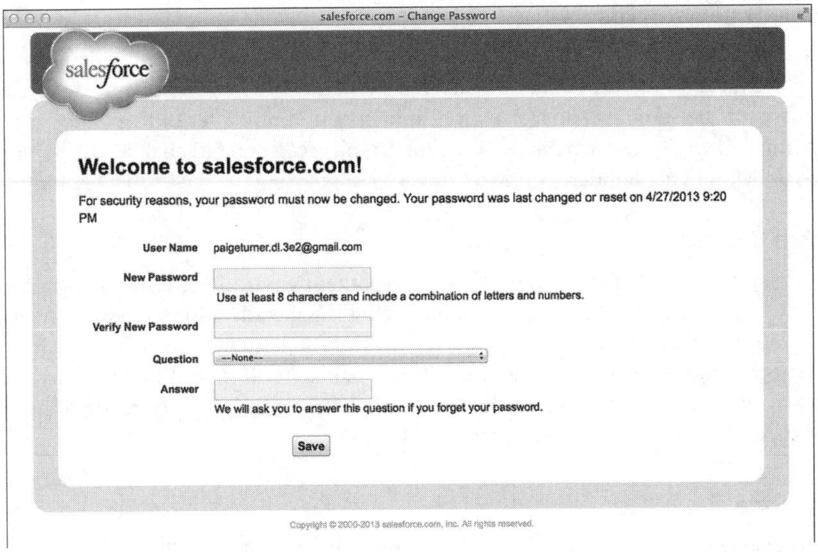

Figure 2.2   Force.com password change page

Tools for Custom Objects

Many tools are available that work with Force.com, created by Salesforce and independent software vendors. But if you're new to Force.com, it's best to start with the free tools supported by Salesforce. Unless noted otherwise, all tools are available from the DeveloperForce Web site (http://developer.force.com). After you're comfortable with the standard tools, explore the range of solutions offered by the Force.com independent software vendor (ISV) community.

Tools for Metadata

Metadata is the description of a Force.com application, from the data model to the user interface and everything in between. In this chapter, the focus is on the data model, and there are three tools available from Salesforce for building it.

Force.com App Builder Tools

App Builder Tools are built in to the native Web user interface of Force.com. They are the easiest and most full-featured tools for working with objects and many other features. When new features are added to Force.com's database, you'll find them in the App Builder Tools first. To use App Builder Tools, log in to Force.com and click Setup. In the App Setup area, click Create, Objects.

Force.com Schema Builder

The Schema Builder is a drag-and-drop interface for building and maintaining database schemas. It renders objects and relationships in a standard entity-relationship diagram style. The database for the Services Manager sample application, found later in this chapter, is built with Schema Builder. To use Schema Builder, log in to Force.com and click Setup. In the App Setup area, click Schema Builder.

Force.com IDE

The Force.com IDE is a plug-in to the Eclipse development environment. Its strength is developing Apex code and Visualforce pages and managing the metadata for larger deployments involving multiple Force.com organizations. It provides some functionality for working with custom objects, but the objects are presented in raw metadata XML, not in a friendly user interface. For more information about the Force.com IDE and installation instructions, visit http://wiki.developerforce.com/page/Force.com_IDE.

Tools for Data

Data tools enable you to import and export data in bulk. They are usually used in a migration, in which data from an existing system is loaded into Force.com.

Force.com Data Loader

Data Loader has the richest data import features of any Salesforce-provided data tool. To get the Windows version login to Force.com, visit the Administration Setup area, and click Data Management, Data Loader. There is also a community-supported Mac OS X version at http://www.pocketsoap.com/osx/lexiloader.

Import Wizard

The Import Wizard is a tool built in to the native user interface. It allows bulk data to be imported as new or updated records of custom objects. To use it, log in to Force.com and click Setup. In the Administration Setup area, click Data Management, Import Custom Objects. The Import Wizard walks you through a seven-step process for getting the data from a comma separated values (CSV) file into Force.com.

Force.com Excel Connector

Excel Connector is an add-in to Microsoft Excel that allows bidirectional data movement between a worksheet and a Force.com object. You can fill an Excel worksheet with records from a Force.com object. In the worksheet, you can change values by simply editing the corresponding cells. The modified values can then be written back to the Force.com object. If you're an Excel power user, you will appreciate this tool. You can download it at http://wiki. developerforce.com/page/Force.com_Excel_Connector.

Object Creation

The easiest way to understand the object creation process is to try it. Log in to Force.com using your DE account and click Setup. In the App Setup area, click Create, Objects. Figure 2.3 shows the screen as it appears in a new Force.com organization, with no objects yet defined.

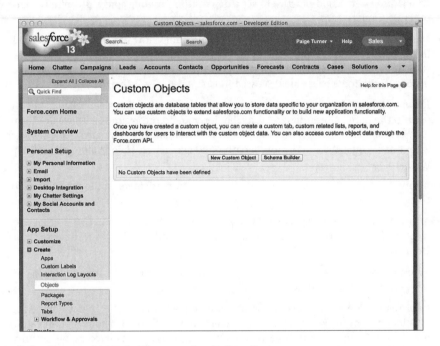

Figure 2.3   Custom objects in Force.com App Builder Tools

To begin, click the New Custom Object button.

Object Definition

The first step of building the custom object is its definition screen. The inputs to this screen are as follows:

- **Label**—This label is a human-readable name of your custom object.

- **Object Name**—This is a very important name. It's how you refer to your custom object when you write Apex code, formula fields, and validation rules. It's automatically populated from the label, but it can be set manually. Although not shown on this screen, internally Force.com appends the Object Name with "__c" to designate it as a custom object rather than a standard object.

> **Tip**
>
> Avoid naming your custom object something overly terse or common, and avoid the names of standard objects. It can be difficult to differentiate multiple objects with the same name.

- **Description**—It's good practice to set a description for your object if you're working with other developers.

- **Context-Sensitive Help Setting**—This setting dictates how the Help for This Page link in the corner of every page behaves on your custom object. By default, it shows the standard Force.com help. You can configure it to display a custom Visualforce page instead. Visualforce pages are discussed in Chapter 6, "User Interfaces."

- **Record Name Label and Format**—Every object has a standard field called Name. It's used in the native user interface as a label for your record. Name can have an Auto Number data type, which causes names to be automatically generated from a pattern, or a Text data type with a maximum length of 80 characters. Name values are not required to be unique.

- **Allow Reports**—If checked, this custom object can participate in the reporting feature of Force.com.

- **Allow Activities**—If this is checked, users can associate calendar events and tasks to records of your custom object. You can find the calendar and tasks features on the Home tab.

- **Track Field History**—If this option is checked, Force.com creates an additional object to store changes to selected fields.

- **Deployment Status (in development, deployed)**—If an object is in development status, it's hidden from the users in your org, except those with the Customize Application permission. Deployed objects become visible to any user, as dictated by the security configuration of the object and org.

- **Object Creation Options**—Unlike the other options, which can be changed later, these options are available only when a custom object is first created. Add Notes and Attachments Related List to Default Page Layout allows external documents to be attached to records of your custom object, like attachments on an email. Launch New Custom Tab Wizard is a shortcut for building a custom tab at the same time as you define your object.

After you've clicked the Save button on the definition page and clicked through pages concerning the object's behavior in the user interface, the detail page of your new custom object is shown. It contains a series of bordered boxes with titles. Each box contains configuration options for a different aspect of the object. Most aspects are described in the following subsections.

Standard Fields

Standard fields are automatically part of every object. They are used for platform-wide functions. The Created By, Last Modified By, Name, and Owner fields help provide record-level access control of your data. Data security is discussed further in Chapter 3, "Database Security."

Custom Fields and Relationships

Custom fields are created by you, the developer, to store data specific to your applications. Custom relationships express associations between the records in a pair of objects, such as a purchase order and its line items. Initially, your object does not contain any custom fields or relationships. After you've added some, they are listed here and can be edited and deleted.

Validation Rules

Validation rules define what constitutes a valid record, preventing records that do not conform from being stored in the database. When a validation rule is added, it applies to data coming from anywhere: a bulk import process, a user interface, a Web service call from another application. When validation rules are defined, they are shown in this list and can be edited and deleted.

Triggers

Triggers are much like triggers in relational databases, except written in Apex code. They fire before or after a data manipulation action such as insert, update, delete, and undelete. They can inhibit the action or extend it by acting on other database objects, modifying data, or even calling out to external Web services.

Page Layouts

A page layout brings together all the native user interface elements for a custom object. This includes the buttons along the top and bottom of the screen, the fields displayed, and related lists, which are records of child objects.

Page layouts are assigned to profiles. This allows different user interfaces to be shown to different types of users. For example, you need one user interface for entering a contact for a support case, but a different one for entering job applicant information. Both end up as records in the Contact object, but the user interfaces can appear very different.

Search Layouts

In this section, you can customize the display of your object in the native search user interfaces. Make a point of editing the Tab layout. It's the most frequently used and worth customizing to save yourself time. The Tab layout displays recently viewed, created, or modified objects on your custom tab. By default, it contains only the Name field.

Standard Buttons and Links

When a custom object is created, a native user interface is also created for that object to enable CRUD operations without coding. The native user interface contains a collection of standard buttons, and this list allows you to override their behavior. With overrides, you can use Visualforce to develop a custom user interface to be shown for actions that require special treatment, such as the creation of a new record in your object.

Custom Buttons and Links

This section allows the definition of one or more custom buttons to appear in the native user interface for your object. For example, you might want to add a Verify button, which would pop up a new window and allow the user to view the results of some analysis performed on the record.

Field Creation

As in object creation, the easiest way to understand field creation is to try it. Return to your custom object detail page and click the New button in the Custom Fields & Relationships section. The first page of the New Custom Field Wizard prompts for field type. The data types can be thought of in terms of seven categories:

1. **Text, Text Area, Text Area (Long), Text Area (Rich), Text (Encrypted)**—Text fields are varying lengths of Unicode text. Force.com does not allow fields with other encodings. Text stores 1 to 255 characters, Text Area stores the same number of characters but allows line breaks, and Text Area (Long) and Text Area (Rich) store up to 32,000 characters. The Rich Text Area field allows images, links, and basic formatting information to be stored in-line with the text. One limitation of both the Long and Rich Text Areas is that Force. com's full-text search feature looks at only the first 2,048 characters. The encrypted text field stores up to 175 characters using the Advanced Encryption Standard (AES) algorithm with a 128-bit master key.

2. **Picklist, Picklist (Multi-Select)**—A picklist is a list of suggested values that is presented to the user. Multi-select enables a user to select multiple values. Record Types can be used to create multiple lists of suggested values for the same field, to be shown to different types of users. Picklist values are not enforced at the database level without the addition of a trigger or validation rule.

3. **Number, Percent, Currency, Geolocation**—Number can store signed values from 1 to 18 digits long, decimal places included. Currency and Percent are also Numbers but add type-specific formatting, such as a dollar sign. Geolocation stores a latitude and longitude pair formatted as a decimal or in degrees, minutes, and seconds.

4. **Checkbox**—Checkbox is a Boolean field. It stores a true or false value, and is represented in the native user interface as a check box.

5. **Date, Date/Time**—In the native user interface, dates are rendered with a calendar picker component and times with a separate, time-masked field with AM/PM selector.

6. **Email, Phone, URL**—These types are provided to enhance the experience in the native user interface. For example, uniform resource locators (URLs) are clickable and open in a new Web browser window.

7. **Relationship (Lookup, Master-Detail)**—These define relationships between two objects. They are covered in more detail in the subsection, "Relationship Fields."

After you've established the field type, the detail page is shown. The settings on this page are described here. Note that not all settings are relevant to every data type.

- **Label**—The label is the human-readable name of your field.

- **Field Name**—Like Object Name, this is an important name. It's the name used to refer to your field in Apex code, formula fields, and validation rules. It's automatically populated from the label, but it can be set manually. Field names cannot contain spaces. Although it's not shown on this screen, internally Force.com appends the Field Name with "__c" to differentiate it from standard fields.

- **Description**—Use this text area to document the purpose of your field to other developers.

- **Help Text**—If you provide help text for your field, a small blue circle icon containing the letter *i* is shown beside it in the native user interface. If a user hovers the mouse over this icon, your help text is displayed.

- **Required**—If this is checked, a record cannot be saved unless this field contains a value. This applies to records created anywhere, in the native user interface, imported from other systems, and programmatically.

- **Unique**—Text and Number fields allow a uniqueness constraint to be applied. If this is checked, new records must contain a unique value for this field, one that does not occur in other records, or it cannot be saved. Like the Required attribute, this is enforced at the database level.

- **External ID**—Text and Number fields can be designated as External IDs. By default, the only unique identifier on an object is the standard Id field. But if External ID is checked, your custom field can be used to uniquely identify records. External IDs are also searchable from the Search sidebar. Note that each object can have at most three External ID fields.

- **Default Value**—If no value is provided for this field in a new record, this optional expression is evaluated and shown as a default value, but can be overwritten by the user. The expression is written in the same language as formula fields and validation rules. It can be as simple as a static value or a series of calculations performed on other fields.

Relationship Fields

Relationship fields can express one-to-one, one-to-many, and many-to-many relationships between objects. Creating relationships keeps data normalized, but also adds to the complexity of the data model, causing greater complexity in code and user interfaces that rely on it.

There are two types of relationship fields: Lookup and Master-Detail. Lookup relationships are the default choice. They are the most flexible and transparent in their operation. You can create up to 20 of them on a single object, they maintain their own record of ownership, and child records can be reassigned to a new parent. By default, deleting a related record clears the value of the field referencing it. Optionally, the Lookup relationship can be defined to prevent a related record from being deleted.

Master-Detail relationships are useful for enforcing mandatory relationships, in which a child record cannot exist without its parent record. All child records in a Master-Detail relationship must have a parent record specified. When the master record in a Master-Detail relationship is deleted, all associated detail records are also deleted. Up to four nested levels of Master-Detail relationships can be created, counting from the master object to the most deeply nested child object. Master-Detail relationships have some other special behaviors, such as allowing aggregation of child records through roll-up summary fields, discussed later in this chapter.

> **Tip**
>
> When moving to Force.com from a relational database, resist the urge to create an object for every table and expect to join them all together with relationships. Force.com has hard limits on the distance between objects that can be joined together for purposes of user interface, reporting, formulas, and triggers. Queries on a child object can reference a maximum of five levels of parent objects. In the reverse scenario, queries against a parent object can reference only a single level of child objects. There are workarounds, such as using formula fields to consolidate fields from distant objects, but keeping your object and relationship count low pays dividends later in the development process.

Table 2.2 summarizes the differences between Lookup and Master-Detail relationships.

Table 2.2   Comparing Lookup and Master-Detail Relationships

Lookup Relationship	Master-Detail Relationship
Child records exist independent of parent	Child records cannot exist without parent
Child records can always be reparented	Child records can be reparented if the option to do so is enabled when the relationship is created
Independent ownership	Always owned by parent record
One of three user-defined options: Deletion of parent clears Lookup value (default), deletion of parent is prohibited, or deletion of parent cascades to delete children (custom objects only)	Deletion of parent cascades to delete children
No roll-up fields	Roll-up summary fields supported
Unlimited nesting, although limited by SOQL	Up to four nested levels

Additional Field Types

Some field types have special behavior, different than simply storing a value. These are listed here:

- **Auto Number**—Most databases have an identity or sequence field, a field that automatically increments itself when a new record is added. In Force.com, Auto Number fields are read-only text fields with a maximum length of 30 characters. You define the length, a display format used to generate values, and the starting number. For example, if you define an Auto Number field with a display format of Project-{0000} and a starting number of 100, the Auto Number field in your first record will contain a value of Project-0100.

- **Formula**—Formula fields are read-only fields that are calculated by Force.com based on an expression you provide when defining the field. The output of a formula can be a currency, date, date/time, number, percent, or text value.

- **Roll-Up Summary**—Roll-up summary fields allow child records in a Master-Detail relationship to be summarized and the result stored in the parent record.

Entering and Browsing Data

One of the happy consequences of building a database in Force.com is that you receive a full-featured data maintenance user interface with near-zero development cost. It is the "native" Force.com user interface. It allows users immediate access to your data with a consistent look and feel, and helps developers visualize and test decisions related to database design.

It's good practice to use the native user interface to test your data model by creating records with dummy values. This helps identify missing fields, nonintuitive page layouts, and additional validation rules needed. After your object contains some records, browse them using Views and Search. Customize Views to show the optimal set of columns. Usable Views are helpful later in the development process for troubleshooting data problems.

Getting Started

Salesforce often adds new features that users must opt in to use. For example, users must opt in to features that involve significant changes to the user interface. Salesforce recently released a faster, more powerful user interface for working with lists of records and for editing records with fewer clicks. Before starting this section, check to make sure your org has these features enabled. Go to the Setup, App Setup area, click Customize, User Interface, and then check the Enable Enhanced Lists and Enable Inline Editing options; click the Save button.

Entering Data

Custom tabs are containers for developer-defined user interfaces. These tabs, such as the Home tab, are displayed at the top of the page. Tabs are the gateway to the native list view and CRUD user interfaces for an object and can also present entirely custom user interfaces built in Visualforce.

If you have not created a custom tab for your object, do so now by going to Setup and, in the App Setup area, clicking Create, Tabs. Click the New button in the Custom Object Tabs section. In the details page, select your custom object from the drop-down list, pick a tab style, and optionally enter a description. Skip through the remaining pages, accepting the default values.

To create a new record in your custom object, click the Create New drop-down on the left side of the screen and select your object from the list. An edit screen is shown, as in Figure 2.4, which shows editing a new record in the standard object named Contact. This screen is defined by the page layout. Make note of things you don't like as you enter test data and return to the page layout to fix them. This process is identical for standard and custom objects.

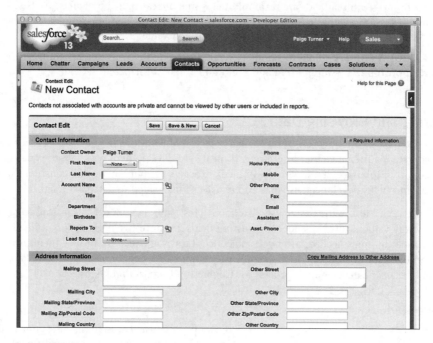

Figure 2.4   Creating a new record in the Contact object

When your new record is saved, the page changes to a view mode. This is also controlled by the page layout. If you've enabled Inline Editing, you can double-click the editable fields to change their values.

Browsing Data

Your first encounter with a list of records is usually on the home page of your custom object. Click your custom object's tab, and you'll see a section listing recently viewed records. It shows only the Name of your records. To customize this list of recently viewed records to show more fields, go to the custom object definition, Search Layouts section, and edit the tab layout to add more fields. Figure 2.5 shows an example of the Contacts Home tab layout with Name, Account Name, Title, Phone, and Email fields visible.

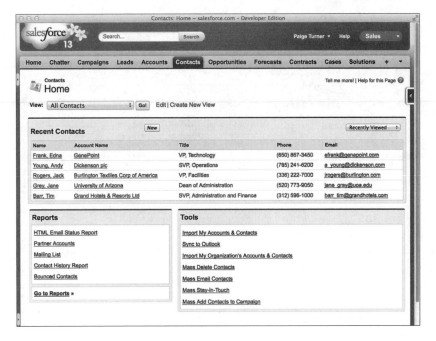

Figure 2.5   Contacts Home tab

Another way to browse data is a View. A View is a native user interface that displays the records of a single object as a list. It includes such features as sorting, pagination, columns that can be dragged to reorder, and the capability to delete and edit data in-line without switching to another user interface. To define a View, you specify the list of fields to be displayed and, optionally, filter criteria to restrict the list to a manageable size.

To show a View on your own object's data, click its tab and then click the Go button. This displays the selected View, which is All by default. Unless you've already customized your All View, it contains only the Name field. Customizing Views is another task, like building tabs and page layouts, that can increase developer productivity, even if you don't plan to use the native user interface outside of administration. Figure 2.6 shows a custom object's View.

Additional Database Features

This section introduces a set of features of the Force.com database that are unique to the way the Force.com platform works. Their configuration and behavior build on the definition of objects and fields, extending them to support more complex native user interfaces, calculations performed on groups of records, and the storage of configuration data.

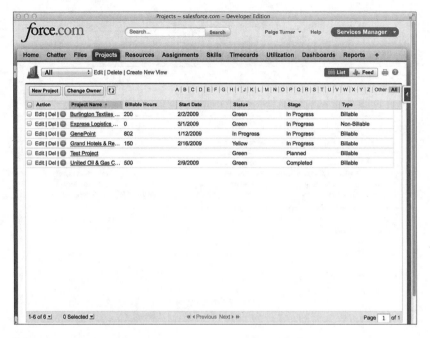

Figure 2.6   View of custom object

The following features are discussed in this section:

- **Roll-up summary fields**—Roll-up summary fields are like formula fields that operate on a group of records, calculating their sum, minimum, maximum, or a record count.

- **Dependent fields**—Dependent fields enable the standard "cascading picklist" user interface pattern, in which user selection in one picklist filters the available values in a second.

- **Record types**—Record types allow records in a single object to take on multiple personalities in the native user interface. For example, the standard object Account is designed to store information on businesses, but with minor adjustments can support data on individuals as well. This can be accomplished with record types.

- **Custom settings**—Custom settings store and manage user preferences, aspects of an application that can be configured by users rather than hard-coded by developers.

Roll-Up Summary Fields

Summarizing data in SQL databases is a routine matter of invoking GROUP BY and an aggregate function like SUM. Force.com's ad hoc query functionality in SOQL provides data grouping and aggregation, but it is subject to limits regarding the number of records aggregated. For the flexibility to obtain aggregate data regardless of data volume, Force.com requires that it be calculated incrementally, either by the database itself or in Apex code. As a result, it's best to plan for summary-level data as the database is designed.

Roll-up summary fields are the mechanism for instructing the database that you'd like summary data to be calculated without custom code. You specify the child object to summarize, the function to apply to the child records, and filter criteria on the child records. The database then takes care of keeping the roll-up summary values up to date as child records are created, modified, and deleted. For example, given an Invoice Header object and Invoice Line Item child object, you could use a roll-up summary field on the Invoice Header to maintain a running count of invoice line items.

Roll-up summary fields are added to objects using the same process as adding other types of custom fields. There are additional options to define the summary calculation, which consists of three parts:

- **Summarized object**—A drop-down list contains the objects you are permitted to summarize. This is restricted to child objects in a Master-Detail relationship with the object you're creating the roll-up summary field on. Lookup relationships are not supported.

- **Roll-up type**—Select the calculation to be performed on the child records and the field of the child object to perform it on. The fields available in this list depend on the calculation. If your calculation is Sum, the list contains fields of type Number, Currency, and Percent. With Min or Max, you can also summarize Date and Date/Time fields. Note that you cannot roll up other roll-up summary fields or formula fields that contain references to other objects, merge fields, or functions returning dynamic values such as TODAY and NOW.

- **Filter criteria**—By default, all records are included in the summary calculation. Alternatively, you can also specify one or more filter criteria to restrict the records involved in the calculation. Build filter criteria by selecting a field to filter, the operator to apply, and the value. If you add more than one criterion, the effect is additive. All filter criteria must be satisfied for the record to be included in the summary calculation.

After you have specified the summary calculation and saved the new field, Force.com begins calculating the summary values on existing records. This can take up to 30 minutes. An icon is displayed beside the field to indicate that the calculation is running.

You can define at most ten roll-up summary fields per object. Make a point of creating them toward the end of your database design process because they make it more difficult to change your objects. For example, you can't convert a Master-Detail relationship to a Lookup relationship without first removing the roll-up summary fields.

Dependent Fields

Dependent fields are primarily used to define cascading picklists. Cascading picklists are a user interface pattern in which the values in one picklist depend on the selection in another picklist. For example, a picklist for state/province might depend on another picklist for country.

When a user selects a country, the state/province picklist is populated with a set of values that make sense given the selected country. In Force.com, the first picklist is called the dependent field, and the second is the controlling field. The controlling field can be a standard or custom picklist (with at least 1 and fewer than 300 values) or a check box field, but cannot be a multi-select picklist. The dependent field can be a custom picklist or multi-select picklist.

A dependent field is an ordinary picklist field with an additional attribute to relate it to a controlling field. To visualize the relationship between the fields, modify your object's page layout so that the controlling field appears above the dependent field. Then perform the following steps to define the relationship between their values:

1. Navigate to the Custom Field Definition Detail page for the dependent field.

2. In the Picklist Options subsection, click the New link next to the label for Controlling Field.

3. Select the controlling field and click the Continue button.

4. Use the grid to specify which values of the controlling field should be included in the dependent field. Picklist values of the controlling field are shown as columns. Values of the dependent field appear as rows. Double-click individual values to include or exclude them or hold down the Shift key while clicking multiple values and click the Include Values and Exclude Values buttons to make changes in bulk.

Record Types

Record types overload the native user interface behavior of a single object. This allows you to get more mileage out of your existing objects or limit the complexity of a new data model.

For example, Salesforce uses this feature in its CRM product. Person Accounts are a record type of the Account object. Accounts ordinarily store information about businesses, but the Person Account record type adapts Account to store information about individuals. Salesforce opted to overload Account with a record type rather than creating an entirely new object.

Before creating a separate object to represent every business entity, ask yourself if the entity is truly new or merely a slight variation of another entity. Where you find slight variations, consider using a single object to do the work of many. The single object contains a superset of the objects' fields. The record type of each record determines which variation of the business entity is stored. Force.com consults the record type and the user's profile to display the correct page layout.

Even if you don't plan to use the native user interface, record types can expand the flexibility of your data model. By using record types, you gain an additional standard field called RecordTypeId. In custom user interfaces, you can use this to drive different functionality. Of course, you can always add your own custom field to accomplish the same thing, but record types force you to make your design explicit at the native Force.com level and provide tight integration with native Force.com security.

Creating a Record Type

Record types are defined at the object level after an object is created. To manage Record types for custom objects, go to the App Setup area and click Create, Objects; then find the section called Record Types. For standard objects, find the standard object in the App Setup, Customize menu, and within it, click Record Types.

Every object has a default record type called Master. It contains the master list of values for all picklist fields in the object. New record types are cloned from the Master record type if no other record types exist, and given a name, label, and description. Normally, record types are in an active state, which makes them available to users who are creating and editing records. Deactivating a record type is required before it can be deleted.

After a record type is saved, it enters an edit mode. Edit mode permits the maintenance of picklist values for the record type. The list of picklist type fields in the object is shown, with Edit links beside each. These Edit links take you to a screen that allows picklist values to be customized. Here, you can select all, or a subset of the picklist values, and provide a custom default value.

This is just one way to manipulate the picklist values of a record type. When adding new picklist values in an object with more than one record type defined, you are asked which record types they apply to. By default, new picklist values are added only to the Master record type, leaving other record types unchanged.

Custom Settings

Custom settings are a special data storage feature designed for relatively simple, frequently accessed data. The type of data stored in custom settings is ancillary, used to configure or control your application rather than the operational data itself, which belongs in standard and custom objects. For example, user preferences in a Java application might be stored in an XML or properties file. In Force.com, they would be stored in custom settings. Once data is stored in a custom setting, it's readily accessible throughout the Force.com platform in Apex, Visualforce, formula fields, validation rules, and Web Services API. As an example, a custom setting named Expert might indicate whether a given user receives the default or advanced version of a user interface.

A custom setting is an object definition, much like a standard or custom database object. It consists of a name, a type, and one or more fields. There are two types of custom settings: List and Hierarchy:

- **List**—The List is the simpler form, behaving like a database object except for the fact that records are accessed one at a time, by unique name. For example, you might define a custom setting with fields representing configurable options in your application, and each named record representing a collection of those options, such as Test and Production.

- **Hierarchy**—The Hierarchy type expands upon the List type, adding the ability to relate data to organization, profile, and user. If a value is not provided for a given level, it defaults to the levels above it. With Hierarchy types, you can create applications that manage settings for individual users, but defer to a profile or organization-wide default when necessary without storing and maintaining redundant, overlapping information.

Using List Custom Settings

The following steps describe how to build a simple custom settings object and manage the values stored in it:

1. Go to the App Setup area and click Develop, Custom Settings. This is where custom settings are defined and their values maintained.

2. Click the New button to define a new custom settings object. Label is the display name for your object, Object Name is the name by which you'll refer to it in programs. Enter Config Setting as the Label and ConfigSetting as the Object Name. For Setting Type, select List. Visibility controls how this setting behaves when packaged. Leave it as Protected. Use the Description field to explain the purpose of your custom setting to other developers in your organization.

> **Tip**
>
> It's a good practice to follow a naming convention for your custom settings so that they can be easily differentiated from custom objects. For example, append the word *Setting* to the end of any custom setting name. The value of naming conventions will become more apparent when you write Apex code that interacts with the database.

3. Click the Save button. Your custom setting is now created and needs some fields and data. Each custom setting can have up to 300 fields.

4. In the Custom Fields section, click the New button to create a new field. Custom settings fields use a subset of the data types available to custom object fields. They are Checkbox, Currency, Date, Date/Time, Email, Number, Percent, Phone, Text, Text Area, and URL. Select Checkbox for your field and click the Next button. For the field label, enter Debug. The Field Name, used to refer to the field in code, is automatically populated. Click the Next button.

5. Click the Save button to finish your field definition.

You're ready to store values in your custom settings object. Force.com provides a standard user interface for this purpose. Click the Manage button and then the New button. There is a field for the Name of the setting record, which serves as a human-readable identifier for the record. Following the name are the custom fields you've defined on the custom setting. In this case, you have a single check box field named Debug. Enter Default for the name, check the Debug box, and click the Save button.

Using Hierarchy Custom Settings

Hierarchy type custom settings provide additional options when storing values. To see them in action, create a new custom settings object called Hierarchy Setting with an object name of HierarchySetting. Again, add a check box field named Debug. The default value of Debug selected here is the organization-level setting, which applies if there are no values defined for a user or profile.

When you've finished creating the custom setting, add a new value to it. You are prompted to set the value of the Debug field as with the List custom setting example. But there is an additional system field called Location. Location determines at which level in the hierarchy the setting applies. There are two options: Profile and User. Try to create two custom setting records, one with Debug checked for the System Administrator profile and the other a user in that profile with Debug unchecked.

> **Caution**
>
> There are storage limits on custom settings data. For example, in a Developer Edition organization, you cannot store more than 2MB total in all of your custom settings. To view your current storage usage and the storage limit for your organization, go to the App Setup area and select Develop, Custom Settings.

Sample Application: Data Model

In this section, you'll build the Force.com database for the Services Manager sample application and import records into it. It begins with a discussion of design goals and a specification of the Services Manager data model. The remainder of the section describes how to implement the data model specification on Force.com and load sample data.

Data Model Design Goals

At a high level, the purpose of the Services Manager sample application is to staff consultants on customer projects based on their skills, and bill the customers for the consultants' time. This means the Force.com data model must store and manage information about the consultants, customers, projects, staffing assignments of consultants to projects, time spent on projects, and the skills of the consultants. This data model forms the foundation of the Services Manager sample application, implemented piecewise throughout this book, designed to illustrate features of the Force.com platform.

Two other, more tactical goals are described in the subsections to follow.

Optimized for Force.com Developer Edition

A guiding principle of this book is to focus on features available in the free, Developer Edition of the Force.com platform. Although it is possible to build a more realistic version of the Services Manager, one that could form the basis of a production application, it is likely to introduce dependencies on a premium version of the platform. The most notable example of a design decision that impacts licensing cost is user authentication, and it is worth discussing in depth.

In a real-world implementation, each consultant in the Services Manager would be its own user (a record in the standard object named User). This would enable that consultant to log in and view only the information he or she has access to. This granular user identity, authentication, and data access control (covered in Chapter 3) is one of the most valuable features of the Force.com platform, so naturally it is not free for unlimited use. Salesforce charges per user for its product.

Rather than using the standard User object and being subject to license restrictions, the Services Manager implementation is designed around the Contact object. There is no relevant limit on the number of free Contact records, and they are easy to create, with no passwords or activation codes required.

If you have a premium Force.com organization and would like to experiment with the User object, it is a simple migration path from the Contact object. Create a Lookup field on the User object, referring to the Contact object. That way, you can always restrict the Contact to the corresponding User who is currently logged in to Salesforce.

Leverage Standard Objects

There are many advantages to using standard objects wherever possible. They are shared by Salesforce's CRM applications such as Service Cloud and Sales Cloud, so there are many special features built in to the platform that you can benefit from. Also, if you plan to build or install other applications in your Force.com environment, they likely also leverage these objects. It's much simpler for applications to interoperate and coexist when they share the same core data objects.

The Services Manager tracks data about consultants and the companies that hire them. This is an excellent fit for the standard objects Contact and Account, respectively. They contain many standard fields for such things as name, addresses, phone numbers, and email address, which can be customized to meet the needs of any application. If the standard fields are not sufficient, you can also add custom fields, the same types of fields you add to custom objects.

Data Model Specification

This section provides the blueprint for building out the data model. As you learn to use the Schema Builder (described in the subsequent section) or an equivalent tool, refer back to this section for the details of the objects, fields, and relationships needed for Services Manager.

The first five subsections cover the objects and their fields. Although relationships are displayed alongside fields in Force.com's user interface, they are kept intentionally separate from the fields here. Instead, they are covered in the final subsection. It is easier to create relationships when all of the objects being related to each other already exist.

Contact

In the Services Manager application, a Contact record represents a consultant, an employee of the fictional professional services company. Contacts can also store information about a client of the services company. Contacts contain basic information, such as first and last name, email address, phone number, and mailing address. This is already captured by the standard Contact object. Contacts also have information specific to services delivery, such as primary skill, number of years of experience, education, and the hourly cost rate. The full list of custom fields to add to the Contact object is shown in Table 2.3.

Table 2.3 **Contact Custom Fields**

Field Name	Type	Type Options	Description
Active	Checkbox	Default Value: Checked	If false, this consultant has left the company or is otherwise unavailable
Education	Text	Length: 255	College(s) attended
Highest Education Level	Picklist	Values: High School, AA, BS, MS, MA, PhD	Most advanced degree attained
Home Office	Text	Length: 255	Office that this consultant typically works out of and/or lives nearest to
Hourly Cost Rate	Currency	Length: 16, Decimal Places: 2	Internal cost of resource, per hour
Industry Start Date	Date		Date started in the field
Region	Picklist	Values: Unspecified, East, West, Central	Area in the country this consultant works in
Start Date	Date		Date started with consulting company
Years of Experience	Formula	Return Type: Number, Decimal Places: 0, Formula: `FLOOR((TODAY() - Industry_ Start_Date__c) / 365)`	Calculated from Industry Start Date

Project

A project is a unit of work that the customer has contracted. It has financial attributes, such as the number of hours allocated for its completion, the expected revenue, and how billing is to be handled. It also has attributes for tracking its lifecycle, such as start and end date, status, stage, and notes. Table 2.4 contains the list of fields in the Project custom object.

Table 2.4   **Project Fields**

Field Name	Type	Type Options	Description
Name	Text	Length: 80	Project name
Type	Picklist	Values: Billable, Non-Billable	Type of project
Start Date	Date		Date project begins
End Date	Date		Date project ends
Billable Hours	Number	Length: 7, Decimal Places: 0	Number of billable hours allocated for this project, usually specified in the SOW
Consulting Budget	Currency	Length: 16, Decimal Places: 2	Amount budgeted for consulting portion of this project
Expense Budget	Currency	Length: 16, Decimal Places: 2	Amount budgeted for expenses
Invoiced	Checkbox	Default Value: Unchecked	Has the customer been invoiced?
Location	Text	Length: 255	Geographic location of this project
Project ID	Auto Number	External ID, Display Format: `Project-{00000}`, Starting Number: 1	Human-readable unique ID for this project
Notes	Long Text Area	Length: 32,000	General notes on the project
Stage	Picklist	Values: Planned, In Progress, Completed, Canceled	Stage of the project
Status	Picklist	Values: Green, Yellow, Red	Status of the project
Status Notes	Text Area		Explanation of the project status

Assignment

Projects are staffed with resources by the creation of assignments. Assignments associate a resource with a project for a specified period. Assignments contain a status, the role the resource is performing on the project, information about the hours billed and remaining, and expected and actual revenue. All Assignment fields are listed in Table 2.5.

Table 2.5 **Assignment Fields**

Field Name	Type	Type Options	Description
Name	Auto Number	Display Format: {MMDDYYYY}-{000}, Starting Number: 1	Assignment
Start Date	Date		Date that the assigned resource begins work on the project
End Date	Date		Date that the assigned resource finishes work on the project
Currently Assigned	Formula	Return Type: Text, Formula: IF(AND(Start_Date__c <= TODAY(), End_Date__c >= TODAY()), "Yes", "No")	If true, today is between Start Date and End Date
Description	Text	Length: 255	Description of this assignment (e.g., Design, Development)
Hourly Cost	Currency	Length: 4, Decimal Places: 2	Internal cost of the assigned resource
Hourly Rate	Currency	Length: 4, Decimal Places: 2	Rate at which the assigned resource is billed out
Total Hours	Number	Length: 5, Decimal Places: 2	Number of hours to be worked during this assignment
Planned Cost	Formula	Return Type: Currency, Decimal Places: 2, Formula: Total_Hours__c * Hourly_Cost__c	Expected cost of this assignment, equal to Total Hours multiplied by Hourly Cost
Planned Revenue	Formula	Return Type: Currency, Decimal Places: 2, Formula: Total_Hours__c * Hourly_Rate__c	Expected revenue from this assignment, equal to Total Hours multiplied by Hourly Rate
Planned Margin	Formula	Return Type: Currency, Decimal Places: 2, Formula: Planned_Revenue__c - Planned_Cost__c	Expected margin from this assignment, equal to Planned Cost minus Planned Revenue

Field Name	Type	Type Options	Description
Role	Text	Length: 255	Role of the resource on this project (e.g., Developer, Instructor)
Status	Picklist	Values: Tentative, Scheduled, Closed	Status of the assignment

Skill

To ensure that projects are staffed with qualified resources, the application must store information about the skills of each resource. A skill contains a name, type, and numeric rating of the competency level of the associated resource. Table 2.6 provides the list of fields in the Skill entity.

Table 2.6   **Skill Fields**

Field Name	Type	Type Options	Description
Name	Auto Number	Display Format: `skill-{00000}`, Starting Number: 1	Skill name
Notes	Text	Length: 255	Additional detail to back up the rating
Rating	Picklist	Values: 0 - None, 1 - Minimal, 2 - Below Average, 3 - Average, 4 - Above Average, 5 - Expert	Proficiency of associated Contact in this skill
Type	Picklist	Validation Rule: `ISPICKVAL(Type__c, '')`, Values: Amazon Web Services, Apex, Application Design, C#, Data Modeling, Documentation, Facebook, Google Data, GUI Design, Java, Perl, PHP, Project Management, Ruby, Training	Type of skill (e.g., Java), nonempty value required

Timecard

As resources work on projects, they keep track of their time. The hours spent each day are logged to a timecard. Each timecard represents a week of work on the project. Multiplying the number of hours worked by the internal cost of the consultant produces a cost. You can find the full list of fields in the Timecard custom object in Table 2.7.

Table 2.7   **Timecard Fields**

Field Name	Type	Type Options	Description
Name	Auto Number	Display Format: {MMDDYYYY}-{00000}, Starting Number: 1	Timecard name
Billable	Checkbox		If true, hours in this timecard are billable
Sunday Hours	Number	Length: 2, Decimal Places: 2	Hours worked on Sunday
Monday Hours	Number	Length: 2, Decimal Places: 2	Hours worked on Monday
Tuesday Hours	Number	Length: 2, Decimal Places: 2	Hours worked on Tuesday
Wednesday Hours	Number	Length: 2, Decimal Places: 2	Hours worked on Wednesday
Thursday Hours	Number	Length: 2, Decimal Places: 2	Hours worked on Thursday
Friday Hours	Number	Length: 2, Decimal Places: 2	Hours worked on Friday
Saturday Hours	Number	Length: 2, Decimal Places: 2	Hours worked on Saturday
Invoiced	Checkbox		If true, this timecard has been invoiced
Invoice Number	Text	Length: 255	Invoice number associated with this timecard
Invoice Date	Date		Date timecard was invoiced
Status	Picklist	Values: Saved, Submitted, Approved, Rejected	Status of this timecard
Notes	Long Text Area	Length: 32,000	Any comments on the timecard, entered by the consultant
Week Ending	Date		Last day in the week recorded by this timecard (a Saturday)

Field Name	Type	Type Options	Description
Total Hours	Formula	Return Type: Number, Decimal Places: 2, Formula: `Sunday_Hours__c +` `Monday_Hours__c +` `Tuesday_Hours__c +` `Wednesday_Hours__c` `+ Thursday_Hours__c` `+ Friday_Hours__c +` `Saturday_Hours__c`	Total number of hours worked this week, equal to the sum of the individual hours columns (Sunday to Saturday)

Summary of Data Relationships

Table 2.8 lists the data relationships in the Services Manager and the Force.com relationship types corresponding to them.

Table 2.8   Relationships in Services Manager

Parent	Child	Child Requires Parent?	Force.com Relationship Type
Account	Project	No	Lookup
Timecard	Assignment	No	Lookup
Contact	Skill	Yes	Master-Detail
Project	Timecard	Yes	Master-Detail
Contact	Timecard	Yes	Master-Detail
Project	Assignment	Yes	Master-Detail
Contact	Assignment	Yes	Master-Detail

Figure 2.7 shows the same relationships in a diagram format.

The two Lookup relationships in the Services Manager are between Account and Project, and Timecard and Assignment. They are Lookup relationships because they are optional. An Account does not require a Project, and a Project does not require an Account. An Assignment does not require a Timecard.

The remainder of the relationships are Master-Detail. In all of them, the child record requires a parent record. For example, Timecard records cannot exist without a corresponding Contact and Project. For mandatory relationships like this, Master-Detail is a good starting point because referential integrity is enforced. If a Project record is deleted, all child Timecard records are also deleted.

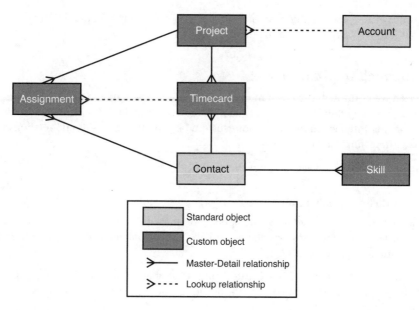

Figure 2.7   Relationship diagram

You might wonder why Contact and Skill are not a many-to-many relationship. It would be the more normalized way to go. But with the simpler, single Master-Detail relationship, the only repeated field is Skill Type. You can use a picklist field to keep users working from the same list of valid skills and a validation rule to increase data integrity. If Skill had a larger set of its own attributes and they could not be expressed as picklists, it would be a good candidate for a many-to-many relationship.

You should be aware of the following limitations of Master-Detail relationships:

- Force.com supports a maximum of four levels of cascading Master-Detail relationships. So a child object in a Master-Detail relationship can be the parent of another Master-Detail relationship, and so on. The four-level limit in genealogical terms means that a child can have a great-grandparent object but not a great-great-grandparent. The canonical example of cascading Master-Detail is the purchase order: A purchase order contains one or more line items, and each line item contains one or more line item details.

- A single object cannot be the child in more than two Master-Detail relationships. When an object is the child of two Master-Detail relationships, that object is referred to as a junction object. It joins two parent objects in a many-to-many relationship. In the Services Manager data model, Assignment and Timecard are junction objects.

In Force.com as in any technology, there are many ways to do the same things, some better than others. Given this first cut of the Services Manager data model, these restrictions on Master-Detail do not seem to be a problem. Incidentally, all the reasons that Master-Detail relationships were chosen can be also satisfied using Lookup fields in conjunction with other Force.com features, to be discussed in later chapters.

Implementing the Data Model

This section walks through the creation of the Services Manager data model in Force.com using Force.com App Builder Tools and Schema Builder. This includes a custom application to contain the user interface components, four custom objects, and the fields and relationships on both the custom and standard objects.

To begin, log in to your DE account and click Setup.

Creating a Custom Application

It's a good practice to define your custom application first so that you can add tabs to it as you build them. The following steps describe how to create a custom application, assign its tabs, and determine which users can see it:

1. In the App Setup section, click Create, Apps. A list of applications is displayed. Ignore the built-in applications. Most come with the DE account and cannot be removed. Click the New button.

2. Enter a label for the application, a name, and a description, and then click the Next button. The label is the human-readable label for the application, displayed to users. Name is an internal name, used by Force.com at the API level.

3. Optionally, select an image to be displayed as the logo for your application. This image is shown in the upper-left corner when your application is active. When you're done, click the Next button.

> ### Tip
>
> To prepare an image for use as an application logo, first go to the Documents tab and click the New button. Check the Externally Available Image check box, enter a name to identify the image, and click the Browse button to locate a file on your computer. Click the Save button to upload the image.

4. This screen is for selecting the tabs to be included in the custom application. Home tab is a system-provided tab included in every application and cannot be removed. There are no tabs defined for the application yet, so do nothing here. Click the Next button.

5. You can restrict access to your application by profile, a grouping of user permissions discussed in Chapter 3. For now, grant access to System Administrator by clicking the last check box in the Visible column. Then click the Save button.

You are returned to the list of applications, but it now contains your new application. If you activate your application by selecting it from the list in the upper-right corner drop-down, you'll see that it contains a single tab, the Home tab.

Creating a Custom Object

The following steps define the custom object for Project:

1. In the App Setup section, click Schema Builder. Initially, all objects, standard and custom, are shown on the canvas. System objects, a subset of standard objects, are not shown.

2. Click the Clear All link to hide all objects from the canvas. This makes it easier to focus on the task.

3. Click the Elements tab. Drag the Object item from the palette on the left onto the canvas. The dialog in Figure 2.8 is shown to capture the details of the new object.

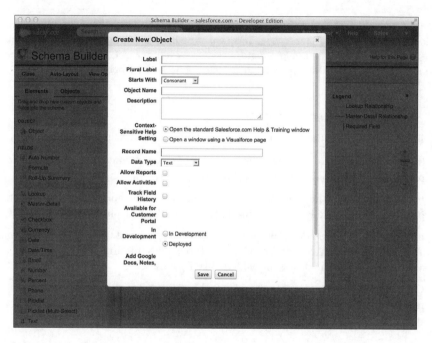

Figure 2.8   Create New Object dialog

4. Enter Project for the Label and Projects for the Plural Label. The Object Name defaults to Project. Enter a one-line description of the object in the Description field. Enter Project Name for the Record Name Label, and leave the data type Text. Check Allow Reports, Allow Activities, and Track Field History; then click the Save button.

5. Now that the object has been created, it's time to create the fields. Start with the Type field. It is a picklist field, so drag a picklist from the palette on the left to the canvas, dropping it directly onto the Project object.

6. In the resulting dialog, enter Type for the label. When your cursor exits the label, the Field Name is automatically populated. For the list of values, enter Billable. Press Enter

to start a new line, and then enter Non-Billable. Click to enable the Use First Value as Default Value option. Click the Save button. You should see the Type field added to the top of the Project object.

Repeat steps 5 and 6 until all the fields of Project, listed in Table 2.4, are created. There will be different options in step 6 depending on the type of the field.

At this point, you have finished defining the first custom object of the Services Manager sample application. To create the remainder of the objects, follow the same steps.

> **Note**
>
> A few of the objects require that the standard field Name be changed from its default type (Text of length 80) to an Auto Number type. This cannot be done within the Schema Builder. Instead, visit the App Builder Tools (Setup, Create, Objects), click the object, click the Edit link beside the standard Name field, and proceed to set the type to Auto Number.

Creating Relationship Fields

The following steps create the Lookup relationship between Project and Account:

1. In the Elements tab in Schema Builder, drag the Lookup relationship type from the palette. Drop it onto the child object. In this case, the child object is Project.

2. In the dialog, enter the Field Label and Field Name. This is typically the name of the parent object. For the Project-Account relationship, the name is Account.

3. In the Related To drop-down list, select the parent object and then click the Next button. The parent object is Account. The Child Relationship Name and Related List Label are automatically set. The dialog should look like Figure 2.9.

4. Click the Save button to create the relationship field. A line will indicate the new relationship between the two objects. The fork symbol at one end of the line indicates the child object. In this case, the fork appears on the Project side.

Repeat these steps until all the Lookup relationships listed in Table 2.8 are created. The steps to create Master-Detail relationships are slightly different. The following steps create the Master-Detail relationship between Project and Timecard:

1. In the Elements tab in Schema Builder, drag the Master-Detail relationship type from the palette. Drop it onto the child object. In this case, the child object is Timecard.

2. In the dialog, enter the Field Label and Field Name. This usually refers to the parent object. In the Project-Timecard relationship, the name is Project.

3. In the Related To drop-down list, select the parent object and then click the Next button. The parent object is Project. The Child Relationship Name and Related List Label fields are automatically set, in this case to Timecards. The dialog should look like Figure 2.10.

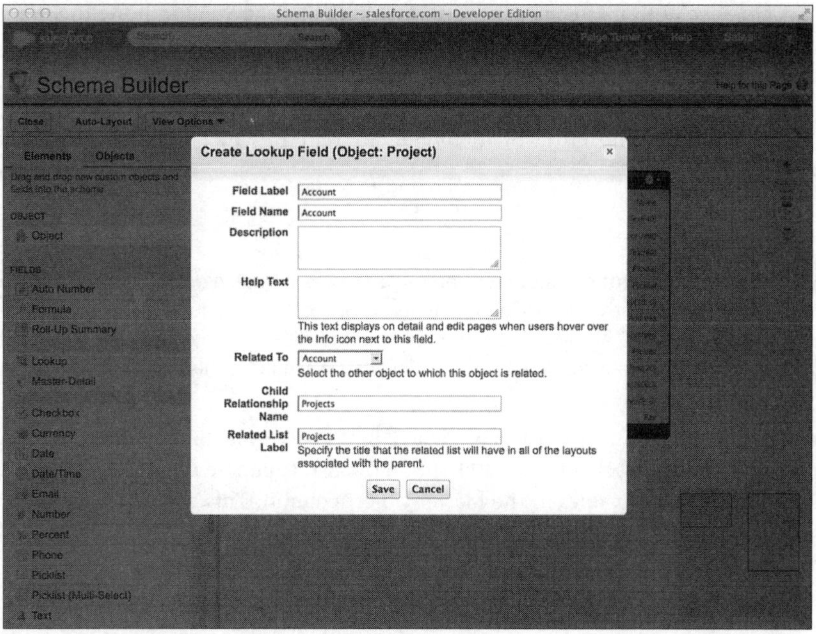

Figure 2.9   Create Lookup Field dialog

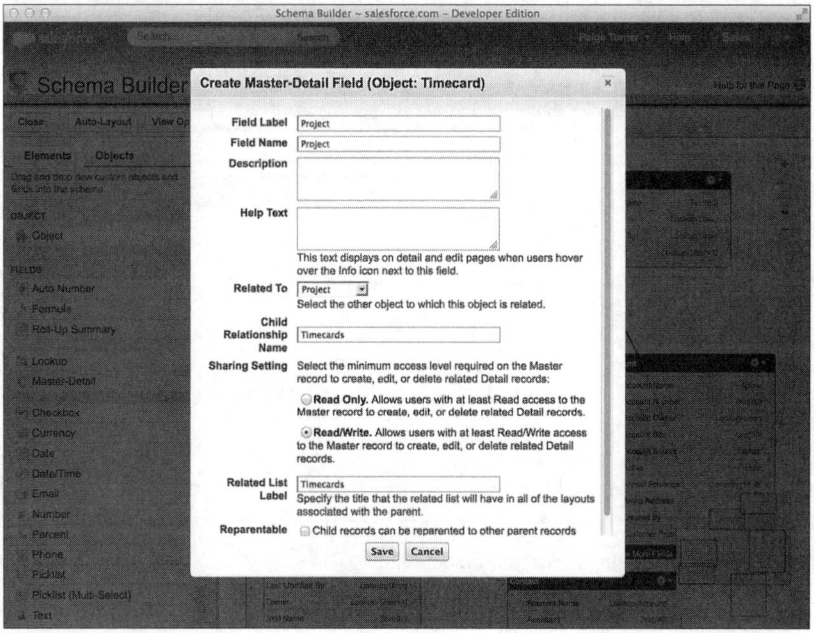

Figure 2.10   Create Master-Detail Field dialog

4. Click the Save button to create the relationship field. A line will indicate the new relationship between the two objects. The fork symbol at one end of the line indicates the child object. In this case, the fork appears on the Timecard side.

As you build the relationships, the visual representation in Schema Builder should resemble the diagram in Figure 2.7.

> **Tip**
>
> One of the most important parts of creating relationships is making sure that they are created on the correct object. In the one-to-many relationship, the "one" side is the parent, and the "many" side is the child. Always create the relationship field on the child, relating it to the parent. You can always delete the field and start over if you make a mistake.

Repeat these steps for each relationship in Table 2.8. When you're done, visit the list of custom objects (Setup, Create, Objects). Figure 2.11 shows the list. Compare it with yours, paying particular attention to the values in the Master Object column. This column is showing the Master-Detail relationships. There should be a total of five master objects listed across all of the relationships.

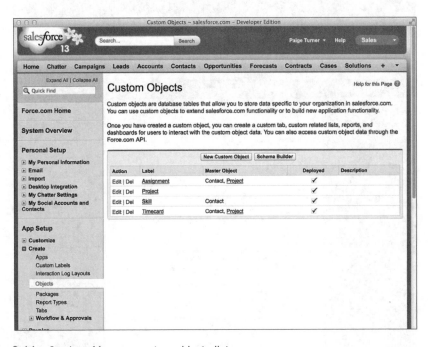

Figure 2.11   Services Manager custom objects list

Creating a Validation Rule

The Skill object requires a new validation rule to enforce that Skill Type field contains a nonempty value. Although this requirement could be configured at the user interface level via a page layout, placing it on the object itself ensures that it is applied consistently across all user interfaces and other channels for data input, such as importing tools. It doesn't make sense to have a Skill record without a Skill Type. Follow these steps to create the validation rule:

1. Go to the Objects list in App Builder Tools (Setup, Create, Objects) and click the Skill object.

2. Find the Validation Rules heading and click the New button.

3. Set the name to Type.

4. The code in Listing 2.9 checks for an empty picklist value. Enter it in the Error Condition Formula text area.

Listing 2.9 **Error Condition Formula for Skill Type Field**

```
ISPICKVAL(Type__c, '')
```

5. In the Error Message text area, enter "Type must contain a value."

6. Click the Save button to create the validation rule.

Creating a Custom Object Tab

Custom object tabs are the gateway to all the native user interface functionality for managing data in your custom object. The following steps create a custom object tab for the Project object:

1. Go to the Objects list in App Builder Tools (Setup, Create, Tabs) and click the New button in the Custom Object Tabs heading.

2. The New Custom Object Tab Wizard is now displayed. Select the Project object from the Object field. Click the Lookup icon (magnifying glass) to select a style for the tab and then click the Next button.

3. Visibility of this tab by profile is easy to change later, so leave this screen unchanged and click the Next button. This means the new tab is visible for all profiles.

4. In the Add to Custom Apps screen, click the Include Tab check box at the top to uncheck it for all applications, and then check it for Services Manager only. Click the Save button to complete the creation of the custom tab.

Repeat these steps to create custom object tabs for all four custom objects in the Services Manager.

Setting Field Visibility

New custom fields are hidden by default. They are not visible in user interfaces in Force.com, and they are also invisible to external tools such as Data Loader. To start using these fields, you must first make them visible.

Perform the following steps to make the custom fields in Contact visible:

1. In the Administration Setup area, click Manage Users, Profiles.

2. Click the System Administrator profile.

3. Scroll down to the heading Field-Level Security, and click the View link beside the Contact object.

4. Click the Edit button, and enable all of the check boxes in the Visible column.

5. Click the Save button to commit your changes to the object's field visibility.

Repeat these steps for the other four objects.

Importing Data

In this section, you will import sample project and resource data into the Force.com database using the Data Loader tool. This process is divided into three stages: preparing the data, importing it, and then verifying it visually using the native user interface. This is certainly not the only way to import data into Force.com, and probably not the easiest. But it employs a free, widely used, fully supported tool from Salesforce that can scale up to support large numbers of records and complex objects.

Data Preparation

Data Loader operates on CSV files. The first line of the file contains a header listing the columns present in the data. The following lines are the body of the data, with each line a record, values separated by commas. You should have access to Microsoft Excel or an equivalent tool for working with CSV files.

To begin, export CSV files for the Project and Contact objects. Because there is no data yet in the database, these files will be empty except for the header line. This serves as a template for the import file, providing an example of the data layout expected by the Data Loader.

To export, perform the following steps:

1. Launch Data Loader. Click the Export button.

2. Enter your username and password and click the Log In button. Make sure your password includes a Security Token appended to it. If you have not yet obtained a Security Token, log in to Force.com using your Web browser; navigate to Setup, My Personal Information, Reset My Security Token; click the Reset Security Token button; and get the Security Token from the email sent to you by Force.com. Click the Next button when your login is completed.

3. Select the Project object to export. Click the Browse button to name the export file and specify its directory. Name the file the same as the object name, and save it where you'll readily find it, such as the desktop. Then click the Next button.

4. Click the Select All Fields button. Then remove the system fields, which are Id, OwnerId, IsDeleted, CreatedDate, CreatedById, LastModifiedDate, LastModifiedById, and SystemModstamp. Click the Finish button.

5. Answer Yes to the confirmation dialog. The export is performed, and a summary dialog is shown. Click the OK button to dismiss it. You now have a CSV file on your desktop containing a single line with the names of the exported fields.

Repeat this process for the Contact object, but this time remove all the standard fields in step 4 except for Id.

You should have two files on your desktop. Create a new worksheet and import contact.csv into it. Repeat this for project.csv.

Listing 2.10 is a sample import file containing five Contact records. In the first column, use the actual Id values from your contact.csv instead of the values shown here. Listing 2.11 contains five sample Project records. Make sure you save the Project and Contact Excel worksheets as two separate CSV files when you're done. (Note: Only a certain number of code characters will fit on one line on the page. The arrow symbol indicates where code that should be entered as one line is wrapped to the next line.)

Listing 2.10   CSV Import File for Contact

```
ID,ACTIVE__C,EDUCATION__C,HIGHEST_EDUCATION_LEVEL__C,
➡HOURLY_COST_RATE__C,HOME_OFFICE__C,REGION__C,START_DATE__C,
➡INDUSTRY_START_DATE__C,YEARS_OF_EXPERIENCE__C
003i0000008TTBqAAO,TRUE,
➡University of Chicago,MS,100,Chicago,Central,2/3/2003,6/1/1983,
003i0000008TTBrAAO,TRUE,St. Edwards
➡University,BS,50,Austin,Central,5/15/2006,5/15/2006,
003i0000008TTBsAAO,TRUE,Cascade College,BS,40,Portland,West,
➡7/1/2008,1/1/2005,
003i0000008TTBtAAO,TRUE,University of
➡Arizona,PhD,120,Tucson,West,10/15/2004,3/1/1992,
003i0000008TTBuAAO,TRUE,Fordham University,MS,125,New
➡York,East,6/28/2007,5/1/1979,
```

Listing 2.11   CSV Import File for Project

```
NAME,TYPE__C,START_DATE__C,END_DATE__C,BILLABLE_HOURS__C,
➡CONSULTING_BUDGET__C,EXPENSE_BUDGET__C,INVOICED__C,LOCATION__C,
➡PROJECT_ID__C,NOTES__C,STAGE__C,STATUS__C,STATUS_NOTES__C
GenePoint,Billable,1/12/2015,,800,
```

➡200000,20000,FALSE,"Mountain View, CA",
➡,Phase 2,In Progress,Green,
Grand Hotels & Resorts Ltd,Billable,2/16/2015,,100,
➡30000,0,FALSE,"Chicago, IL",
➡,,In Progress,Green,
United Oil & Gas Corp.,Billable,2/9/2015,,500,
➡75000,10000,FALSE,"New York, NY",
➡,,In Progress,Green,
Burlington Textiles Corp of America,Billable,2/2/2015,,200,
➡40000,5000,FALSE,"Burlington, NC",
➡,,In Progress,Green,
Express Logistics and Transport,Non-Billable,3/1/2015,,0,
➡0,0,FALSE,"Portland, OR",
➡,Presales,In Progress,Green,

Data Import

Now that the data is prepared, you're ready to import it. Launch Data Loader again, log in, and then follow these steps:

1. From the File menu, select Update.

2. Select Contact from the list of Salesforce objects.

3. Click the Browse button and locate your `contact.csv` file, and then click the Next button.

4. The file structure is verified, and a small dialog is displayed showing the number of records contained in the file. Check to make sure that this matches the number of records you expected. Click the OK button to continue.

5. The mapping dialog takes columns from your file and matches them with fields in the Force.com object. Click the Create or Edit a Map button.

6. The easiest way to create the mapping is to click the Auto-Match Fields to Columns button. Because the import files were actually once export files, the columns should match perfectly. Figure 2.12 shows the result of this mapping. All the available Force.com fields except for OwnerId were mapped to columns of the CSV file. The YEARS_OF_EXPERIENCE__C column has no mapping because it is a Formula field and cannot be modified. Click the OK button to continue.

7. The new mapping is copied to the current mapping screen. Click the Next button.

8. Click the Browse button to locate a directory to save the results of the import. Data Loader creates two files, one containing errors and another containing success messages. Click the Finish button to begin the import and click Yes to confirm.

9. A dialog is shown with the results of the import. If you received errors, click the View Errors button to examine them, fix your import file accordingly, and try the import again.

Repeat this process for `project.csv`.

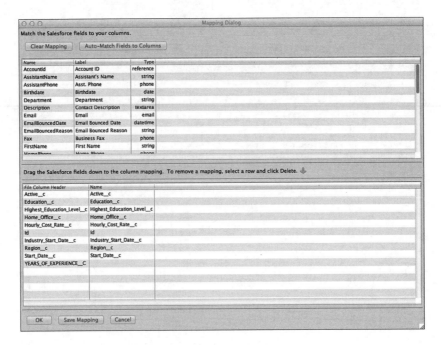

Figure 2.12   Column-to-field mapping for `contact.csv`

Data Verification

Data Loader outputs a CSV file containing the records successfully imported. But a more friendly way to look at the successfully imported data is to log in to Force.com and browse the records using the native user interface.

After you log in, select the Services Manager application from the application drop-down list in the upper-right corner of the screen. It contains six tabs, one for each of the custom objects defined in this chapter plus the standard Accounts and Contacts tabs. Click the Contacts tab and then click the Go button to display the view named All Contacts, which contains all the records of the Contact object.

You should see a list of the contact records you just imported. By default, only the names are shown. You can modify this view to show more fields by clicking the Edit link to the left of the Create New View link and then adding fields in the Select Fields to Display section. Figure 2.13 shows a modified All Contacts View.

Figure 2.14 shows the detail of an individual Contact record. Verify that the currency and dates imported correctly. Notice that the number of years of experience was calculated from the Industry Start Date field.

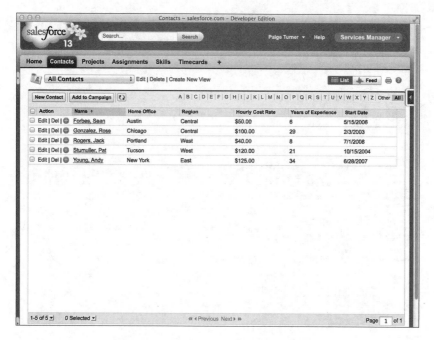

Figure 2.13   Modified All Contacts View

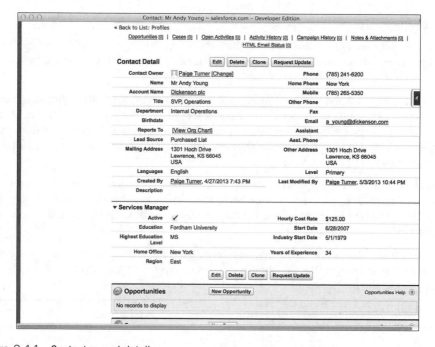

Figure 2.14   Contact record detail

To complete your rounds, browse to the Projects tab. Manually associate each Project with a parent Account of your choice, and verify that all the field types were imported correctly.

Summary

This chapter engaged you with the Force.com database in areas essential for application development. The skills covered in this chapter should enable you to build various data-driven applications, all through configuration rather than coding. Here are some key points to take forward:

- The Force.com database is not a standard relational database. It's a logical database based on Objects and Fields, like Tables and Columns but tuned for business applications and integrated into every feature of the platform.

- Custom objects are the backbone of development in Force.com. By defining them and their fields, you are also defining a user interface that is programmatically generated by Force.com. This interface allows data to be entered and browsed without coding, while preserving the data integrity called for in your object definition.

- Services Manager consists of four custom objects and leverages two standard objects: Account and Contact.

3

Database Security

For many developers, securing an application is the drudge work left after the fun and challenging development work is done. The good news is that Force.com makes security relatively painless, whether you think about it before, during, or after an application is built. The concepts of user identity, data ownership, and fine-grained access control are baked into the platform, requiring configuration rather than coding in most cases.

You might wonder why this chapter is about only database security rather than being a general discussion of security. After all, Force.com is more than a database. The reason is that the database is the center of Force.com development. Just as object definitions are leveraged throughout the platform to construct native user interfaces and strongly typed procedural code expressions, data security measures are equally pervasive.

This chapter contains the following sections:

- **Overview of database security**—Take a high-level view of the database security features available in Force.com and how they interact to protect your data.

- **Object-level security**—Get in depth on the methods for protecting individual data objects and their fields.

- **Record-level security**—Learn how to control access to individual records within your Force.com database.

- **Sample application**—Walk through the design and implementation of the security model for the Services Manager.

Overview of Database Security

Force.com provides a multilayered approach to data security. Each layer secures data using a different approach, and the layers build on each other to provide a deep, configurable defense. Figure 3.1 identifies the layers of security and their relationship to data and other layers.

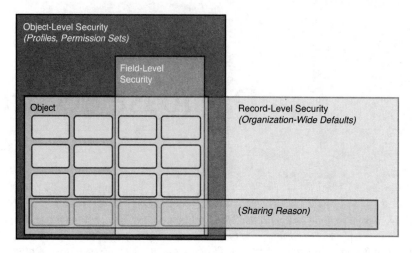

Figure 3.1   Security architecture

The box enclosing the Object represents object-level security, which is provided by profiles and permission sets. A profile is a unit of Force.com metadata used to group users with common data access requirements. It contains a set of permissions for every object defined in the Force. com organization. These permissions determine whether users belonging to the profile are authorized to read, create, edit, and delete records of each object. Also within the profile are rules determining access to individual fields of an object. Fields can be hidden entirely or defined as read-only directly in the profile or in page layouts.

Permission sets contain the same permission-related metadata as profiles, but a user can be assigned to many of them at once. In contrast, a user is assigned to a single profile at a time. Permission sets are generally used to override profiles on an individual user basis.

Record-level security is layered on top of object-level security. It further restricts access to data based on the concept of record ownership. But it can never override object-level security. Organization-wide defaults define the default, most restrictive sharing behavior of each object, and sharing reasons create exceptions to this default behavior, granting access to specific groups of users.

Another way to think about Force.com security features is to imagine them as a funnel, as shown in Figure 3.2. Requests for data enter the top of the funnel and descend, filtered through successive layers of security technology. If the requests survive until the bottom of the funnel, they have passed security clearance and are granted.

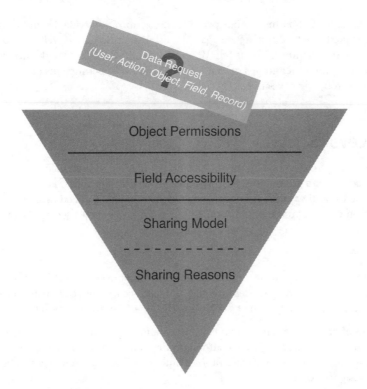

Figure 3.2   Security architecture as a funnel

The four filters in the funnel are described here:

1. **Object permissions**—At the top of the funnel, the data request is evaluated against the object permissions. They ensure that the requesting user is authorized by its profile to take the desired action on this object. The solid line under this level indicates that requests denied at this point stop moving through the funnel.

2. **Field accessibility**—The requesting user's profile is consulted again to determine whether fields are included in the request that are read-only or hidden.

3. **Sharing model**—If the user is not the owner of this record or otherwise privileged with an administrative profile, organization-wide defaults are applied. These defaults designate records of each object as private, public with Read and Write access, or public with read-only access. In a slight break of the funnel concept indicated by the dashed line, if the sharing model prohibits access, the request has one more chance to be granted through exceptions called sharing reasons.

4. **Sharing reasons**—Sharing reasons override the organization-wide defaults. The owner of the requested record is matched against a list of sharing reasons relevant to its group affiliation. If a sharing reason is found, access is granted. Groups are defined as simple lists of users and other groups or as a hierarchy, allowing permissions of subordinates to be inherited by their superiors.

Object-Level Security

Object-level security is governed by the profile and permission sets assigned to the user. Profiles control data access for a group of users on the level of objects and fields. Permission sets also control data access at the object and field level, but are designed to maximize reuse and flexibility. This section describes profiles and permission sets and how they are configured.

Profiles

Profiles are the primary way to customize the Force.com user experience. They contain a large number of settings to control the user interface and data security of your organization. Users are assigned to profiles based on the tasks they need to perform in your system.

The two types of profiles are standard and custom. Standard profiles are provided with Force.com and cannot be renamed or deleted, although they can be reconfigured. Custom profiles have the same functionality as standard profiles but can be named. They can also be deleted if no users are assigned to them.

To manage profiles, click Setup, and in the Administration Setup area, click Manage Users, Profiles. In the realm of data security, the two primary sections to focus on are Administrative Permissions and Object Permissions.

> **Tip**
>
> Make sure Enhanced Profile List Views and Enhanced Profile User Interface options are enabled for your organization. The Enhanced Profile List Views feature allows up to 200 profiles at a time to be compared and modified easily, with far fewer clicks than the default user interface. The Enhanced Profile User Interface organizes profile settings by common administrative tasks and makes them searchable. To enable these features, click Setup, and in the App Setup area, click Customize, User Interface.

Administrative Permissions

Two administrative privileges in a profile trump all other security features in Force.com: Modify All Data and View All Data. Users of a profile with these permissions can modify and view all records of all objects, overriding all Force.com security measures. These permissions are powerful, so grant them with extreme care in a production environment. Developers need these permissions to work with tools such as the Force.com IDE, but this applies only in a sandbox or development environment.

Object Settings

Object permissions are divided into two sections: one for standard objects and another for custom objects. They have identical functionality. Note that object permissions cannot be edited on standard profiles. Figure 3.3 shows the section of a custom profile that defines object permissions.

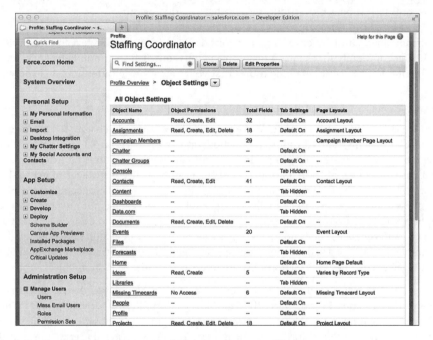

Figure 3.3   Configuring object permissions on a custom profile

Each object name is followed by a list of its permissions. The permissions are described in the following list:

- **Read**—The Read permission allows users to view records of this object.

- **Create**—The Create permission permits Read access and the addition of new records to the object.

- **Edit**—The Edit permission allows records in this object to be read and modified, unless overridden by field-level permissions.

- **Delete**—The Delete permission enables users to read, edit, and remove records from this object. Deleted records are moved to the Recycle Bin, where they can be undeleted or permanently erased.

- **View All**—The View All permission is like the systemwide View All administrative permission but scoped to a single object. It's designed for use in exporting data because it circumvents other security features of the platform, ensuring that all records are accessible.

- **Modify All**—Like View All, the Modify All permission is intended for bulk data operations such as migration and cleansing. It allows users to modify all fields of all records in this object, overriding every other security measure.

New custom objects initially have all permissions disabled for all profiles, except those with View All Data or Modify All Data administrative permissions. This platform behavior of defaulting to the most secure configuration ensures that your data is not unintentionally exposed.

Licensing

Profiles are associated with a user license. Licenses are how Salesforce charges for the Force.com platform when you're ready to go into production with an application. Salesforce has many license types to provide flexibility in pricing, including low-priced options for external customers and partners known as "portal licenses," but the most basic licenses are Salesforce and Salesforce Platform. The Salesforce Platform license allows full use of Force.com but disables the business domain-specific functionality, such as CRM or Sales Force Automation (SFA). For example, a Salesforce license grants you the use of the Opportunity and Case objects, but a Salesforce Platform license does not. Sometimes even infrastructure features are downgraded. For example, profiles for a full Salesforce license can delegate administration on standard and custom objects. The Salesforce Platform license limits this feature to custom objects only.

Planning ahead pays in regard to licensing Force.com. If you are sure you do not need the extra features of the Salesforce license, select the Salesforce Platform license for your profiles. This cuts down on the number of objects and features you see during development and prevents you from accidentally referencing one of them. Also, in order to assign a user to a profile, that user must have a user license that matches the profile. Your custom profile cannot be associated with a different license after it has been created.

Permission Sets

Permission sets are a powerful complement to profiles. They contain the same user interface and data security settings as profiles, but are designed to address situations in which the settings do not apply to a large enough population of users to justify the use of a profile, or there are too many valid combinations of settings to create a profile for each one.

For example, if one special sales rep was allowed to tentatively staff consultants to projects, he or she would require the permissions resulting from a partial combination of the Sales Rep profile and the Staffing Coordinator profile. It is not possible to combine profiles or partially apply them, so without permission sets you would need to create a whole new one-off profile for this situation. Permission sets provide an elegant, maintainable solution. You would create a permission set to grant access to the Assignment object only. The special sales rep would get assigned to this permission set, leaving his or her profile unchanged.

To manage permission sets, click Setup, and in the Administration Setup area, click Manage Users, Permission Sets. The overview page of a permission set is shown in Figure 3.4. It provides links to all of the configurable areas of a permission set. They are divided into settings specific to applications and settings that apply to all applications. After a permission set is created, it can be assigned to users using the related list on the user page labeled Permission Set Assignments.

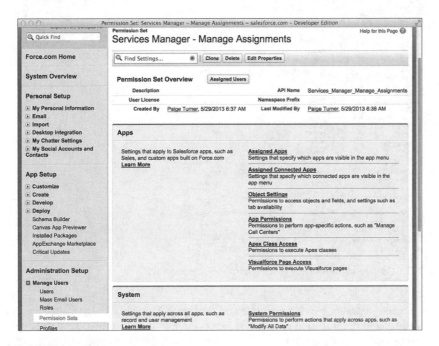

Figure 3.4   Permissions set overview

Field-Level Security

Security of fields is determined by a combination of the profile and the page layout. The more restrictive of the two always takes precedence. The two ways to edit field-level security are through the profile directly using the Field-Level Security section or through a feature called Field Accessibility. Field Accessibility is a bit more sophisticated because it provides a consolidated view of fields across page layouts and profiles.

Field-Level Security in Profiles

To reach the Field-Level Security section, click Setup, and in the Administration Setup area, click Manage Users, Profiles. Select a profile by clicking its name and scroll down to the Field-Level Security section. Click the View link next to the object name, such as Project, shown in Figure 3.5.

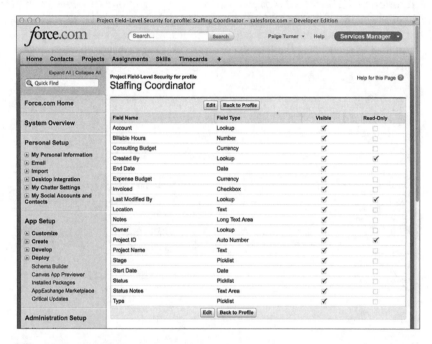

Figure 3.5   Configuring field-level security for the Project object

The two possible states for a field are visible and read-only. Fields marked as visible are available for display and modification on page layouts belonging to this profile. Read-only fields might also be visible on a page layout, but values in these fields cannot be modified.

Field Accessibility

Field Accessibility addresses the finer control of fields provided through the combination of page layout and profile. The more restrictive of two settings always wins. So, if a page layout defines a field as read-only that is defined in the profile as being invisible, the profile takes precedence, and the field is hidden. Field Accessibility provides an easy way to see this behavior in action.

To use Field Accessibility, click Setup, and in the Administration Setup area, click Security Controls, Field Accessibility. Select an object and then drill in by Field or Profile to see the corresponding field accessibility table. Each field has one of four accessibility values:

- **Required**—If a field is defined as required in its page layout and visible in its profile, it is a required field. This means for a record to be saved, it must contain a value for this field.

- **Editable**—A field defined as visible in both the page layout and the profile is designated as editable. This field appears to the user and can be modified.

- **Read-only**—If a field is declared read-only on its profile or visible in its profile and read-only in its page layout, then it is a read-only field. It appears in the page layout, but its value cannot be modified.

- **Hidden**—Fields that are set to invisible on their profile or page layout are hidden. Hidden fields are never shown to the users of this profile.

Try marking a field as read-only in its page layout but invisible in its profile. Then hover the cursor over the word *Hidden* in the field accessibility table. You'll see the message that the field is hidden because of field security. If you edit the field again and make it visible via the profile, the field becomes read-only per the page layout.

Record-Level Security

In Force.com, individual data records within an object are secured through a combination of three concepts:

1. **Record ownership**—All records except those on the child side of a Master-Detail relationship have a single named owner. Record owners are individual users or groups of users. Ownership of a record can be transferred manually to another user or group.

2. **User groups**—Users can be organized into flat lists and placed in a hierarchy. Groups can contain individual users as well as other groups.

3. **Sharing model**—The sharing model consists of two parts: organization-wide defaults and sharing reasons. The organization-wide defaults can be configured to lock down all records by object, regardless of their owner. Sharing reasons selectively override the defaults to allow access based on record ownership or arbitrary criteria.

This section discusses each concept in more depth.

Record Ownership

When a new record is created, it's owned by the user who created it. The owner has full control over the record. The owner can read, edit, and delete the record; share with other users; and transfer ownership to a different user.

You can experiment with record ownership by creating a record in the native user interface and examining its detail. Notice that its owner field is set to your user, the user creating the record. To share the record with others, click the Sharing button. To transfer ownership, click the Change link beside the owner name.

Owners are typically individual users, but a queue can also be an owner. A queue is a holding area for records to which users are assigned. When a user takes ownership of a record in queue, it leaves the queue and is assigned directly to that user. To configure queues, go to the Administration Setup area and click Manage Users, Queues.

Most objects support record ownership. The notable exception is child objects in a Master-Detail relationship. Records in these child objects have no owners. They inherit ownership from their parent records, and changes in ownership must be made on the parent record.

User Groups

Record-level sharing operates on groups of users, not individual users. Force.com provides two mechanisms for grouping users relevant to sharing: public groups and roles.

Public Groups

At its simplest level, a public group is a named list of users included in the group. This list can also contain other public groups. To define a public group, click Setup. In the Administration Setup area, click Manage Users, Public Groups.

A best practice for public groups is to keep the membership list as short as possible. This improves performance and simplifies maintenance. Build larger groups up from smaller subgroups rather than working with individual users.

Roles

Roles are also groups of users but are organized in a hierarchy. Users in roles can inherit the privileges of the roles below them in the hierarchy. This includes record ownership.

A user belongs to one role at a time, and all applications in your Force.com organization use a single role hierarchy.

To define roles, click Setup. In the Administration Setup area, click Manage Users, Roles. The first time you use this feature, Force.com asks you to select a sample set of roles to get started.

Sharing Model

The sharing model defines how record-level privileges are granted to users who do not own the record. Configuring the sharing model is a two-part process. Organization-wide defaults are used to establish the most restrictive level of access for each object. Sharing reasons override the defaults to grant access to individual records.

Organization-Wide Defaults

Every object that allows record ownership has an organization-wide default setting dictating how records are shared between the owner and other users. Custom objects have several default settings:

- **Private**—Records belong to the owner and only the owner. With the exception of the data administration-level privileges View All and Modify All, records are accessible only to their owners.

- **Public Read-Only**—Any user can view records in this object but cannot edit or delete them. Only the owner and users with administrative privileges have rights to edit and delete.

- **Public Read/Write**—Any user can view, edit, and delete records in this object. All newly created custom objects default to this setting.

- **Controlled by Parent**—This option is available only to child objects in Lookup relationships. It delegates record-sharing decisions to the parent record. The child records behave as if they lack an owner. Objects with this default setting have the same record-sharing behavior as children in a Master-Detail relationship.

When setting organization-wide defaults, begin with the user to receive the minimum access to data. Set the organization-wide default settings with this user in mind. All users then have at least this level of access to records. To configure organization-wide defaults, click Setup. In the Administration Setup area, click Security Controls, Sharing Settings. Figure 3.6 shows the screen with organization-wide defaults.

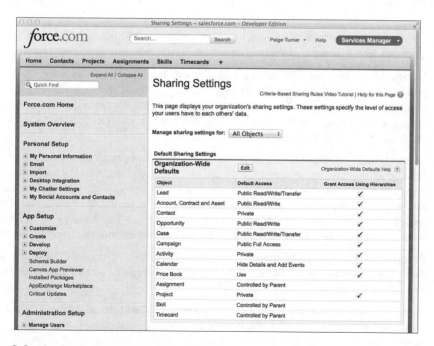

Figure 3.6   Configuring organization-wide defaults

The rightmost column of check boxes called Grant Access Using Hierarchies determines whether the role hierarchy is used on this object to propagate permissions upward to superior roles. By default, this behavior is enabled. Disabling it causes roles to function like public groups. Record permissions are shared only between a pair of roles, never aggregated up the role hierarchy.

Sharing Reasons

Sharing reasons override the organization-wide defaults to allow individual records to be shared between groups of users. The groups can be roles or public groups. The behavior of the sharing reason depends on the groups involved and the type of sharing reason.

Sharing between roles results in asymmetric privileges. Users in subordinate roles do not receive any privileges of their superiors, but superiors receive all the privileges of their subordinates. Sharing with public groups is symmetric, granting equal rights to both parties. In other words, a user has access to all records that are accessible to its descendants in the role hierarchy.

> **Note**
>
> Objects with the most permissive organization-wide default (public read/write) cannot use sharing reasons.

Objects with the most permissive organization-wide default (public read/write) cannot use sharing reasons. The four types of sharing reasons are as follows:

1. **Manual**—The owner of a record can elect to manually share it with another user or group of users. The owner specifies the level of access (Read Only or Read/Write) to be granted. To configure manual sharing, click the Sharing button on a detail record in the Force.com native user interface. Figure 3.7 shows the user interface for sharing a record named GenePoint in the Project object.

2. **Sharing rules**—Sharing rules allow records to be shared automatically by Force.com based on group membership or arbitrary criteria. In Figure 3.8, a sharing rule is being created for the Project object. It specifies that members of the West business unit can automatically read and write all Project records owned by their colleagues in the same business unit. In Figure 3.9, a criteria-based sharing rule is being defined to provide users in the Executive role with Read and Write access to billable projects.

3. **Procedural**—Records can be shared programmatically using Apex code. This allows a developer to define the conditions that govern the sharing of a record. This is discussed in Chapter 5, "Advanced Business Logic."

4. **Delegated administration**—Profiles contain two special systems permissions called View All Data and Modify All Data. If these are granted, they exempt users in that profile from all sharing rules, giving them access to all records regardless of owner. This privilege is intended for data import, export, and cleansing programs that need to run unencumbered by sharing rules.

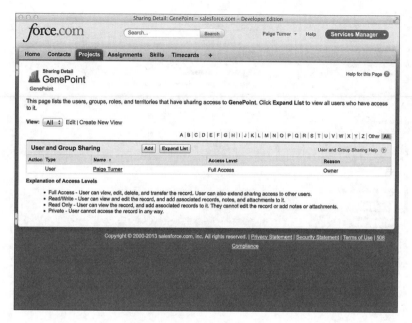

Figure 3.7   Manually sharing a Project record

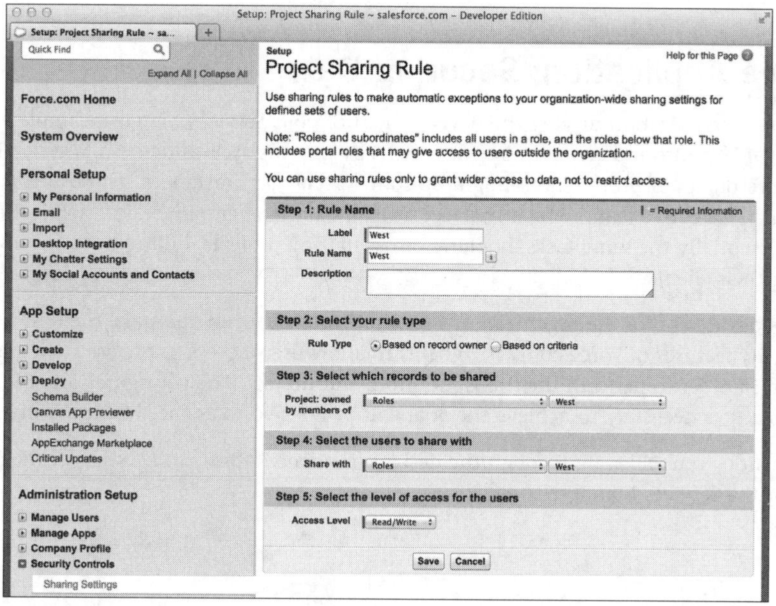

Figure 3.8   Creating a sharing rule for projects

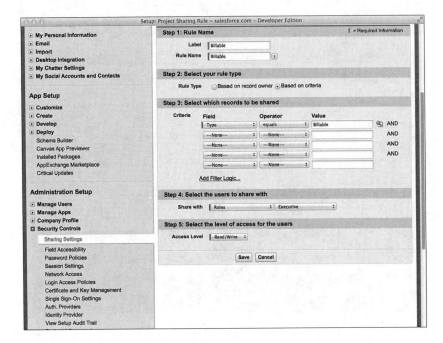

Figure 3.9   Creating a criteria-based sharing rule for projects

Sample Application: Securing Data

The fictional organization driving the development of your Services Manager sample application is organized into independent business units by geography. Business units generally do not share resources or projects, but might do so in special circumstances. All business units roll up to an executive team, which has access to all data. The employees of each business unit perform essentially the same tasks: booking deals, staffing projects, billing time on projects, and invoicing their clients.

From this description of the organization's structure, consider how to make the best use of the data security features of Force.com. The goal is to allow users access to precisely the right data they need in order to perform their jobs, no more and no less. The configuration of Force.com security features necessary to achieve the goal will be referred to as the security model.

In this section, you will walk through the design, implementation, and testing of the security model for the Services Manager application.

Designing the Security Model

To begin the design process, review the fundamentals of Force.com security and the sample application's security requirements:

- Force.com data security has two facets: profiles and the sharing model. Profiles protect objects and their fields, and the sharing model controls access to individual records.

- Data security in the sample application is determined by an employee's job function and business unit. Job functions are identical across business units, and business units do not normally share data.

The design strategy followed in the remainder of this section examines each of the sample application's security requirements and discusses the configuration of the Force.com security features necessary to satisfy them.

Security by Job Function

Job functions dictate what type of data a user is allowed to view and modify. For example, consultants should not create projects or assignments. A staffing coordinator creates projects and assigns resources to them. But a consultant is allowed to create and edit timecards.

As you're thinking about job functions, you're naturally discussing the objects that make up the application. In Force.com, profiles control access to objects and fields. To design profiles for the Services Manager application, start by listing all job functions and objects in a grid. At the intersection of each job function and object, determine the level of access needed. The level of access is expressed as a series of permissions. The permissions are read, create, edit, and delete. Table 3.1 shows the output of this exercise.

Table 3.1 **Services Manager Profiles**

Profile	Project	Contact	Timecard	Assignment	Skill	Account
Sales Rep	Read	Read			Read	Read
		Create				Create
		Edit				Edit
		Delete				Delete
Staffing Coordinator	Read	Read		Read	Read	Read
	Create	Create		Create		Create
	Edit	Edit		Edit		Edit
	Delete	Delete		Delete		

Profile	Project	Contact	Timecard	Assignment	Skill	Account
Project Manager	Read	Read	Read	Read	Read	Read
	Edit		Create		Create	
			Edit		Edit	
			Delete		Delete	
Consultant	Read	Read	Read	Read	Read	Read
			Create		Create	
			Edit		Edit	
					Delete	
Accounts Receivable	Read	Read	Read	Read	Read	Read
	Create	Create	Edit			Create
	Edit	Edit				Edit
	Delete					
Vice President	Read	Read	Read	Read	Read	Read
	Create	Create	Create	Create	Create	Create
	Edit	Edit	Edit	Edit	Edit	Edit
	Delete	Delete	Delete	Delete	Delete	Delete

Security by Business Unit

Business units are autonomous minicompanies that have a somewhat competitive relationship with each other. All business units report to an executive team. The sample organization is shown in Figure 3.10.

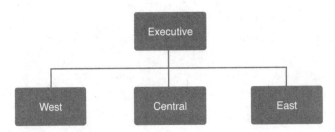

Figure 3.10   Services Manager business units

The Force.com security model must account for the following facts about the organization:

- In normal day-to-day operations, business units do not share data. This includes projects, resources, customers, and contacts. All data is private, belonging to the business unit that created it.

- In some cases, business units might need to share records. For example, a consultant with specialized skills is needed on projects in all three business units.

- Members of the executive team are able to read and write all data.

In the preceding section, you designed profiles to provide each job function in the organization with access to objects and fields. Now you must look at the requirements to protect each record of data. This is where Force.com's record-level security features come into play. To design for record-level security, use the following three steps:

1. **Establish the sharing model**—For each object, determine the most restrictive mode of sharing that is called for on its records. For the custom objects found in Services Manager, the options are Private, Public Read Only, and Public Read/Write. Private means that records remain under the control of their owners. Do not consider objects on the Detail side of Master-Detail relationships because records in these objects inherit ownership from their parent record. The output of this step is a list of objects, each with a default access setting (Private, Public Read Only, or Public Read/Write).

2. **Build groups of users**—Identify scenarios in which users need to share data outside of the restrictive defaults defined in the sharing model. Look for groups of users involved in these exceptions to the sharing model. Examine the flow of information between the two groups. It can be symmetric, with both groups getting equal access to the data. Or it can be one-sided, with one group receiving elevated rights to another group's data without reciprocation. The output of this step is a list of roles and public groups. Use roles where the sharing relationship is one-sided, and public groups where the relationship is equal.

3. **Set sharing rules**—Using the list of roles and public groups from the preceding step, build a list of sharing rules. To build each rule, follow three steps, as shown here:

    a. Determine which group owns the record to be shared.

    b. Identify the other group requiring access to the records owned by the first group.

    c. Decide whether the other group requires Read Only or Read/Write access to the shared record.

Following the first step creates the results given in Table 3.2, which shows the sharing model chosen for each object.

Table 3.2   **Sharing Model for Services Manager**

Object	Sharing Model
Project	Private
Contact	Private
Account	Private

In the second step, the groups of users are defined. In Services Manager, the only groups relevant to sharing are the business units. Each business unit will become a role, including the executive team.

For the final step of defining sharing rules between the groups, the requirement is to allow users in the same business unit to collaborate on records. To accomplish this task, grant each business unit Read/Write access to records owned by users in its business unit.

Implementing the Security Model

In the preceding section, you designed the sharing model for the Services Manager sample application. In this section, you will implement it in your Force.com DE organization. The implementation involves five separate tasks:

1. **Create profiles**—Profiles control access to objects and fields. The profiles in Services Manager are modeled after job functions such as Consultant and Project Manager.

2. **Configure field accessibility**—Profiles also provide fine-grained control over the fields within an object. In Services Manager, several cases exist in which a particular type of user needs Read access to an object, but not the whole object. Some fields are sensitive and should be hidden. Supporting these cases using field-level accessibility settings is easy.

3. **Set organization-wide defaults**—This is the first step in defining record-level control over data. All records have an owner, initially the user who created the record. Organization-wide defaults are defined on each object and dictate which users besides the owner, if any, also receive access to the records.

4. **Establish role hierarchy**—Roles provide a way to group users into a hierarchy. Users at higher levels in the hierarchy receive access to all records owned by their subordinates. In the Services Manager example, roles are used to model geographically distinct business units. By default, business units do not share data with each other. An executive team at the top of the hierarchy receives access to all data.

5. **Add sharing rules**—Sharing rules are one way to override the organization-wide defaults. They automatically share records between two groups of users based on record ownership and group membership. In Services Manager, sharing rules are used to allow record owners in the same business unit to collaborate on the same data. For example, if two

Project Managers are in the West, they should be able to see each other's Project records because they work on the same team.

Create Profiles

On the Setup screen in the Administration Setup area, click Manage Users, Profiles. For each profile identified in Table 3.1, follow these steps:

1. Click the New Profile button.

2. Select an existing profile to use as the starting point for the new custom profile. Standard Platform User is a good choice because the Services Manager sample application can work with a Salesforce Platform user license.

3. Enter the profile name and click the Save button.

4. The new profile is created—a copy of the existing one. Click the Edit button to customize it.

5. In Custom App Settings, select Services Manager as the default.

6. Scroll down to the Standard Object Permissions section. Check off the boxes as appropriate to grant access to Accounts and Contacts. Repeat the same process in the Custom Object Permissions section for the four custom objects in the Services Manager application.

7. Click the Save button. As a shortcut to create more profiles, click the Clone button and start building the next profile from step 3.

When you're done, your Profiles page should resemble Figure 3.11.

Configure Field Accessibility

In addition to object-level security, you also need to protect sensitive fields. Newly created custom fields are always invisible. They must be explicitly made visible using a profile or permission set. You need to consider the sensitivity of each field to each type of user, an excellent security best practice enforced by Force.com. For example, a Consultant can see all of the fields on a Project object except the finance-related fields Consulting Budget, Expense Budget, and Invoiced.

Follow this procedure to set the visibility of fields in an object:

1. Click Setup, and in the Administration Setup area, click Security Controls, Field Accessibility.

2. Click the object to configure—for example, Project.

3. Click View by Profiles.

4. Select the profile—for example, Consultant. At a glance, you can see the access level of every field in the profile.

5. For each field to change, click its corresponding field access value.

6. Click the first Visible check box to make the field visible to this profile.

7. Click the Save button.

8. Repeat from step 4 until every profile is assigned the correct access levels for this object.

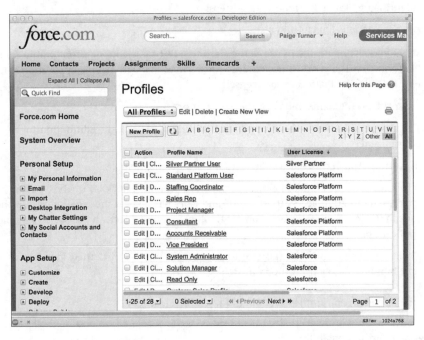

Figure 3.11   Services Manager profiles

Make all fields on the object visible for the remaining profiles. When you're done with these steps for the Project object, your Field Accessibility screen for the Consultant profile should resemble that shown in Figure 3.12.

Repeat this process on the following objects:

- **Timecard**—All fields visible, but invoice-related fields (Invoiced, Invoice Number, Invoice Date) are hidden from the Consultant profile.

- **Assignment**—All fields visible, but finance-related fields (Hourly Cost, Hourly Rate, Planned Cost, Planned Margin, Planned Revenue) are hidden from the Consultant profile.

- **Contact**—All fields visible, but the Hourly Cost Rate field is hidden from the Consultant profile.

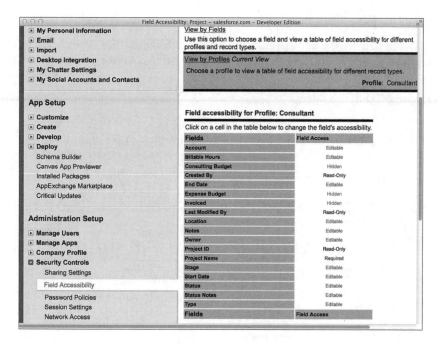

Figure 3.12   Accessibility of Project fields to Consultant profile

Set Organization-Wide Defaults

Follow these steps to configure the organization-wide defaults:

1. Click Setup. In the Administration Setup area, click Security Controls, Sharing Settings.

2. Click the Edit button.

3. In the Project row, select Private. Repeat this for Contact.

4. Click the Save button.

All Projects and Contacts are now private. This means that only the owner of a Project or Contact is able to see it. Although this is not the desired behavior, it is the most restrictive setting. From there, you will use sharing rules to open access to members of the same business unit.

Establish Role Hierarchy

In the Services Manager sample application, business units are represented using roles. Roles are chosen over public groups because they provide the one-way sharing needed between business units and the executive team.

To configure the roles, follow these steps:

1. Click Setup. In the Administration Setup area, click Manage Users, Roles. If you've never used this feature before, click the Set Up Roles button to continue past the display of sample role hierarchies.

2. Rename CEO to Executive.

3. Rename three of the roles reporting to Executive to West, Central, and East.

4. Delete the unneeded roles, starting with those at the lowest level of the hierarchy.

When you're done, your role hierarchy should appear as shown in Figure 3.13.

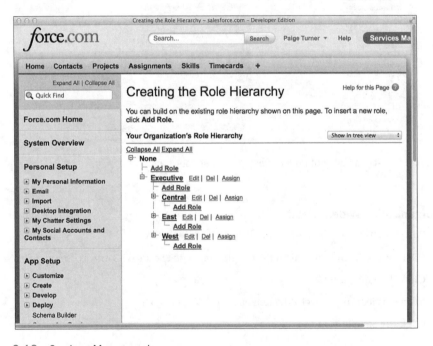

Figure 3.13   Services Manager roles

Add Sharing Rules

The goal in using sharing rules is to allow users in the same business unit to collaborate and share data. A record created by one user should be available to all users in the same business unit and their superiors, the executive team.

To configure sharing rules, follow these steps:

1. Click Setup. In the Administration Setup area, click Security Controls, Sharing Settings.

2. Scroll to the bottom of the screen. Click the New button in the Project Sharing Rules section.

3. Enter a rule label, and its name will be automatically set based on the label—for example, West.

4. The first pair of drop-down lists identifies the record owners who will be sharing. Select Roles from the first drop-down list and a role from the second—for example, West.

5. Select the group of users to share with. To share records within the same business unit, set this pair of drop-downs to the same values as those in the preceding step—for example, Roles and West.

6. The final drop-down list, Access Level, specifies the level of access that the second group of users receives to the shared records. Select Read/Write.

Repeat this process to share Project records within the other two business units, Central and East. Records are automatically shared with executives because they lie above the business units on the role hierarchy. Figure 3.14 shows the completed list of sharing rules.

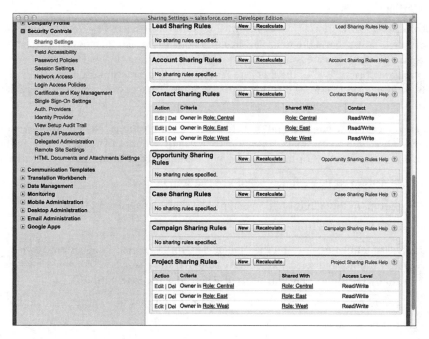

Figure 3.14   Services Manager sharing rules

Testing the Security Model

Although Services Manager is a sample application, it's a good idea to get into the habit of testing the security of all Force.com applications before you go into production with them. If you do not take the time to test methodically, a user or group of users could be unable to perform their jobs or become exposed to confidential data intended for other users.

Security testing requires the same level of patience and attention to detail as the actual configuration. If you've kept a spreadsheet or another document with the details of your configuration, you can use it to construct a test plan. Where feasible, make sure you test from the perspective of every group of uniquely privileged users. The native user interface is a great tool for security testing because it exposes the underlying security model accurately, without the distortion of potentially buggy custom code found in custom user interfaces.

Test object and field visibility by visiting tabs. Test access levels by looking for buttons that modify the state of the record on the pages in these tabs. Test sharing rules by creating records with different owners and checking their visibility to other users.

In the following subsections, you will create three additional users for testing, prepare some test data, verify object and field visibility for three profiles, and test manual sharing between two roles.

Create Additional Users

Force.com Developer Edition provides you with up to seven free users for your testing. Two of the users are licensed to use the full Salesforce functionality, which includes all the standard objects. Three of the users are Salesforce Platform Users, meaning they have access to a subset of the standard objects. Two of the users are Force.com - App Subscription users, which are roughly equivalent to Salesforce Platform Users. Services Manager can be tested using Salesforce Platform Users.

Although you could use one user and cycle him through the various roles and profiles, creating as many users as you can makes testing more efficient and intuitive. Start with a Staffing Coordinator in the West, a Consultant in the West, and a Vice President in the Executive team.

Follow these steps to create each new Salesforce Platform user:

1. Click Setup. In the Administration Setup area, click Manage Users, Users.

2. Click the New User button.

3. Enter First and Last name and then Email. Set Profile to one of the custom Services Manager profiles and select a role. Make sure that the check box Generate New Password and Notify User Immediately is selected. Then click the Save button.

4. You will receive an email with a link to log in as your new user. Visit this login link.

5. Set your new password.

6. Click Setup. In the Personal Setup area, click My Personal Information, Grant Login Access.

7. Grant login access to your administrator by entering a date in the second input field and clicking the Save button. This is a time-saving step that allows you, the administrator, to log in temporarily as the user without going through the full login process of entering a username and password.

Repeat this process for each new user. When you're done, you should have a list of users resembling the one shown in Figure 3.15.

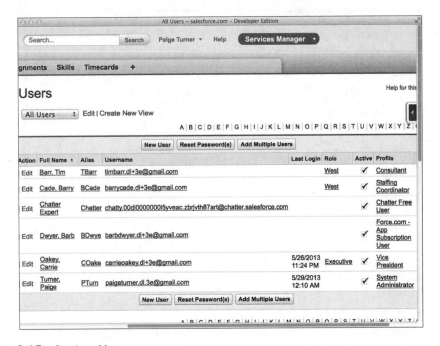

Figure 3.15   Services Manager users

Prepare Data

If you log in as a nonadministrator, you'll notice that no Project records are visible. But you imported some in the preceding chapter, so where are they? Because your sharing model is set to Private, they are accessible only to the owner, which is the administrator user you used to import them.

To get started with testing profiles, you need to transfer ownership of some records. Log in as the administrator. Grant your Consultant user ownership of a Contact record by visiting the record and clicking the Change link beside the owner name. Figure 3.16 shows the record with a new owner. Note that the owner is different from the user who created the record.

Figure 3.16   Contact record with new owner

Repeat the same process to transfer ownership of a Project to your user in the Staffing Coordinator profile.

Test the Consultant Profile

Now log in as a user in the Consultant profile. Click the Contacts tab and click the Go button. You should see the Contact record. Using the Timecard tab, verify that you can create a new record. Do the same for the Skills tab. Note that the Assignment tab does not contain a New button. That's because the Consultant profile prohibits this user from creating an Assignment record. Also notice that the Hourly Cost field is hidden.

Before you leave this record, click the New Skill button and add a few skills to the consultant. Then click around in the other tabs to verify that the consultant cannot create a Project or Contact and cannot see the hidden fields in these objects.

Test the Staffing Coordinator Profile

When you're satisfied with the Consultant, log out and log in as a Staffing Coordinator. Verify the following behaviors of this profile:

- Can create, edit, and delete Projects and view all their fields
- Can create, edit, and delete Assignments

- Can create, edit, and delete Contacts

- Cannot create, edit, or delete Skills

- Cannot create, read, edit, or delete Timecards

Test the Executive Role, Vice President Profile

Log in as your Executive VP user and verify that this user has full access to any of the records owned by the other users. This includes the ability to edit, delete, and change ownership and share the records.

Recall that the privileged access of this user stems from a combination of two Force.com security features:

1. **Executive role**—The Executive role is at the top of the role hierarchy. All Project and Resource records owned by users below this level are automatically shared with users belonging to the Executive role.

2. **Vice President profile**—The Vice President profile has full access to all the objects and fields used in the Services Manager.

Test Business Unit Collaboration

Say that the Central business unit's Staffing Coordinator requests a specialized consultant for a high-profile project, but this consultant works in the West. Verify that the security model supports this scenario using the following steps:

1. Log in as the System Administrator or an Executive VP user.

2. Locate the record of a Contact working in the West. Verify this by clicking the Contact record's Owner field and examining the value of that user's role.

3. Click the Sharing button.

4. Click the Add button.

5. In the Search drop-down list, select Roles.

6. Select Role: Central and click the Add button. The Share With list now contains Role: Central. Keep the Access Level at Read Only because you do not want the Central users to be modifying this West-owned Contact.

7. Click the Save button.

The sharing detail screen for this Contact should look like Figure 3.17. Note the presence of both the sharing rule and the newly added manual share.

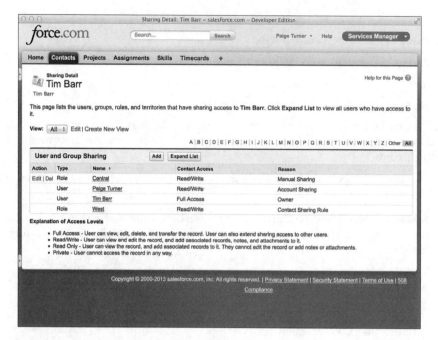

Figure 3.17   Sharing detail for a Contact record

Now that the record is shared with Central, it's time to test it. Make sure you're logged in as the System Administrator. Modify the Staffing Coordinator user so that it belongs to the Central role, and log in as that user. Staff the West consultant to a project by creating an Assignment, setting this consultant as the Contact. If you are able to do this, the manual share is working as intended.

Summary

This chapter introduced the data security features provided by the Force.com platform. These features can eliminate much of the effort required in traditional application development to build basic security infrastructure. Here are a few points to consider before moving on:

- Data can be protected at the object, field, and record level.

- Profiles control access to objects and fields. A combination of object and field permissions plus page layouts determines the degree to which a field is accessible to users.

- Most records have a built-in concept of ownership. The record's owner, plus organization-wide defaults and sharing reasons that override these defaults, determines nonowners' rights to view and modify records.

4

Business Logic

Business logic in Force.com is developed in Apex, a programming language designed for the Force.com platform. Through Apex code, many platform features, such as the database and user interface, can be customized to meet the needs of individual users and companies.

This chapter introduces Apex as a language for writing business logic, specifically where it interacts with the Force.com database. It uses a combination of explanatory text and code snippets to introduce concepts and encourage experimentation. This approach assumes you're already experienced in some other high-level, object-oriented programming language and would like to see for yourself how Apex is different.

The chapter consists of the following sections:

- **Introduction to Apex**—Learn basic facts about Apex and how it differs from other programming languages.

- **Introducing the Force.com IDE**—Take a brief tour of the Force.com IDE, a user interface for developing, debugging, and testing Apex code.

- **Apex language basics**—Learn the building blocks of the Apex language, such as data types and loops.

- **Database integration in Apex**—Incorporate the Force.com database into your Apex programs through queries, statements that modify data, and code executed automatically when data is changed.

- **Debugging Apex using Developer Console**—With Developer Console, you can directly inspect the state of your Apex code as it runs.

- **Unit tests in Apex**—Write tests for your code and run them in Developer Console.

- **Sample application**—Walk through the implementation of a data validation rule for the Services Manager sample application.

Note

The code listings in this chapter are available in a GitHub Gist at http://goo.gl/evtet.

Introduction to Apex

Apex is a stored procedure-like language that runs entirely on the Force.com platform. It provides object-oriented features and tight integration with the Force.com database. It's mainly used in custom user interfaces and in triggers, code that is executed when data is changed in the database.

Apex is not a general-purpose programming language like Java or C. Its scope is limited to business and consumer applications that operate on relational data and can benefit from the feature set of the surrounding Force.com platform.

Apex programs exist in a multitenant environment. The computing infrastructure used to execute Apex is operated by Salesforce and shared among many developers or tenants of the system. As a result, unlike general-purpose programming languages you are familiar with, the execution of Apex programs is closely controlled to maintain a consistently high quality of service for all tenants.

This control is accomplished through governor limits, rules that Force.com places on programs to keep them operating within their allotted share of system resources. Governor limits are placed on database operations, memory and bandwidth usage, and lines of code executed. Some governor limits vary based on the type of licensing agreement you have in place with Salesforce or the context that the code is running in, and others are fixed for all users and use cases.

> **Note**
>
> The most prevalent governor limits are discussed throughout this book, but it is not a complete treatment of the subject. The authoritative guide to governor limits is the *Force.com Apex Code Developer's Guide*, available at http://developer.force.com. Educate yourself on governor limits early in the development process. This education will alter the way you architect your Apex code and prevent costly surprises. Additionally, test all of your Apex code with production-like data volumes. This helps to expose governor-related issues prior to a production deployment.

Here are a few important facts about Apex:

- **It includes integrated testing features.** Code coverage is monitored and must reach 75% or greater to be deployed into a production environment.

- **It is automatically upgraded.** Salesforce executes all of its customers' unit tests to verify that they pass before deploying a major release of the Force.com platform. Your code is always running on the latest version of Force.com and can take advantage of any and all new functionality without the hassle and risks of a traditional software upgrade process.

- **There is no offline runtime environment for Force.com.** You can edit your code on your desktop computer, but it must be sent to Force.com for execution.

- **Apex is the only language that runs on the Force.com platform.** You can integrate Apex with programs running outside of Force.com using HTTP-based techniques such as REST.

- **The Force.com database is the only database integrated into the Apex language.**
  Other databases can be integrated through Web services or other technology using HTTP.

The two primary choices for developing Apex code are the Web-based App Builder Tools and the Force.com IDE, provided as a stand-alone application as well as a plug-in to the standard Eclipse IDE. The Force.com IDE is the more powerful and developer-friendly of the two, so it is used throughout this book.

Introducing the Force.com IDE

The Force.com IDE is an extension to the standard Eclipse development tool for building, managing, and deploying projects on the Force.com platform. This section covers installation and gives a brief walk-through of the Force.com IDE components used throughout this book.

Installation

The Force.com IDE is distributed in two forms: a stand-alone application and a plug-in to the Eclipse IDE. If Force.com is your primary development language or you are not an existing Eclipse IDE user, the stand-alone version is a good choice. The plug-in version of the Force.com IDE requires Eclipse, which you can find at www.eclipse.org. Only specific versions of Eclipse are supported by the Force.com IDE. If you are already using Eclipse but it's an unsupported version, keep your existing Eclipse version and install the supported version just for use with the Force.com IDE. Multiple versions of Eclipse can coexist peacefully on a single computer.

Visit http://wiki.developerforce.com/index.php/Apex_Toolkit_for_Eclipse to learn how to install the stand-alone and plug-in versions of the Force.com IDE.

Force.com Perspective

A perspective is a concept used by Eclipse to describe a collection of user interface components. For example, Eclipse has built-in perspectives called Java and Java Debug. By installing the Force.com IDE, you've added a perspective called Force.com. Figure 4.1 shows the Force.com perspective, indicated in the upper-right corner.

If you do not see the Force.com perspective, click the menu option Window, Open Perspective, Other; select Force.com from the Open Perspective dialog; and click the OK button. The Open Perspective dialog is shown in Figure 4.2.

The Force.com perspective includes several user interface panels, called Views. You can see two of them at the bottom of Figure 4.1: Execute Anonymous and Apex Test Runner. It also adds a new type of project called the Force.com Project, which is shown in the left-side Navigator tab. The first step to using the Force.com IDE is to create a Force.com Project.

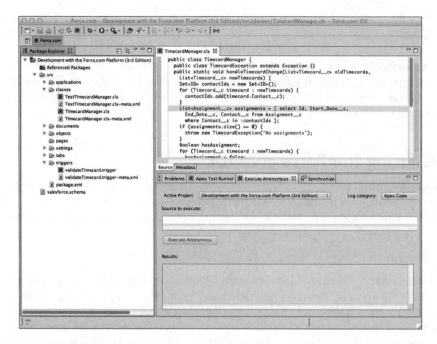

Figure 4.1   Force.com perspective

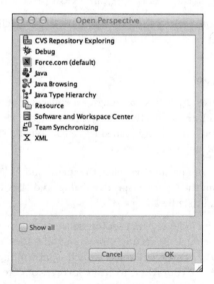

Figure 4.2   Open Perspective dialog

Force.com Projects

A Force.com Project allows you to read and write code, user interfaces, and other metadata objects within a Force.com organization from your local computer. Although this metadata is edited locally, it must be deployed to the Force.com service to run. Deployment to Force.com occurs automatically every time you make a modification to an object in a Force.com Project and save the changes. The contents of a Force.com Project are visible in the Navigator or Package Explorer Views.

> **Note**
>
> Force.com does not provide its own integrated source control system, but Force.com Projects can be integrated into your company's source control system through the built-in Team features of Eclipse. Refer to the Eclipse documentation for more information.

Problems View

The Force.com IDE leverages the standard Eclipse View called Problems to display compilation errors. When you save changes to an object in a Force.com Project, it is sent over the network to the Force.com service for compilation. If compilation fails, Force.com-specific errors are added to the Problems View. In most cases, you can double-click a problem row to navigate to the offending line of code.

Schema Explorer

The Schema Explorer allows direct interaction with the Force.com database. Use it to inspect objects and fields and to execute database queries and preview their results. To open the Schema Explorer, double-click the object named salesforce.schema in any Force.com Project. In Figure 4.3, the Schema Explorer is open and displaying the fields in the Project object in its right panel. In its left panel, a query has been executed and has returned a list of Contact records.

Apex Test Runner View

All business logic written in Force.com must be accompanied by unit tests to deploy it to a production environment. Apex Test Runner View is a user interface to run unit tests and view test results, including statistics on code performance and test coverage. If the Apex Test Runner is not already visible on the bottom of your screen, go to the Window menu and select Show View, Apex Test Runner.

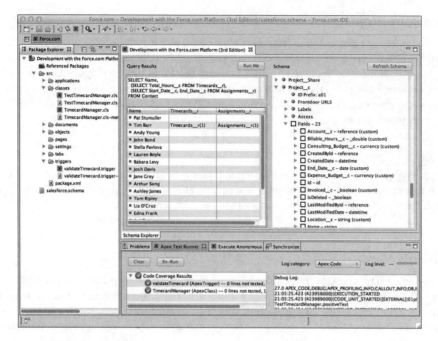

Figure 4.3   Force.com IDE Schema Explorer

Execute Anonymous View

The Execute Anonymous View provides an interactive, immediate way to execute arbitrary blocks of Apex code. Unless noted otherwise, you can execute all the code snippets in this chapter directly from the Force.com IDE using the Execute Anonymous View.

To try the Execute Anonymous View, first create a new Force.com Project. Go to the File menu and select File, New Force.com Project. Enter a project name; enter your Force.com username, password, and security token; and click the Next button. If you receive an error on this step, double-check your username, password, and security token. Also make sure you're providing the credentials for a Developer Edition organization, given that other types of organizations might not have access to the Force.com API. Select the metadata components Apex and Visualforce; then click the Finish button to create the project.

After you've created a project for your Development Edition organization, the Execute Anonymous View should be visible in the lower-right half of the screen. If not, go to the Window menu and select Show View, Execute Anonymous. In the Source to Execute text box, enter the code given in Listing 4.1. If the text box is not visible, resize your Execute Anonymous View until it's tall enough to see it. If the text box is disabled, double-click the Execute Anonymous tab to maximize and enable it. After you've entered the code, click the Execute Anonymous button to run it.

Listing 4.1 **Hello World**

```
String helloWorld(String name) {
  return 'Hello, ' + name;
}
System.debug(helloWorld('Apex'));
```

This sample code defines a function called `helloWorld` that accepts a single `String` parameter. It then invokes it with the name `Apex` and displays the results, `Hello Apex`, to the debug log.

Apex Language Basics

This section describes the building blocks of the Apex language. The building blocks are variables, operators, arrays and collections, and control logic. Basic knowledge of the syntax and operation of Apex is valuable for almost any custom development task in Force.com, including triggers, custom user interfaces, and integration with external systems. The section concludes with an introduction to Apex governor limits. Knowledge of governor limits is a critical part of writing business logic that scales from Developer Edition organizations to production organizations with real-world data volumes.

Variables

This subsection covers variable declaration, data types, constants and enums, and type conversions. It also provides detail on rounding numbers and converting dates to and from strings, common tasks in business applications.

Variable Declaration

Apex is a strongly typed language. All variables must be declared before they're referenced. At minimum, a variable declaration consists of the data type followed by the variable name. For example, Listing 4.2 is a valid statement.

Listing 4.2 **Variable Declaration**

```
Integer i;
```

The variable `i` is declared to be an Integer. Apex does not require variables to be initialized before use, but doing so is good practice. The variable `i` initially contains a null value.

Variable names cannot start with numbers or symbols, cannot contain two or more consecutive underscore characters, and must not conflict with Apex reserved words. These are special keywords used by the Apex language itself. The list of reserved words is available in the *Force.com Apex Code Developer's Guide*.

Variable names are not case sensitive. Try defining two variables with the same name, one in uppercase and one in lowercase, to prove this, as in Listing 4.3. If you try to execute this code, you will receive a compilation error citing a duplicate variable.

Listing 4.3   **Case Insensitivity of Variable Names**

```
Integer i;
String I;
```

Data Types

In Apex, all data types are objects. There is no concept of a primitive type such as an `int` in Java. Table 4.1 lists Apex's standard atomic data types. These types contain a single value at a time or a null value.

Table 4.1   **Standard Atomic Data Types**

Data Type	Valid Values
String	Zero or more Unicode characters.
Boolean	True or false.
Date	Date only; no time information is included.
Datetime	Date and time value.
Time	Time only; no date information is included.
Integer	32-bit signed whole number (–2,147,483,648 to 2,147,483,647).
Long	64-bit signed whole number (–263 to 263–1).
Decimal	Signed number with whole (m, Integer) and fractional components (n), expressed as $m.n$. Total length of number, including sign and decimal point, cannot exceed 19 characters.
Double	64-bit signed number with a decimal point (–263 to 263–1).
Blob	Binary data.
ID	ID is a variation of the String type to store the unique identifiers for Force.com database records. ID values are restricted to 18 characters. Values are checked at compile and runtime, and a `StringException` is thrown if they do not conform.
Object	Object is the generic type. Variables defined as Object are essentially type-less and can receive any value. Typeless code is vulnerable to runtime errors because it is invisible to the compiler's type checking functionality.

Constants and Enums

A constant is a variable that cannot be modified after it has been initialized. It is declared using the `final` keyword and can be initialized only in constructors, in initializers, or in the declaration itself.

An enum is a set of identifiers. Listing 4.4 provides an example of a constant as well as an enum. The constant is an Integer type; the enum is named `MyConstants` and contains three members. The variable x is initialized to the first member, and its data type is the enum itself, which can be thought of as a user-defined data type.

Listing 4.4   **Defining an Integer Constant and an Enum**

```
final Integer MAGIC_NUMBER = 42;
Enum MyConstants { One, Two, Three }
MyConstants x = MyConstants.One;
```

After it has been declared, an enum can be referenced in Apex code like any built-in data type. It can also be converted into an Integer from its zero-indexed position using its `ordinal` method or into a String using its `name` method.

Converting Data Types

The two ways to convert one data type to another are implicit and through conversion methods. Implicit conversion means that no method calls or special notation is required to convert one type into another. Conversion methods are functions that explicitly convert a value from one type to another type.

Implicit conversion is supported for numeric types and String types. For numbers, the rule is this: Integer → Long → Double → Decimal. Conversions can move from left to right without casting, as Listing 4.5 demonstrates.

Listing 4.5   **Implicit Conversion of Numeric Types**

```
Integer i = 123;
Long l = i;
Double d = l;
Decimal dec = d;
```

For Strings, ID and String are interchangeable, as shown in Listing 4.6. If conversion is attempted from String to ID but the String is not a valid ID, a `System.StringException` is thrown.

Listing 4.6   **Converting between ID and String**

```
String s = 'a0I80000003hazV';
ID id = s;
String s2 = id;
```

When implicit conversion is not available for a pair of types, you must use a conversion method. Data type objects contain a static conversion method called valueOf. Most conversions can be handled through this method. Listing 4.7 is a series of statements that convert a string into the various numeric types.

Listing 4.7   **Type Conversion Methods**

```
String s = '1234';
Integer i = Integer.valueOf(s);
Double d = Double.valueOf(s);
Long l = Long.valueOf(s);
Decimal dec = Decimal.valueOf(s);
```

When a type conversion method fails, it throws a TypeException. For example, when the code in Listing 4.8 executes, it results in an error: System.TypeException: Invalid integer: 1234.56.

Listing 4.8   **Type Conversion Error**

```
String s = '1234.56';
Integer i = Integer.valueOf(s);
```

Rounding Numbers

Rounding occurs when the fractional component of a Decimal or Double is dropped (round), or when a Decimal is divided (divide) or its scale (number of decimal places) reduced (setScale). Apex has a set of rounding behaviors called rounding modes that apply in all three of these situations. By default, the rounding mode is HALF_EVEN, which rounds to the nearest neighbor, or to the even neighbor if equidistant. For example, 0.5 rounds to 0, and 0.6 to 1. For the complete list of rounding modes, refer to the *Force.com Apex Code Developer's Guide* at www.salesforce.com/us/developer/docs/apexcode/index.htm.

Listing 4.9 demonstrates the three operations that can cause rounding.

Listing 4.9   **Three Rounding Operations**

```
Decimal d = 123.456;
Long rounded = d.round(RoundingMode.HALF_EVEN);
Decimal divided = d.divide(3, 3, RoundingMode.HALF_EVEN);
Decimal reducedScale = d.setScale(2, RoundingMode.HALF_EVEN);
```

Converting Strings to Dates

Strings can be converted to Date and Datetime types using the `valueOf` conversion methods, but the string values you're converting from must be in a specific format. For Date, the format is `YYYY-MM-DD`; for Datetime, `YYYY-MM-DD HH:MM:SS`, regardless of the locale setting of the user. Time does not have a `valueOf` method, but you can create one with its `newInstance` method, providing hours, minutes, seconds, and milliseconds. Listing 4.10 shows the creation of all three types.

Listing 4.10 **Creating Date, Datetime, and Time**

```
Date d = Date.valueOf('2015-12-31');
Datetime dt = Datetime.valueOf('2015-12-31 02:30:00');
Time t = Time.newInstance(2,30,0,0);
```

Converting Dates to Strings

Dates can be converted to strings through the `String.valueOf` method. This applies a default format to the date values. If you want control over the format, Datetime has a `format` method that accepts a Date pattern. This pattern follows the `SimpleDateFormat` pattern found in the Java API, which is documented at the following URL: http://download.oracle.com/javase/1.4.2/docs/api/java/text/SimpleDateFormat.html. For example, the code in Listing 4.11 outputs `Thu Dec 31, 2020`.

Listing 4.11 **Formatting a Datetime**

```
Datetime dt = Datetime.valueOf('2020-12-31 00:00:00');
System.debug(dt.format('E MMM dd, yyyy'));
```

Operators

Apex supports the standard set of operators found in most languages. Each operator is listed in Table 4.2 along with its valid data types, precedence if mathematical, and a brief description. In an expression with two operators, the operator with lower precedence is evaluated first.

Table 4.2 **Operators, Their Data Types, and Precedence**

Operators	Operands	Precedence	Description
=	Any compatible types	9	Assignment
+, -	Date, Datetime, Time	4	Add or subtract days on Date, Datetime, milliseconds on Time, argument must be Integer or Long
+	String	N/A	String concatenation

Operators	Operands	Precedence	Description
+, -, *, /	Integer, Long, Double, Decimal	4	Numeric add, subtract, multiply, divide
!	Boolean	2	Logical negation
-	Integer, Long, Double, Decimal	2	Arithmetic negation
++, --	Integer, Long, Double, Decimal	1	Unary increment, decrement
&, |, ^	Integer, Long, Boolean	10	Bitwise AND, OR, XOR
<<, >>, >>>	Integer, Long	10	Signed shift left, signed shift right, unsigned shift right
==, <, >, <=, >=, !=	Any compatible types	5 (<, >, <=, >=), 6 (==, !=)	Not case sensitive, locale-sensitive comparisons: equality, less than, greater than, less than or equal to, greater than or equal to, not equal to
&&, ||	Boolean	7 (&&), 8 (||)	AND, OR, with short-circuiting behavior (second argument is not evaluated if first argument is sufficient to determine result)
===, !==	Map, List, Set, Enum, SObject	N/A	Exact equality, exact inequality
()	Any	1	Group an expression and increase its precedence
? :	Boolean	N/A	Shortcut for if/then/else expression

Operators not included in Table 4.2 are the assignment variations of date, string, and numeric (+=, -=, *=, /=) and bitwise (|=, &=, ^=, <<=, >>=, >>>=) arithmetic. For example, x = x + 3 assigns x to itself plus 3, but so does x += 3.

Arrays and Collections

Arrays and collections are a family of data types that contain a sequence of values. It includes Lists and Arrays, Sets, and Maps. This subsection covers each of the three types and describes how to create them and perform some basic operations. Each collection type is different, but there are four methods you can invoke on all of them:

1. **clear**—Removes all elements from the collection

2. **clone**—Returns a copy of the collection

3. **isEmpty**—Returns false if the collection has elements, true if empty

4. **size**—Returns the number of elements in the collection as an Integer

Lists and Arrays

Lists and Arrays contain an ordered sequence of values, all the same type. Duplicate values are allowed. Unlike Lists, the length of an Array is fixed when you initialize it. Lists have a dynamic length that is adjusted as you add and remove elements.

To declare a List variable, use the `List` keyword followed by the data type of its values in angle brackets. Because Lists and Arrays are containers for other values, they must be initialized before values can be added to them. The `new` keyword creates an instance of the List. Listing 4.12 declares a variable called `stringList` that contains Strings, initializes it, and adds a value.

Listing 4.12 Creating a List

```
List<String> stringList = new List<String>();
stringList.add('Hello');
```

To create an Array, specify a variable name, data type, and length. Listing 4.13 creates an Array of Strings named `stringArray`, initializes it to accommodate five elements, and then assigns a value to its first element.

Listing 4.13 Creating an Array

```
String[] stringArray = new String[5];
stringArray[0] = 'Hello';
```

Multidimensional Arrays are not supported. But you can create a two-dimensional List object by nesting a List within another List. In Listing 4.14, `list2` is defined as a List containing Lists of Strings. A String List called `childList` is initialized, populated with a value, and added to `list2`.

Listing 4.14 Nested List Usage

```
List<List<String>> list2 = new List<List<String>>();
List<String> childList = new List<String>();
childList.add('value');
list2.add(childList);
```

Arrays and Lists have interchangeable behavior and syntax in Apex, as demonstrated in Listing 4.15. Lists can be initialized using an Array initializer, and its elements accessed using the square-bracket notation. Arrays can be initialized using the List constructor, and accessed using the List getters and setters. But for the sake of code clarity, picking one usage style and sticking with it is a good idea. In this book, List is the standard because it better reflects the object-oriented nature of these collection types.

Listing 4.15   **Mixed Array and List Syntax**

```
List<Integer> intList = new Integer[3];
intList[0] = 123;
intList.add(456);
Integer[] intArray = new List<Integer>();
intArray.add(456);
intArray.set(0, 123);
```

Arrays and Lists preserve the order in which elements are inserted. They can also be sorted in ascending order using the sort method of the List object. For custom sorting behavior, you can implement the Comparable interface on the classes in your list. This interface allows you to examine two objects and let Force.com know if the objects are equal or if one occurs before the other.

Sets

The Set is another collection type. Like a List, a Set can store only one type of element at a time. But Sets do not allow duplicate values and do not preserve insertion order. Sets are initialized like Lists. In Listing 4.16, a set named stringSet is created, and two values are added.

Listing 4.16   **Basic Set Usage**

```
Set<String> stringSet = new Set<String>();
stringSet.add('abc');
stringSet.add('def');
System.debug(stringSet.contains('abc'));
```

The final statement in Listing 4.16 outputs true, illustrating one of the most valuable features of the Set collection type: its contains method. To test whether a particular String exists in an Array or a List, every element of the List must be retrieved and checked. With a Set, this test can be done more efficiently thanks to the contains method.

Maps

The Map type stores pairs of keys and values and does not preserve their insertion order. It maintains the relationship between key and value, functioning as a lookup table. Given a key stored in a Map, you can retrieve its corresponding value.

Maps are initialized with a key data type and value data type. Listing 4.17 initializes a new Map called myMap to store Integer keys and String values. It inserts a single value using the put method and then retrieves it using the get method. The last line of code prints abc because that is the value associated with the key 123.

Listing 4.17   **Basic Map Usage**

```
Map<Integer, String> myMap = new Map<Integer, String>();
myMap.put(123, 'abc');
System.debug(myMap.get(123));
```

Other useful methods of Maps include `containsKey` (returns `true` if the given key exists in the Map), `remove` (returns and removes an element by key), `keySet` (returns a Set of all keys), and `values` (returns an Array of all values).

Control Logic

This subsection describes how to control the flow of Apex code execution. It covers conditional statements, loops, exception statements, recursion, and asynchronous execution.

Conditional Statements

Conditional statements evaluate a Boolean condition and execute one code block if true, another if false. Listing 4.18 provides an example, defining a function that prints `true` if an Integer argument is greater than 100, `false` otherwise.

Listing 4.18   **Conditional Statement Usage**

```
void testValue(Integer value) {
   if (value > 100) {
    System.debug('true');
   } else {
    System.debug('false');
   }
}
testValue(99);
testValue(101);
```

In addition to this simple `if`, `else` structure, you can chain multiple conditional statements together using `else if`.

> **Note**
>
> In conditional code blocks that contain a single statement, the curly braces around them can be omitted. This is true of all the control logic types in Apex. For example, `if (a > 0) return 1 / a; else return a;` is a valid statement.

Loops

Loops in Apex behave consistently with other high-level languages. Table 4.3 lists the loop statements available in Apex.

Table 4.3   **Types of Loops**

Name	Syntax	Description
Do-While Loop	`do { code_block }` `while (condition);`	Executes code block as long as Boolean condition is `true`. Evaluates `condition` after running code block, executing the code block at least once.
While Loop	`while (condition) {` `code_block; }`	Executes code block as long as Boolean condition is `true`. Evaluates `condition` before running code block, so code block might not be executed at all.

Traditional For Loop	`for (init; exit`
	`condition; increment)`
	`{ code_block; }`
		Executes `init` statement once. Loops on the following steps: exit loop if Boolean exit `condition` evaluates to `false`, executes code block, executes `increment` statement.

List/Set Iteration For Loop	`for (var : list/set)` `{ code_block }`	For every element of the list or set, assigns `var` to the current element and executes the code block. Cannot modify the collection while iterating.

The keywords `break` and `continue` can be used to further control the loops. To immediately exit a loop at any point in its execution, use `break` in the code block. To abort a cycle of loop execution in the middle of a code block and move to the next cycle, use `continue`.

Exception Statements

Exceptions are classes used to signal a problem at runtime. They abort the normal flow of code execution, bubbling upward until explicitly handled by some other code, carrying with them information about the cause of the problem.

Apex allows custom exception classes to be defined that are meaningful to your programs. It also provides system exception classes corresponding to areas of the Force.com platform. Some common system exceptions are `DmlException` (issues with changes to the database), `NullPointerException` (attempt to dereference a null value), `QueryException` (issues with database queries), and `TypeException` (issues converting data types).

The two ways to use exceptions in your code are to raise an exception with the `throw` keyword and handle an exception with the `try`, `catch`, and `finally` keywords:

1. **Raise an exception**—When your code cannot proceed due to a problem with its input or other issue, you can raise an exception. An exception stops execution of the code and provides information about the problem to its callers. Only custom exceptions,

classes that are subclasses of Force.com's `Exception` class, can be raised. The names of all custom exception classes must end with the word *Exception*. Construct an instance of your exception class using an optional message or another exception as the preceding cause and provide it as an argument to the `throw` keyword.

2. **Handle an exception**—An exception handler in Apex is a code block defined to expect and take action on one or more named exception classes. It consists of a `try` code block, zero or more `catch` code blocks, and optionally a `finally` code block. The `try` code block is executed first. If an exception is raised, Apex looks for a `catch` code block that matches the exception class. If it's found, execution skips to the relevant `catch`. If not, the exception is bubbled upward to the caller. After the code in the `try` completes, successfully or not, the `finally` code block is executed.

Listing 4.19 demonstrates both forms of exception statements. It inserts a Timecard record within a `try` block, using a `catch` block to handle a database exception (`DmlException`). The code to handle the database exception itself raises an exception, a custom exception class called `MyException`. It ends by printing a final message in the `finally` block.

Listing 4.19   **Sample Exception Statements**

```
class MyException extends Exception {}
Timecard__c timecard = new Timecard__c();
try {
  insert timecard;
} catch (DMLException e) {
  throw new MyException('Could not create Timecard record: ' + e);
} finally {
  System.debug('Exiting timecard creation code');
}
```

Recursion

Apex supports the use of recursion in code. The maximum stack depth is not documented, so experiment with your own code before committing to a recursive algorithm. For example, the code in Listing 4.20 fails with `System.Exception: Maximum stack depth reached: 1001`.

Listing 4.20   **Recursion with Unsupported Depth**

```
Integer counter = 0;
void recursive() {
  if (counter < 500) {
    counter++;
    recursive();
  }
}
recursive();
```

Asynchronous Execution

Code in Apex normally is executed synchronously. From the user's point of view, there is a single thread of execution that must complete before another can begin. But Apex also supports an asynchronous mode of execution called future methods. Code entering a future method completes immediately, but the body of the method isn't executed until later, at a time determined by the Force.com platform.

The code in Listing 4.21 declares a future method called `asyncMethod` with a single parameter: a list of strings. It might use these strings to query records via SOQL and perform DML operations on them.

Listing 4.21 **Future Method Declaration**

```
@future
public static void asyncMethod(List<String> idsToProcess) {
  // code block
}
```

Future methods typically are used to perform expensive tasks that are not time-critical. A regular synchronous method can begin some work and invoke a future method to finish it. The future method starts fresh with respect to governor limits.

Future methods have many limitations, as follows:

- You cannot invoke more than ten future methods in a single scope of execution. There is no guarantee of when these methods will be executed by Force.com or in what order.

- Future methods cannot call other future methods.

- Future method signatures are always static and return void. They cannot use custom classes or database objects as parameters—only primitive types such as String and Integer and collections of primitive types.

- You cannot test future methods like ordinary methods. To write testable code that includes future methods, keep your future methods limited to a single line of code that invokes a normal method to perform the actual work. Then in your test case, call the normal method so that you can verify its behavior.

- Force.com limits your usage of future methods in a 24-hour period to 250,000 or 200 per licensed user, whichever is greater. This limit is shared with Batch and Scheduled Apex.

> **Note**
>
> Batch Apex is an additional feature for asynchronous execution. It provides much greater control than future methods and supports processing of millions of records. Batch Apex is covered in Chapter 9, "Batch Processing."

Object-Oriented Apex

Apex is an object-oriented language. This subsection describes Apex in terms of five standard characteristics of object-oriented languages, summarized here:

- **Encapsulation**—Encapsulation combines the behavior and internal state of a program into a single logical unit.

- **Information hiding**—To minimize tight coupling between units of a program, information hiding limits external visibility into the behavior and state of a unit.

- **Modularity**—The goal of modularity is to establish clear boundaries between components of a program.

- **Inheritance**—Inheritance allows one unit of code to define its behavior in terms of another.

- **Polymorphism**—Polymorphism is the capability to interact with multiple units of code interchangeably without special cases for each.

These principles of object-oriented programming help you learn the Apex syntax and behaviors from a language-neutral point of reference.

Encapsulation

Encapsulation describes the bundling of a program's behavior and state into a single definition, usually aligned with some real-world concept. In Apex that definition is a class.

When a class is defined, it becomes a new data type in Apex. Classes contain variables, methods, properties, constructors, initializers, and inner classes. These components are summarized in the following list, and their usage is demonstrated in Listing 4.22:

- **Variables**—Variables hold the state of an object instance or class. By default, variables declared inside a class are scoped to individual object instances and are called member variables. Every instance of an object gets its own member variables and can read and write their values independently without interfering with the values stored in other object instances. There are also class variables, also known as static variables. They are declared using the `static` keyword. Static variables are shared across all instances of the object.

- **Methods**—Methods define the verbs in a class, the actions to be taken. By default, they operate within the context of individual object instances, able to access all visible member variables. Methods can also be static, operating on the class itself. Static methods have access to static variables but never member variables.

- **Properties**—A property is a shortened form of a method that provides access to a static or instance variable. An even shorter form is called an automatic property. These are properties with no code body. When no code is present, the logic is implied. Getters return their value; setters set their value.

- **Constructors**—A constructor is a special method executed when a class is instantiated. Constructors are declared much like methods, but share their name with the class name, and have no return type declaration.

- **Initializers**—An initializer contains code that runs before any other code in the class.

- **Inner classes**—An inner class is a class defined within another class.

Listing 4.22   **Class Definition**

```
class MyClass {
  static Integer count; /* Class variable */
  Integer cost; /* Member variable */
  MyClass(String c) { /* Constructor */ }
  void doSomething() { /* Method */ }
  Integer unitCost { get { return cost; } set { this.cost = value; } }
  Integer q { get; set; }
  { /* Initializer */ }
  class MyInnerClass { /* Inner class */ }
}
```

> **Tip**
>
> Code listings containing static variables or inner class declarations cannot be tested in the Execute Anonymous View of the Force.com IDE. Create a stand-alone class and then invoke it from the Execute Anonymous view. To create a stand-alone class in the Force.com IDE, select your Force.com Project and then select New, Apex Class from the File menu.

Information Hiding

Class definitions include notation to limit the visibility of their constituent parts to other code. This information-hiding notation protects a class from being used in unanticipated and invalid ways and simplifies maintenance by making dependencies explicit. In Apex, information hiding is accomplished with access modifiers. There are two places to use access modifiers: on classes, and on methods and variables:

- **Classes**—An access modifier of `public` makes a class visible to the entire application namespace, but not outside it. A `global` class is visible to Apex code running in every application namespace.

- **Methods and variables**—If designated `private`, a method or variable is visible only within its defining class. This is the default behavior. An access modifier of `protected` is visible to the defining class and subclasses, `public` is visible to any Apex code in the same application namespace but not accessible to other namespaces, and `global` can be used by any Apex code running anywhere in the organization, in any namespace.

Modularity

Apex supports interfaces, which are skeletal class definitions containing a list of methods with no implementation. A class built from an interface is said to implement that interface, which requires that its method names and the data types of its argument lists be identical to those specified in the interface.

The proper use of interfaces can result in modular programs with clear logical boundaries between components, making them easier to understand and maintain.

Inheritance

Apex supports single inheritance. It allows a class to extend one other class and implement many interfaces. Interfaces can also extend one other interface. A class extending from another class is referred to as its subclass.

For a class to be extended, it must explicitly allow it by using the `virtual` or `abstract` keyword in its declaration. Without one of these keywords, a class is final and cannot be subclassed. This is not true of interfaces because they are implicitly virtual.

By default, a subclass inherits all the functionality of its parent class. All the methods defined in the parent class are also valid on the subclass without any additional code. This behavior can be selectively overridden if the parent class permits. Overriding a method is a two-step process:

1. The parent class must specify the `virtual` or `abstract` keywords on the methods to be overridden.

2. In the subclass, the `override` keyword is used on the virtual or abstract methods to declare that it's replacing the implementation of its parent.

After it's overridden, a subclass can do more than replace the parent implementation. Using the `super` keyword, the subclass can invoke a method in its parent class, incorporating its functionality and potentially contributing its own.

Polymorphism

An object that inherits a class or implements an interface can always be referred to in Apex by its parent class or interface. References in variable, property, and method declarations treat the derived objects identically to objects they are derived from, even though they are different types.

This polymorphic characteristic of object types can help you write concise code. It works with the hierarchy of object types to enable broad, general statements of program behavior, behavior applying to many object types at once, while preserving the option to specify behavior per object type.

One example of using polymorphic behavior is method overloading, in which a single method name is declared with multiple argument lists. Consumers of the method simply invoke it by name, and Apex finds the correct implementation at runtime based on the object types.

Understanding Governor Limits

Governor limits are imposed on your running Apex code based on the type of resource consumed. When a governor limit is encountered, your code is immediately terminated with an exception indicating the type of limit reached. Examples of resource types are heap (memory used during execution) and SOQL queries.

Table 4.4 lists a few of the most important governor limits. Additional governor limits are introduced later in the book.

Table 4.4   **Subset of Governor Limits**

Resource Type	Governor Limit
Heap	6MB
Apex code	1,000,000 lines of code executed, 3MB code size
Database	50,000 records retrieved via SOQL

> **Note**
>
> Namespaces are used to separate and isolate Apex code and database objects developed by different vendors so that they can coexist and interoperate in a single Force.com organization. Governor limits are applied independently to each namespace. For example, if you install a package from Force.com AppExchange, the resources consumed by code running inside that package do not count against the limits applied to your code.

Database Integration in Apex

In Apex, the Force.com database is already integrated into the language and runtime environment. There are no object-relational mapping tools or database connection pools to configure. Your Apex code is automatically aware of your database, including all of its objects and fields and the security rules protecting them.

This section examines the five ways the database is exposed in Apex code, which are summarized here:

1. **Database records as objects**—Database objects are directly represented in Apex as classes. These classes are implicitly imported into your code, so you're always developing from the latest database schema.

2. **Database queries**—SOQL is a concise expression of the records to be queried and returned to your programs.

3. **Persisting database records**—Apex has a built-in Data Manipulation Language (DML), providing verbs that create, update, or delete one or more records in the database.

4. **Database triggers**—Triggers are code that register interest in a specific action or actions on a database object, such as an insert or delete on the Account object. When this action occurs, the trigger code is executed and can inhibit or enhance the behavior of the database action.

5. **Database security in Apex**—Normally, Apex code runs in a privileged mode, granting it full access to all the data in the system. Alternatively, you can configure it to run under the same restrictions imposed on the current user, including object and record-level sharing rules.

Database Records as Objects

All database objects, standard and custom, are available as first-class members of the Apex language, automatically and transparently. This eliminates the mind-numbing, error-prone work of importing, mapping, and translating between relational and program data structures, chores commonly required in general-purpose programming languages. In Apex, references to database objects are verified at compile time. This reduces the possibility of runtime surprises caused by field or object mismatches. Listing 4.23 shows an example of creating a record in the Contact object and setting its first name field.

Listing 4.23 **Creating a Record**

```
Contact contact = new Contact();
contact.FirstName = 'Larry';
```

Database relationships are also exposed in Apex. The __r syntax refers to a relationship field, a field that contains a reference to another object or list of objects. Listing 4.24 builds on the previous listing, creating an Assignment record and associating it with the Contact record.

Listing 4.24 **Creating a Record with Relationship**

```
Assignment__c assignment = new Assignment__c();
assignment.Contact__r = contact;
```

The Force.com IDE's Schema Explorer can take the mystery out of relationship fields like Contact__r. It displays the correct syntax for referring to fields and relationships, based on the actual schema of the database object. Its Schema list on the right side displays all objects, custom and standard. Drilling into an object, the Fields folder lists all fields in the object and their types. A reference type indicates that a field is the child object in a Lookup relationship. Expand these fields to reveal their parent object's type and name. For example, in the Project custom object, Account__r is the foreign key to the Account object. This is demonstrated in Figure 4.4.

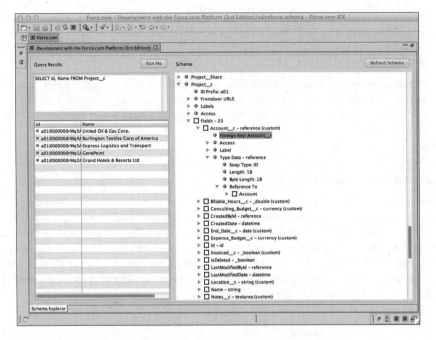

Figure 4.4   Viewing relationships in Schema Explorer

Data integrity is protected in Apex at compile and runtime using object metadata. For example, Name is defined as a read-only field in Contact, so the code in Listing 4.25 cannot be compiled.

Listing 4.25   **Attempted Assignment to Read-Only Field**

```
Contact c = new Contact();
c.Name = 'Larry';
```

After a database object is referenced in Apex code, that object cannot be deleted or edited in a way that invalidates the code. This protects your code from changes to the database schema. Impacted code must be commented out before the database objects are modified.

Database Queries

You've seen how data structures in Apex are implicitly defined by the objects in your database. Force.com provides two query languages to populate these objects with data: Salesforce Object Query Language (SOQL) and Salesforce Object Search Language (SOSL). SOSL, addressed in Chapter 5, "Advanced Business Logic," provides unstructured, full-text search across many objects from a single query.

The focus of this section is SOQL because it is the workhorse of typical business applications. This section includes subsections on the basics of SOQL, filtering and sorting, how to query related objects, and how to use SOQL from Apex code.

As you read this section, you can experiment with the sample SOQL queries using the Force. com IDE's Schema Explorer. In the Navigator or Package Explorer View, expand the node for your Force.com Project and double-click salesforce.schema. Enter a query in the text box in the upper-left corner and click the Run Me button. The results appear in the table below the query. In Figure 4.5, a query has been executed against the Project object, returning four records. Note that many of the queries rely on objects from the Services Manager sample application rather than standard Force.com objects.

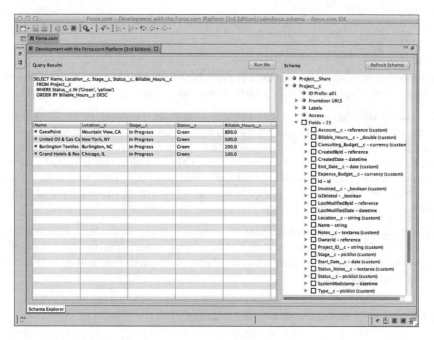

Figure 4.5   Running SOQL queries in Schema Explorer

> **Note**
>
> This book does not cover every feature and nuance of SOQL. For the complete specification, visit http://developer.force.com and download the latest Force.com SOQL and SOSL Reference.

SOQL Basics

Despite being one letter away from SQL and borrowing some of its syntax, SOQL is completely different and much easier to understand on its own terms. Just as Apex is not a general-purpose programming language like Java, SOQL is not a general-purpose database query language like SQL. SOQL is specifically designed and optimized for the Force.com database.

A SOQL statement is centered on a single database object, specifying one or more fields to retrieve from it. The fields to select are separated by commas. Listing 4.26 is a simple SOQL statement that returns a list of Account records with Id and Name fields populated. SOQL is not case sensitive. SOQL keywords are shown throughout the book in uppercase and metadata objects in title case for readability only.

Listing 4.26 **Simple SOQL Statement**

```
SELECT Id, Name
  FROM Account
```

Filtering Records

SOQL supports filter conditions to reduce the number of records returned. A filter condition consists of a field name to filter, an operator, and a literal value.

Valid operators are > (greater than), < (less than), >= (greater than or equal to), <= (less than or equal to), = (equal to), != (not equal to), IN and NOT IN (matches a list of literal values, and supports semi-joins and anti-joins), and INCLUDES and EXCLUDES (match against multi-select picklist values). On String fields, the LIKE operator is also available, which applies a pattern to filter records. The pattern uses the % wildcard to match zero or more characters, _ to match one character, and the \ character to escape the % and _ wildcards, treating them as regular characters.

Multiple filters are combined in a single SOQL statement using the Boolean operators AND and OR and grouped with parentheses. Listing 4.27 returns the names of accounts with a type of direct customer, a modification date sometime during the current year, and more than $100 million in annual revenue.

Listing 4.27 **SOQL Statement with Filter Conditions**

```
SELECT Name
  FROM Account
  WHERE AnnualRevenue > 100000000
  AND Type = 'Customer - Direct'
  AND LastModifiedDate = THIS_YEAR
```

Notice the way literal values are specified. Single quotation marks must be used around String literals but never with other data types. THIS_YEAR is a built-in relative time function. The values of relative time functions vary based on when the query is executed. Other relative time functions are YESTERDAY, TODAY, TOMORROW, LAST_WEEK, THIS_WEEK, NEXT_WEEK, and so forth.

Absolute dates and times can also be specified without single quotation marks. Dates must use the YYYY-MM-DD format. Datetimes can be YYYY-MM-DDThh:mm:ssZ,

YYYY-MM-DDThh:mm:ss+hh:mm, or YYYY-MM-DDThh:mm:ss-hh:mm, indicating the positive or negative offset from Coordinated Universal Time (UTC).

In addition to filter conditions, SOQL supports the LIMIT keyword. It sets an absolute upper bound on the number of records that can be returned from the query. It can be used in conjunction with all the other SOQL features. For example, the SOQL statement in Listing 4.28 returns up to ten Account records modified today.

Listing 4.28 **SOQL Statement with Record Limit**

```
SELECT Name, Type
  FROM Account
  WHERE LastModifiedDate = TODAY
  LIMIT 10
```

Sorting Query Results

Results of a query can be sorted by up to 32 fields in ascending (ASC, the default) or descending (DESC) order. Sorting is not case sensitive, and nulls appear first unless otherwise specified (NULLS LAST). Multi-select picklists, long text areas, and reference type fields cannot be used as sort fields. The SOQL query in Listing 4.29 returns records first in ascending order by Type and then in descending order by LastModifiedDate.

Listing 4.29 **SOQL Statement with Sort Fields**

```
SELECT Name, Type, AnnualRevenue
  FROM Account
  ORDER BY Type, LastModifiedDate DESC
```

Querying Multiple Objects

The result of a SOQL query can be a simple list of records containing rows and columns or hierarchies of records containing data from multiple, related objects. Relationships between objects are navigated implicitly from the database structure. This eliminates the work of writing accurate, efficient join conditions common to development on traditional SQL databases.

The two ways to navigate object relationships in SOQL are child-to-parent and parent-to-child. Listing 4.30 is an example of a child-to-parent query, returning the name, city, and Force.com username creating its contact of all resources with a mailing address in the state of California. It selects and filters fields of the Project object, the parent object of Account. It also selects the Name field from the User object, a parent two levels removed from Project via the Account's CreatedBy field.

Listing 4.30   **SOQL with Child-to-Parent Relationship**

```
SELECT Name, Account__r.Name, Account__r.CreatedBy.Name
  FROM Project__c
  WHERE Account__r.BillingState = 'CA'
```

> **Caution**
>
> The results of child-to-parent relationship queries are not completely rendered in the Force.
> com IDE. You can double-click a row and column to view fields from a parent record, but this is
> limited to direct parents only. Fields from parent-of-parent objects, such as the `Contact__r`.
> `CreatedBy` relationship in Listing 4.29, are omitted from the results. This is a limitation not of
> SOQL, but of the Force.com IDE.

At most, five levels of parent objects can be referenced in a single child-to-parent query, and the query cannot reference more than 25 relationships in total.

The second form of relationship query is the parent-to-child query. Listing 4.31 provides an example. The parent object is Resource, and the child is Timecard. The query selects from every Contact its Id, Name, and a list of hours from its Timecards in the current month.

Listing 4.31   **SOQL with Parent-to-Child Relationship**

```
SELECT Id, Name,
  (SELECT Total_Hours__c
    FROM Timecards__r
    WHERE Week_Ending__c = THIS_MONTH)
  FROM Contact
```

A parent-to-child query cannot reference more than 20 child objects. Double-clicking the parent record in the results table brings up the child records for viewing in the Force.com IDE.

Using SOQL in Apex

Like database objects, SOQL queries are an integrated part of the Apex language. They are developed in-line with your code and verified at compile time against your database schema.

Listing 4.32 is an example of a SOQL query used in Apex. It retrieves a list of Project records for this year and loops over them, summing their billable hours in the variable totalHours. Note the usage of the variable named statuses directly in the SOQL query, preceded by a colon. This is known as a *bind variable*. Bind variables can appear on the right side of a WHERE clause, as the value of an IN or NOT IN clause, and in the LIMIT clause.

Listing 4.32 **SOQL Query in Apex**

```
Decimal totalHours = 0;
List<String> statuses = new String[] { 'Green', 'Yellow' };
List<Project__c> projects = [ SELECT Billable_Hours__c
  FROM Project__c
  WHERE Start_Date__c = THIS_YEAR and Status__c IN :statuses ];
for (Project__c project : projects) {
  totalHours += project.Billable_Hours__c;
}
System.debug(totalHours);
```

This code relies on a List to store the results of the SOQL query. This means the entire SOQL query result must fit within the heap size available to the program. A better syntax for looping over SOQL records is a variation of the List/Set Iteration For Loop called a SOQL For Loop. The code in Listing 4.33 is a rewrite of Listing 4.32 using the SOQL For Loop. This allows it to run when the Project object contains up to 50,000 records for this year without consuming 50,000 records' worth of heap space at one time.

Listing 4.33 **SOQL Query in Apex Using SOQL For Loop**

```
Decimal totalHours = 0;
for (Project__c project : [ SELECT Billable_Hours__c
  FROM Project__c
  WHERE Start_Date__c = THIS_YEAR ]) {
  totalHours += project.Billable_Hours__c;
}
System.debug(totalHours);
```

An additional form of the SOQL For Loop is designed for use with Data Manipulation Language (DML). Consider how the code in Listing 4.32 could be adapted to modify Project records returned from the SOQL query rather than simply summing them. With the existing code, one Project record would be modified for each loop iteration, an inefficient approach and a quick way to run afoul of the governor limits. But if you change the type of variable in the For Loop to a list of Project records, Force.com provides up to 200 records per loop iteration. This allows you to modify a whole list of records in a single operation.

> **Note**
>
> Looping through a list of records to calculate the sum of a field is provided as an example of using SOQL with Apex. It is not an optimal way to perform calculations on groups of records in the database. Chapter 5 introduces aggregate queries, which enable calculations to be returned directly from a SOQL query, without Apex.

Any valid SOQL statement can be executed in Apex code, including relationship queries. The result of a child-to-parent query is returned in a List of objects whose types match the child object. Where fields from a parent object are included in the query, they are available as nested variables in Apex code. For example, running the query in Listing 4.30 within a block of Apex code returns a `List<Project__c>`. If this List is assigned to a variable named `projects`, the first Account record's billing state is accessible by `projects[0].Account__r.BillingState`.

Parent-to-child queries are returned in a List of objects, their type matching the parent object. Each record of the parent object includes a nested List of child objects. Using Listing 4.31 as an example, if `results` contains the `List<Contact>` returned by the query, `results[0].Timecards__r[0].Total_Hours__c` accesses a field in the first Contact's first Timecard child record.

> **Note**
>
> Usage of SOQL in Apex is subject to governor limits. For example, you are limited to a total of 100 SOQL queries, or 300 including parent-to-child queries. The cumulative maximum number of records returned by all SOQL queries, including parent-to-child, is 50,000.

Persisting Database Records

Changes to database records in Force.com are saved using Data Manipulation Language (DML) operations. DML operations allow you to modify records one at a time, or more efficiently in batches of multiple records. The five major DML operation types are listed next. Each is discussed in more detail later in this subsection.

- **Insert**—Creates new records.
- **Update**—Updates the values in existing records, identified by Force.com unique identifier (`Id`) field or a custom field designated as an external identifier.
- **Upsert**—If records with the same unique identifier or external identifier exist, this updates their values. Otherwise, it inserts them.
- **Delete**—Moves records into the Recycle Bin.
- **Undelete**—Restores records from the Recycle Bin.

DML operations can be included in Apex code in one of two ways: DML statements and database methods. Beyond the syntax, they differ in how errors are handled. If any one record in a DML statement fails, all records fail and are rolled back. Database methods allow for partial success. This chapter uses DML statements exclusively. Chapter 5 provides information on database methods.

> **Note**
>
> Usage of DML in Apex is subject to governor limits. For example, you are limited to a total of 150 DML operations. The cumulative maximum number of records modified by all DML operations is 10,000.

Insert

The `Insert` statement adds up to 200 records of a single object type to the database. When all records succeed, they contain their new unique identifiers. If any record fails, a `DmlException` is raised and the database is returned to its state prior to the `Insert` statement. For example, the code in Listing 4.34 inserts a Contact record and uses it as the parent of a new Resource record.

Listing 4.34   **Inserting a Record**

```
try {
  Contact c = new Contact(FirstName = 'Justin', LastName = 'Case',
    Hourly_Cost_Rate__c = 75, Region__c = 'West');
  insert c;
} catch (DmlException e) {
  System.debug(LoggingLevel.ERROR, e.getMessage());
}
```

Update

`Update` saves up to 200 existing records of a single object type. Existing records are identified by unique identifier (`Id`). Listing 4.35 illustrates the usage of the `Update` statement by creating a Resource record for Doug and updating it. Refresh the Resources tab in the native user interface to see the new record.

Listing 4.35   **Updating Records**

```
Contact doug = new Contact(FirstName = 'Doug', LastName = 'Hole');
insert doug;
doug.Hourly_Cost_Rate__c = 100;
doug.Home_Office__c = 'London';
update doug;
```

Upsert

`Upsert` combines the behavior of the `Insert` and `Update` operations on up to 200 records of the same object type. First, it attempts to locate a matching record using its unique identifier or external identifier. If one is found, the statement acts as an `Update`. If not, it behaves as an `Insert`.

The syntax of the Upsert statement is identical to Update and Insert, but adds a second, optional argument for specifying an external identifier. If an external identifier is not provided, the record's unique identifier is used. The code in Listing 4.36 upserts a record in the Contact object using the field Resource_ID__c (created in Chapter 11, "Advanced Integration") as an external identifier. If a Contact record with a Resource_ID__c value of 1001 exists, it is updated. If not, it is created.

Listing 4.36 **Upserting a Record**

```
Contact c = new Contact(Resource_ID__c = 1001,
  FirstName = 'Terry', LastName = 'Bull');
upsert c Resource_ID__c;
```

Delete and Undelete

Delete and Undelete statements move up to 200 records of the same object type to and from the Recycle Bin, respectively. Listing 4.37 shows an example of the Delete statement. A new Resource record named Terry is added and then deleted.

Listing 4.37 **Deleting Records**

```
Contact terry = new Contact(FirstName = 'Terry', LastName = 'Bull');
insert terry;
delete terry;
```

Listing 4.38 builds on Listing 4.37 to undelete the Terry record. Concatenate the listings in the Execute Anonymous view to test. The database is queried to prove the existence of the undeleted record. Try running the code a second time with the undelete statement commented out to see that it is working as intended.

Listing 4.38 **Undeleting Records**

```
undelete terry;
Contact terry2 = [ SELECT Id, Name
  FROM Contact WHERE Name LIKE 'Terry%' LIMIT 1 ];
System.debug(terry2.Name + ' exists');
delete terry;
```

Database Triggers

Triggers are Apex code working in concert with the Force.com database engine, automatically invoked by Force.com when database records are modified. Trigger code can perform any necessary processing on the modified data before or after Force.com completes its own work. The following list describes scenarios commonly implemented with triggers:

- A validation rule is required that is too complex to define on the database object using formula expressions.

- Two objects must be kept synchronized. When a record in one object is updated, a trigger updates the corresponding record in the other.

- Records of an object must be augmented with values from another object, a complex calculation, or external data via a Web service call.

This subsection covers the essentials of trigger development, including definition, batch processing, and error handling.

Definition

A trigger definition consists of four parts:

1. A unique trigger name to differentiate it from other triggers. Multiple triggers can be defined on the same database object.

2. The name of the database object on which to create the trigger. You can create triggers on standard and custom objects.

3. A comma-separated list of one or more trigger events that cause the trigger code to be executed. An event is specified using two keywords. The first keyword is either `before` or `after`, indicating that the trigger is to be executed before or after the database operation is saved. The second keyword is the DML operation: `insert`, `update`, `delete`, or `undelete`. For example, the trigger event `before update` means that the trigger is fired before a record is updated. Note that `before undelete` is an invalid trigger event.

4. The block of Apex code to execute when the trigger event occurs. The code typically loops over the list of records in the transaction and performs some action based on their contents. For `insert` and `update` triggers, the list of records in the transaction is provided in the variable `Trigger.new`. In a `before` trigger, these records can be modified. In `update`, `delete`, and `undelete` triggers, `Trigger.old` contains a read-only list of the original versions of the records. Also available to your trigger code is a set of Boolean variables indicating the event type that fired the trigger. They are useful when your trigger is defined on multiple events yet requires separate behavior for each. These variables are `Trigger.isBefore`, `Trigger.isAfter`, `Trigger.isInsert`, `Trigger.isUpdate`, `Trigger.isDelete`, and `Trigger.isUndelete`.

Listing 4.39 is an example of a trigger named `validateTimecard`. It is triggered before inserts and updates to the Timecard custom object. It doesn't do anything yet because its code block is empty.

Listing 4.39 **Trigger Definition**

```
trigger validateTimecard on Timecard__c(before insert, before update) {
  // code block
}
```

Triggers cannot be created in the Execute Anonymous view. Create them in the Force.com IDE by selecting File, New, Apex Trigger. To test triggers, use the native user interface to manually modify a relevant record, or write a unit test and invoke it from the Apex Test Runner or Execute Anonymous view.

> **Tip**
>
> A best practice for organizing trigger logic is to place it in an Apex class rather than the body of the trigger itself. This does not change anything about the behavior of the trigger or its governor limits, but encourages code reuse and makes the trigger easier to test.

Batch Processing in Triggers

Manual testing in the native user interface and simplistic unit tests can lull you into the false belief that triggers operate on a single record at a time. Not to be confused with Batch Apex, triggers can always be invoked with a list of records and should be optimized accordingly. Many ways exist to get a batch of records into the Force.com database, including the Data Loader and custom user interfaces. The surest way to a production issue with governor limits is to write a trigger that operates inefficiently when given a batch of records. The process of hardening a trigger to accept a batch of records is commonly called *bulkifying* the trigger.

Batches can be up to 200 records. When writing your trigger code, look at the resources consumed as you loop over `Trigger.new` or `Trigger.old`. Study the governor limits and make sure your code splits its work into batches, doing as little work as possible in the loop. For example, if you have some additional data to query, build a set of IDs from the trigger's records and query them once. Do not execute a SOQL statement for each loop iteration. If you need to run a DML statement, don't put that in the loop either. Create a List of objects and execute a single DML statement on the entire List. Listing 4.40 shows an example of looping over a batch of Contact records (in the variable `contacts`) to produce a list of Assignment records to insert.

Listing 4.40   **Batching DML Operations**

```
List<Assignment__c> toInsert = new List<Assignment__c>();
for (Contact contact : contacts) {
  toInsert.add(new Assignment__c(
    Contact__r = contact));
}
insert toInsert;
```

Error Handling

Errors are handled in triggers with `try`, `catch` blocks, consistent with other Apex code. But uncaught errors within a trigger differ from other Apex code in how they can impact execution of the larger database transaction the trigger participates in.

A common use of errors in triggers is for validation. Strings describing validation errors can be added to individual records or fields using the `addError` method. Force.com continues to process the batch, collecting any additional errors, and then rolls back the transaction and returns the errors to the initiator of the transaction.

> **Note**
>
> Additional error-handling behavior is available for transactions initiated outside of Force.com; for example, through the SOAP API. Records can fail individually without rolling back the entire transaction. This is discussed in Chapter 10, "Integration with Force.com."

If an uncaught exception is encountered in a trigger, whether thrown by the system or the trigger code itself, the batch of records is immediately aborted, and all changes are rolled back.

Database Security in Apex

Outside of Anonymous blocks, Apex always runs in a privileged, system context. This gives it access to read and write all data. It does not honor object-, field-, and record-level privileges of the user invoking the code. This works well for triggers, which operate at a low level and need full access to data.

Where full access is not appropriate, Apex provides the `with sharing` keyword. For example, custom user interfaces often require that access to data is limited by the privileges of the current user. Using `with sharing`, the sharing rules applying to the current user are evaluated against the data requested by queries and updated in DML operations. This option is discussed in detail in Chapter 6, "User Interfaces."

Debugging Apex Using Developer Console

Because Apex code cannot be executed on your local machine, debugging Apex requires some different tools and techniques than traditional software development. This section describes how to debug your code using two features of the Force.com's Developer Console. Developer Console allows you to set checkpoints to capture a snapshot of the state of your program. It also records execution logs when users perform actions in your application, allowing you to step through the logic and resources consumed.

Checkpoints

Checkpoints allow you to freeze variables at a specific point of execution in your program and examine them later. The point in the code at which the checkpoint is captured is called a checkpoint location. It is similar to a breakpoint in a standard development environment.

To work with checkpoints, open Developer Console and click the Checkpoints tab. To set a checkpoint location, locate the code using the Tests or Repository tab and click to the left of the desired line. In Figure 4.6, a checkpoint location has been set at line 10, indicated by the dot to the left of the line number.

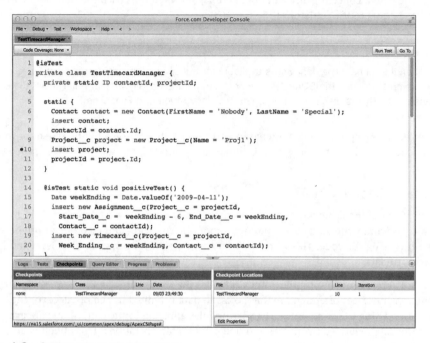

Figure 4.6   Setting a heap dump location

When code is executed at a checkpoint location, a checkpoint is generated. It can be viewed by double-clicking on a row in the Checkpoints tab, as shown in Figure 4.7. A checkpoint has been selected in the Checkpoints tab at the bottom, and its details shown in the top panel. The Symbols tab lists the program's variables and their values at the point in time of the checkpoint.

Execution Logs

Testing or debugging code from a user's point of view, directly from the native user interface, is often necessary. With the Developer Console pop-up window open, you can continue using Force.com in the main browser window. Actions you perform in the application result in execution log entries. Click the Logs tab in Developer Console to examine them.

In Figure 4.8, the user's action has resulted in a log entry, shown in the top table, which is selected and opened by double-clicking it. The top and middle of the screen display the raw execution log on the right panel, and an analysis in the left panels. The Stack Tree, Execution Overview, and Execution Stack provide different views of the Force.com resources consumed and their impact on response time.

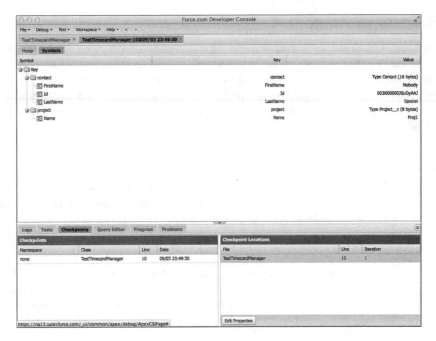

Figure 4.7   Examining a heap dump

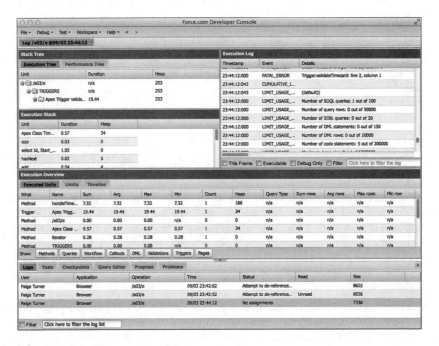

Figure 4.8   Examining the execution log

Unit Tests in Apex

Testing Apex code consists of writing and executing unit tests. Unit tests are special methods written to exercise the functionality of your code. The goal of testing is to write unit tests that execute as many lines as possible of the target code. The number of lines of code executed during a test is called *test coverage* and is expressed as a percentage of the total lines of code. Unit tests also typically perform some pretest preparation, such as creating sample data, and posttest verification of results.

Test Methods

Test methods are static Apex code methods, annotated with `@isTest`. They are written within an outer class, also annotated with `@isTest`. Tests are subject to the same governor limits as all Apex code, but every test method is completely independent for the purposes of limit tracking, not cumulative. Also, test classes are not counted against the code size limit for a Force.com organization.

A test is considered successful if its method is executed without encountering an uncaught exception. A common testing pattern is to make a series of assertions about the target code's state using the built-in method `System.assert`. The argument of `assert` is a Boolean expression. If it evaluates to `true`, the program continues; otherwise, a `System.Exception` is thrown and causes the test to fail.

Listing 4.41 shows a simple test method. It asserts two statements. The second is false, so the test always fails.

Listing 4.41   **Test Method**

```
@isTest static void negativeTest() {
  Integer i = 2 + 2;
  System.assert(i == 4);
  System.assert(i / 2 == 1);
}
```

Rather than adding two numbers together, most unit tests perform substantial operations in one or more other classes. Sometimes it's necessary to examine the contents of a private variable or invoke a protected method from a test. Rather than relaxing the access modifiers of the code to make them visible to tests, annotate the code you are testing with `@TestVisible`. This annotation provides your test code with privileged access but otherwise preserves the access modifiers in your code.

Test Data

With the exception of users and profiles, tests do not have access to the data in the Force.com database. You can annotate a class or method with `@isTest(SeeAllData=true)` to make the organization's data visible to tests, but this is not a best practice. The recommended approach is for tests to create their own temporary test data. All database modifications occurring during execution of a test method are automatically rolled back after the method is completed. Create your own test data in a setup phase before your tests are executed, and limit your assertions to that test data.

Running Tests

All tests are automatically executed when migrating code to a production environment, even unchanged and existing tests not included in the migration. Tests can and should be executed manually throughout the development process. Three ways to run tests are described in the following list:

1. The Force.com native user interface includes a test runner. In the App Setup area, click Develop, Apex Classes, and then click the Run All Tests button.

2. In the Force.com IDE, right-click an Apex class containing test methods and select Force. com, Run Tests.

3. From Developer Console, click the Tests tab and the New Run button. Select the tests to include, and click the Run button. Alternatively, right-click on the Classes folder in Eclipse and select Force.com, Run Tests to execute all tests in your organization. Figure 4.9 shows Developer Console after running a test.

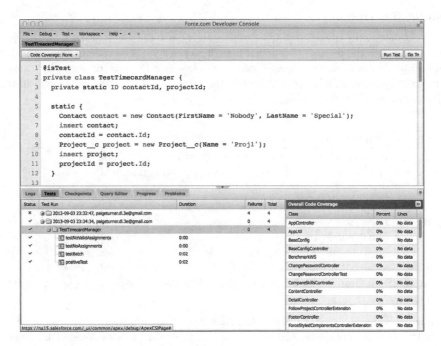

Figure 4.9   Viewing test results in Developer Console

Sample Application: Validating Timecards

This section applies Apex, SOQL, DML, and triggers to ensure that timecards entered into the Services Manager sample application have a valid assignment. An *assignment* is a record indicating that a resource is staffed on a project for a certain time period. A consultant can enter a timecard only for a project and time period he or she is authorized to work. Triggers are one way to enforce this rule.

The following subsections cover the process of configuring the Force.com IDE for Apex development, creating the trigger code to implement the timecard validation rule, and writing and running unit tests.

Force.com IDE Setup

Begin by creating the Force.com IDE Project for the Services Manager sample application, if you have not already done so. Select the menu option File, New, Force.com Project. Enter a project name, username, password, and security token of your Development Edition organization and click the Next button and then the Finish button. The Force.com IDE connects to Force.com, downloads the metadata in your organization to your local machine, and displays a new project node in your Navigator view.

Creating the Trigger

Listing 4.42 defines the trigger to validate timecards. It illustrates a best practice for trigger development: Keep the trigger's code block as small as possible. Place code in a separate class for easier maintenance and to encourage code reuse. Use naming conventions to indicate that the code is invoked from a trigger, such as the `Manager` suffix on the class name and the `handle` prefix on the method name.

Listing 4.42   **Trigger** validateTimecard

```
trigger validateTimecard on Timecard__c(before insert, before update) {
  TimecardManager.handleTimecardChange(Trigger.old, Trigger.new);
}
```

To create this trigger, select File, New, Apex Trigger. Enter the trigger name, select the object (`Timecard__c`), enable the two trigger operations (`before insert`, `before update`), and click the Finish button. This creates the trigger declaration and adds it to your project. It is now ready to be filled with the Apex code in Listing 4.42. If you save the trigger now, it will fail with a compilation error. This is because the dependent class, `TimecardManager`, has not yet been defined.

Continue on to creating the class. Select File, New, Apex Class to reveal the New Apex Class Wizard. Enter the class name (`TimecardManager`), leave the other fields (Version and Template) set to their defaults, and click the Finish button.

Listing 4.43 is the `TimecardManager` class. It performs the work of validating the timecard on behalf of the trigger. First, it builds a Set of resource Ids referenced in the incoming set of timecards. It uses this Set to query the Assignment object. For each timecard, the assignment List is looped over to look for a match on the time period specified in the timecard. If none is found, an error is added to the offending timecard. This error is ultimately reported to the user or program initiating the timecard transaction.

Listing 4.43 `TimecardManager` **Class**

```
public with sharing class TimecardManager {
  public class TimecardException extends Exception {}
  public static void handleTimecardChange(List<Timecard__c> oldTimecards,
    List<Timecard__c> newTimecards) {
    Set<ID> contactIds = new Set<ID>();
    for (Timecard__c timecard : newTimecards) {
      contactIds.add(timecard.Contact__c);
    }
    List<Assignment__c> assignments = [ select Id, Start_Date__c,
      End_Date__c, Contact__c from Assignment__c
      where Contact__c in :contactIds ];
    if (assignments.size() == 0) {
      throw new TimecardException('No assignments');
    }
    Boolean hasAssignment;
    for (Timecard__c timecard : newTimecards) {
      hasAssignment = false;
      for (Assignment__c assignment : assignments) {
        if (assignment.Contact__c == timecard.Contact__c &&
          timecard.Week_Ending__c - 6 >= assignment.Start_Date__c &&
          timecard.Week_Ending__c <= assignment.End_Date__c) {
          hasAssignment = true;
          break;
        }
      }
      if (!hasAssignment) {
        timecard.addError('No assignment for contact ' +
          timecard.Contact__c + ', week ending ' +
          timecard.Week_Ending__c);
      }
    }
  }
}
```

Unit Testing

Now that the trigger is developed, you must test it. During development, taking note of the code paths and thinking about how they are best covered by unit tests is a good idea. An even better idea is to write the unit tests as you develop.

To create unit tests for the timecard validation code using the Force.com IDE, follow the same procedure as that for creating an ordinary Apex class. An optional variation on this process is to select the Test Class template from the Create New Apex Class Wizard. This generates skeleton code for a class containing only test methods.

Listing 4.44 contains unit tests for the `TimecardManager` class. Before each unit test, test data is inserted in a static initializer. The tests cover a simple positive case, a negative case in which no assignments exist for the timecard, a second negative case in which no valid assignments exist for the time period in a timecard, and a batch insert of timecards. The code demonstrates a best practice of placing all unit tests for a class in a separate test class with an intuitive, consistent naming convention. In our example, the `TimecardManager` class has a test class named `TestTimecardManager`, the class name prefaced by the word *Test*.

Listing 4.44   **Unit Tests for** `TimecardManager` **Class**

```
@isTest
private class TestTimecardManager {
  private static ID contactId, projectId;

  static {
    Contact contact = new Contact(FirstName = 'Nobody', LastName = 'Special');
    insert contact;
    contactId = contact.Id;
    Project__c project = new Project__c(Name = 'Proj1');
    insert project;
    projectId = project.Id;
  }

  @isTest static void positiveTest() {
    Date weekEnding = Date.valueOf('2015-04-11');
    insert new Assignment__c(Project__c = projectId,
      Start_Date__c =  weekEnding - 6, End_Date__c = weekEnding,
      Contact__c = contactId);
    insert new Timecard__c(Project__c = projectId,
      Week_Ending__c = weekEnding, Contact__c = contactId);
  }

  @isTest static void testNoAssignments() {
    Timecard__c timecard = new Timecard__c(Project__c = projectId,
      Week_Ending__c = Date.valueOf('2015-04-11'),
      Contact__c = contactId);
```

```
  try {
    insert timecard;
  } catch (DmlException e) {
    System.assert(e.getMessage().indexOf('No assignments') > 0);
    return;
  }
  System.assert(false);
}

@isTest static void testNoValidAssignments() {
  Date weekEnding = Date.valueOf('2015-04-04');
  insert new Assignment__c(Project__c = projectId,
    Start_Date__c = weekEnding - 6, End_Date__c = weekEnding,
    Contact__c = contactId);
  try {
    insert new Timecard__c(Project__c = projectId,
    Week_Ending__c = Date.today(), Contact__c = contactId);
  } catch (DmlException e) {
    System.assert(e.getMessage().indexOf('No assignment for contact') > 0);
    return;
  }
  System.assert(false);
}

@isTest static void testBatch() {
  Date weekEnding = Date.valueOf('2015-04-11');
  insert new Assignment__c(Project__c = projectId,
    Start_Date__c =  weekEnding - 6, End_Date__c = weekEnding,
    Contact__c = contactId);
  List<Timecard__c> timecards = new List<Timecard__c>();
  for (Integer i=0; i<200; i++) {
    timecards.add(new Timecard__c(Project__c = projectId,
      Week_Ending__c = weekEnding, Contact__c = contactId));
  }
  insert timecards;
}
}
```

After saving the code in the unit test class, run it by right-clicking in the editor and selecting
Force.com, Run Tests. After a few seconds, you should see the Apex Test Runner view with a
green check box indicating that all tests passed, as shown in Figure 4.10. Expand the results
node to see 100% test coverage of the TimecardManager, and scroll through the debug log to
examine performance information and resource consumption for each of the tests.

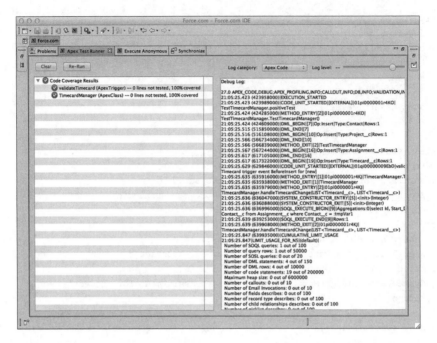

Figure 4.10   Viewing test results

Summary

This chapter is arguably the most important chapter in the book. It describes core Apex concepts and syntax that form the basis of all subsequent chapters. Absorb this chapter, augmenting it with the information available through the developer.force.com Web site and community, and you will be well prepared to write your own Force.com applications.

Before moving on, take a few minutes to review these major areas:

- Apex is the only language that runs inside the Force.com platform and is tightly integrated with the Force.com database. Apex is strongly typed and includes object-oriented features.

- The Force.com database is queried using SOQL and SOSL, and its records are modified using DML. All three languages can be embedded directly inside Apex code.

- Resources consumed by Apex programs are tightly controlled by the Force.com platform through governor limits. Limits vary based on the type of resource consumed. Learn the relevant governor limits as early as possible in your development process. This ensures that you write efficient code that scales up to production data volumes.

5

Advanced Business Logic

In the preceding chapter, you learned the basics of the Apex language for developing business logic. This chapter extends your knowledge of Apex to reach more features of the Force.com platform. The following topics are covered:

- **Aggregate SOQL queries**—*Aggregate queries operate on groups of records, summarizing data declaratively at the database level rather than in Apex.*

- **Additional SOQL features**—*SOQL includes features for querying related objects and multi-select picklists.*

- **Salesforce Object Search Language (SOSL)**—*SOSL is a full-text search language, a complement to SOQL, that allows a single query to search the textual content of many database objects and fields.*

- **Transaction processing**—*Apex includes database methods to enable the partial success of transactions, saving and restoring of database state, and locking of records returned from a query.*

- **Apex managed sharing**—*Managed sharing allows programmatic control over record-level sharing.*

- **Sending and receiving email**—*Apex programs can send and receive email with support for text and binary attachments and templates for standardizing outbound messages.*

- **Dynamic Apex**—*Execute database queries that aren't hard-coded into your programs, query Force.com for your database's metadata, and write generic code to manipulate database records regardless of their type.*

- **Custom settings in Apex**—*Data from custom settings can be retrieved, created, updated, and deleted from Apex.*

- **Sample application**—*The Services Manager sample application is enhanced to send email notifications to users when a business event occurs.*

> **Note**
>
> The code listings in this chapter are available in a GitHub Gist at http://goo.gl/q65M4.

Aggregate SOQL Queries

SOQL statements that summarize or group records are called *aggregate queries*. Aggregate queries in SOQL run at the database level rather than in Apex. This results in much better performance and simpler code. This section covers three aspects of aggregate SOQL queries:

- **Aggregate functions**—Rather than simply returning the discrete values of a database field in a SELECT statement, aggregate functions such as SUM apply a simple calculation on each record and return the accumulated result.

- **Grouping records**—The GROUP BY syntax works with aggregate functions to return a set of summarized results based on common values.

- **Grouping records with subtotals**—SOQL provides two special forms of the GROUP BY syntax to calculate subtotals and return them in the query results.

Aggregate Functions

Aggregate functions in SOQL work much like their SQL counterparts. They are applied to fields in the SELECT list. After you include an aggregate function in a query, nonaggregate fields in the same query are not allowed. The six aggregate functions available in SOQL are

- **AVG**—Calculates an average of the values in a numeric field.

- **COUNT**—Counts the values in a numeric, date, or string field, including duplicate values but not nulls. Unlike all other aggregate functions, the argument to COUNT is optional.

- **COUNT_DISTINCT**—Counts the unique values in a numeric, date, or string field, excluding nulls.

- **MIN**—Returns the minimum value in a numeric, date, or string field. The minimum of a string field is the first value when values are sorted alphabetically. If the string is a picklist type, the minimum is the first value in the picklist.

- **MAX**—Returns the maximum value in a numeric, date, or string field. The maximum of a string field is the last value when values are sorted alphabetically. If the string is a picklist type, the maximum is the last value in the picklist.

- **SUM**—Computes the sum of values in a numeric field.

All queries containing aggregate functions return a special Apex object called AggregateResult, except the no-argument form of COUNT, which returns an integer. The AggregateResult object contains the aggregate values calculated by running the query. They have default field names expr0 for the first field, expr1, and so forth. Alternatively, you can provide an alias immediately following the aggregate function column to provide a friendlier label for the value in your code. Aggregate result fields are accessed using the get method.

To get started with aggregate functions in Apex, open Force.com IDE's Execute Anonymous view and type in and run the code given in Listing 5.1.

Listing 5.1   **Returning the Record Count**

```
Integer i = [ SELECT COUNT() FROM Timecard__c ];
System.debug(i);
```

This code prints the number of records contained in the Timecard__c object to the debug log. The SOQL query returns an integer because it uses the no-argument form of the COUNT aggregate function. In contrast, the example in Listing 5.2 uses the SUM aggregate function and returns an AggregateResult object, with an alias Total specified on the aggregate column. Note that if an alias were not specified, the aggregate column would be named expr0.

Listing 5.2   **Calculating a Sum**

```
AggregateResult r = [ SELECT SUM(Total_Hours__c) Total
  FROM Timecard__c ];
System.debug(r.get('Total'));
```

> **Note**
>
> Normal SOQL governor limits apply to aggregate functions. The number of records used to compute an aggregate result are applied toward the limit on records returned. So although your COUNT query returns a single result record, if it counted more than 50,000 records, your query will fail with an exception. If such a failure is disruptive to your application, make sure you use a WHERE clause to reduce the number of records that are processed in the query. The LIMIT keyword is not allowed in queries with aggregate functions, except for the special form of the COUNT function that has no field argument.

Grouping Records

SOQL provides the GROUP BY syntax for grouping records by one or more fields. When a query contains a grouping, its results are collapsed into a single record for each unique value in the grouped field. Because you can no longer return individual field values, all fields not specified as grouped must be placed within aggregate functions.

Listing 5.3 shows a simple example of grouping records without aggregate functions. It examines all the records in the Contact object and returns only the unique values of the field Region__c.

Listing 5.3   **Returning Unique Records by Grouping Them**

```
for (AggregateResult r : [ SELECT Region__c FROM Contact
  GROUP BY Region__c ]) {
  System.debug(r.get('Region__c'));
}
```

Although aggregate functions can be used alone in a simple query, they are much more powerful when used in conjunction with record groupings. Listing 5.4 demonstrates aggregate functions with record groupings. It groups all Timecard records by the geographic region of the consultant (Contact) who performed the work, and sums their reported hours. This results in one record per geographic region with the region's name and a sum of their timecard hours.

Listing 5.4   **Using Aggregate Functions with Record Groupings**

```
for (AggregateResult r : [ SELECT Contact__r.Region__c,
  SUM(Total_Hours__c) FROM Timecard__c
  GROUP BY Contact__r.Region__c ]) {
  System.debug(r.get('Region__c') + ' ' + r.get('expr0'));
}
```

You're already familiar with the WHERE keyword in SOQL for filtering query results using Boolean expressions. Filtering on the results of aggregate functions requires the HAVING keyword. It works just like WHERE, but the field being filtered must be wrapped with an aggregate function and included in the GROUP BY list.

The code in Listing 5.5 outputs the average hourly cost rates for consultants by education level, but excludes records at or below an average cost rate of $100. The filtering of the average cost rates is specified by the HAVING keyword.

Listing 5.5   **Filtering Grouped Records by Aggregate Function Values**

```
for (AggregateResult r : [ SELECT Highest_Education_Level__c ed,
  AVG(Hourly_Cost_Rate__c) FROM Contact
  GROUP BY Highest_Education_Level__c
  HAVING AVG(Hourly_Cost_Rate__c) > 100 ]) {
  System.debug(r.get('ed') + ' ' + r.get('expr0'));
}
```

Grouping Records with Subtotals

Two special forms of grouping in SOQL produce subtotals and grand totals for the record groupings specified in the query. They are GROUP BY ROLLUP and GROUP BY CUBE, and they replace GROUP BY syntax and support up to three grouped fields. These functions make it easier for developers to produce cross-tabular or pivot-style outputs common to reporting tools, where groups become the axes and aggregate values are the cells. The Force.com database calculates the totals and provides them in-line, in the results, eliminating the need to write Apex to post-process the data.

Listing 5.6 demonstrates GROUP BY ROLLUP to add subtotals to combinations of two fields: Status__c and Region__c. Because Status__c appears first in the GROUP BY ROLLUP function, the subtotals are calculated for each of its unique values. The function GROUPING is used to identify subtotal records, and also to order the results so that the subtotals appear last.

Listing 5.6   **Subtotals on Two Field Groupings**

```
for (AggregateResult r : [ SELECT Project__r.Status__c, Contact__r.Region__c,
  SUM(Total_Hours__c) hours, COUNT(Id) recs,
  GROUPING(Project__r.Status__c) status, GROUPING(Contact__r.Region__c) region
  FROM Timecard__c
  GROUP BY ROLLUP(Project__r.Status__c, Contact__r.Region__c)
  ORDER BY GROUPING(Project__r.Status__c), GROUPING(Contact__r.Region__c) ]) {
  System.debug(LoggingLevel.INFO,
    r.get('Status__c') + ' ' + r.get('Region__c') + ' ' +
    r.get('region') + ' ' + r.get('status') + ' ' +
    r.get('hours') + ' ' + r.get('recs'));
}
```

Listing 5.7 shows the result of running the code in Listing 5.6 on a database containing 13 Timecard records spread across West and Central regions' projects in Yellow and Green status. Note the third and fourth columns contain the value of the GROUPING function. Here, a 1 indicates that the record is a subtotal, and 0 indicates a normal record. For example, the fifth record from the top is a subtotal on status because the 1 appears in the status column. The other values in that record indicate the sum of all Timecard hours for projects in Yellow status is 109, and that this constitutes three records' worth of data. The final record contains the grand totals, which you can verify by adding the record count of the Green subtotal (10) to the Yellow subtotal (3).

Listing 5.7   **Excerpt of Debug Log after Running Code in Listing 5.6**

```
16:04:43.207|USER_DEBUG|[7]|INFO|Green West 0 0 230.0 6
16:04:43.207|USER_DEBUG|[7]|INFO|Green Central 0 0 152.0 4
16:04:43.207|USER_DEBUG|[7]|INFO|Yellow Central 0 0 109.0 3
16:04:43.207|USER_DEBUG|[7]|INFO|Green null 1 0 382.0 10
16:04:43.207|USER_DEBUG|[7]|INFO|Yellow null 1 0 109.0 3
16:04:43.207|USER_DEBUG|[7]|INFO|null null 1 1 491.0 13
```

To experiment with GROUP BY CUBE, replace the word ROLLUP with CUBE in Listing 5.6 and run the code. The GROUP BY CUBE syntax causes all possible combinations of grouped fields to receive subtotals. The results are shown in Listing 5.8. Note the addition of two records, subtotals on the Region__c field indicated by a 1 in the region column.

Listing 5.8   Excerpt of Debug Log after Changing Listing 5.6 to `Group By Cube`

```
16:06:56.003|USER_DEBUG|[7]|INFO|Green Central 0 0 152.0 4
16:06:56.003|USER_DEBUG|[7]|INFO|Green West 0 0 230.0 6
16:06:56.004|USER_DEBUG|[7]|INFO|Yellow Central 0 0 109.0 3
16:06:56.004|USER_DEBUG|[7]|INFO|Green null 1 0 382.0 10
16:06:56.004|USER_DEBUG|[7]|INFO|Yellow null 1 0 109.0 3
16:06:56.004|USER_DEBUG|[7]|INFO|null West 0 1 230.0 6
16:06:56.004|USER_DEBUG|[7]|INFO|null Central 0 1 261.0 7
16:06:56.005|USER_DEBUG|[7]|INFO|null null 1 1 491.0 13
```

Additional SOQL Features

Although SOQL doesn't allow arbitrary joins, it provides some control over how related objects are navigated. This section discusses inner and outer joins, as well as semi-joins and anti-joins:

- **Inner join and outer join**—SOQL statements that include related objects normally do so by outer join, but can perform an inner join instead using a WHERE clause.

- **Semi-join and anti-join**—Semi-join and anti-join are types of relationship queries that use the results of a subquery to filter the records returned from the parent object.

- **Multi-select picklists**—A multi-select picklist is a form of picklist field that allows multiple values to be stored for a single record. The standard conditional filters of the SOQL WHERE clause do not suffice for handling multiple values within a single record and column, so SOQL provides special syntax to handle this case.

Inner Join and Outer Join

A SOQL statement consists of a single base object, specified using the FROM keyword. All fields in the base object can be retrieved in the query, as well as fields from parent and child objects depending on their distance away from the base object. Force.com takes care of joining related objects together to retrieve the requested fields.

These implicit joins are always outer joins. An outer join returns all records from the base object, including records that do not refer to a related object. To get a feel for this behavior, create a new Project record in the native user interface and leave all of its fields blank, but enter **Test Project** for the Name. Open Force.com IDE's Schema Explorer and enter and run the query given in Listing 5.9.

Listing 5.9   SOQL Outer Join

```
SELECT Name, Account__r.Name
  FROM Project__c
```

This query returns the name and account name of the Projects. Account is the parent object of Project through a Lookup relationship. Because it is a Lookup relationship and not Master-Detail, it can contain a null value in `Account__c`, the Account foreign key field. With no foreign key to Account, `Account__r`, the foreign object reference, is also null.

You should see the five records imported from Listing 2.11 in Chapter 2, "Database Essentials," plus the newly added record, named Test Project. Figure 5.1 shows the result of running the query. The Test Project record contains no value for `Account__r` yet was included in the results anyway. This is due to the outer join behavior.

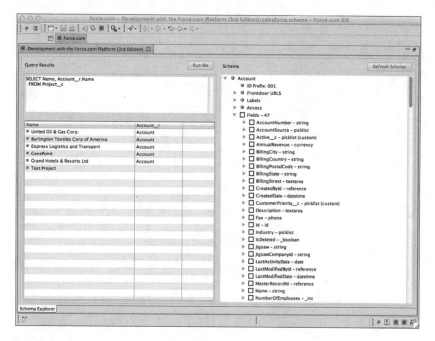

Figure 5.1   Outer join results in Schema Explorer

In a relational database, this same query translated to SQL would result in five rows. The Test Project row would not be returned because it does not match a row in the Account table. Joins in SQL are inner by default, returning only rows that match both tables of the join.

To duplicate this inner join behavior in SOQL, simply add a filter condition to eliminate records without a matching record in the related object. For example, Listing 5.10 adds a filter condition to Listing 5.9 to exclude Project records without a corresponding Account.

Listing 5.10   **SOQL Inner Join**

```
SELECT Name, Account__r.Name
  FROM Project__c
  WHERE Account__c != null
```

The results of this query are shown in Figure 5.2. It has returned five records, each one with a corresponding parent Account record. The newly added Project record without the Account is correctly omitted.

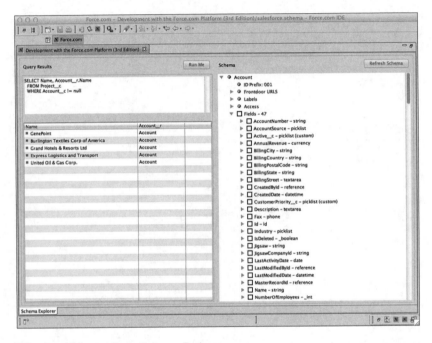

Figure 5.2   Inner join results in Schema Explorer

Semi-Join and Anti-Join

In Chapter 4, "Business Logic," you learned the two ways related objects can be included in SOQL: parent-to-child and child-to-parent queries. Semi-join and anti-join queries enhance the functionality of both queries, and add the ability to make child-to-child queries. In general, they allow records from one object to be filtered by a subquery against another object.

For example, suppose you need a list of all Account records that have at least one Project record in a yellow status. To make sure you have a valid test case, edit one of the Project records in the native user interface to set it to a yellow status. Try to write a query to return its Account, with Account as the base object.

You can't do this without using a semi-join. Listing 5.11 shows one attempt. But it returns the unique identifiers and names of all Accounts and the unique identifiers of any Projects in yellow status. You would still have to write Apex code to filter through the Account records to ignore those without Project child records.

Listing 5.11   **Parent-to-Child Query, Filter on Child**

```
SELECT Id, Name,
 (SELECT Id FROM Projects__r WHERE Status__c = 'Yellow')
  FROM Account
```

Figure 5.3 shows the result of executing this query. Grand Hotels & Resorts Ltd is the Project in yellow status, and you can see that its Project record has been returned in the relationship field Projects__r.

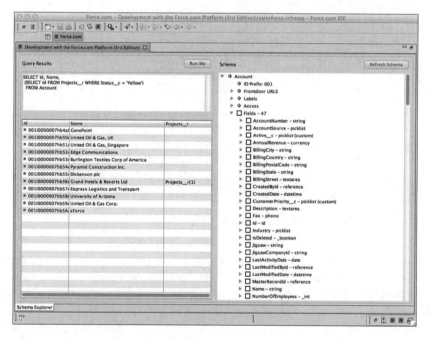

Figure 5.3   Parent-to-child query, filter on child

Listing 5.12 rewrites this query using a semi-join. Read it from the bottom up. A subquery identifies Projects in yellow status, returning their Account unique identifiers. This set of Account unique identifiers is used to filter the Account records returned by the query. The result is a single Account, as shown in Figure 5.4.

Listing 5.12   **SOQL with Semi-Join**

```
SELECT Id, Name
  FROM Account
  WHERE Id IN
    (SELECT Account__c FROM Project__c WHERE Status__c = 'Yellow')
```

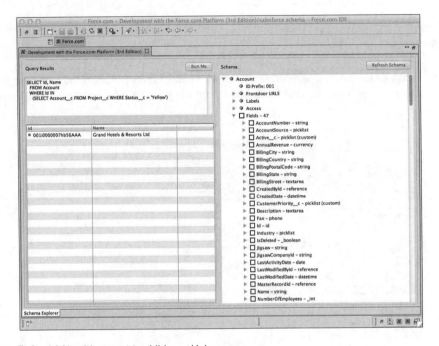

Figure 5.4   SOQL with parent-to-child semi-join

An anti-join is the negative version of a semi-join. It uses the NOT IN keyword to allow the subquery to exclude records from the parent object. For example, Listing 5.13 returns all Accounts except those containing Projects in a green status. Note that the results include the Project in yellow status, as well as all Account records not associated with a Project.

Listing 5.13   **SOQL with Anti-Join**

```
SELECT Id, Name
  FROM Account
  WHERE Id NOT IN
    (SELECT Account__c FROM Project__c WHERE Status__c = 'Green')
```

Returning to semi-joins, Listing 5.14 provides an example of another type, called child-to-child. It joins two child objects that aren't directly related by relationship fields. The records in the Timecard object are filtered by contacts that have at least one assignment as a consultant. This means Timecards logged by contacts who are not assigned to a project as a consultant are excluded from the results. Child-to-child refers to the Timecard and Assignment objects, which are related to each other only in so much as they are children to other objects.

Listing 5.14   SOQL with Child-to-Child Semi-Join

```
SELECT Project__r.Name, Week_Ending__c, Total_Hours__c
  FROM Timecard__c
  WHERE Contact__c IN
    (SELECT Contact__c FROM Assignment__c WHERE Role__c = 'Consultant')
```

Listing 5.15 demonstrates a third type of semi-join, the child-to-parent. Timecards are filtered again, this time to include consultants with an hourly cost rate of more than $100. Child-to-parent refers to the relationship between the Timecard and Contact objects. Contact is the parent object, and it is being used to restrict the output of the query on Timecard, the child object.

Listing 5.15   SOQL with Child-to-Parent Semi-Join

```
SELECT Project__r.Name, Week_Ending__c, Total_Hours__c
  FROM Timecard__c
  WHERE Contact__c IN
    (SELECT Id FROM Contact WHERE Hourly_Cost_Rate__c > 100)
```

Several restrictions are placed on semi-join and anti-join queries:

- The selected column in the subquery must be a primary or foreign key and cannot traverse relationships. It must be a direct field on the child object. For example, it would be invalid to rewrite the subquery in Listing 5.12 to return Account__r.Id in place of Account__c.

- A single query can include at most two semi-joins or anti-joins.

- Semi-joins and anti-joins cannot be nested within other semi-join and anti-join statements, and are not allowed in subqueries.

- The parent object cannot be the same type as the child. This type of query can always be rewritten as a single query without a semi-join or an anti-join. For example, the invalid query SELECT Name FROM Project__c WHERE Id IN (SELECT Id FROM Project__c WHERE Status__c = 'Green') can be expressed without a subquery: SELECT Name FROM Project__c WHERE Status__c = 'Green'.

- Subqueries cannot be nested and cannot contain the OR, count(), ORDER BY, or LIMIT keywords.

Multi-Select Picklists

Multi-select picklists are interchangeable with ordinary picklists in queries, except for being prohibited in the ORDER BY clause. SOQL includes two additional features for filtering multi-select picklists, described in the following list:

- **Semicolon AND operator**—The semicolon is used to express multiple string literals. For example, 'Java;Apex' means that the multi-select picklist has both Java and Apex items selected in any order. The semicolon notation can be used with the = and != SOQL operators to make assertions about the selected items of multi-select picklists.

- **INCLUDES and EXCLUDES keywords**—The INCLUDES and EXCLUDES keywords are followed by comma-separated lists of literal values. The INCLUDES keyword returns records in which the selected values of a multi-select picklist are included in the list of values. The EXCLUDES keyword returns records that match none of the values.

The semicolon notation can be combined with the INCLUDES and EXCLUDES keywords to express any combination of multi-select picklist values.

To try this out, create a multi-select picklist named Requested Skills on the Project object. Run the SOQL statement given in Listing 5.16 using the Force.com IDE's Schema Explorer. It returns Project records with the multiple selection of Apex, Java, and C# in the Requested Skills field and also records with only Python selected. Populate Project records with matching values to see them returned by the query.

Listing 5.16   **SOQL with Multi-Select Picklist**

```
SELECT Id, Name
  FROM Project__c
  WHERE Requested_Skills__c INCLUDES ('Apex;Java;C#', 'Python')
```

Salesforce Object Search Language (SOSL)

Data stored in the Force.com database is automatically indexed to support both structured and unstructured queries. SOQL is the language for structured queries, allowing records from a single object and its related objects to be retrieved with precise, per-field filter conditions. SOSL is a full-text search language for unstructured queries. It begins by looking across multiple fields and multiple objects for one or more search keywords, and then applies an optional SOQL-like filter on each object to refine the results.

To decide which query language to use, consider the scope of the query. If the query spans multiple unrelated objects, SOSL is the only practical choice. If the query searches for words within many string fields, it can probably be expressed more concisely in SOSL than SOQL. Use SOQL for queries on a single object with filters on various data types.

SOSL Basics

At the highest level, a SOSL query specifies search terms and scope. The search terms are a list of string literals and can include wildcards. The search scope is fields containing string data from one or more objects. This excludes Number, Date, and Checkbox fields from being searched with SOSL.

SOSL query syntax consists of four parts:

- **Query**—The query is one or more words or phrases to search on. The query can include the wildcards * (matches any number of characters) and ? (matches any single character) at the middle or end of search terms. Enclose a search term in quotation marks to perform an exact match on multiple words. Use the logical operators AND, OR, and AND NOT to combine search terms and parentheses to control the order in which they're evaluated. Note that searches are not case sensitive.

- **Search group**—The search group is an optional part of the SOSL query indicating the types of fields to search in each object. Valid values are ALL FIELDS (all string fields), NAME FIELDS (the standard Name field only), EMAIL FIELDS (all fields of type Email), and PHONE FIELDS (all fields of type Phone). The default value is ALL FIELDS.

- **Field specification**—The field specification is a comma-separated list of objects to include in the result. By default, the Id field of each object is included. Optionally, you can specify additional fields to return by enclosing them in parentheses. You can also specify conditional filters using the same syntax as the SOQL WHERE clause, set the sort order with the ORDER BY keyword, and use the LIMIT keyword to limit the number of records returned per object.

- **Record limit**—This optional value specifies the maximum number of records returned by the entire query, from all the objects queried. If a record limit is not provided, it defaults to the maximum of 200.

These four parts are combined in the following syntax: FIND *'query'* IN *search group* RETURNING *field specification* LIMIT *record limit*. The single quotation marks around query are required.

SOSL in Apex

SOSL in Apex works much like SOQL in Apex. Queries are enclosed in square brackets and compiled directly into the code, ensuring that the query syntax is correct and references valid fields and objects in the database.

As with SOQL, bind variables can be used to inject variable values from the running program into select parts of the query. This injection of values is performed in a secure manner because Apex automatically escapes special characters. Bind variables are allowed in the search string (following FIND), filter literals (in the WHERE block), and the LIMIT keyword.

SOSL is not allowed in triggers. It will compile, but will fail at runtime. It is allowed in unit tests and custom user interfaces, as covered in Chapter 6, "User Interfaces." In this chapter, you can experiment with SOSL using the Execute Anonymous view.

> **Note**
>
> You are limited to 20 SOSL queries returning a maximum of 2,000 rows per query.

Listing 5.17 is a sample SOSL query in Apex. It returns the names of records in the Project and Contact objects that contain the word *Chicago* in any of their fields.

Listing 5.17 **SOSL in Apex**

```
List<List<SObject>> result = [
  FIND 'Chicago'
  RETURNING Project__c(Name), Contact(Name)
];
List<Project__c> projects = (List<Project__c>)result[0];
for (Project__c project : projects) {
  System.debug('Project: ' + project.Name);
}
List<Contact> resources = (List<Contact>)result[1];
for (Contact resource : resources) {
  System.debug('Contact: ' + resource.Name);
}
```

Figure 5.5 shows the results of running this code in the Execute Anonymous view. If your debug log is cluttered with too many other entries to see the output of the query, set Apex code to the Debug level and all other Log categories to None.

Transaction Processing

This section covers three features of Apex that control how transactions are processed by the database:

- **Data Manipulation Language (DML) database methods**—DML database methods are much like DML statements from Chapter 4, but add support for partial success. This allows some records from a batch to succeed while others fail.

- **Savepoints**—Savepoints designate a point in time that your code can return to. Returning to a savepoint rolls back all DML statements executed since the establishment of the savepoint.

- **Record locking**—Apex provides a SOQL keyword to protect records from interference by other users or programs for the duration of a transaction.

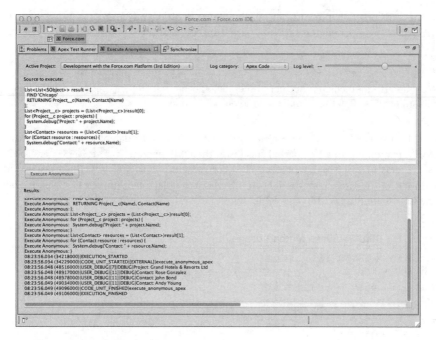

Figure 5.5   Results of SOSL in Apex

Data Manipulation Language (DML) Database Methods

All database operations in Apex are transactional. For example, an implicit transaction is created when a trigger fires. If the code in a trigger completes without error, DML operations performed within it are automatically committed. If the trigger terminates prematurely with an uncaught exception, all DML operations are automatically rolled back. If multiple triggers fire for a single database operation, all trigger code succeeds or fails as a group.

In Chapter 4, you were exposed to DML statements. These statements accept a single record or batch of records. When operating on a batch, they succeed or fail on the entire group of records. For example, if 200 records are inserted and the last record fails with a validation error, none of the 200 records are inserted.

Apex offers a second way of making DML statements called DML database methods. DML database methods allow batch DML operations to fail on individual records without impacting the entire batch. To do this, they do not throw exceptions to indicate error. Instead they return an array of result objects, one per input record. These result objects contain a flag indicating success or failure, and error details in the event of failure.

A DML database method exists for each of the DML statements. Each method takes an optional Boolean parameter called opt_allOrNone to specify batch behavior. The default value is true, indicating that the behavior is "all or none." This makes the method identical to a DML

statement, with one failed record causing the failure of all records and a `DmlException`. But if
the `opt_allOrNone` parameter is `false`, partial success is allowed.

> **Note**
>
> DML database methods are subject to the same governor limits and general restrictions as
> DML statements. Refer to Chapter 4 for more information.

Listing 5.18 inserts a batch of two Skill records using the `insert` database method. It passes
`false` as an argument to allow partial success of the DML operation. The `insert` method
returns an array of `SaveResult` objects. They correspond one-to-one with the array passed as
an argument to the `insert` method. Each `SaveResult` object is examined to check for failure,
and the results are displayed in the debug log.

Listing 5.18   **DML Database Method Usage**

```
Contact tim = [ SELECT Id
  FROM Contact
  WHERE Name = 'Tim Barr' LIMIT 1 ];
Skill__c skill1 = new Skill__c(Contact__c = tim.Id,
  Type__c = 'Java', Rating__c = '3 - Average');
Skill__c skill2 = new Skill__c(Contact__c = tim.Id,
  Rating__c = '4 - Above Average');
Skill__c[] skills = new  Skill__c[] { skill1, skill2 };
Database.SaveResult[] saveResults =
  Database.insert(skills, false);
for (Integer i=0; i<saveResults.size(); i++) {
  Database.SaveResult saveResult = saveResults[i];
  if (!saveResult.isSuccess()) {
    Database.Error err = saveResult.getErrors()[0];
    System.debug('Skill ' + i + ' insert failed: '
      + err.getMessage());
  } else {
    System.debug('Skill ' + i + ' insert succeeded: new Id = '
      + saveResult.getId());
  }
}
```

The result of executing this code is shown in Figure 5.6. The debug log indicates the first record
is inserted, but the second failed because it doesn't contain a value for the `Type__c` field. This
is enforced by a validation rule created in Chapter 2. If you edit this code and remove the
second argument to `Database.insert`, which enables partial success, the failure of the second
record raises an exception and rolls back the successful insertion of the first record.

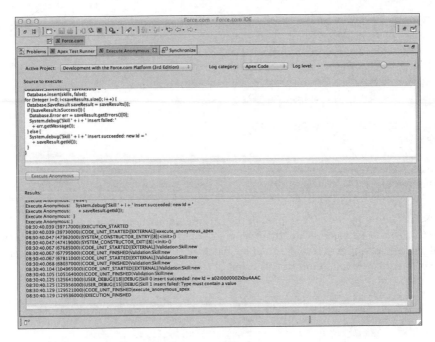

Figure 5.6   Results of `insert` DML database method

Savepoints

Savepoints are markers indicating the state of the database at a specific point in the execution of your Apex program. They allow the database to be restored to a known state in case of error or any scenario requiring a reversal of all DML operations performed since the savepoint.

Set a new savepoint using the `Database.setSavepoint` method, which returns a Savepoint object. To restore the database to a savepoint, call the `Database.rollback` method, which takes a Savepoint object as its only argument.

Several limitations exist on the use of savepoints. The number of savepoints and rollbacks contributes toward the overall limit on DML statements, which is 150. If you create multiple savepoints and roll back, all savepoints created after the savepoint you roll back to are invalidated. Finally, you cannot share a savepoint across triggers using a static variable.

Listing 5.19 is an example of using the `setSavepoint` and `rollback` methods. First, a savepoint is set. Then, all the Project records in your database are deleted, assuming your database doesn't contain more than the governor limit of 10,000 records for DML. Finally, the database is rolled back to the savepoint. The number of records in the Project object is counted before each operation in the program to illustrate its behavior.

Listing 5.19   **Savepoint and Rollback Usage**

```
void printRecordCount() {
  System.debug([ SELECT COUNT() FROM Project__c ] + ' records');
}
printRecordCount();
Savepoint sp = Database.setSavepoint();

delete [ SELECT Id FROM Project__c ];
printRecordCount();

Database.rollback(sp);
printRecordCount();
```

The results of running the code snippet in the Execute Anonymous view are shown in
Figure 5.7. The debug log indicates that the Project object initially contains five records. They
are all deleted, leaving zero records. Then the database is rolled back to the savepoint established before the deletion, resulting in a count of five records again.

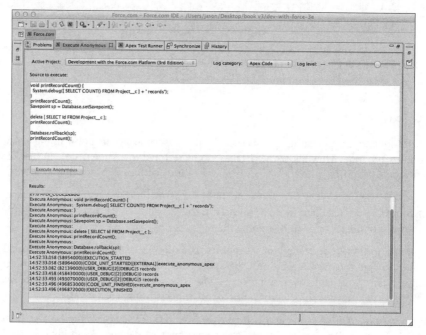

Figure 5.7   Results of savepoint and rollback sample code

Record Locking

Apex code has many entry points. Code can be invoked from outside of Force.com via a Web service call, by modifying a record with a trigger on it in the native user interface, inside Force.com IDE in an Execute Anonymous view, or in a unit test. Additionally, multiple users or programs can be running the same code simultaneously or code that uses the same database resources.

DML operations using values returned by SOQL or SOSL queries are at risk for dirty writes. This means values updated by one program have been modified by a second program running at the same time. The changes of the second program are lost because the first program is operating with stale data.

For example, if your code retrieves a record and then modifies its value later in the program, it requires a write lock on the record. A write lock prevents the record from being concurrently updated by another program. Write locks are provided in Apex via the SOQL FOR UPDATE keyword. This keyword indicates to Apex that you intend to modify the records returned by the SOQL query. This locks the records, preventing them from being updated by another program until your transaction is complete. No explicit commit is necessary. The records are unlocked, and changes are automatically committed when the program exits successfully or is rolled back otherwise.

> **Note**
>
> You cannot use the ORDER BY keyword with FOR UPDATE. Query results are automatically ordered by Id field.

Listing 5.20 is an example of record locking in Apex. Tim Barr is given a raise of $20. His Resource record is retrieved and locked, the hourly cost is incremented, and the database is updated. The use of FOR UPDATE ensures that this code running simultaneously in two contexts still results in the correct outcome: a $40 increase in hourly cost rate, $20 from each of the two independent execution contexts, serialized with FOR UPDATE. Without the locking, a dirty write could cause one of the updates to be lost. For this example to execute without errors, make sure you have a Contact record named Tim Barr with a non-null value for the Hourly_Cost_Rate__c field.

Listing 5.20   **Record Locking Example**

```
Contact tim = [ SELECT Id, Hourly_Cost_Rate__c
  FROM Contact
  WHERE Name = 'Tim Barr' LIMIT 1
  FOR UPDATE ];
tim.Hourly_Cost_Rate__c += 20;
update tim;
```

Apex Managed Sharing

Apex managed sharing allows Apex code to add, edit, and delete record sharing rules. This is the third and most advanced type of record sharing provided by Force.com. It provides the Apex developer with full control of record sharing. Apex managed sharing uses the same infrastructure as the other two types of record sharing, discussed in Chapter 3, "Database Security," and briefly reviewed here:

- **Force.com managed sharing**—These are record sharing rules maintained by Force.com. A native user interface enables administrators to add, edit, and delete these rules. Rules are based on user, group, or role membership and defined individually on each object. They are configured in the Administration Setup area, Security Controls, Sharing Settings.

- **User managed sharing**—Users who own records can grant permission to additional users from the native user interface. This is a manual process. The owner visits a record to share and clicks the Sharing button to add, edit, or remove its sharing rules.

This section is divided into two parts, described next:

- **Sharing objects**—Sharing objects are where Force.com stores record sharing rules. The fields of sharing objects are described, as well as restrictions on their use.

- **Creating sharing rules in Apex**—This walks you through the infrastructure behind sharing rules, finishing with a code sample to add a sharing rule in the Services Manager sample application schema.

Sharing Objects

Every custom object, except Detail objects in a Master-Detail relationship, has a corresponding sharing object to store its record-level sharing rules. The sharing object is created automatically by Force.com and is invisible to the native user interface. It can be seen in the Force.com IDE's Schema Explorer. Its name is the name of your object with `__Share` appended. For example, the sharing object for the `Project__c` object is `Project__Share`.

The sharing object contains explicit sharing rules. These are created by Force.com managed sharing, user managed sharing, and Apex managed sharing. It does not contain implicit shares such as organization-wide defaults.

Four fields of the sharing object control how records are shared between users and groups, as follows:

- **ParentID**—`ParentId` is the unique identifier of the record being shared.

- **UserOrGroupId**—This is the unique identifier of the user or group that the sharing rule is granting access to. Groups are public groups or roles.

- **AccessLevel**—This field stores the level of access granted to the user or group for this record. The three valid values are `Read` (Read Only), `Edit` (Read and Edit), and `All` (Full Control). Apex managed sharing cannot set a record to `All`. The value of `AccessLevel` must be more permissive than the organization-wide default or a runtime exception is thrown.

- **RowCause**—The purpose of the RowCause field is to track the origin of the sharing rule. Valid values are Manual (the default) or a custom sharing reason, defined on the object in the Apex Sharing Reasons related list. Manual sharing rules can be edited and removed by the record owner and are reset when record ownership changes. Sharing records with a custom reason are not reset when ownership changes and cannot be edited or removed without the administrative permission Modify All Data.

Restrictions

Two important restrictions exist on Apex managed sharing:

- Objects with an organization-wide default sharing level of Public Read/Write, the most permissive setting, cannot use Apex managed sharing. Set the level to Private or Public Read Only instead.

- After a sharing record is created, the only field that can be updated is the access level. If you need to change other fields, delete the sharing record entirely and re-create it.

Caution

When the organization-wide sharing default is changed for an object, all sharing rules are recalculated. This causes your Apex managed sharing rules to be deleted. To re-create them, you must implement an Apex class to participate in the recalculation event. This code uses the Apex batch processing feature to allow processing of millions of records in smaller groups of records, to stay within governor limits. The Apex batch processing functionality is covered in Chapter 9, "Batch Processing."

Creating Sharing Rules in Apex

Figure 5.8 shows the Force.com managed sharing settings for the Project object, configured in Chapter 3. The sharing rules specify that projects owned by members of one role are shared by all users in that role. This is defined three times because three separate roles exist, one for each region in the sample company.

Navigate to an individual Project record and click the Sharing button. Figure 5.9 is an example of the resulting screen. It lists the sharing rules in effect for this record. The first sharing rule is the default one, specifying that the owner has full control over the record. The second is the sharing rule maintained by Force.com managed sharing, configured using the screen shown in Figure 5.8, which allows users in the same role as the owner (West) to edit the record.

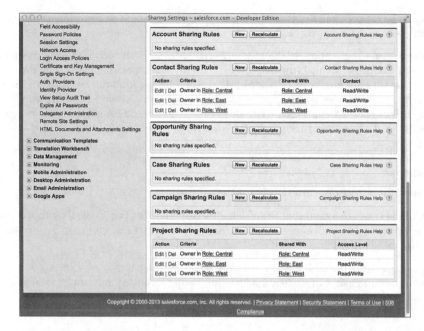

Figure 5.8   Sharing rules for Project object

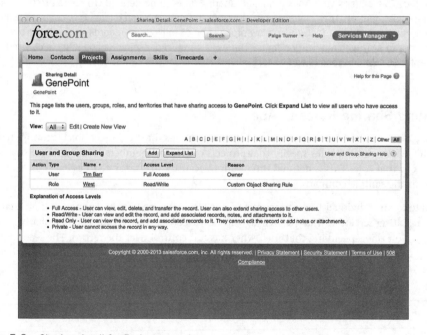

Figure 5.9   Sharing detail for Project record

You've visited screens in the native user interface where record sharing is taking place. Next, look a level deeper at the data driving the sharing behavior. Open the Force.com IDE's Schema Explorer and run the query shown in Listing 5.21. It illustrates how Force.com stores the information for the sharing rules in Figure 5.9 and what you will be manipulating with Apex managed sharing.

Listing 5.21   **SOQL Query on Project Share Object**

```
SELECT ParentId, UserOrGroupId, AccessLevel
  FROM Project__Share
  WHERE Parent.Name = 'GenePoint'
```

Figure 5.10 is the result of running the query. Note that the identifiers in your Force.com organization will be different from those in the figure.

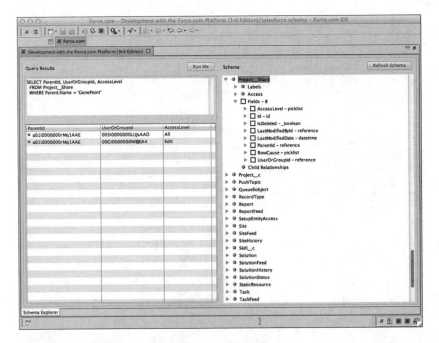

Figure 5.10   Results of SOQL query on Project Share object

Try to decode the meaning of each record. The `ParentId` field contains the unique identifier of the record being shared. The query has filtered by the name GenePoint, which is a Project record. The `UserOrGroupId` field contains the unique identifier of a User or Group record. The `AccessLevel` field is one of the four access levels (All, None, Edit, View), although only Edit and View can be set using Apex managed sharing.

The first record has All access, so it's the default sharing rule granting the owner of the record full access. The second record might be a mystery at first. The `UserOrGroupId` does not match up with the unique identifier of the West region's role record. Run the query shown in Listing 5.22 to track down the meaning of this value.

Listing 5.22   **SOQL Query on Group Object**

```
SELECT Id, Type, RelatedId
    FROM Group
```

The Group object stores information about roles and other groups in Force.com. Figure 5.11 displays the results of the query. The `RelatedId` field contains the same value as the `UserOrGroupId` value of the second sharing record. This is where Force.com managed sharing has stored the fact that the Project record named GenePoint is shared with other members of the West role.

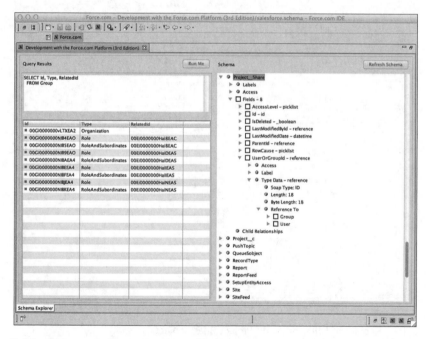

Figure 5.11   Results of SOQL query on Group object

Apex managed sharing allows you to insert new rows into the `Project__Share` object, and other sharing objects, and specify custom sharing reasons that are meaningful to your application. Custom sharing reasons are maintained for each object individually. To try adding one, go to the App Setup area and click Create, Objects and select the Project object. Scroll to the bottom of the page. In the Apex Sharing Reasons list, add a new reason with a label of My

Sharing Reason. Force.com automatically suggests a Name, converting spaces to underscores. Refer to the custom sharing reason in your Apex code by adding __c to the end of the name.

Listing 5.23 contains sample code you can run in the Execute Anonymous view. It shares the GenePoint record with an additional user, specifying the custom sharing reason, with Read-only access.

Listing 5.23   **Inserting Sharing Rule on Project Object**

```
User carrie = [ SELECT Id FROM User
  WHERE Name = 'Carrie Oakey' LIMIT 1 ];
Project__c genePoint = [ SELECT Id FROM Project__c
  WHERE Name = 'GenePoint' LIMIT 1 ];
Project__Share share = new Project__Share(
  ParentId = genePoint.Id,
  UserOrGroupId = carrie.Id,
  rowCause = Project__Share.rowCause.My_Sharing_Reason__c,
  AccessLevel = 'Read');
insert share;
```

After executing this code, refresh the Sharing Details for GenePoint and you should see the screen shown in Figure 5.12. It shows that the new custom sharing rule has been added. Because the sharing rule was created by Apex code and uses a custom sharing reason, it's preserved across changes of record ownership and cannot be edited or deleted by users unless they have the Modify All Data administrative permission in their profile.

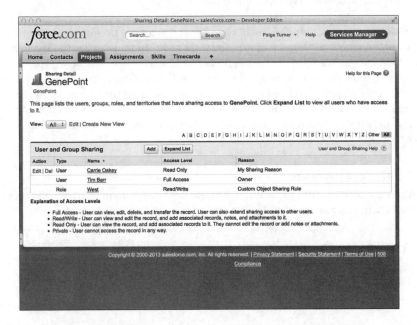

Figure 5.12   Sharing detail for Project record with Apex managed sharing rule

Sending and Receiving Email

Force.com allows emails to be sent and received in Apex code. This functionality can be helpful in many scenarios. For example, you could send an email from within a trigger to notify users of events occurring in the application, such as work that requires their attention. You could write code to automate the classification of incoming emails to customer support, searching for keywords and routing them to the proper support employees. This section describes how to use the objects and methods built in to Apex to process inbound and outbound email and introduces the administration screens of the native user interface that support them.

Sending Email

The three ways to send email in Apex are the following:

- **SingleEmailMessage**—Sends an email to up to ten receivers. The email addresses of receivers are provided as strings. A string containing HTML or plain text is used as the message body.

- **SingleEmailMessage with template**—Sends to up to ten receivers, but the unique identifiers of Contact, Lead, or User objects must be used instead of strings to provide the receivers' email addresses. The message body is constructed from a template. Templates are globally available to an organization as defined by an administrator or private to an individual user. Templates can include merge fields to dynamically substitute field values from the receiver's record and, optionally, field values from an additional, related object.

- **MassEmailMessage**—Behaves like a SingleEmailMessage with template but can send email to up to 250 receivers in a single call.

Each of these three ways of sending email contributes toward the maximum of 10 email calls within a single context, an instance of running Apex code. To translate that to the number of email messages, if you use the SingleEmailMessage object with 10 recipients, you can reach a maximum of 100 recipients (10 recipients times the 10 invocation maximum) within a single execution of your program. You can reach 2,500 recipients using the MassEmailMessage. Force.com imposes a daily limit on mass emails, which varies based on the edition of Force.com being used. If this limit is exceeded, an exception is thrown with the exception code MASS_MAIL_LIMIT_EXCEEDED.

Using SingleEmailMessage

You can run the code in Listing 5.24 directly in the Execute Anonymous view. It looks up the User record for the current user and sends a test message to its email address.

Listing 5.24   **Sending Email**

```
User you = [ SELECT Email
  FROM User
  WHERE Id = :UserInfo.getUserId()
```

```
  LIMIT 1 ];
Messaging.SingleEmailMessage mail =
  new Messaging.SingleEmailMessage();
mail.setToAddresses(new String[] { you.Email });
mail.setSubject('Test message');
mail.setPlainTextBody('This is a test');
Messaging.sendEmail(new Messaging.SingleEmailMessage[] { mail });
```

Check the email account associated with your Force.com user for the new message. If you do not see the message, it might be in your junk mail folder. If it's not in your inbox or junk mail folder, your email server might have refused its delivery. In this case, Force.com will send you the returned message with any delivery error information, given that you are both the sender and the receiver.

> ### Note
> Force.com provides online tools to help you authorize its mail servers to ensure that its messages are delivered. Go to the Administration Setup area and click Email Administration, Deliverability and Test Deliverability for more information.

Notice that the sender and receiver of the email are identical. You have sent a message to yourself via Force.com. By default, Apex email methods run using the identity of the current user. The current user's email address becomes the "from" address in outbound emails. Alternatively, you can define an organization-wide email address and use it to set the "from" address. This enables all of your outbound emails to be sent from a single set of authorized, public email addresses. To define an organization-wide email address, go to the Administration Setup area and click Email Administration, Organization-Wide Addresses.

Using `SingleEmailMessage` with Template

Templates standardize the appearance and content of emails. They also make including dynamic content in messages without cumbersome, hard-to-maintain code full of string concatenations simple. To add a new email template, go to the Personal Setup area and click Email, My Templates.

When a template is used to send a message, you must provide a `targetObjectId` value. This is the unique identifier of a Lead, Contact, or User record. The email address associated with this record becomes the recipient of the email.

Optionally, a `whatId` can be provided. This is the unique record identifier of an Account, Asset, Campaign, Case, Contract, Opportunity, Order, Product, Solution, or any custom object. The fields from this record can be referenced in your template using merge fields. When the message is sent, the record is retrieved and its data substituted into the message body in the locations specified by the merge fields.

Listing 5.25 sends an email using a template. Before trying it, create a template with the unique name of `Test_Template`. Set its text or HTML content to `Hello {!User.FirstName}!` or the equivalent to demonstrate the use of merge fields. Mark the template as available for use. In Listing 5.25, a SOQL query is used to retrieve the template's unique identifier so that it isn't hard-coded into the program.

Listing 5.25   **Sending Email Using a Template**

```
User you = [ SELECT Email
  FROM User
  WHERE Id = :UserInfo.getUserId()
  LIMIT 1 ];
EmailTemplate template = [ SELECT Id
  FROM EmailTemplate
  WHERE DeveloperName = 'Test_Template'
  LIMIT 1 ];
Messaging.SingleEmailMessage mail =
  new Messaging.SingleEmailMessage();
mail.templateId = template.Id;
mail.targetObjectId = you.Id;
mail.setSaveAsActivity(false);
Messaging.sendEmail(new Messaging.SingleEmailMessage[] { mail });
```

> **Note**
>
> The `setSaveAsActivity` method was called in Listing 5.25 to disable the HTML email track-ing feature, which is not compatible with the User object (`targetObjectId`). The `setSaveAsActivity` method is described in the upcoming subsection, "Additional Email Methods."

Using `MassEmailMessage`

Mass emails can be sent to 250 recipients in a single method call. The code for sending a mass email is similar to that for sending a single email with a template. The difference is that a `MassEmailMessage` object is created instead of a `SingleEmailMessage`. At minimum, you must provide a value for `targetObjectIds` (an array of Lead, Contact, or User record unique identifiers) and a `templateId`.

Optionally, you can provide `whatIds`, an array of record unique identifiers corresponding to the array of `targetObjectIds`. Field values from these records add dynamic content to the message body. The records are limited to Contract, Case, Opportunity, and Product types. Note that none of these object types are available in a Force.com platform-only license.

Listing 5.26 demonstrates the use of the `MassEmailMessage`. It selects one Contact in the system and sends an email using the same template created for Listing 5.25.

Listing 5.26 **Sending a Mass Email**

```
User you = [ SELECT Email
  FROM User
  WHERE Id = :UserInfo.getUserId()
  LIMIT 1 ];
EmailTemplate template = [ SELECT Id
  FROM EmailTemplate
  WHERE DeveloperName = 'Test_Template'
  LIMIT 1 ];
Messaging.MassEmailMessage mail = new Messaging.MassEmailMessage();
mail.templateId = template.Id;
mail.targetObjectIds = new Id[] { you.Id };
mail.setSaveAsActivity(false);
Messaging.sendEmail(new Messaging.MassEmailMessage[] { mail });
```

Transactional Email

The transactional behavior of the `sendEmail` method is consistent with that of Force.com database DML methods. When an invocation of Apex code is completed without error, email is sent. If an uncaught error causes the program to be terminated prematurely, email is not sent. If multiple emails are sent, by default they all fail if one fails. Setting the optional `opt_allOrNone` parameter of the `sendEmail` method to `false` enables partial success of a group of outbound messages. In this case, the `sendEmail` method returns an array of `SendEmailResult` objects. These objects can be used to determine the success or failure of each message and include error details in case of failure.

Additional Email Methods

The following list describes useful methods that apply to both `SingleEmailMessage` and `MassEmailMessage` objects:

- **setCcAddresses**—This method accepts a string array of email addresses to carbon copy on the email.

- **setSenderDisplayName**—The sender display name is shown in email reading programs as a label for the sender email address.

- **setReplyTo**—The reply-to address is the email address designated to receive replies to this message. If not specified, it's always the sender's email address.

- **setBccSender**—If this is set to `true`, Force.com blind-carbon-copies the sender's email address. In a mass email, the sender is copied only on the first message. Force.com prevents use of this feature if an administrator has enabled Compliance BCC Email. You can do this in the Administration Setup area by clicking Email Administration, Compliance BCC Email.

- **setUseSignature**—By default, Force.com appends the sending user's signature to the end of outbound emails. You can edit this signature in the Personal Setup area by clicking Email, My Email Settings. To turn off this feature, pass `false` to this method.

- **setFileAttachments**—The argument to this method is an array of `EmailFileAttachment` objects. These objects contain the names and data of attachments to be sent with the message. They provide a method to set the attachment body (`setBody`) and filename (`setFileName`). The total size of the attachments for a single message cannot exceed 10MB.

- **setDocumentAttachments**—Force.com has a native object type for storing content called Document. You can find it in the native user interface by clicking the Documents tab. Here you can create, edit, and delete Documents and group them into folders. Each Document record has a unique identifier, and this method accepts an array of them. Each Document specified is sent as an attachment to the message. All attachments in a single message, including file attachments, cannot exceed 10MB.

- **setOrgWideEmailAddressId**—Use this method to specify the unique identifier of an organization-wide email address. This email address is used as the "from" address rather than the address of the current user. To define organization-wide email addresses and obtain their unique identifiers, go to the Administration Setup area and click Email Administration, Organization-Wide Addresses.

- **setSaveAsActivity**—Force.com's outbound email can be configured to track the behavior of email recipients who are Leads or Contacts in the system. This is accomplished with an invisible image embedded in messages sent using templates. When receivers who haven't blocked multimedia content in their email readers open the message, the Force.com service is contacted and tracks this information. By visiting the receiver's Lead or Contact record, you can see the date the email was first opened, the number of times it was opened, and the date it was most recently opened. By default, this setting is enabled. To disable or enable it for the organization, go to the App Setup area and click Customize, Activities, Activity Settings and select Enable Email Tracking. To disable it for a specific message, pass `false` to this method.

Receiving Email

The two steps for configuring Force.com to process inbound emails are as follows:

1. Write an Apex class that implements a specific interface (`Messaging.InboundEmailHandler`) and method (`handleInboundEmail`). This provides your code access to the envelope (`Messaging.InboundEnvelope`) and content (`Messaging.InboundEmail`) of inbound emails, including mail headers and attachments. It is otherwise standard Apex code with no special restrictions. The return value of this method is a `Messaging.InboundEmailResult`. To indicate processing failure, set the `success` field of this object to `false`. Any explanatory message set in the `message` field is returned to the sender as an email response.

2. Create an Email Service using the native user interface. An Email Service is associated with one or more Force.com-issued email addresses that serve as the gateways to your Apex class. When email arrives at the email address, your Apex class is invoked to process it.

If your Apex code fails with an uncaught exception while processing an incoming email, Force.com treats the email as undeliverable. This is much like a mail gateway behaves when presented with an unknown recipient email address. An email is returned to the sender with diagnostic information about the problem, including the error message from your Apex code.

To personalize email processing based on the identity of the sender, use one of these strategies:

- Have all users share a single inbound email address. Your Apex code reads the sender's "from" address and customizes behavior based on that, perhaps by querying Contact or Lead for more information about them.

- Issue each user or group of users a unique email address. Your Apex code can adjust its behavior based on the "to" address of the incoming message.

Caution

There are governor limits on inbound email. The maximum size of each inbound message, attachments included, is 10MB. The maximum size of each message body, text and HTML combined, is 100KB. The maximum size of each binary attachment is 5MB and 100KB for text attachments. The maximum heap size for Apex email handlers is 18MB. If any of these limits are reached, your Apex code will not be invoked, and the offending message will be returned to its sender.

Getting Started with Inbound Email Processing

Follow these next steps to create a new Apex class to process inbound email in the Force.com IDE. This is a simple example that sends a reply to the inbound message with the original message quoted in the body.

1. Make sure your Force.com project is selected and click New, Apex Class in the File menu.

2. Enter MyEmailService for the name and select the Inbound Email Service template.

3. Click the Finish button. Enter the code given in Listing 5.27, skipping the class, method, and result declarations because they are provided by the template. Save your changes.

Listing 5.27   **Receiving Email**

```
global class MyEmailService implements
  Messaging.InboundEmailHandler {
  global Messaging.InboundEmailResult
    handleInboundEmail(Messaging.InboundEmail email,
      Messaging.InboundEnvelope envelope) {
```

```
Messaging.InboundEmailResult result = new
  Messaging.InboundEmailresult();
Messaging.SingleEmailMessage outbound = new
  Messaging.SingleEmailMessage();
outbound.toAddresses = new String[] { email.replyTo };
outbound.setSubject('Re: ' + email.subject);
outbound.setHtmlBody('<p>This reply was generated by Apex.'
  + 'You wrote:</p><i>' + email.plainTextBody + '</i>');
Messaging.sendEmail(new Messaging.SingleEmailMessage[]
  { outbound });
return result;
}
}
```

4. In the native user interface, go to the App Setup area and click Develop, Email Services.

5. Click the New Email Service button.

6. Enter a service name. Enter MyEmailService as the Apex class. Leave the other options set to their defaults and click the Save button.

7. Click the Activate button. Then click the New Email Address button to create a Force.com-generated email address.

8. This screen allows you to whitelist email addresses and domains that are allowed to use this email service. By default, it's configured to allow emails only from the current user's email address. Accept this setting by clicking the Save button.

9. You should now see an email address listed at the bottom of the page, as shown in Figure 5.13. Copy the address to your Clipboard, open your favorite email application, and send a test message to this address. Within a minute, you should receive an email in response, generated by your Apex class.

Dynamic Apex

Dynamic Apex describes features of Apex that bypass its typically strongly typed nature. For example, database queries, objects, and fields are part of the language, and references to them are strongly typed, validated at compile time. Dynamic Apex allows you to work with these objects as ordinary strings rather than compiled parts of your program. This has its advantages in that your program can be more dynamic and generic. It also has disadvantages, the primary one being that your code can suffer a greater variety of errors at runtime.

This section describes three dynamic Apex features. Dynamic database queries are SOQL and SOSL queries executed at runtime from strings rather than from compiled code. Schema metadata allows Apex code to introspect the structure of the Force.com database, including its objects, fields, and relationships. Type methods allow introspection of an object's type, including creation of a new instance.

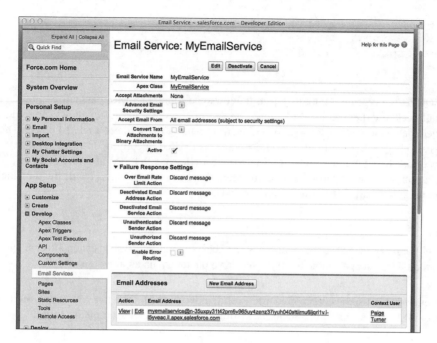

Figure 5.13   Email service configuration

Dynamic Database Queries

In Chapter 4, you learned about bind variables. They are variables whose values are injected into SOQL and SOSL statements in predefined locations, notated with colons. But bind variables are not powerful enough to support an entirely dynamic WHERE clause, one that includes conditional filters added and subtracted based on the behavior of the program. You could write every combination of WHERE clause and use long strings of conditional statements to pick the right one. An alternative is a completely dynamic query, executed using the `Database.query` method.

Listing 5.28 provides an example of two dynamic queries. The first is on the Contact object. The results of the query are returned in a list of Contact records. Other than the dynamic query itself, this code should be familiar. The second query selects Project records but treats them as a list of SObject objects.

Listing 5.28   **Dynamic SOQL Queries**

```
List<Contact> resources = Database.query(
  'SELECT Id, Name FROM Contact');
for (Contact resource : resources) {
  System.debug(resource.Id + ' ' + resource.Name);
}
```

```
List<SObject> projects = Database.query('SELECT Id, Name FROM Project__c');
for (SObject project : projects) {
  System.debug(project.get('Id') + ' ' + project.get('Name'));
}
```

The SObject is a typeless database object. It allows you to interact with database records without declaring them as a specific type. The get method of the SObject allows the retrieval of a field value by name. The getSObject method returns the value of a related object. These values also have setter methods: set and setSObject. Used in conjunction with DML statements or database DML methods, you can write generic code that operates on a series of database objects. This is particularly useful when you have several objects with the same field names because it can reduce the amount of code.

> **Tip**
>
> Use the escapeSingleQuotes of the String object to prevent SOQL injection attacks. This method adds escape characters (\) to all single quotation marks in a string.

SOSL queries can also be constructed and executed dynamically. The Search.query method returns a list of lists containing SObjects. Listing 5.29 provides an example of its use.

Listing 5.29   **Dynamic SOSL Query**

```
List<List<SObject>> result = Search.query(
  'FIND \'Chicago\' '
  + 'RETURNING Contact(Name), Project__c(Name)');
for (List<SObject> records : result) {
  for (SObject record : records) {
    System.debug(record.get('Name'));
  }
}
```

The SOSL query returns the names of Project and Contact records containing the word *Chicago*. The outer loop is executed for each type of object specified in the RETURNING clause. The inner loop runs over the matching records of that object type. For example, the first iteration of the loop assigns records to a list of Contact records that matched the search term. The second iteration assigns it to the matching Project records.

> **Note**
>
> Dynamic queries have all the same governor limits as their static counterparts.

Schema Metadata

Schema metadata is information about the Force.com database, available to your Apex code dynamically, at runtime. It has many potential uses, such as customizing the behavior of Apex code installed in multiple organizations, driving the construction of dynamic queries, or verifying that the database is configured in a certain way. This section describes the five types of schema metadata (object, field, child relationship, picklist, and record type) and includes code that can be run in the Execute Anonymous view to demonstrate accessing them.

> **Note**
>
> You are limited to a maximum of 100 calls to schema metadata methods. All five types of schema metadata methods contribute equally to the limit.

Object Metadata

Object metadata is information about the database objects in the Force.com organization. It includes custom as well as standard objects. Listing 5.30 provides an example of retrieving object metadata. The metadata of all objects in the database is retrieved, and their names and labels are printed to the debug log.

Listing 5.30   **Retrieving Object Metadata**

```
Map<String, Schema.SObjectType> objects = Schema.getGlobalDescribe();
Schema.DescribeSObjectResult objInfo = null;
for (Schema.SObjectType obj : objects.values()) {
  objInfo = obj.getDescribe();
  System.debug(objInfo.getName() + ' [' + objInfo.getLabel() + ']');
}
```

Field Metadata

Field metadata provides access to all the attributes of fields you configure on a database object. Listing 5.31 demonstrates how to access field metadata. The fields of the Project__c object are retrieved, including standard and custom fields. The getDescribe method is invoked on each to return its metadata, a Schema.DescribeFieldResult object. The name, label, data type, precision, and scale of each field are displayed in the debug log.

Listing 5.31   **Retrieving Field Metadata**

```
Map<String, Schema.SObjectField> fields =
  Schema.SObjectType.Project__c.fields.getMap();
Schema.DescribeFieldResult fieldInfo = null;
for (Schema.SObjectField field : fields.values()) {
  fieldInfo = field.getDescribe();
  System.debug(fieldInfo.getName()
```

```
        + ' [' + fieldInfo.getLabel() + '] '
        + fieldInfo.getType().name()
        + '(' + fieldInfo.getPrecision()
        + ', ' + fieldInfo.getScale() + ')');
}
```

> **Tip**
>
> If you do not know the type of an object, you can still retrieve its metadata using
> `getSObjectType`. For example, if `a01i0000000rMq1` is the unique identifier of a Project
> record, the result of `Id.valueOf('a01i0000000rMq1').getSObjectType()` can replace
> `Schema.SObjectType.Project__c` in the second line of Listing 5.31.

Child Relationship Metadata

Child relationship metadata contains the child's object type, the relationship name, and an
object identifying the field in the child object that relates it to the parent. Listing 5.32 demonstrates the retrieval of child relationship metadata from the Contact object. Compare the results
with what you see in the Force.com IDE's Schema Explorer for the Contact object.

Listing 5.32 **Retrieving Child Relationship Metadata**

```
Schema.DescribeSObjectResult res = Contact.SObjectType.getDescribe();
List<Schema.ChildRelationship> relationships = res.getChildRelationships();
for (Schema.ChildRelationship relationship : relationships) {
  System.debug(relationship.getField() + ', ' + relationship.getChildSObject());
}
```

Picklist Metadata

Picklist metadata provides access to the master list of available picklist values for a picklist
or multi-select picklist field. It does not include the assignments of picklist values to record
types, nor does it provide any information about the relationship between picklist values in
dependent picklists. Listing 5.33 is an example of its use, printing the picklist values of the Skill
object's Type field to the debug log.

Listing 5.33 **Retrieving Picklist Metadata**

```
Schema.DescribeFieldResult fieldInfo =
  Schema.SObjectType.Skill__c.fields.Type__c;
List<Schema.PicklistEntry> picklistValues = fieldInfo.getPicklistValues();
for (Schema.PicklistEntry picklistValue : picklistValues) {
  System.debug(picklistValue.getLabel());
}
```

Record Type Metadata

Record type metadata contains the names and unique identifiers of record types defined on an object. It also indicates the availability of the record type to the current user (isAvailable) and whether the record type is the default record type for the object (isDefaultRecordTypeMapping).

Listing 5.34 provides an example of using record type metadata. It retrieves the record types in the Contact object and prints their names to the debug log.

Listing 5.34   **Retrieving Record Type Metadata**

```
Schema.DescribeSObjectResult sobj = Contact.SObjectType.getDescribe();
List<Schema.RecordTypeInfo> recordTypes = sobj.getRecordTypeInfos();
for (Schema.RecordTypeInfo recordType : recordTypes) {
  System.debug(recordType.getName());
}
```

Dynamic Instance Creation

Sometimes it can be useful to create an object instance without hard-coding its type in a program. For example, your program might include an extensibility mechanism for other developers to add or customize its behavior. One way to do this is to expose an Apex interface, document it, and allow users to provide the name of a custom Apex class that implements the interface. Listing 5.35 is a simplified version of this scenario that can run in the Execute Anonymous window.

Listing 5.35   **Creating Instance from Type Name**

```
interface MyType { void doIt(); }
class MyTypeImpl implements MyType {
  public void doIt() { System.debug('hi'); }
}
Type t = MyTypeImpl.class;
if (t != null) {
  MyType mt = (MyType)t.newInstance();
  mt.doIt();
}
```

Notice that MyTypeImpl is defined as the type to be created in the program on line 5, so it isn't dynamic. The dynamic form is Type.forName('MyTypeImpl'), which is invalid in the Execute Anonymous window because MyTypeImpl is transient, defined in the scope of the Execute Anonymous code block only. To try the dynamic type lookup, create the interface and class using the Force.com IDE.

Custom Settings in Apex

You are not limited to using the native user interface for managing data in custom settings, as demonstrated in Chapter 2. Custom settings can also be created, updated, and deleted using standard DML methods. This means you can build your own user interfaces for managing them, or use them to store frequently accessed, simple configuration values needed by your programs. Force.com provides increased performance for custom settings access versus ordinary database access, and custom settings are exempt from the governor limits placed on database access. For example, you might use a custom setting named Debug as a global switch to enable verbose logging within your Apex code.

To get started with custom settings in Apex, run the code in Listing 5.36. It inserts a custom setting record, setting its name and its field value. It assumes you already have defined a List type custom setting object named ConfigSetting containing a single Checkbox field named Debug.

Listing 5.36　**Creating a Custom Setting Record**

```
insert new ConfigSetting__c(Name = 'Default', Debug__c = false);
```

Now that your custom setting has a value, try retrieving it. Run the code in Listing 5.37 in the Force.com IDE's Execute Anonymous view.

Listing 5.37　**Retrieving a Custom Setting Value**

```
ConfigSetting__c cfg = ConfigSetting__c.getValues('Default');
System.debug(cfg.Debug__c);
```

The first line retrieves the named record, Default, which you created in Listing 5.36. The second line prints the value of the custom field to the debug log. You can also retrieve a Map of all fields and values using the getAll method.

To update a custom setting value, retrieve it by name, and then update it as you would a database record. Listing 5.38 provides an example.

Listing 5.38　**Updating a Custom Setting Record**

```
ConfigSetting__c cfg = ConfigSetting__c.getValues('Default');
cfg.Debug__c = true;
update cfg;
```

You can also delete custom setting records using the delete DML method, as shown in Listing 5.39.

Listing 5.39 **Deleting a Custom Setting Record**

```
ConfigSetting__c cfg = ConfigSetting__c.getValues('Default');
delete cfg;
```

Hierarchy type custom settings allow a user or profile to be related to them. If no user or profile is specified, they become organization-wide defaults. The code in Listing 5.40 assumes you have created a Hierarchy type custom setting named HierarchySetting with a single text field named Field. It creates a new record and relates it to the current user by setting the system field SetupOwnerId to the current user's unique identifier. This same field also accepts a profile unique identifier to make the custom setting apply to a profile instead of a user. And if SetupOwnerId is set to null, it becomes an organization-wide default.

Listing 5.40 **Creating a Hierarchy Type Custom Setting Record**

```
insert new HierarchySetting__c(
  SetupOwnerId = UserInfo.getUserId(),
  Field__c = 'My user preference value');
```

To retrieve a Hierarchy type custom setting value, use the getInstance method of the custom setting object. By default, it returns the "lowest" level of setting value, meaning the value most specific to the current user. If a user-level setting is available, it is returned. Otherwise, the return value is the setting associated with the user's profile. If no user or profile-level settings are present, the organization-wide default is returned. This behavior can be overridden by passing a user or profile unique identifier as an argument to the getInstance method.

Sample Application: Adding Email Notifications

This section applies your knowledge of Apex's outbound email features to enhance the Services Manager sample application. Many scenarios in Services Manager could benefit from email notifications. For example, consultants have requested that they get an email when a timecard is approved or rejected by their project managers.

To implement this change, add a trigger on the after update event of the Timecard object. If the new value of the Timecard's Status field is Approved or Rejected, query the Contact record that created the Timecard. Send an email notification of the change to the Contact.

Listing 5.41 is a sample implementation. It begins by checking to make sure that the updated Timecard contains a new value for the Status field and that the new status is either Approved or Rejected. If so, it makes three queries to retrieve data to send the notification email: the email address of the Contact logging the Timecard, the name of the Project, and the name of the user modifying the Timecard record. It constructs the email message and sends it.

Listing 5.41   **Email Notification Trigger on Timecard**

```
trigger handleTimecardNotifications
  on Timecard__c (after update) {
  for (Timecard__c timecard : trigger.new) {
    if (timecard.Status__c !=
      trigger.oldMap.get(timecard.Id).Status__c &&
      (timecard.Status__c == 'Approved' ||
      timecard.Status__c == 'Rejected')) {
      Contact resource =
        [ SELECT Email FROM Contact
          WHERE Id = :timecard.Contact__c LIMIT 1 ];
      Project__c project =
        [ SELECT Name FROM Project__c
          WHERE Id = :timecard.Project__c LIMIT 1 ];
      User user = [ SELECT Name FROM User
          WHERE Id = :timecard.LastModifiedById LIMIT 1 ];
      Messaging.SingleEmailMessage mail = new
        Messaging.SingleEmailMessage();
      mail.toAddresses = new String[]
        { resource.Email };
      mail.setSubject('Timecard for '
        + timecard.Week_Ending__c + ' on '
        + project.Name);
      mail.setHtmlBody('Your timecard was changed to '
        + timecard.Status__c + ' status by '
        + user.Name);
      Messaging.sendEmail(new Messaging.SingleEmailMessage[]
        { mail });
    }
  }
}
```

This implementation is not batch-safe. It makes four SOQL queries per Timecard. Even if this were addressed, the code could easily reach the limit of ten email invocations.

To fix this problem, you could change the code to use the `MassEmailMessage`, building a list of recipient Contact objects from the batch. Unfortunately, the `MassEmailMessage`'s `whatIds` field cannot be used with custom objects, so you'll have to forgo the customized message detailing the changes to the Timecard.

An alternative is to anticipate the governor limit. If a batch of Timecards requires more than ten email notifications, send the ten and suppress subsequent notifications.

Summary

This chapter has introduced some of the advanced features of Apex, features that you might not need in every application but that contribute to your knowledge of what is possible with Apex. Before moving on to the next chapter, consider these final points:

- Aggregate queries provide a standard, declarative way to perform calculations on groups of records in the database.

- Rules governing record sharing can be controlled in Apex code using Apex managed sharing.

- You can send and receive emails in Apex code. This provides your applications an additional way to interact with users.

- Although Apex features strongly typed database objects and queries, you can also write code that uses database resources dynamically. This carries with it the risk of runtime errors but opens up new possibilities of dynamic behavior to your applications. It is particularly powerful when writing custom user interfaces.

- You can read and write custom settings from Apex like any database object, but without the governor limits.

6

User Interfaces

Force.com's native user interface provides a consistent and simple way to search, create, update, and delete database records. It combines the definition of database objects with user interface metadata such as page layouts to produce user interfaces through configuration rather than code. For developers and administrators, this makes customization straightforward. For users, the uniformity means that learning to use one screen in Force.com provides the experience to learn all screens with minimal incremental effort.

For applications that require a greater level of control over the appearance and behavior of the user interface, Visualforce offers a solution. Visualforce is a technology in the Force.com platform for building custom user interfaces. Visualforce user interfaces can be built to look nothing like Force.com, exactly like Force.com, or your own unique blend of the two.

This chapter covers the basics of Visualforce in the following sections:

- ***Introduction to Visualforce**—Learn the concepts and terminology of Visualforce.*

- ***Visualforce controllers**—See how controllers contain the business logic that drives the user interface.*

- ***View components**—Learn how view components define the appearance of Visualforce pages.*

- ***Visualforce and the native user interface**—Understand where and how Visualforce pages coexist with the native user interface of Force.com.*

- ***Visualforce in production**—Look at how security, governor limits, error handling, and testing are handled with Visualforce.*

- ***Sample application**—Implement a feature of the Services Manager sample application called the Skills Matrix. It is a Visualforce page for viewing and editing the skill sets of consultants.*

> **Note**
>
> The code listings in this chapter are available in a GitHub Gist at http://goo.gl/SQAl0.

Introduction to Visualforce

This section presents an introduction to Visualforce. It covers the following topics:

- **Overview of Visualforce**—Examine the pieces of Visualforce and how they're put together to aid in understanding this chapter and online reference materials.

- **Getting started with Visualforce**—Take a brief look at how Visualforce development projects work, learn the tools for Visualforce development, and build a "hello world" example.

Overview of Visualforce

Visualforce is a combination of a page containing the presentation and Apex classes containing the business logic. The presentation is usually HTML rendered in the Web browser, but Visualforce also supports content types such as XML and PDF. HTML output is typically interactive, building up state by collecting user input across a series of related pages.

Force.com processes Visualforce pages on its servers. Only the final rendered page and partial page updates are returned to the Web browser—never the raw data or business logic. Visualforce is driven by metadata. It can use the definition of fields in the database to provide the appropriate user interface, without custom code. For example, a Visualforce page with an input field mapped to a Date field in the database is rendered with a calendar picker component, consistent with the Force.com native user interface.

The architecture of Visualforce follows the Model-View-Controller (MVC) pattern. This pattern dictates the separation of presentation (View), business logic (Controller), and data (Model). In Visualforce, business logic and data are combined in the controller, named after its MVC counterpart. The presentation lives in the page.

Figure 6.1 shows the relationship between the page and the controller in Visualforce, as well as some of Visualforce's internals.

Controller

The controller is Apex code that reads and writes data in the model, typically the Force.com database. The interaction of the controller with the user interface is accomplished through variables and action methods. Variables are exposed to the presentation layer through getter and setter methods. Getter methods allow the page to retrieve the value of a variable and display it for the user. Setter methods allow the user to modify the value of a variable through a user interface component such as a text input box.

Action methods perform the processing work on behalf of the user. They are wired up to buttons, links, and even asynchronous events on the user interface.

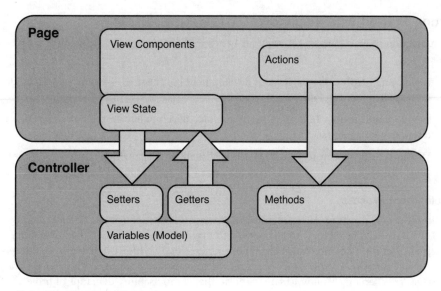

Figure 6.1   Visualforce architecture

Force.com provides default controller implementations, called *standard controllers*. Standard controllers replicate the behavior of the native user interface, such as editing and creating records, but allow customization of its user interface without code. Custom behavior can be added to standard controllers using controller extensions, which are classes written in Apex. You can also implement a controller from scratch in Apex. This is called a *custom controller*.

Page

The Visualforce page defines the appearance of your user interface using a mixture of standard HTML and Visualforce-specific XML markup. The XML markup is used to add view components to the page. View components bind the controller to the page, defining how data and user actions are to be rendered in the user interface. Force.com provides a standard set of view components to support common HTML user interface patterns and supports user-defined components.

In Figure 6.1, the arrows between the page and the controller represent expressions. Expressions are embedded in view components to allow the page to reference methods in the controller or in system classes such as `UserInfo`. Expressions in Visualforce use the same language as formula fields in the database, with a special prefix and suffix added. For example, `{!save}` is an expression that invokes the save method of the controller.

Note

Visualforce maintains a strict separation of business logic and presentation. No business logic is allowed in a Visualforce page, not even for trivial formatting tasks.

Getting Started with Visualforce

This subsection offers a path to getting your hands on Visualforce, divided into three parts, as follows:

1. **Development process**—Begin your development contrasting Visualforce with standard Web application development.

2. **Development tools**—Take a look at Visualforce development in the Force.com IDE and the native user interface.

3. **"Hello World" example**—Build your first Visualforce page with a custom controller.

Development Process

Visualforce development projects are much like standard Web application development projects. They have server-side logic to be coded, and user interfaces to be designed, wired up, and tested. User interface developers must collaborate closely with their server-side counterparts to make sure that the necessary data and logic are available to them. The user interfaces themselves are changing rapidly to satisfy the aesthetic and usability demands of project stakeholders.

Unlike with other Web application projects, Force.com eliminates much of the work of choosing and integrating Web frameworks. In terms of simply serving data-driven Web content, Force.com is the only framework you need. The important task then becomes strategizing on how best to use the platform to minimize custom development effort and maintenance cost while maximizing reuse and flexibility.

Walk through the native user interface and think carefully about what features you can reuse, extend, and override. Force.com offers a lot of user interface functionality by default and exposes a variety of hooks into it. Work with the native user interface where possible, rather than circumventing it. The further your project goes toward a fully custom user interface, the more work you spend to implement things that are potentially already provided, maintained, and constantly improved by Force.com.

Development Tools

The two tools for working with Visualforce are the native user interface and the Force.com IDE. The examples in this book can be built in either tool, but all screenshots are shown from the Force.com IDE.

In the native user interface, developers can enable a footer on the bottom of all Visualforce pages that includes syntax highlighting and an integrated help system. Called development mode, it's enabled on a per-user basis; you can enable it by visiting the Personal Setup area and clicking My Personal Information, Personal Information and checking both the Development Mode and Show View State in Development Mode boxes. You must have Customize Application permission enabled on your profile to select these options. With development mode enabled, you can create new Visualforce pages on the fly by visiting them (for example, /apex/myPage) as well as edit existing pages. Figure 6.2 shows an example of editing a Visualforce page in development mode.

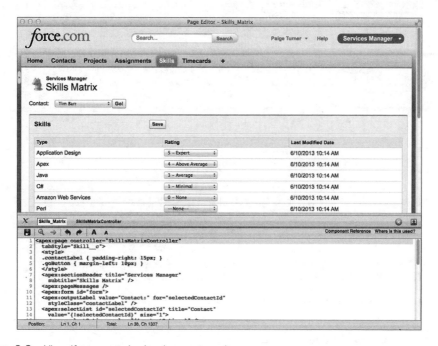

Figure 6.2   Visualforce page in development mode

Force.com IDE integrates Visualforce pages and controllers into the familiar Eclipse user interface. In Figure 6.3, the Visualforce page editor is active. You've already worked with the Force.com IDE to create triggers. Visualforce controllers are displayed in the folder named `classes`. Visualforce pages are in a separate folder named `pages`.

"Hello World" Example

To get a sense for Visualforce controllers and pages, follow these steps to create a simple working example:

1. Open the Force.com IDE, select a Force.com Project, and select File, New, Visualforce Page. Alternatively, you can right-click any object within a Force.com Project to reach the New menu.

2. Enter MyPage6_1 for the label, press Tab, and click the Finish button.

3. In the page editor, enter the code shown in Listing 6.1. Do not save it yet. If you do, it will fail to compile because it references a controller class that doesn't exist.

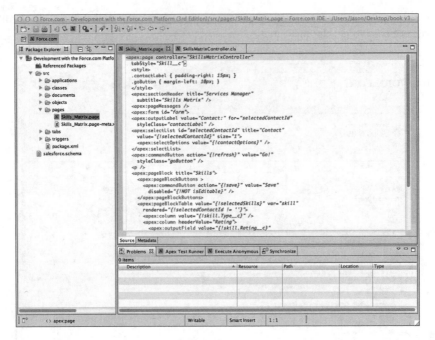

Figure 6.3   Force.com IDE's Visualforce page editor

Listing 6.1   **MyPage6_1 Code**

```
<apex:page controller="MyPageController6_1">
  <apex:form>
    Your name: <apex:inputText value="{!name}" />
    <apex:outputText value="{!message}" />
    <apex:commandButton action="{!hello}" value="Say Hi" />
  </apex:form>
</apex:page>
```

4. Select File, New, Apex Class. Enter MyPageController6_1 for the name and click the Finish button.

5. In the Apex code editor, enter the code shown in Listing 6.2. Select File, Save All to save both the controller and the page code. Check the Problems view to make sure that there are no compilation errors.

Listing 6.2   **MyPageController6_1 Code**

```
public class MyPageController6_1 {
  public String name { get; set; }
  public String message { get; private set; }
```

```
  public PageReference hello() {
    message = 'Hello, ' + name;
    return null;
  }
}
```

6. In your Web browser, log in to Force.com and edit the URL to remove everything after the hostname, replacing it with /apex/MyPage6_1. Your URL should look something like this: https://na6.salesforce.com/apex/MyPage6_1. You should see your custom Visualforce page. Enter your name and click the Say Hi button to see the hello message.

Visualforce Controllers

Controllers provide the business logic behind Visualforce pages. They supply data to the page, accept input from users through the page, perform actions on behalf of the user, and redirect the browser to new pages. Controllers come in three flavors:

- **Standard controllers**—Force.com provides default controller implementations called standard controllers. They contain the same functionality as found in the native user interface. No custom Apex code is involved in a standard controller.

- **Custom controllers**—Custom controllers are the opposite of standard controllers, providing no default functionality and consisting entirely of custom Apex code.

- **Controller extensions**—Controller extensions are the middle ground between standard and custom controllers. They begin with a standard controller and extend or override its functionality with custom Apex code.

Standard Controllers

Every database object, both standard and custom, has a standard controller. Its name is simply the name of the object. No Apex code exists for a standard controller. The controller implementation is already provided by Force.com.

Working with a Single Record

By default, the standard controller operates on a single record at a time. It receives this record from the `id` parameter in the URL. Try this for yourself by creating a new Visualforce page named MyPage6_3 with the code in Listing 6.3.

Listing 6.3 **Visualforce Page Using Standard Controller**

```
<apex:page standardController="Project__c">
  The current project is: {!Project__c.Name}
  <apex:form >
```

```
    <apex:commandButton action="{!edit}" value="Edit {!Project__c.Name}" />
    <apex:commandButton action="{!list}" value="Go To List" />
  </apex:form>
</apex:page>
```

If you visit the page in your browser (/apex/mypage6_3) without providing an id, you'll
see no current project named in the page. If you append an id value for a Project record (for
example, /apex/MyPage6_3?id=a008000000CTwEw), you can get the name of the project and
working edit and list buttons.

Listing 6.3 demonstrates a few actions provided by the standard controller, leveraged using
expression language in view components. For example, access to the current project record
is provided through {!Project__c}, and access to the navigation actions through {!edit}
and {!list}. In general, the following expressions are available in a page that uses a standard
controller:

- **Data**—{!id} is the unique identifier of the current record, and {!object} is the current
  record itself, where *object* is the lowercase name of your object. All fields of the object
  are automatically available, including related child objects but not parent objects.

- **Navigation**—{!cancel} navigates to the cancel page, {!edit} to the standard edit page,
  and {!view} to the standard view page.

- **Action and navigation**—{!delete} deletes the current record and navigates to the
  standard delete page, and {!save} saves the current record and refreshes the page.

- **Action only**—{!quicksave} saves the current record without navigation.

Working with Multiple Records

A variation of the standard controller exists called the standard set controller. It operates on
a list of records rather than a single record. The list is produced by executing a view, a user-
defined set of column names, filter criteria, and sort criteria for an object. To try it, create
another Visualforce page named MyPage6_4 with the code given in Listing 6.4.

Listing 6.4   **Visualforce Page with Standard Set Controller**

```
<apex:page standardController="Project__c" recordSetVar="projects">
  <apex:repeat value="{!projects}" var="p">
    {!p.Name}<br />
  </apex:repeat>
</apex:page>
```

Visit /apex/myPage6_4 with your browser, and you'll see a list of all projects. Force.com has
used the user's most recently executed view to obtain a list of project records, sorted by the
first column in the view, even if that column is not displayed in the Visualforce page. The
records are available to your page in the variable projects, specified by the page attribute

recordSetVar. The recordSetVar indicates to Force.com that the standard set controller should be used.

The standard set controller allows you to work with up to 10,000 records at once and supports pagination with a variable page size. It also supports multiple selection and actions on a selected set of records.

The following expressions are valid in any page that uses a standard set controller:

- **Data**—The variable name you set in recordSetVar is bound to the current list of records, {!selected} is an array of SObjects that are selected, {!resultsSize} sets or gets the number of records currently displayed, and {!completeResult} is a Boolean containing false if more than 10,000 records exist.

- **Pagination**—Navigate across multiple pages of data using the {!first}, {!last}, {!next}, and {!previous} actions. {!pageNumber} sets or gets the current page number, and {!pageSize} sets or gets the number of records in a page. {!hasPrevious} returns true if a previous page exists, and {!hasNext} returns true if a subsequent page exists.

- **Filters**—{!filterId} is the unique identifier of the currently selected filter (list view), and {!listViewOptions} is an array of SelectOption objects containing the names and identifiers of the available list views.

- **Navigation**—{!cancel} navigates to the cancel page, and {!edit} to the standard edit page.

- **Action and navigation**—{!delete} deletes the current record and navigates to the standard delete page, and {!save} saves the current record and refreshes the page.

- **Action only**—{!quicksave} saves the current record without navigation.

Custom Controllers

Custom controllers provide complete control over the behavior of a page with no default implementation. A custom controller is simply an Apex class designed to be bound to a Visualforce page. There is no new syntax to learn. At a high level, building a custom controller consists of defining the data to make available to the page and the actions that the page can invoke.

Exposing Data

The purpose of exposing data in a controller is to make it available to the page. Within a page, page components can use expressions to bind to it and render HTML or some other representation of the data. This binding is by reference, so data modified in the page can also be modified in the controller.

Simply making a variable public does not provide a Visualforce page access to it. The variable must have a getter method, a setter method, or both, depending on whether you intend to provide read-only or read and write access to the data.

For example, the page component inputText is an input and output component. It renders any existing or default value by invoking the getter and then invokes the setter to update the value after it is changed by the user and the page is submitted.

Expression language allows traversal of an object through dot notation, so providing separate getters and setters for every field in a database record, for example, is not necessary. Expose the object itself and use dot notation to access its fields. For example, the code in Listing 6.5 exposes a Project record for read-only access using the automatic properties feature of the Apex language. The read-only access is accomplished using the private access modifier keyword for the set accessor. Thanks to the Project getter, the page can contain expressions like {!project.Name} and even {!project.Account__r.BillingCity} because you've made the parent object's field available through a SOQL statement in the constructor.

Listing 6.5   **Custom Controller, Read-Only Access to Project Record**

```
public class MyPageController6_5 {
  public Project__c project { get; private set; }
  public MyPageController() {
    project = [ SELECT Name, Account__r.BillingCity FROM Project__c
      WHERE Name = 'GenePoint' LIMIT 1 ];
  }
}
```

> **Caution**
>
> Placing business logic in the getter and setter methods is bad practice and, in many cases, prohibited at runtime. Make a habit of exposing data through Apex automatic properties rather than full getter or setter methods. Automatic properties do not allow a code body to be added.

Expressions are the closest you can get to business logic on the page without resorting to JavaScript. For example, you can combine expressions to form more complex expressions. The expression {!isVisible && isEditable} invokes both the getIsVisible and getIsEditable methods on the controller and evaluates to true if they are both true. Conditionals are also supported. For example, the condition expression {!IF(tabSelected, 'currentTab', 'secondaryPalette')} uses the value of the tabSelected method to determine whether to return one string (currentTab if true) versus another (secondaryPalette if false).

Writing Action Methods

Actions on a page are wired up to action methods in the controller, again by expression language. Action methods are public, nonstatic controller methods that return a

`PageReference` object or null. If null, the current page is refreshed. If not, the `PageReference` is used to determine the location of the new page.

Actions have three purposes:

1. **Preserve view state**—The view state is maintained by Force.com within your page at runtime and posted back to its servers for the invocation of an action. It consists of the values of all of your controllers' accessible, nontransient variables. It allows you to build stateful interactions consisting of multiple pages without writing boilerplate code to copy values around in hidden fields, in the URL, or by using stateful patterns in the controller such as session objects, which are not supported by Force.com. You can opt out of actions entirely, redirecting the user at a browser level using standard HTML anchors and forms. But by doing so, you're circumventing some of the value provided by Visualforce and giving yourself extra work.

2. **Invoke custom logic**—Actions can perform some custom logic, such as using DML methods to upsert a record to the database. Other than the constructor, action methods are the only place you should write new business logic or call existing Apex code in a Visualforce controller.

3. **Trigger page navigation**—The `PageReference` object returned by an action determines the page to be refreshed in the browser. Construct a `PageReference` from a page name, such as `new PageReference('MyPage')`. The URL of the browser remains the same, but the body is refreshed with the contents of `MyPage`. This is not always desirable behavior, because a user can click the Reload button in the browser and potentially trigger the same action with the same input data. For example, this would result in duplicate records if the action code performs an insert DML operation. You can tell Force.com to redirect the user to the new page by calling the `setRedirect` method on the `PageReference` and passing `true`. A redirect updates the browser's URL and resets the view state, giving the user a fresh start and preventing any problems with the browser's Reload button.

Listing 6.6 is a sample controller to illustrate a common pattern in Visualforce: wrapping a database object with an Apex class. The wrapper object allows you to enhance a class for participation in user interface tasks, such as formatting data. In Listing 6.6, the wrapper exists to add a `selected` attribute. This attribute is bound to an `inputCheckbox` view component, shown in Listing 6.7, allowing the user to select multiple items. The action can then perform a mass update based on the selection. In the sample code, it simply outputs the unique identifier of each selected Project record to the debug log.

Listing 6.6 Controller with Wrapper Pattern

```
public class MyPageController6_6 {
  public List<ContactWrapper> contacts { get; set; }
  public MyPageController6_6() {
    contacts = new List<ContactWrapper>();
    List<Contact> records = [ SELECT Name FROM Contact ];
    for (Contact record : records) {
```

```
        contacts.add(new ContactWrapper(record));
      }
    }
    public PageReference doSomething() {
      for (ContactWrapper wrapper : contacts) {
        if (wrapper.selected) {
          System.debug(wrapper.data.Id);
        }
      }
      return null;
    }
    class ContactWrapper {
      public Contact data { get; private set; }
      public Boolean selected { get; set; }
      public ContactWrapper(Contact data) {
        this.data = data;
        this.selected = false;
      }
    }
  }
}
```

Listing 6.7   **Page with Wrapper Pattern**

```
<apex:page controller="MyPageController6_6">
<apex:form>
  <apex:pageBlock title="Sample Code">
    <apex:pageBlockButtons >
      <apex:commandButton action="{!doSomething}"
        value="Do Something" />
    </apex:pageBlockButtons>
    <apex:pageBlockTable
      value="{!contacts}" var="contact">
      <apex:column headerValue="Selected">
        <apex:inputCheckbox value="{!contact.selected}" />
      </apex:column>
      <apex:column headerValue="Contact Name">
        {!contact.data.Name}
      </apex:column>
    </apex:pageBlockTable>
  </apex:pageBlock>
</apex:form>
</apex:page>
```

> **Tip**
>
> To clearly differentiate your controller code from triggers and other Apex code, adopt a naming convention and stick to it. A good one is to suffix your class name with the word *Controller*.

Controller Extensions

The final type of controller is the controller extension. A controller extension is a custom controller that extends the behavior of a standard controller. Controller extensions are primarily used to integrate Visualforce more tightly with the native user interface. Many features of Visualforce integration such as overriding standard buttons are not supported for pages that use custom controllers.

Custom controllers can be easily retrofitted to become controller extensions. Multiple extensions can be used in a single page, enabling a large monolithic controller to be divided into smaller controllers by behavior, where some pages might use only a subset of the behaviors.

Listing 6.8 illustrates a trivial controller extension class, and Listing 6.9 shows a page that uses it. The only difference between it and a custom controller is that a constructor is required, allowing the standard controller (`StandardController` for a single record or `StandardSetController` for multiple records) to be passed to the class. In a page that uses the controller extension, all the built-in actions from the standard controller are available implicitly, without any code.

Listing 6.8   **Sample Controller Extension with Single Action Method**

```
public class MyPageController6_8 {
  private ApexPages.StandardController controller;
  public MyPageController6_8(ApexPages.StandardController controller) {
    this.controller = controller;
  }
  public PageReference doSomething() { return null; }
}
```

Listing 6.9   **Page Using Sample Controller Extension**

```
<apex:page standardController="Project__c"
  extensions="MyPageController6_8">
  <apex:form>
    <apex:commandButton action="{!doSomething}"
      value="Do Something" />
  </apex:form>
</apex:page>
```

View Components

View components work with the controller to define the appearance and behavior of a Visualforce user interface. They connect variables in the controller to input and output elements, such as text boxes and labels, and methods in the controller to action-oriented elements, such as buttons and links. Force.com provides a library of standard view components to support common Web user interface design patterns.

This section contains the following subsections:

- **View component basics**—Here, you'll learn how to add any view component to a page and some of the common characteristics. This material is preparation for the five subsections to follow, which cover specific types of standard view components.

- **Data components**—Data components enable Visualforce pages to move data in and out of the controller using standard HTML elements.

- **Action components**—Action components invoke methods on the controller, updating the view state and refreshing the page or navigating to a new page.

- **Primitive components**—Several components exist with similar syntax to HTML tags, bridging the gap between Visualforce functionality and standard HTML.

- **Force.com-styled components**—These components allow Visualforce pages to inherit the appearance of the Force.com native user interface.

- **Force.com user interface components**—The Force.com UI components inherit the appearance of the native user interface as well as its behavior. They are large-scale building blocks for incorporating native Force.com user interface functionality wholesale into your custom pages.

View Component Basics

The three important areas to understand about view components are the following:

- **View component syntax**—View components are embedded in a Visualforce page using XML markup.

- **Page definition**—Every user interface page must begin with the `page` component. All Visualforce components must be declared within the `page` component.

- **Component visibility**—The `rendered` attribute, present on most components, allows conditional rendering of its HTML.

View Component Syntax

Adding view components to a Visualforce page involves constructing XML markup. The markup consists of three parts: the component name, an optional set of attributes, and an optional component body. Listing 6.10 is a sample usage of the view component `dataList`. It demonstrates all three parts of referencing a view component in a Visualforce page.

Listing 6.10   **Sample View Component Usage**

```
<apex:dataList value="{!contacts}" var="contact">
  <b>{!contact.Name}</b>
</apex:dataList>
```

Component Name

The component name is specified in the name of the tag. The component is `dataList`, prefaced with the `apex` namespace to instruct Force.com that this is a standard view component. The `dataList` component renders an HTML list, which is a series of `LI` tags within a `UL` tag.

Attributes

Each view component has its own shape. The shape is the set of attributes accepted by the view component and their data types. Attribute values are either static names or expressions.

The `dataList` component iterates over the values in the controller, creating `LI` HTML tags for each. The `value` attribute specifies the source of these values. The value `{!contacts}` is expression language syntax that retrieves the reference of the `contacts` variable from the controller using its getter method, `getContacts`. If this method is not available, its access modifier is not public, or it returns an incompatible data type, then the Visualforce page cannot be compiled. The `var` attribute specifies a variable name that can be referenced in the component body to access each element of the collection.

> **Note**
>
> Almost every Visualforce component accepts an `id` attribute. This attribute is used to provide a unique identifier to the component. The unique identifier can be used to obtain a reference to the component at runtime, from JavaScript or other Visualforce components. Chapter 7, "Advanced User Interfaces," includes more information on using the `id` attribute.

Component Body

The component body is the text between the start and the end of the XML tag. If no component body is specified, the tag is said to be self-closing. Each component can define its own treatment of the component body.

For example, `dataList` uses the component body to format its list elements. In the sample code, the name of each resource in the list is displayed in bold. The behavior of a self-closing instance of `dataList` depends on the collection type. If you pass a list of primitive types, Force.com can simply return their string representation in the page. But if you pass a list of complex types such as Contact records as in this example, how to dereference the records to produce text for the list items is not clear. If this example had no component body, a list of empty `LI` tags would be produced.

Page Definition

Every Visualforce user interface page must begin with the `page` component. Its main purpose is to connect the page to a controller and optionally override the global appearance of the page.

The `page` component requires either a standard or a custom controller to be specified. The `standardController` attribute is used to reference a standard controller, and its value is the name of a standard or custom object. Optionally, an `extensions` attribute can be provided with a comma-separated list of custom Apex classes that extend the standard controller. To specify a custom controller instead, set the `controller` attribute to the name of a custom controller class.

By default, pages are styled consistently with the Force.com native user interface. They include its stylesheet, sidebar, and header region containing application tabs, banner, and drop-down list of applications. You can override this behavior by setting the `standardStylesheets`, `sidebar`, and `showHeader` Boolean attributes.

Controlling Component Visibility

The `rendered` attribute is available on most standard Visualforce components. It is a Boolean value that indicates whether the component is included in the page. Setting `rendered` to `false` does not hide the component using CSS. It omits it entirely from the rendered page.

For some applications, this server-side approach to visibility is a strong alternative to CSS or JavaScript techniques such as using the `display: none` style directive to hide page elements. The `rendered` attribute is especially powerful when used in conjunction with the partial page refresh feature of Visualforce, discussed in Chapter 7.

Data Components

Data components allow fields and records from the Force.com database to be manipulated within a Visualforce page. They are divided into three categories:

- **Metadata-aware components**—The HTML rendered by these smart components varies based on the definition of the field. These components are valid only when bound to database objects.

- **Primitive data components**—If your field data is contained in a variable in Apex code rather than a database object, use primitive data components to render input and output HTML elements bound to their values.

- **Repeating components**—If you have a list of any type of object, you can iterate over it with a repeating component to render its contents.

Metadata-Aware Components

Metadata-aware components use the definition of database objects to determine the appearance of the component on the page. There are two components: one for input (`inputField`) and one for output (`outputField`).

The inputField component displays the appropriate input element in HTML for the database field it's bound to. Its value attribute defines the binding. For example, an inputField bound to a picklist renders HTML including the valid picklist values and selected value. The inputField also provides a visual indicator when the database field is required, consistent with the native user interface. The inputField component must be contained within a form component. Listing 6.11 shows an example of its usage.

Listing 6.11   **Sample Usage of inputField Component**

```
<apex:form>
  <apex:inputField value="{!project.Stage__c}" />
</apex:form>
```

The outputField formats the value of a field using the correct pattern for that field's data type. For example, an outputField bound to a currency field displays the currency type and decimal point. The value attribute binds the component to data in the controller. In Listing 6.12, the page expression {!project.Billable_Hours__c} provides the source of data for the outputField.

Listing 6.12   **Sample Usage of outputField Component**

```
<apex:outputField value="{!project.Billable_Hours__c}" />
```

Primitive Data Components

Primitive data components add Visualforce functionality to standard HTML tags. Use these components when you are working with data that is not contained in a database object or when the standard Visualforce rendering or behavior is not desirable.

Table 6.1 describes the primitive data components. With the exception of outputLabel, all components listed in the table must be contained in a form component or a compilation error results.

Table 6.1   **Primitive Data Components**

Component	Sample Usage	Value Data Type	Sample HTML Output
outputLabel	`<apex:outputLabel value="outputLabel" />`	String	`<label>outputLabel</label>`
inputCheckbox	`<apex:inputCheckbox value="{!booleanValue}" />`	Boolean	`<input type="checkbox" checked="checked"/>`

inputFile	`<apex:inputFile value="{!blobValue}" />`	Blob	`<span>`
			`<input type="file"/>`
			`</span>`

Component	Sample Usage	Value Data Type	Sample HTML Output
inputHidden	`<apex:inputHidden value="{!hiddenValue}" />`	String	`<input type="hidden" value="hiddenValue"/>`
inputSecret	`<apex:inputSecret value="{!secretValue}" />`	String	`<input type="password" value=""/>`
inputText	`<apex:inputText value="{!textValue}" />`	String	`<input type="text" value="textValue"/>`
inputTextArea	`<apex:inputTextArea value="{!textAreaValue}" />`	String	`<textarea>textArea Value </textarea>`
selectList	`<apex:selectList value="{!selectedItem}">` `<apex:selectOptions value="{!optionValues}" />` `</apex:selectList>`	String or String[] if multiselect (selectList), SelectOption[] (selectOptions)	`<select size="1">` `<option value="">` `optionValue` `</option>` `</select>`
selectRadio	`<apex:selectRadio value="{!selectedItem}">` `<apex:selectOptions value="{!optionValues}" />` `</apex:selectRadio>`	String (selectRadio), SelectOption[] (selectOptions)	`<input type="radio"/>` `<label>optionValue </label>`
selectCheckboxes	`<apex:selectCheckboxes value="{!selectedItem}">` `<apex:selectOptions value="{!optionValues}" />` `</apex:selectCheckboxes>`	String or String[] if multiselect (selectCheckboxes), SelectOption[] (selectOptions) []	`<input type="checkbox" />` `<label>optionValue</ label>`

Repeating Components

Repeating components are bound to a list or set of values. They iterate over them, rendering the component body for each child in the collection.

The three types of repeating components are dataList, dataTable, and repeat. They all require two attributes: value, a binding to the collection, and var, the name of the variable that contains a reference to the current child.

The difference between the three components is in how the HTML is rendered. The dataList component is rendered as an HTML list, with each element of the collection rendered as a list item (LI tag). The dataTable component is rendered as an HTML table, with each element in a table row (TR tag). The repeat component provides no HTML formatting, leaving that entirely up to the Visualforce developer.

Listing 6.13 demonstrates usage of the repeat component to loop over the elements of the collection Skills__r. Each element of the collection is assigned to the variable skill. This variable is valid within the body of the repeat so that you can render its data—in this case, using an outputField component to display each child's Type__c field. A common use of the repeat component is in conjunction with a custom controller method that returns a list of records. You can iterate over the list with repeat, outputting HTML elements as you go.

Listing 6.13 **Sample Usage of repeat Component**

```
<apex:repeat value="{!Skills__r}" var="skill">
  <apex:outputField value="{!skill.Type__c}" />
</apex:repeat>
```

Action Components

Action components allow the page to invoke a method on the controller. The controller method typically performs some operation on the contents of the page, such as updating the database, and then either refreshes the page or navigates to a new page.

Before any refreshing or navigation takes place, the state of the user interface input elements on the page is injected into the variables of the controller using setters. This way, they are accessible from within your action code.

The two basic action components are commandButton and commandLink. The commandButton is rendered as an HTML button, whereas the commandLink is rendered as an anchor. Both are valid only inside a form component. They are typically used with an action attribute that specifies the name of the controller method to invoke or the URL of a new page to navigate to and a value attribute that displays a label to the user. Listing 6.14 is an example of using the commandButton, which invokes the doSomething method of the controller when clicked.

Listing 6.14 **Sample Usage of commandButton Component**

```
<apex:form>
  <apex:commandButton action="{!doSomething}"
    value="Do Something" />
</apex:form>
```

The `page` component also has an action, specified in the `init` attribute. This action is called automatically upon page load but should not be used for initialization code. Its purpose is to immediately redirect the user to a new page.

Before invoking a controller method, all action components perform validation on data components, accepting user input that is contained within their parent `form`. For example, if an input component is required but no value is provided, an error results. Errors can be displayed using the `pageMessages` or `messages` component (described in the "Error Handling" subsection of this chapter) and beside any `inputField` components if their database field is defined to do so. You can disable this validation behavior by setting the action component's `immediate` attribute to `true`.

> **Note**
>
> Visualforce includes actions that operate asynchronously, allowing modifications to the page without a full page refresh. These actions are discussed in Chapter 7.

Primitive Components

Many standard components mirror standard HTML tags, summarized in Table 6.2. These primitive components might seem unnecessary because you can always write the equivalent HTML without using a Visualforce component. But one thing plain HTML cannot do is server-side conditional rendering.

Table 6.2   **Primitive Components**

Component	Sample Usage	Sample HTML Output

outputPanel	`<apex:outputPanel>`
	`outputPanel`
	`</apex:outputPanel>`
		`<span>outputPanel</span>`

outputText	`<apex:outputText>`
	`outputText`
	`</apex:outputText>`
		`outputText`

outputLink	`<apex:outputLink value=`
	`"http://developer.force.com">`
	`Click here`
	`</apex:outputLink>`
		`<a href="http://developer.`
		`force.com">Click here</a>`

image	`<apex:image` `value="myimage.png" />`	`<img src="myimage.png"/>`

iframe	`<apex:iframe src="http://`
	`developer.force.com" />`
		`<iframe width="100%"`
		`scrolling="no" height="600"`
		`frameborder="0"`
		`title="Content" src="http://`
		`developer.force.com"></iframe>`

With regular HTML, your markup always appears in the page, increasing its size and load time, and hiding it requires JavaScript or CSS. Visualforce provides the `rendered` attribute, allowing you to improve the performance of your pages by conditionally rendering markup based on the state of the controller.

There are two additional primitive components: `includeScript` and `stylesheet`. They both accept a `value` attribute to specify the URL of a script or stylesheet resource to load. These components do not have a `rendered` attribute, but using them instead of their HTML counterparts can improve page performance and maintainability. The script and stylesheets are included directly in the HTML HEAD tag for the page, which is not possible to do from a Visualforce page using HTML. Additionally, these components ensure that scripts and stylesheets are not duplicated on the page.

Force.com-Styled Components

Force.com's native user interface makes heavy use of CSS and JavaScript within its Web pages to provide a consistent look and feel across the platform. Many Visualforce components deliver this same styling to developers, without requiring any knowledge of Force.com's CSS or other implementation details. The following list groups these components into five categories based on their function:

- **Page structure**—`sectionHeader`, `pageBlock`, `pageBlockSection`, and `pageBlockSectionItem` are the native structural elements used by Force.com to organize a page into a hierarchy of clearly identifiable sections, subsections, and sets of label/field pairs.

- **Action containers**—`pageBlockButtons` and `toolbar/toolbarGroup` organize a series of buttons or links for performing actions on the page.

- **Table**—`pageBlockTable` is used like a `dataTable` but renders rows and columns in the Force.com native style.

- **Paging components**—`panelBar/panelBarItem` and `tab/tabPanel` group components into pages that can be dynamically shown and hidden.

- **Notifications**—`pageMessages` displays errors and information.

Figure 6.4 illustrates all the components in use on a single Visualforce page.

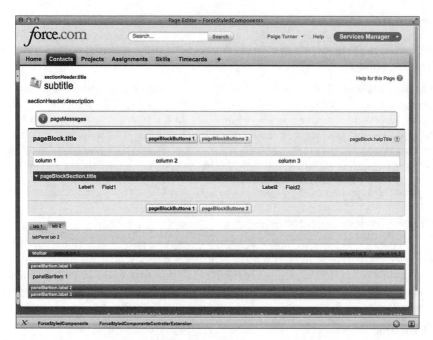

Figure 6.4   Force.com-styled components

Listings 6.15 and 6.16 implement the controller and page shown in Figure 6.4.

Listing 6.15   Sample Controller with Force.com-Styled Components

```
public class ForceStyledComponentsControllerExtension {
  private final List<Contact> contacts;
  public ForceStyledComponentsControllerExtension(
    ApexPages.StandardSetController stdController) {
    this.contacts = (List<Contact>)stdController.getRecords();
  }
  public PageReference initPage() {
    ApexPages.addMessage(new ApexPages.Message(
      ApexPages.Severity.INFO, 'pageMessages'));
    return null;
  }
}
```

Listing 6.16   **Sample Page with Force.com-Styled Components**

```
<apex:page standardController="Contact"
  recordSetVar="contacts"
extensions="ForceStyledComponentsControllerExtension"
  action="{!initPage}">
<apex:form>
<apex:sectionHeader title="sectionHeader.title"
  subtitle="subtitle"
  description="sectionHeader.description"
  help="http://developer.force.com" />
<apex:pageMessages />
<apex:pageBlock title="pageBlock.title"
  helpUrl="http://developer.force.com"
  helpTitle="pageBlock.helpTitle">
  <apex:pageBlockButtons>
    <apex:commandButton action="{!save}"
      value="pageBlockButtons 1"/>
    <apex:commandButton action="{!save}"
      value="pageBlockButtons 2" disabled="true" />
  </apex:pageBlockButtons>
  <apex:pageBlockTable var="r" value="{!contacts}"
    title="pageBlockTable.title" rows="1">
    <apex:column>column 1</apex:column>
    <apex:column>column 2</apex:column>
    <apex:column>column 3</apex:column>
  </apex:pageBlockTable>
  <p />
  <apex:pageBlockSection title="pageBlockSection.title"
    columns="2">
    <apex:pageBlockSectionItem>
      <apex:outputPanel>Label1</apex:outputPanel>
      <apex:outputPanel>Field1</apex:outputPanel>
    </apex:pageBlockSectionItem>
    <apex:pageBlockSectionItem>
      <apex:outputPanel>Label2</apex:outputPanel>
      <apex:outputPanel>Field2</apex:outputPanel>
    </apex:pageBlockSectionItem>
  </apex:pageBlockSection>
</apex:pageBlock>
<p />
<apex:tabPanel switchType="client" selectedTab="name2">
  <apex:tab label="tab 1"
    name="name1">tabPanel tab 1</apex:tab>
  <apex:tab label="tab 2"
    name="name2">tabPanel tab 2</apex:tab>
</apex:tabPanel>
```

```
<p />
<apex:toolbar>
  <apex:outputText>toolbar</apex:outputText>
  <apex:outputLink value="http://developer.force.com">
    outputLink 1</apex:outputLink>
  <apex:toolbarGroup itemSeparator="line" location="right">
    <apex:outputLink value="http://">outputLink 2</apex:outputLink>
    <apex:outputLink value="http://">outputLink 3</apex:outputLink>
  </apex:toolbarGroup>
</apex:toolbar>
<p />
<apex:panelBar>
  <apex:panelBarItem label="panelBarItem.label 1">panelBarItem 1
  </apex:panelBarItem>
  <apex:panelBarItem label="panelBarItem.label 2">panelBarItem 2
  </apex:panelBarItem>
  <apex:panelBarItem label="panelBarItem.label 3">panelBarItem 3
  </apex:panelBarItem>
</apex:panelBar>
</apex:form>
</apex:page>
```

Force.com User Interface Components

Four view components are available that each replicate coarse-grained areas of Force.com's native user interface functionality. These components are a single reference on your Visualforce page, but they expand to produce many subordinate user interface elements when rendered to users. They are summarized in the following list:

1. **listViews**—The listViews component is rendered by Force.com on the list page of an object tab when the Enable Enhanced Lists option is disabled for the organization.

2. **enhancedList**—The enhancedList component consists of a drop-down list of view names and a table of records returned by executing the view.

3. **relatedList**—The relatedList component renders the records of any one of an object's child objects.

4. **detail**—The detail component provides a subset of the native user interface's detail page for an object.

listViews Component

The listViews component includes the capability to create and edit list views, as well as execute them and render their records. The only required attribute of listViews is type, which binds a database object type to the component.

enhancedList Component

The enhancedList component is a more modern version of the listViews component. It has the same functionality but also includes drag-and-drop reorderable columns, sortable columns, and results pagination with dynamic page sizes. It appears in the native user interface only when Enable Enhanced Lists is enabled for the organization.

The required attributes of enhancedList are height (the height of the component in pixels) and either type (the database object type displayed by the component) or listId (the unique identifier of the list view).

relatedList Component

The relatedList component renders a list of child records. It is the same component that appears in the native interface below the detail for a record. It is paginated and allows related records to be edited, deleted, and created, depending on the object permissions of the current user.

The required attributes of relatedList are list, the name of the child relationship to be rendered in the list, and subject, an expression language reference to the parent record on the controller (defaults to the id parameter of the page if not provided). Both Master-Detail and Lookup relationships are supported by relatedList.

detail Component

The detail component replicates the functionality of the native user interface on the detail page of a record. It respects the page layout of the record, including page layouts defined per record type. It also supports in-line editing for the edit mode of an object.

Like the relatedList component, detail requires a subject or it attempts to read a record identifier from the page's id URL parameter. By default, all related lists are rendered below the detail section unless the relatedList parameter is set to false.

Visualforce and the Native User Interface

Force.com provides many places for Visualforce pages to be integrated into its native user interface. You can embed Visualforce pages inside standard user interface pages, override the buttons that navigate between pages, override the standard pages entirely, and add buttons and tabs to navigate to an entirely custom user interface. Areas of the native user interface extensible through Visualforce are summarized here:

- **Standard pages**—Standard pages provide the default user interface for maintaining records in the Force.com database. These pages can be overridden with your custom Visualforce pages.

- **Standard buttons**—Standard buttons normally navigate the user to standard pages, such as the New button, which moves the user to the edit page for a new record. But these buttons can be remapped to your custom Visualforce pages, to inject an additional visual step before the standard page or to hide it altogether.

- **Page layouts**—Page layouts define the position of fields, buttons, and related lists in the native user interface. Visualforce pages can be embedded within page layouts.

- **Custom buttons and links**—Custom buttons appear at the top and bottom of standard pages and links within a detail page. They can navigate the user to a Visualforce page.

- **Custom tabs**—Custom tabs are added to an application and appear at the top of the Web browser under the application banner. A Visualforce page can be configured as a custom tab.

Standard Pages

The native user interface consists of four standard pages for working with database records. These can all be overridden, as described here:

1. **Tab**—The tab page appears when a custom object tab is clicked. Figure 6.5 provides an example of this page.

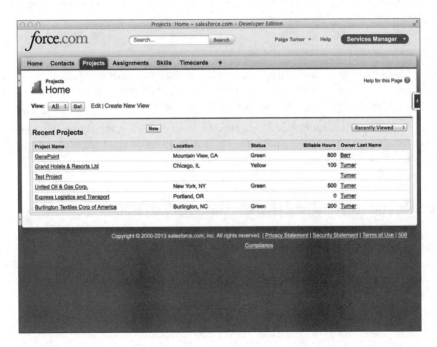

Figure 6.5   Standard tab page

2. **List**—The list page displays a series of records in a tabular view, as shown in Figure 6.6. You reach it by clicking the Go button from the tab page.

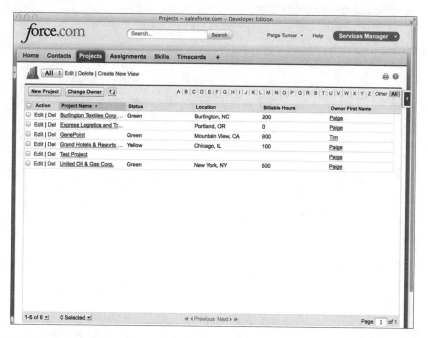

Figure 6.6   Standard list page

3. **View**—The view page is a read-only view of a single record and its related records. Figure 6.7 is the view page for the Contact object. A page layout, determined by profile and optionally record type, is used to determine the appearance of the view page.

4. **Edit**—The edit page uses the same layout as the view page but allows the values of a record to be modified and saved. This is shown in Figure 6.8 for the Contact object.

Caution

Override the standard edit page with caution. The standard edit page provides deep functionality, such as page layouts and record types, that cannot be replicated in a Visualforce page without a significant amount of custom code.

To override a standard page, go to the App Setup area and click Create, Objects and select the object. Scroll to the Buttons, Links, and Actions section. Tab, view, and edit pages can be overridden only with Visualforce pages that use a standard, single record controller. The list page must use a standard set controller. Controller extensions are supported in all pages.

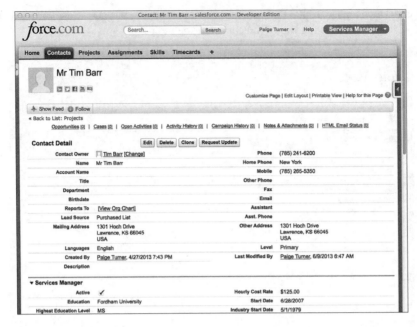

Figure 6.7   Standard view page

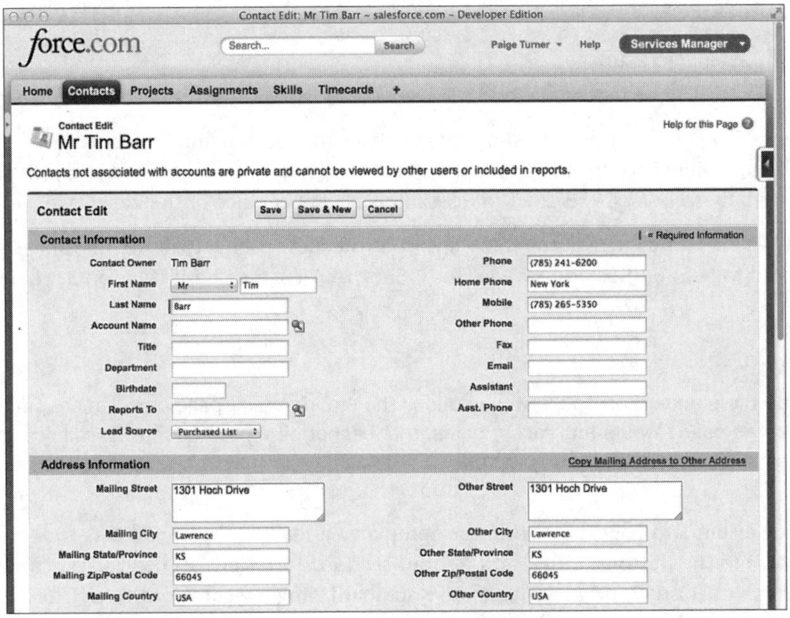

Figure 6.8   Standard edit page

Standard Buttons

Visualforce pages can be shown as the result of clicking a native user interface button, overriding the button's standard behavior. The following standard buttons can be overridden:

- **New**—The New button normally navigates the user to the edit page on a new record.
- **Delete**—This is the page navigated to after a record is deleted. The default behavior is to navigate to the tab page.
- **Clone**—The Clone button copies the values from the current record into a new record and places the user in edit mode on that record. This behavior can be customized by overriding the Clone button.
- **Accept**—The Accept button applies to records owned by a queue rather than a single user. It enables a user to remove a record from the queue, assigning ownership of the record to himself. This button appears on the list page only when it is displaying records owned by a queue.

To override a standard button, go to the App Setup area and click Create, Objects and select the object. Scroll to the Buttons, Links, and Actions section. Your Visualforce page must use a standard, single record controller, with or without extensions.

Page Layouts

A Visualforce page can be embedded in an object's page layout alongside its fields. Figure 6.9 shows a new section called My Section, defined using the page layout editor. My Page is the name of a Visualforce page that has been dragged into My Section and is now visible whenever a record of that object is viewed or edited.

The result of adding the Visualforce page called My Page to the layout for the Contact object is shown in Figure 6.10. The text "Hello Visualforce" is being rendered by the Visualforce page embedded within the record's detail page.

To add a Visualforce page to a page layout, go to the App Setup area and click Create, Objects and select the object. Scroll to the Page Layouts section and click the Edit link for the page layout. For your Visualforce pages to appear in the page layout editor, they must conform to the following guidelines:

- They cannot already be in use by a tab.
- They use a standard, single record controller, with or without extensions.
- Their controller's object type matches that used by the page layout. For example, for a Visualforce page to appear on the Contact page layout, it must use a standard Contact controller.

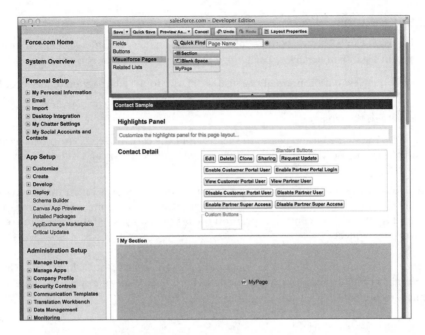

Figure 6.9   Adding a Visualforce page to page layout

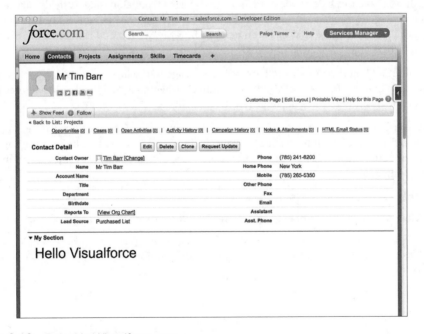

Figure 6.10   Embedded Visualforce page

Custom Buttons and Links

You can configure buttons and links that navigate to any Visualforce page. These buttons and links are then added to page layouts. Buttons and links are defined on the database object. In the App Setup area, click Create, Objects, and then click the object. Scroll to the Buttons, Links, and Actions area and click the New button.

Custom buttons and links tied to Visualforce pages can be added to the object's detail page layout or a related list page layout. The detail page layout requires a standard controller. The related list layout requires a standard set controller. Controller extensions can be used with either.

Custom Tabs

You can configure any Visualforce page as a new tab in the Force.com native user interface. To add a new Visualforce tab, go to the App Setup area and click Create, Tabs. Click the New button in the Visualforce Tabs section to create a tab. Select a Visualforce page, give the new tab a unique label and name, select a tab label and style, set tab visibility on profiles and applications, and click Save.

Visualforce in Production

This section describes areas of focus for real-world user interfaces written in Visualforce. It includes the following subsections:

- **Debugging and tuning**—Force.com provides Web-based tools for debugging and tuning Visualforce pages.

- **Security**—Securing Visualforce pages is an important task. Visualforce pages can expose users to records they should not see under record sharing rules and cause runtime errors due to lack of object or field visibility.

- **Error handling**—Error handling in Visualforce is a process of catching all exceptions and handling them thoughtfully, with both the integrity of the database and the user experience in mind.

- **Governor limits**—The code running in Visualforce controllers is subject to governor limits, applied within the scope of each user-initiated action.

- **Unit tests**—Force.com requires test coverage on the code in Visualforce controllers and provides system methods to assist.

Debugging and Tuning

Developer Console is the first place to look to troubleshoot unexpected behavior from a Visualforce user interface. While Developer Console is open, every interaction with

Force.com is logged and can be examined in depth. In Figure 6.11, Developer Console is active and contains six entries, shown in the bottommost table.

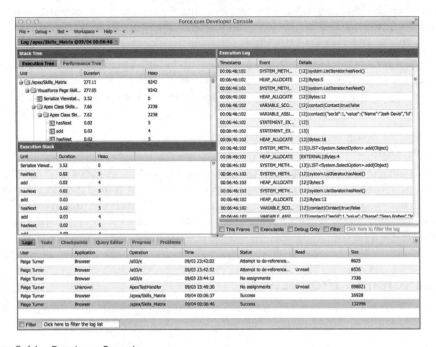

Figure 6.11   Developer Console

The last log entry has been clicked, and the other panels of Developer Console are refreshed with detailed information. This information is centered around the Apex code executed in the controller associated with the page, as well as any Apex code executed as a result of controller code. If a bug exists in your controller code, it should be obvious in the Execution Tree, Execution Log, and Stack Tree panels as you trace the flow of instructions.

The next place to look for bugs is the Visualforce page markup. If Force.com encounters something invalid in the course of rendering a Visualforce page, such as a null reference in your controller, it can interrupt the processing of your page entirely and display an error message. Trial and error can be helpful in these situations. Comment out portions of your Visualforce page using HTML comment tags (`<!-- sample comment -->`) until the page functions again and you've isolated the troublesome portion. An in-browser development tool such as Firebug or Chrome Developer Tools is also helpful if the page renders successfully but has a client-side presentation or logic issue. These tools enable close inspection of the JavaScript, HTML, and CSS in the page.

When you're ready to improve the performance of your Visualforce page, examine the view state. The view state contains the values of local variables in your controller. They are encoded and embedded in the page itself in a hidden field and sent back to Force.com upon every user action. Sending the view state back and forth to the browser and processing it in Force.com can reduce the responsiveness of your user interface. View state is limited to 128K, but performance can be impacted well before the limit is reached.

The Visualforce development mode footer contains a tab called View State, shown in Figure 6.12. With it, you can examine the contents of the view state: the variables saved there, along with their sizes and contents. Double-clicking one of the folders opens a dialog with charts showing the contribution of various types of view state toward the limit.

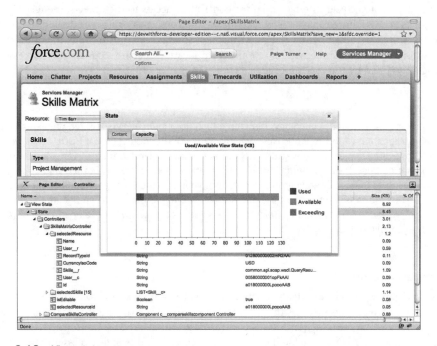

Figure 6.12   View state

Your goal is to minimize the view state. Look for controller variables that do not need to persist across page views, and add the `transient` keyword to them. The `transient` keyword tells Force.com not to save the state of the variable in the Web page, removing the round-trip cost of transporting that data to and from the Web browser. Avoid querying extraneous information from the database in your SOQL calls. Also, simplify and streamline any nested data structures that are required in the view state.

> **Note**
>
> Performance tuning Visualforce pages is a complex subject beyond the scope of this book. An excellent resource is a best-practices document from Salesforce itself, available at http://www.salesforce.com/docs/en/cce/salesforce_visualforce_best_practices/salesforce_visualforce_best_practices.pdf. Learning these best practices early in the development process can prevent costly rework. Additionally, test all of your Visualforce pages with realistic data volumes. This helps to expose performance issues prior to a production deployment.

Security

Securing a Visualforce user interface involves controlling access to the objects, the records, and the page itself. Visualforce obeys the object and field-level security rules configured in profiles. Record security is handled by the controller through special keywords in Apex in conjunction with custom code that can be written to enforce application-specific security rules. Access to the page is granted by the user's profile.

> **Note**
>
> As Visualforce is a Web technology, it's also critical to guard your Visualforce pages against vulnerabilities native to the Web. This includes Cross-Site Scripting (XSS), SOQL Injection, and Cross-Site Request Forgery (CSRF). There are many built-in features of Visualforce and Apex that address these vulnerabilities transparently to the developer, but it's a good idea to be aware of them. Depending on the nature of your Visualforce pages, additional effort may be needed to protect against them. For more information, consult the *Secure Coding Guideline* document published by Salesforce, available at http://wiki.developerforce.com/page/Secure_Coding_Guideline.

Object-Level Security

Access to database objects and fields is determined by the profile and is consistent with the native user interface. This protects the database and maintains the centralized control of data security, but also exposes the user interface to various runtime errors if improperly configured. For example, if the user's profile denies all access to an object, this object is essentially invisible. When a Visualforce controller attempts to select from it, the page fails with an exception. Other configuration problems are handled more transparently to the user. If the user's profile lacks edit access on an object and a Visualforce page binds an `inputField` to that object, it is automatically rendered as an `outputField`, appropriately blocking user input.

When developing a controller, check that the SOQL, SOSL, and DML operations are fully compatible with the set of profiles expected to use the page. As a developer, you have full visibility to every object and field, but do not assume that your users have the same level of access. Test the Visualforce pages by logging in as a test user or cycling through profiles on a single test user. You can also write unit tests that run under the privileges of a specific user using the `System.runAs` method, covered in more detail in the "Unit Tests" subsection.

Record-Level Security

Standard controllers always honor the record-level security of the current user. But by default, record sharing rules are ignored by code in custom controllers. These controllers run in a system context, like a trigger.

> **Note**
>
> Record sharing rules are still honored by the methods of standard controllers that have extensions defined, but the code in an extension class itself still runs in system mode.

For example, if a user's profile grants the user access to a particular object, your custom controller queries it, and your Visualforce page displays the results, the user can read every record in the object, regardless of the sharing settings.

You can change this behavior in the controller code by specifying a security mode in the class definition. Two security modes are available: with sharing and without sharing. The controller definition in Listing 6.17 uses with sharing to configure the controller to honor record sharing rules.

Listing 6.17   **Custom Controller Using Record Sharing Rules**

```
public with sharing class MyController {
  // the code in this controller honors record sharing rules
}
```

The without sharing security mode indicates that a class should not obey record sharing rules, which is the default state. You do not need to change this unless your code accesses objects that have record sharing rules defined that you would like to enforce in your user interface. Subclasses inherit the security mode from their parent class, but inner classes do not. In nested calls, where one class calls another class, the current security mode is applied unless explicitly specified.

After a security mode is chosen, no additional work is required. SOSL and SOQL statements automatically return the correct subset of records based on the sharing rules for each object. But if a record is referenced directly that is not shared with the user, such as through a DML method updating a foreign key, a runtime error is thrown. Use a try, catch block around DML methods to make sure that this situation is properly handled.

Page-Level Security

Profiles determine which users are able to use a Visualforce page. Pages must be explicitly enabled for each profile that requires access. If this is not done, users will receive an error page titled Insufficient Privileges when attempting to view the page.

To grant a profile access to a page, go to the Administration Setup and click Manage Users, Profiles. Select the desired profile, scroll to the Enabled Visualforce Page Access section and click the Edit button. Select pages from the Available Visualforce Pages list and click the Add button to add them to the Enabled Visualforce Pages list. Click Save when you're done.

> **Note**
> Users with the Customize Application permission can access all Visualforce pages in the organization.

Error Handling

The two main concerns when handling errors in Visualforce are how uncaught exceptions impact the user interface and how to communicate caught exceptions to users.

Uncaught Exceptions

Allowing an uncaught exception in a trigger is often an appropriate way to notify the user of a problem because Force.com displays a nicely formatted error message to the user in the native user interface. But in a Visualforce page, uncaught exceptions result in an alarming, generic Force.com error page whose appearance cannot be controlled or customized in any way.

As this is typically not consistent with the usability and look and feel of a custom user interface, one of the goals of error handling in Visualforce is to avoid these uncaught exceptions. Place a `try`, `catch` block around every action method, or at least those that perform SOSL, SOQL, or DML operations.

A benefit of uncaught exceptions in triggers is that they roll back the current transaction. Catching all exceptions in your Visualforce controller forces your code to roll back explicitly if required by your application. For example, if your controller has two DML statements in an action method and fails on the second with a caught exception, the first statement is still committed to the database at the conclusion of the method. If this leaves the database in an undesirable state for your application, set a savepoint at the beginning of the method and roll back to it in the `catch` block. For an example of using savepoints, refer to Listing 5.19 in Chapter 5, "Advanced Business Logic."

Error Communication

Visualforce provides page components and corresponding data objects for communicating errors to the user in a consistent way. The page components are `messages` and `pageMessages`, which display the page-level errors returned by a controller. These components are placed on pages, typically at the top, and render the `ApexPages.Message` objects added to the page. `Message` objects contain a message and optional severity. Severity is used to style the message when displayed in the `pageMessages` component and can also be filtered on in test methods.

Listing 6.18 is an example of code to add an error-severity message to the page. To be visible, it must be rendered by a `messages` or `pageMessages` component.

Listing 6.18   **Sample Usage of Page Messages**

```
ApexPages.addMessage(new ApexPages.Message(
  ApexPages.Severity.ERROR, 'Something went wrong'));
```

Governor Limits

Visualforce controllers have the same set of governor limits as all Apex code. Table 6.3 reviews these limits.

Table 6.3   **Subset of Governor Limits**

Resource Type	Governor Limit
Visualforce Iteration Components (e.g., `apex:repeat`)	1,000 items per collection
Heap	6MB
Apex code	200,000 lines of code executed, 3MB code size
SOQL	100 queries
Records from SOQL	50,000 records cumulatively for all SOQL queries
DML	150 DML statements
Records in DML	10,000 records cumulatively for all DML statements

Governor limits apply during execution of user-initiated actions and are not cumulative. When an action is complete, the governor limits reset. For example, if your controller contains a `save` method bound to a `commandButton`, the governor limits apply during the execution of the `save` method. When the user clicks the button again or takes another action that invokes a method, the governor limits begin counting your resource consumption again from zero.

If you need to work with larger data sets in your Visualforce pages and are bumping into governor limits, consider whether you can partition the user interface into a series of read-only and read-write subpages. If so, you can take advantage of higher governor limits on the read-only pages by adding the `readOnly="true"` attribute to the `apex:page` element. The governor limit increases are shown in Table 6.4.

Table 6.4   **Relaxed Governor Limits for Read-Only Visualforce Pages**

Resource Type	Governor Limit
Visualforce Iteration Components (e.g., `apex:repeat`)	10,000 items per collection
Records from SOQL	1,000,000 records cumulatively for all SOQL queries

Unit Tests

Unit tests are mandatory for all Apex code, including Visualforce controllers but not the pages themselves. Your application code must have at least 75% test coverage before it can be deployed to a production environment.

The mechanics of writing unit tests for controllers is similar to that of triggers, with some additional system methods for test setup. But the strategy for testing controllers is unique, because controller code normally relies on the Web browser to drive it.

Listing 6.19 provides an example of the test setup code. It starts by creating an instance of the controller class and getting a reference to the Visualforce page to test. This is a `PageReference` instance, created by passing the page name as an argument. The `Test.setCurrentPage` method sets the context of the test method to the page you want to test.

Listing 6.19   **Sample Controller Test Method**

```
static testMethod void sampleTestMethod() {
  MyPageController controller = new MyPageController();
  PageReference page = new PageReference('MyPage');
  Test.setCurrentPage(page);
}
```

The body of your tests can employ one or more of the following test strategies to exercise code in the controller:

- Directly invoke controller methods and getters/setters.
- Add a test harness to constructor code to read URL arguments to establish controller state or perform actions.
- Verify data in the database using SOQL and SOSL queries.
- Use `System.runAs` blocks to simulate different users, such as `System.runAs(user) { block; }`.

> **Caution**
>
> Even 100% test coverage on the controller class does not guarantee a bug-free user interface. Testing Visualforce pages is like testing any Web application. Test it manually with your Web browser or with an automated Web testing tool.

Sample Application: Skills Matrix

One of the features of the Services Manager sample application is skill set management. The skills of consultants are tracked using the Skill object, a child of the Contact object. Entering skills in the native user interface involves navigating to the Contact's record and clicking the New button in the Skills related list and then selecting a skill type and a rating.

Users of the application have requested a more streamlined way to enter and view skills, called the Skills Matrix. The requirements of the Skills Matrix follow:

- **Reduce navigation clicks**—Provide a single screen for entering and viewing all skill-related information. The screen shows the skills and ratings of a single contact at a time in tabular format: skill types as rows and a single column to view and edit ratings.

- **Encourage data completeness**—All skill types are shown at all times. This is in contrast with the native user interface, which shows only the skills containing ratings. Showing all skill types, including those lacking a rating, encourages users to treat the user interface like a survey and should increase data completeness.

- **Allow all to view, restrict editing**—Whether a rating is editable or read-only depends on the current user. If the user is editing her own contact record, all ratings are editable. If the user is a manager, vice president, or system administrator (by profile), the user is allowed to edit the skills of any contact. If the user does not meet any of the previous criteria, the skill ratings are read-only.

This section describes building the feature in three parts. The first part is a basic implementation, to allow the selection of a contact and editing of its skills. The second part adds the finishing touches to implement the full set of requirements. The final section provides a sample, full implementation of the feature, shown in Figure 6.13, and comments on portions of the code.

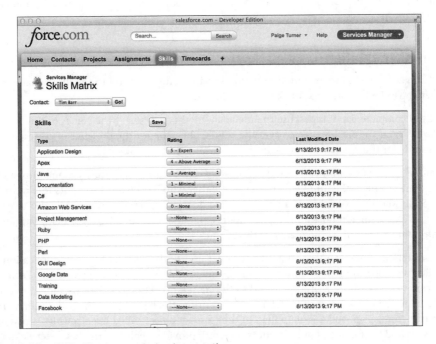

Figure 6.13   Skills Matrix sample implementation

Basic Implementation

In the basic implementation, build a Visualforce page with a drop-down list at the top containing contact names and a table below it with the skills and ratings. The only skills shown are those that already contain ratings for the contact. The ratings can be edited and saved by any user.

Start by creating the page and controller in the Force.com IDE. Add a `selectList` component and a corresponding getter in the controller to return a list of `SelectOption` objects, constructed from the names and unique identifiers of records of the `Contact` object. Add a refresh `commandButton` to fetch the skills for the currently selected contact.

Build and test the drop-down list of contacts before moving on to the list of skills. Then flesh out the controller, querying the `Type__c` and `Rating__c` fields of the `Skill__c` records belonging to the selected contact. Iterate over that list in the page, displaying the ratings as drop-down lists. Add an action method to the controller to save changes to the skills list. Use the upsert database method, as later your skills list will contain both new and edited records. Add a `commandButton` on the page to invoke the action method.

Test your user interface frequently during development. Add your page to the native user interface with a Visualforce tab or override the Skills custom object tab. To override the tab, in the App Setup area, click Create, Objects and select Skill. Scroll to the Buttons, Links, and Actions section. Click the Edit link for the action Skills Tab. For the Override With, select the Visualforce Page radio button. Select your Skills Matrix page from the drop-down list and click the Save button.

Full Implementation

After you get the basic implementation into a working state, move on to the more challenging requirements: the complete list of skill types and data security.

To get the complete list of types, use the metadata methods to query the values of the `Skill__c.Type__c` picklist. Iterate over the values, checking for the presence of corresponding Skill records for the contact. Create Skill records where they are missing.

For data security, you cannot rely on built-in Force.com record-level security alone. It operates on the `OwnerId` field, the unique identifier of the user who has ownership rights to a record. In the Skills Matrix, ownership of a contact record does not determine who is allowed to edit or view its skills. An administrator might import contact data from a legacy system, or a user in human resources might be the owner of the contact.

The assumption is that every consultant and other user of the Services Manager application has a license to log in to Force.com as an independent user with his own credentials. Each full user license carries with it a unique record in the standard User object. This user identity can be correlated to the contact record to determine at runtime the behavior of the Skills Matrix. To create this correlation, add a lookup field to the Contact object called User, setting its parent to the standard User object. For each contact record, provide a value of the new User field. This lookup of the User from Contact can drive the decision of the controller to make a set of skills editable or not.

When you're done with the implementation, test it against the three user scenarios: privileged user, consultant editing his or her own skills, and consultant viewing the skills of another consultant.

Tip

Only users with the System Administrator profile will have access to your new Skills Matrix page. To open the page to nonadministrative users, in the Administration Setup area, click Manage Users, Profiles and select the profile of the users. Scroll to the Enabled Visualforce Page Access section and click the Edit button. Select your page from the Available Visualforce Pages list and click the Add button to move it to the Enabled Visualforce Pages list. Click the Save button when you're done.

Implementation Walk-Through

This subsection provides the code for a sample implementation of the Skills Matrix. It includes the controller, the page, and controller test cases.

Skills Matrix Controller

Listing 6.20 contains a sample implementation of the Skills Matrix controller class. The controller has four variables, each with a getter method for access by the Visualforce page. The selectedContactId variable contains the unique identifier of the contact selected for editing or viewing. isEditable is a flag used by the page to enable or disable the Save button and to determine whether to render skills as text fields or editable drop-down lists. The selected Contact variable contains several fields from the Contact object needed throughout the controller, queried using the selectedContactId. The selectedSkills list contains the skill types and ratings to be displayed and edited in the user interface, and this same list is used to update the database upon a save action.

The controller has two actions: save and refresh. The save action applies the changes from the drop-down lists of skill ratings by upserting them into the database. The refresh action uses the unique identifier of the currently selected contact (selectedContactId) to query the database for Skill records. It compares them against the complete list of skill types via the database metadata call getPicklistValues. Finally, it updates the isEditable variable based on whether the current user is privileged or is associated with the currently viewed contact.

Several helper methods are in the controller. addError and addInfo are shortcuts for adding notifications to the page, displayed using the pageMessages component. The get CurrentUserContact method queries the Contact record corresponding to the current user. The isManager method returns true if the user is privileged, enabling the user to edit the skills of any contact.

Listing 6.20   **Skills Matrix Controller**

```
public class SkillsMatrixController {
  public String selectedContactId { get; set; }
  public Boolean isEditable { get; private set; }
  public Contact selectedContact { get; private set; }
  public List<Skill__c> selectedSkills { get; private set; }
  public List<SelectOption> getContactOptions() {
    List<SelectOption> options = new List<SelectOption>();
      options.add(new SelectOption(
        '', '-- Select Contact --'));
    List<Contact> contacts = [ SELECT Id, Name
      FROM Contact ORDER BY LastName ];
    for (Contact contact : contacts) {
      options.add(new SelectOption(contact.Id,
        contact.Name));
    }
    return options;
  }
  public PageReference refresh() {
    if (selectedContactId == null) {
      addError('Select a contact');
      return null;
    }
    selectedContact = [ SELECT Id, Name,
      User__r.UserRoleId,
      User__r.ProfileId,
      (SELECT Type__c, Rating__c, LastModifiedDate
        FROM Skills__r ORDER BY Rating__c DESC)
      FROM Contact
      WHERE Id = :selectedContactId
      LIMIT 1 ];
    Set<String> skillTypes = new Set<String>();
    selectedSkills = new List<Skill__c>();
    for (Skill__c skill : selectedContact.Skills__r) {
      skillTypes.add(skill.Type__c);
      selectedSkills.add(skill);
    }
    Schema.DescribeFieldResult field = Skill__c.Type__c.getDescribe();
    String picklistValue = null;
    for (Schema.PicklistEntry entry : field.getPicklistValues()) {
      picklistValue = entry.getLabel();
      if (!skillTypes.contains(picklistValue)) {
        selectedSkills.add(
          new Skill__c(Contact__c = selectedContact.Id,
            Type__c = picklistValue));
      }
    }
    if (isManager()) {
```

```apex
      isEditable = true;
    } else {
      Contact userContact = getCurrentUserContact();
      isEditable =
        selectedContact != null && userContact != null
        && selectedContact.Id == userContact.Id;
    }
    return null;
  }
  private void addError(String msg) {
    ApexPages.addMessage(new ApexPages.Message(
      ApexPages.Severity.ERROR, msg));
  }
  private void addInfo(String msg) {
    ApexPages.addMessage(new ApexPages.Message(
      ApexPages.Severity.INFO, msg));
  }
  public Contact getCurrentUserContact() {
    List<Contact> userContact = [ SELECT Id, Name,
      User__r.UserRoleId, User__r.ProfileId
      FROM Contact
      WHERE User__c = :UserInfo.getUserId()
      LIMIT 1 ];
    if (userContact.size() == 0) {
      addError('No contact associated with user');
      return null;
    } else {
      return userContact.get(0);
    }
  }
  private Boolean isManager() {
    List<Profile> profiles = [ SELECT Id
      FROM Profile WHERE Name IN (
      'Project Manager', 'Vice President', 'System Administrator')
      AND Id = :UserInfo.getProfileId() LIMIT 1 ];
    return profiles.size() == 1;
  }
  public PageReference save() {
    try {
      upsert selectedSkills;
      addInfo('Changes saved');
    } catch(DmlException e) {
      addError('Could not save changes: ' + e.getMessage());
    }
    return null;
  }
}
```

Skills Matrix Visualforce Page

Listing 6.21 contains sample code for the Skills Matrix Visualforce page. It uses Force.com-styled view components to achieve an appearance that resembles the native user interface. The `pageBlock` and `pageBlockButtons` components visually separate the selection of the resource from the skills data and Save button, and the `sectionHeader` component mimics the appearance of a native object tab.

The `pageBlockTable` component iterates over the list of skills, displaying them as a table using standard Force.com styling. Each row of the table includes two columns. The first column contains the skill type. The second contains two components: one for editing the skill rating and another strictly for viewing it. Only one of these components is shown at a time. They are rendered conditionally based on whether the controller has determined the data to be editable. If the skills data is editable, only the `inputField` component is rendered. If the current user does not have the rights to edit the ratings, only the `outputField` is rendered.

Listing 6.21 **Skills Matrix Visualforce Page**

```
<apex:page controller="SkillsMatrixController"
  tabStyle="Skill__c">
  <style>
  .contactLabel { padding-right: 15px; }
  .goButton { margin-left: 10px; }
  </style>
  <apex:sectionHeader title="Services Manager"
    subtitle="Skills Matrix" />
  <apex:pageMessages />
  <apex:form id="form">
  <apex:outputLabel value="Contact:" for="selectedContactId"
    styleClass="contactLabel" />
  <apex:selectList id="selectedContactId" title="Contact"
    value="{!selectedContactId}" size="1">
    <apex:selectOptions value="{!contactOptions}" />
  </apex:selectList>
  <apex:commandButton action="{!refresh}" value="Go!"
    styleClass="goButton" />
  <p />
  <apex:pageBlock title="Skills">
    <apex:pageBlockButtons>
      <apex:commandButton action="{!save}" value="Save"
        disabled="{!NOT isEditable}" />
    </apex:pageBlockButtons>
    <apex:pageBlockTable value="{!selectedSkills}" var="skill"
      rendered="{!selectedContactId != ''}">
      <apex:column value="{!skill.Type__c}" />
      <apex:column headerValue="Rating">
        <apex:outputField value="{!skill.Rating__c}"
```

```
          rendered="{!NOT isEditable}" />
        <apex:inputField value="{!skill.Rating__c}"
          rendered="{!isEditable}" />
      </apex:column>
      <apex:column value="{!skill.LastModifiedDate}" />
    </apex:pageBlockTable>
  </apex:pageBlock>
  </apex:form>
</apex:page>
```

Controller Tests

The test cases in Listing 6.22 achieve 96% coverage of the Skills Matrix controller. They begin with a static initializer and `init` method to prepare the database for the tests by adding test data. This data is not permanent. All database actions during testing are rolled back automatically upon test completion.

The test cases rely on two Contact records: Tim and Barry. To test the behavior of the Skills Matrix on existing data, Tim is given a single Skill record, whereas Barry is left without skills. For testing security, Tim's Contact record is associated with a User record named Tim, whereas Barry's Contact record is not mapped to a User record. Update the query for the users in the static initializer to match two usernames in your own organization.

Listing 6.22 Skills Matrix Unit Test Class

```
@isTest
private class TestSkillsMatrixController {
  static PageReference page;
  static SkillsMatrixController controller;
  static Contact barry, tim;
  static User barryUser, timUser;
  static {
    timUser = [ SELECT Id FROM User WHERE Name = 'Tim Barr' LIMIT 1 ];
    barryUser = [ SELECT Id FROM User WHERE Name = 'Barry Cade' LIMIT 1 ];
    init();
  }
  private static void init() {
    barry = new Contact(FirstName = 'Barry', LastName = 'Cade');
    tim = new Contact(FirstName = 'Tim', LastName = 'Barr',
      User__c = timUser.Id);
    insert new Contact[] { barry, tim };
    Skill__c[] skills = new Skill__c[] {
      new Skill__c(Type__c = 'Java', Rating__c = '3',
        Contact__c = tim.Id) };
    insert skills;
    page = new PageReference('SkillsMatrix');
```

```apex
      Test.setCurrentPage(page);
      controller = new SkillsMatrixController();
  }
  static testMethod void testAsUser() {
    System.runAs(timUser) {
      init();
      controller.selectedContactId = barry.Id;
      controller.refresh();
      System.assert(!controller.isEditable);
      controller.selectedContactId = tim.Id;
      controller.refresh();
      System.assert(controller.isEditable);
    }
  }
  static testMethod void testNoContactForUser() {
    System.runAs(barryUser) {
      init();
      controller.selectedContactId = barry.Id;
      controller.refresh();
      System.assert(ApexPages.hasMessages(ApexPages.Severity.ERROR));
    }
  }
  static testMethod void testNoSkills() {
    controller.getContactOptions();
    controller.selectedContactId = barry.Id;
    controller.refresh();
    System.assert(controller.selectedSkills.size() > 0);
    System.assert(controller.isEditable);
  }
  static testMethod void testWithSkills() {
    controller.getContactOptions();
    controller.selectedContactId = tim.Id;
    controller.refresh();
    System.assert(controller.selectedSkills.size() > 0);
    System.assert(controller.selectedSkills.get(0).Type__c == 'Java');
  }
  static testMethod void testNoContactSelected() {
    controller.selectedContactId = null;
    PageReference ref = controller.refresh();
    System.assert(ApexPages.hasMessages());
  }
  static testMethod void testSave() {
    final String skillRating = '5 - Expert';
    controller.getContactOptions();
```

```
  controller.selectedContactId = barry.Id;
  controller.refresh();
  List<Skill__c> selectedSkills = controller.selectedSkills;
  Skill__c skill = selectedSkills.get(0);
  skill.Rating__c = skillRating;
  String skillType = skill.Type__c;
  controller.save();
  System.assert(ApexPages.hasMessages(ApexPages.Severity.INFO));
  Skill__c savedSkill = [ SELECT Rating__c FROM Skill__c
    WHERE Contact__c = :barry.Id AND
      Type__c = :skillType LIMIT 1 ];
  System.assert(savedSkill != null &&
    savedSkill.Rating__c == skillRating);
  }
}
```

The test methods are described here in the order in which they appear in the code:

- **testAsUser**—This test uses the System.runAs method to assume the identity of Tim. Tim is assigned to a User, so when his corresponding Contact record is selected and the list of skills is refreshed, the isEditable flag should be set to true. If Barry is selected, the flag should be false.

- **testNoContactForUser**—System.runAs is used again, this time to test for an error condition. Barry's user does not have a child Contact record, so he should receive an error when visiting the Skills Matrix. Without a mapping to the User object, the application cannot determine whether the current user has access to edit skills.

- **testNoSkills**—This test method runs as a System Administrator. It selects Barry from the contact list and refreshes, asserting that there are Skills records. These records are created from the Skill object's Type__c field's picklist values. Another assertion is made that the skill ratings are editable because an administrator can edit the skills of all contacts.

- **testWithSkills**—This test retrieves the skills for Tim and asserts that the Java skill is first in the list. This is because Tim already has a Skill record for Java, and existing records should be placed at the top of the user interface.

- **testNoContactSelected**—The selected contact is set to null to verify that an information message is added to the page. This message instructs the user to select a contact.

- **testSave**—This test uses the controller to rate Barry as an expert in the first skill on the skills list. It then queries the database independently to verify that the controller saved the data correctly.

Summary

This chapter has covered the basics of Visualforce. Visualforce is a challenging but rewarding area of the Force.com platform, enabling the development of custom, data-intensive Web user interfaces using high-level languages for both logic and presentation. Mastering Visualforce requires the application of all of your Force.com skills and knowledge: the database, security model, and Apex code.

Use this chapter as a jumping-off point to the online documentation and Visualforce Developer's Guide. The Visualforce Developer's Guide contains the most current and complete information on the standard Visualforce view components.

Before moving on to the next chapter, consider what you've learned about Visualforce:

- A strong distinction exists between the controller and the page. No business logic is allowed on the page.

- The state of your pages at runtime is maintained automatically by Force.com. This enables you to design stateful interactions across one or many pages without writing custom state transfer code, assuming you always use Visualforce action components rather than raw HTML tags such as anchors.

- Custom controller code runs as the system user by default, meaning record-level security is not honored.

7

Advanced User Interfaces

Now that you are familiar with the basics of Visualforce, this chapter introduces features that enable you to build richer, more interactive user interfaces. The features are divided into the following sections:

- *Asynchronous actions—Visualforce has built-in, cross-browser support for Ajax behavior, without requiring you to write JavaScript code or integrate with JavaScript libraries.*

- *Modular Visualforce—Visualforce has a number of features to enable you to write modular pages. You can embed static content, build pages that include other pages, define page templates, and create your own library of custom Visualforce components.*

- *Dynamic Visualforce—Learn how to create Visualforce pages that can change their structure on the fly, based on administrator-maintainable declarative metadata or the results of executing Apex code.*

- *Single-page applications in Force.com—Take a slight detour away from Visualforce to develop high-performance Web applications that use the latest client-side frameworks and Force.com as the data layer.*

- *Introduction to Force.com Sites—Visualforce pages can be accessed by users who do not have accounts in your Force.com organization using a feature called Force.com Sites.*

- *Sample application—The Services Manager sample application's Skills Matrix is enhanced to demonstrate Ajax behavior and the use of JavaScript libraries and custom Visualforce components.*

> **Note**
>
> The code listings in this chapter are available in a GitHub Gist at http://goo.gl/IMfqc.

Asynchronous Actions

So far, you've built Visualforce pages that have a simple interaction with their controller. They display data from the controller, potentially allowing the user to change it, and then submit it using an action component such as a `commandButton`. The action component invokes a method on the controller that returns a `PageReference`, navigating the user to a new page or refreshing the current page.

Visualforce actions also support more complex, asynchronous interactions with the page, commonly referred to as Ajax. Ajax is short for Asynchronous JavaScript and XML. Visualforce supports Ajax in two ways:

1. It allows actions to run in the background. The user is free to continue working with the page while Force.com processes the result. For example, a duplicate checking algorithm could examine the page while the user is inputting data, flagging duplicate records as they are discovered.

2. Actions can refresh a subset of the Visualforce page, such as a table of data, rather than the entire page. This can create a richer, more interactive experience for users and often better-performing pages.

This section explains how to add Ajax behavior to Visualforce pages. It includes the following subsections:

- **Partial page refresh**—Refresh selected elements on the page rather than the whole page.

- **Action as JavaScript function**—Define a JavaScript function that calls an action method on the controller.

- **Action as timed event**—Configure an action method to fire at a predefined time interval.

- **Action as JavaScript event**—Bind a JavaScript event (such as `onclick`) to a controller action method.

- **Indicating action status**—Reflect the status of an asynchronous action on the page.

Partial Page Refresh

Any action component can refresh part of a page using the `reRender` attribute. This attribute contains a comma-separated list of identifiers (the `id` values) of Visualforce view components to be refreshed when the action is completed. The identifiers must be of Visualforce components, not raw HTML elements. If no `reRender` value is provided or the identifiers are invalid, the entire page is refreshed. This is the default behavior of an action component.

Listings 7.1 and 7.2 are a Visualforce page and controller that demonstrate partial page refresh. A `commandButton` is defined to increment an integer value in the controller when clicked, via the `increment` method. The amount to be incremented is passed from the page to controller during the click, using the `param` component. The `increment` method returns a null `PageReference` to remain on the current Visualforce page rather than navigating to a new page. This is a requirement for partial page refreshes.

An `outputPanel` displays the current value of the integer. The `reRender` attribute is set on the `commandButton` to refresh only the `outputPanel` rather than the entire page.

Listing 7.1   **Visualforce Page Using Partial Page Refresh**

```
<apex:page controller="MyPageController7_1">
  <apex:form>
    <apex:commandButton action="{!increment}" value="Increment"
      reRender="result">
      <apex:param assignTo="{!amount}" value="2" />
    </apex:commandButton>
    <apex:outputPanel id="result">The value is: {!value}
    </apex:outputPanel>
  </apex:form>
</apex:page>
```

Listing 7.2   **Visualforce Controller Using Partial Page Refresh**

```
public class MyPageController7_1 {
  public Integer value { get; private set; }
  public Integer amount { get; set; }
  public MyPageController7_1() {
    value = 0;
  }
  public PageReference increment() {
    value += amount;
    return null;
  }
}
```

> **Note**
>
> Not every Visualforce component supports being the target of a `reRender` attribute. If you dis-
> cover a component that is not refreshing properly, enclose it in an `outputPanel` component,
> give the `outputPanel` a unique `id` value, and specify that `id` value in the `reRender` attribute.

Action as JavaScript Function

The action component `actionFunction` allows you to call an Apex method in the controller
as a JavaScript function. This decouples the user interface representation of the action from the
action itself. You've already experienced action components that require a user to click a link
or button to trigger a controller action. With `actionFunction`, you can call an action from
anywhere in your page, including custom JavaScript code.

To use the `actionFunction` component, minimally specify an action to invoke in the `action`
attribute, a JavaScript function name in the `name` attribute, and enclose it in a `form` component. Optionally, you can define arguments on the function by nesting `param` components

inside the `actionFunction` tag. You can also define a JavaScript function to be invoked when the action is complete by using the `oncomplete` attribute.

Listings 7.3 and 7.4 contain page and controller code demonstrating the use of `actionFunction` and partial page refresh. It multiplies a number by two using a controller method exposed as a JavaScript function. The resulting value is displayed on the page using a `pageMessages` component and also refreshed in the call to the JavaScript function. This causes a stateful interaction in which the number is multiplied in a series.

Listing 7.3 **Visualforce Page Using `actionFunction`**

```
<apex:page controller="MyPageController7_3">
  <apex:outputPanel id="result">
    <apex:pageMessages />
    <a onclick="timesTwoFunction('{!value}'); return false;">
      Run
    </a>
  </apex:outputPanel>
  <apex:form>
    <apex:actionFunction name="timesTwoFunction"
      action="{!timesTwo}" reRender="result">
      <apex:param name="arg1" value="" assignTo="{!value}" />
    </apex:actionFunction>
  </apex:form>
</apex:page>
```

Listing 7.4 **Visualforce Controller Using `actionFunction`**

```
public class MyPageController7_3 {
  public Integer value { get; set; }
  public MyPageController7_3() {
    value = 1;
  }
  public PageReference timesTwo() {
    value *= 2;
    addInfo('The result is: ' + value);
    return null;
  }
  private void addInfo(String msg) {
    ApexPages.addMessage(new ApexPages.Message(
      ApexPages.Severity.INFO, msg));
  }
}
```

Action as Timed Event

The `actionPoller` component invokes a method on the controller at a constant time interval. It can be used to perform a long-running operation incrementally, using a series of smaller steps. Another common usage is to perform a repetitive background task such as querying the database for some interesting business event. For example, a user interface designed for project staffers might use an `actionPoller` to automatically refresh a list of available resources once per minute.

To use `actionPoller`, provide a value for the `action` attribute, the controller method to invoke, and enclose it in a `form` component. This usage fires the action method every 60 seconds. Optionally, provide a value for the `interval` attribute, the time in seconds to wait between invocations of the action. This value must be 5 or greater. You can also set the `onsubmit` and `oncomplete` attributes, JavaScript functions to call before the action is invoked and after the action is completed.

Listing 7.5 is a sample page that uses the `actionPoller` along with the controller from Listing 7.4. Rather than requiring the user to click a link to multiply the number by two, the action happens automatically every 5 seconds.

Listing 7.5 **Visualforce Page Using `actionPoller`**

```
<apex:page controller="MyPageController7_3">
  <apex:outputPanel id="result">
    <apex:pageMessages />
  </apex:outputPanel>
  <apex:form>
    <apex:actionPoller interval="5" action="{!timesTwo}"
      reRender="result" />
  </apex:form>
</apex:page>
```

Action as JavaScript Event

To invoke an action on the controller as a result of a JavaScript event, use the `actionSupport` component. This component fires an action whenever the event is detected on the enclosing Visualforce component.

The `actionSupport` component is placed within the body of a Visualforce component that fires the JavaScript event of interest. For example, an `inputField` component renders an HTML input element, so it fires standard JavaScript events such as `onfocus`, `onblur`, `onclick`, and so forth. Placing an `actionSupport` component within the `inputField` component allows it to listen for one of these events and invoke a controller method in response.

To use `actionSupport`, specify the name of the controller method to invoke in its `action` attribute, and a single JavaScript event to listen for in the `event` attribute. By default, `action-Support` overrides the default browser-level handlers for the selected event. To disable this behavior, include a `disableDefault` attribute with the value of `false`. The `onsubmit` and `oncomplete` attributes are also supported to allow pre- or postprocessing of the request using your own JavaScript function.

Reusing the controller code from Listing 7.4, the Visualforce page in Listing 7.6 fires the `timesTwo` action when the text field receives focus. Try it by clicking somewhere else on the page, and then into the text field.

Listing 7.6 **Visualforce Page Using `actionSupport`**

```
<apex:page controller="MyPageController7_3">
  <apex:outputPanel id="result">
    <apex:pageMessages />
  </apex:outputPanel>
  <apex:form>
    <apex:inputText>
      <apex:actionSupport action="{!timesTwo}"
        event="onfocus" reRender="result" />
    </apex:inputText>
  </apex:form>
</apex:page>
```

Indicating Action Status

You've learned how to invoke actions asynchronously. To notify users when asynchronous actions are being performed, use the `actionStatus` component in conjunction with any action component.

The `actionStatus` component can notify users of two states: when an asynchronous action is started and when it is stopped. To use it, place it in the location on your page where you want to show the status message. Use the `startText` and `stopText` attributes to specify the messages to be shown to the user. If you need to pass arguments to the action, use a nested `param` component.

Listing 7.7 provides an example of using the `actionStatus` component, building on the page from Listing 7.6 and the controller from Listing 7.4. When the text field receives focus, the action is fired, and the status message changes to Started. When the action is complete, the status message is set to Stopped.

Listing 7.7 **Visualforce Page Using `actionStatus`**

```
<apex:page controller="MyPageController7_3">
  <apex:outputPanel id="result">
    <apex:pageMessages />
```

```
    </apex:outputPanel>
    <apex:actionStatus id="status"
      startText="Started" stopText="Stopped" />
    <apex:form>
      <apex:inputText>
        <apex:actionSupport action="{!timesTwo}"
          event="onfocus" reRender="result" status="status" />
      </apex:inputText>
    </apex:form>
</apex:page>
```

To display an image or a stylized message, you can use the start and stop facets. Facets are modifiers accepted by some Visualforce components to specify rich values that cannot be contained in XML attributes, such as nested HTML elements. Listing 7.8 is an example of using the facets to mark up the status message with H2 HTML heading elements.

Listing 7.8 **Code Snippet Using `actionStatus` with Facets**

```
<apex:actionStatus id="status">
  <apex:facet name="stop">
    <h2>Stopped</h2>
  </apex:facet>
  <apex:facet name="start">
    <h2>Started</h2>
  </apex:facet>
</apex:actionStatus>
```

To display a dynamic status message, you can write a JavaScript function to modify HTML elements on the page and call it from the actionStatus component. The actionStatus component supports the onStart and onStop attributes, which specify JavaScript functions to be invoked when the associated action is started and stopped. Listing 7.9 provides an example of this usage, using JavaScript to update the HTML content of an outputPanel in response to the actionStatus changing state.

Listing 7.9 **Code Snippet Using `actionStatus` with JavaScript**

```
<apex:page controller="MyPageController7_3">
  <script type="text/javascript">
    function start() {
      document.getElementById("{!$Component.myStatus}").innerHTML = 'Started';
    }
    function stop() {
      document.getElementById("{!$Component.myStatus}").innerHTML = 'Stopped';
    }
  </script>
  <apex:outputPanel id="result">
```

```
    <apex:pageMessages />
  </apex:outputPanel>
  <apex:actionStatus id="status"
    onStart="start();" onStop="stop();" />
  <apex:outputPanel id="myStatus"></apex:outputPanel>
  <apex:form>
    <apex:inputText>
      <apex:actionSupport action="{!timesTwo}"
        event="onfocus" reRender="result" status="status" />
    </apex:inputText>
  </apex:form>
</apex:page>
```

Referencing Visualforce Components from JavaScript

In Listing 7.9, the status of the action invocation is displayed in the element `myStatus` using JavaScript. For the purposes of the example, the element is an `outputPanel` Visualforce component rather than a simple `div` tag. This illustrates an important aspect of using JavaScript in Visualforce pages.

Each Visualforce component is assigned a unique identifier, set in its `id` attribute. When you override this `id` attribute and provide your own value, Visualforce fully qualifies it by affixing the identifiers of any containers included between your component and the root `page` component.

If your JavaScript code attempts to reference a Visualforce component using the raw identifier as it appears in the HTML, it will fail to locate it. Instead, use `{!$Component.id}`, where `id` is the identifier you set on your Visualforce component. When the page is rendered, Visualforce reads this token and replaces it with the fully qualified value of the identifier. If the identifier cannot be found, the token is replaced with an empty string.

If your component is contained within a `form` component, you must provide the form with an `id` value as well and include the form identifier in the component reference. For example, if the form identifier is `myForm` and the component you want to obtain a reference to is `myText`, the usage is `{!$Component.myForm:myText}`.

> **Tip**
> Use the View Source feature of your Web browser or a plug-in such as Firebug to debug component identifier problems.

Modular Visualforce

Visualforce pages that are modular, composed of a number of smaller, reusable building blocks, improve usability by providing consistent appearance and behavior. They are also easier to develop and maintain. Common functionality is defined once in a single place rather than repeated in multiple pages.

Visualforce provides several features you can use to create modular, highly maintainable pages:

- **Static resources**—Reusable images, scripts, stylesheets, and other static content can be stored in static resources, available for embedding in all Visualforce pages in the Force.com organization.

- **Inclusion**—The contents of one Visualforce page can be included in another page. A common use for this is page headers and footers.

- **Composition**—Composition allows one Visualforce page to serve as a template for another. The template specifies the static and dynamic portions of a page. Use the template to inject dynamic content while maintaining a consistent page layout and structure.

- **Custom Visualforce components**—Visualforce provides a library of standard components such as `pageBlock` and `dataTable`, but also allows you to define your own custom components, reusable in any page.

Static Resources

Static resources are containers for content used in Visualforce pages that does not change. Examples of unchanging content include images, stylesheets, and JavaScript files. Although any service that allows storage of URL-accessible data can perform a similar role, static resources have the benefit of being tightly integrated with the Visualforce page. Their names are validated when the page is compiled, preventing the creation of a page that refers to an invalid static resource. They are also inaccessible to anonymous public Internet users. Users not authenticated to your Salesforce organization cannot load your static resources unless you explicitly allow it using Force.com Sites.

A static resource can be a single file or a zip archive consisting of many files. The maximum size of a single static resource is 5MB, and no more than 250MB of static resources can be defined in any single Force.com organization.

To create a new static resource, follow these steps:

1. In the App Setup area, click Develop, Static Resources.

2. Click the New button to add a new static resource.

3. Enter a name for the static resource. The name cannot contain spaces or other nonalphanumeric characters, must begin with a letter, and must be unique. The name is used to refer to the static resource in Visualforce pages.

4. Specify an optional description to explain the purpose of this static resource to other users.

5. Click the Browse button to find a file in your file system to provide the content for the static resource.

6. Leave the Cache Control setting at its default value, Private. This setting is discussed later in the "Introduction to Force.com Sites" subsection.

7. Click the Save button to complete the static resource definition.

If your static resource contains a single file, refer to it in your Visualforce page using the syntax `{!$Resource.name}`, where `name` is the name of the static resource to include.

The syntax is different for referring to a single file within a static resource that is a zip archive. Use `{!URLFOR($Resource.name, 'path/tofile')}`, where `name` is the name of the static resource, and `path/tofile` is the full path to the desired file.

Inclusion

A simple way to create modular Visualforce pages is to use the `include` component. It embeds the content of the included page in the current page. The `pageName` attribute specifies the name of the Visualforce page to include. The included page must be a Visualforce page. You cannot include arbitrary URLs.

Listing 7.10 provides an example of using the `include` component. It embeds the page named SkillsMatrix between two horizontal rules.

Listing 7.10 **Visualforce Page Using `include`**

```
<apex:page>
  <hr />
  <apex:include pageName="SkillsMatrix" />
  <hr />
</apex:page>
```

When a single Visualforce page ends up containing multiple controllers due to the `include` component, controllers are isolated from each other and operate independently. The controller of the included page does not have access to the state of the controller on the parent page, and vice versa. But pages are included inline, so JavaScript functions and DOM references can be made across included pages without security restrictions.

> **Caution**
>
> Be careful when using `messages` and `pageMessages` components in pages that are to be included in other pages. If the included page and parent page both supply one of these components, the same page messages will be rendered in multiple locations.

Composition

Composition is a powerful way to create modular Visualforce pages. It allows a Visualforce page to be defined as a template. The template can contain static content and placeholders for content that can be overridden by an implementing page. This enforces a standard structure for the pages without requiring Visualforce developers to remember a sequence of `include` components. It also places more control over the appearance of many pages within the scope of a single page (the template) for easier maintenance.

In the template page, the `insert` component is used to define a named area that can be over-ridden by a page implementing the template. The implementing page uses the `composition` component to set the name of the page to serve as its template. It then provides content for the named areas of the template using the `define` component.

For example, a template might consist of a header, body, and footer, with horizontal rules between each. Listing 7.11 defines this template page, named `MyPage7_11`. Note that the header area includes its own default content. This optional content is rendered in the event that content is not provided by an implementing page.

Listing 7.11 **Visualforce Page as Template**

```
<apex:page>
  <apex:insert name="header">
    <h1>Header</h1>
  </apex:insert>
  <hr /><apex:insert name="body" />
  <hr /><apex:insert name="footer">
    Inheriting the footer content
  </apex:insert>
</apex:page>
```

The template is not interesting to render by itself, but in Listing 7.12 it's implemented using the `composition` component. The `template` attribute specifies the template defined in Listing 7.11, which should be named `MyPage7_11` for this example to work properly. The three dynamic areas are merged into the template to result in the final rendered output. The header area is provided, so it overrides the content defined by the template. The footer is inherited from the template.

Listing 7.12 **Visualforce Page Using Template**

```
<apex:page>
  <apex:composition template="MyPage7_11">
    <apex:define name="header">
      Overriding the header content
    </apex:define>
    <apex:define name="body">
      This is the body content
    </apex:define>
  </apex:composition>
</apex:page>
```

Composition works with multiple controllers identically to the `include` component. They run independently of each other, but all content is rendered in the same page.

Custom Visualforce Components

Custom components allow you to build a library of reusable user interface elements, encapsulating behavior and appearance while integrating with the data on the page and in the controller using the standard expression language. With custom components, all the functionality of standard components such as `pageBlock` and `inputField` is available to you to define from scratch using Visualforce and Apex code.

Custom components can be used to hide the implementation details of client-side technology like JavaScript. For example, a component can wrap a JavaScript user interface library such as Sencha's Ext JS, freeing Visualforce page developers from the details of integrating Ext JS code into their pages. Custom components can also serve as full-blown pages themselves, reading and writing in the Force.com database through standard or custom controllers.

Defining a Custom Component

To create a new component, select File, New, Visualforce Component in the Force.com IDE. Or, using the Web browser, navigate to App Setup and click Develop, Components.

Custom components are defined with `component` as the root-level element rather than the familiar `page`. Following the `component` tag is an optional set of `attribute` components specifying the names and types of variables that can be shared between the page and the component. Supported types are primitives, standard and custom database objects, one-dimensional arrays, and custom Apex classes. Attributes can be declared as `required`, meaning that a page using the component must provide a value or it fails to compile. Attributes can also be assigned to member variables in a controller using the `assignTo` attribute.

The remainder of the component definition is identical to a standard Visualforce page, containing a combination of JavaScript, CSS, HTML elements, and standard components, as well as other custom components.

Listing 7.13 provides an example of a component for showing an address on a Google Map.

Listing 7.13 **Custom Visualforce Component to Render Google Map**

```
<apex:component >
  <apex:attribute name="address" type="string" required="true"
    description="Address to show on the Google map" />
  <apex:includeScript
    value="https://maps.googleapis.com/maps/api/js?sensor=false" />
  <script>
  var geocoder;
  var map;
  function init() {
```

```
  geocoder = new google.maps.Geocoder();
  var latlng = new google.maps.LatLng(-34.397, 150.644);
  var mapOptions = {
    zoom: 17,
    center: latlng,
    mapTypeId: google.maps.MapTypeId.ROADMAP
  }
  map = new google.maps.Map(document.getElementById("map-canvas"),
    mapOptions);
}

function renderAddress(address) {
  geocoder.geocode( { 'address': address },
  function(results, status) {
    if (status == google.maps.GeocoderStatus.OK) {
      map.setCenter(results[0].geometry.location);
      var marker = new google.maps.Marker({
          map: map,
          position: results[0].geometry.location
      });
    } else {
      alert("Geocode failed: " + status);
    }
  });
}
var previousOnload = window.onload;
window.onload = function() {
if (previousOnload) {
  previousOnload();
}
init();
renderAddress('{!address}');
}
</script>
<div id="map-canvas" style="width: 320px; height: 480px;"></div>
</apex:component>
```

Using a Custom Component

Using a custom component in a page is much like using a standard component. The difference is that instead of prefacing the component with the apex namespace, you use c. Listing 7.14 shows an example of using the custom component defined in Listing 7.13 to render a Google Map for an address. It references the GoogleMap component, followed by a value for its required address attribute containing the street address to render on the map. In this example, the attribute value is hard-coded into the page, but this is not the only way to provide an attribute value. Like standard components, attribute values can include expression language, enabling them to share data with the controller.

Listing 7.14   **Visualforce Page Using Custom Component**

```
<apex:page>
<c:GoogleMap address="1 market st. san francisco, ca" />
</apex:page>
```

Dynamic Visualforce

Normally when a user visits a Visualforce page, Force.com constructs HTML or other content from the Visualforce components and their bindings to the controller. In contrast, dynamic Visualforce features allow the definition of the page itself, both its components and their bindings to the controller, to be determined at runtime, outside of the page. These features are most often used by software vendors who deliver Force.com applications on the Salesforce AppExchange, where the same application code must run within multiple, distinct customer organizations and adapt itself accordingly.

This section covers dynamic Visualforce features in more detail in the following subsections:

- **Dynamic field references**—Dynamic field references allow the fields displayed in a Visualforce page to be injected into the page when viewed by a user. They can be provided by Apex code in the page controller or by Field Sets, a type of declarative metadata configurable without code.

- **Component generation**—Visualforce pages can be constructed dynamically in Apex code. This can be essential for certain specialized user interfaces, but come with trade-offs not present with static pages.

Dynamic Field References

Dynamic field references are designed for situations in which you need to be flexible about which field to render. Ordinary field references are found in Visualforce components and determine their relationship to the controller. For example, an `outputText` component with content `{!project.Name}` renders the `Name` field of the object named `project` in the controller. The equivalent dynamic field reference is `{!project[field]}`, where *field* is a String value containing the name of the field to display.

The data referenced by a dynamic field reference must be available at runtime or an error will occur. If you're using a standard controller, call the method `addFields` to notify the controller about new fields if possible, and it will take care of retrieving the data. For custom controllers, controller extensions, or queries involving related objects, build a dynamic SOQL query string and execute it with `Database.query`.

Listings 7.15 and 7.16 provide the Visualforce controller and page code for a simple example of dynamic field references. The Visualforce page renders a simple XML-encoded collection of Project records, embedded in HTML. The determination of which fields to display from each Project record is determined dynamically inside the controller. The fields are rendered in the page using two nested `repeat` components. The outer `repeat` iterates over an array of Project records returned by the controller. The inner `repeat` cycles through each field name from the controller, combining it with the record reference to obtain the value of that field for the current record.

Listing 7.15   **Visualforce Controller Using Dynamic Field References**

```
public class MyPageController7_16 {
  public List<String> fields { get; set; }
  public List<Project__c> records { get; set; }
  public MyPageController7_16() {
    fields = new String[] { 'Id', 'Name', 'CreatedDate' };
    records = [ SELECT Name, CreatedDate FROM Project__c ];
  }
}
```

Listing 7.16   **Visualforce Page Using Dynamic Field References**

```
<apex:page controller="MyPageController7_16">
<pre>
&lt;projects&gt;
  <apex:repeat value="{!records}" var="record">
  &lt;project&gt;
    <apex:repeat value="{!fields}" var="field">
    &lt;{!field}&gt;{!record[field]}&lt;/{!field}&gt;
    </apex:repeat>
  &lt;/project&gt;
  </apex:repeat>
&lt;/projects&gt;
</pre>
</apex:page>
```

Using Field Sets

Imagine the `fields` variable in Listing 7.15, which contains the list of field names to display on the Visualforce page, must be maintained by a nondeveloper. You could create a custom object to store the fields in the database and build a Visualforce user interface to manage them. Or you could use field sets and avoid all of that work.

A field set is a user-defined ordered list of fields on an object that can be referenced from Visualforce or Apex. A field set is editable using an administrative user interface built in to Force.com, leaving the code that uses it unchanged. For custom objects, go to the App Setup area; click Create, Objects; select the object; and find its Field Sets section. Standard objects are also in the App Setup area under Customize.

Once a field set is created, it can be referenced in a Visualforce component with the syntax `{!$ObjectType.ObjectName.FieldSets.FieldSetName}`, where `ObjectName` is the name of the standard or custom object that the field set is defined on, and `FieldSetName` is the name of the field set.

The fields of a field set are automatically loaded by the standard controller. For custom controllers, add accessors for the fields and dynamically construct SOQL from the field set to ensure the data is available to the page.

Component Generation

Dynamic field references are useful when you do not know what fields to display. Component generation comes into play when you do not know what object to render. It allows the construction of a Visualforce page from Apex code.

To start using component generation, add one or more `dynamicComponent` elements to your Visualforce page. This serves as the container into which the generated components are injected. The `dynamicComponent` is bound to a controller method, specified in the `componentValue` attribute, that must return an instance of `Component.Apex.*` to be rendered.

Listings 7.17 and 7.18 show a controller and page that leverage component generation to display a `detail` component bound to the user's selection of one of three object types. A dynamic SOQL statement is generated using the list of accessible fields from the selected object type to retrieve the most recently modified record. The generated `detail` component is bound to its result.

Listing 7.17   **Visualforce Controller Using Dynamic Components**

```
public class MyPageController7_18 {
  public SObject record { get; set; }
  public String selectedObject { get; set; }
  public List<SelectOption> getAvailableObjects() {
    List<SelectOption> options = new List<SelectOption>();
    options.add(new SelectOption('Project__c', 'Project'));
    options.add(new SelectOption('Timecard__c', 'Timecard'));
    options.add(new SelectOption('Contact', 'Contact'));
    return options;
  }
  public PageReference refresh() {
    Schema.SObjectType targetType =
      Schema.getGlobalDescribe().get(selectedObject);
    Map<String, Schema.SobjectField> fields =
      targetType.getDescribe().fields.getMap();
    List<String> queryFields = new List<String>();
```

```
        for (String s : fields.keySet()) {
            if (fields.get(s).getDescribe().isAccessible()) {
                queryFields.add(s);
            }
        }
        String soql = 'SELECT ';
        for (String s : queryFields) {
            soql += s + ', ';
        }
        soql = soql.substring(0, soql.length() - 2);
        soql += ' FROM ' + selectedObject;
        soql += ' ORDER BY LastModifiedDate DESC LIMIT 1';
        try {
            record = Database.query(soql);
        } catch (QueryException e) {}
        return null;
    }
    public Component.Apex.Detail getComponent() {
        Component.Apex.Detail result =
            new Component.Apex.Detail();
        result.expressions.subject = '{!record.Id}';
        result.title = false;
        result.relatedList = false;
        return result;
    }
}
```

Listing 7.18 **Visualforce Page Using Dynamic Components**

```
<apex:page controller="MyPageController7_18">
  <apex:form >
    <apex:selectList value="{!selectedObject}" size="1">
      <apex:selectOptions value="{!availableObjects}"/>
    </apex:selectList>
    <apex:commandButton value="Refresh" action="{!refresh}" />
  </apex:form>
  <apex:dynamicComponent componentValue="{!component}"/>
</apex:page>
```

> **Note**
>
> Component generation is not a viable substitute for standard static Visualforce pages. Its use should be strictly limited to user interfaces that adapt to user actions in ways that can't be coded in static markup.

Single-Page Applications in Force.com

A single-page application is an application that runs almost entirely within the Web browser. In contrast, older Web application architectures generate the appearance and behavior of Web pages primarily on the server. Single-page applications tend to be more interactive and responsive than Web applications that rely on full or even partial page refreshes from the server.

Single-page applications can be challenging to build as they are heavily reliant on client-side JavaScript code. Many JavaScript frameworks have sprouted up to assist developers. They address the difficulties in implementing complex user interfaces by separating the concerns of Web user interfaces using Model-View-View Model (MVVM) or Model-View-Controller (MVC) patterns. Some examples of frameworks to support single-page application development are Backbone.js, Knockout.js, AngularJS, and Ember.js.

At first glance, this seems to replace much of Visualforce. Although it does replace the Web-rendering portions of Visualforce with its own data binding and templating technologies, Visualforce continues to provide the glue that makes everything work smoothly. For example, it loads the single-page application code, making communication between the user's Web browser and Force.com secure and authenticated without additional development effort. The resulting blend of Force.com and JavaScript performs better than Visualforce for many types of user interfaces, minimizes proprietary code, and keeps back-end dependencies clear and modular to maximize testability.

JavaScript Remoting

JavaScript remoting allows a controller method to be invoked directly from JavaScript with no Visualforce components necessary. Instead, you annotate the controller method with `@RemoteAction` and write a small amount of JavaScript to call it.

Although similar in function to JavaScript remoting, the `actionFunction` Visualforce component differs in some significant ways. The `actionFunction` component is designed for use in a Visualforce page with other native Visualforce components. Like most Visualforce components, it uses a form to create a stateful interaction between the controller and the page. This is not the case with remoting, which makes it a bit more responsive as a result. Remoting is also asynchronous, while the `actionFunction` component is synchronous.

JavaScript remoting is particularly helpful in the development of single-page applications on Force.com. With JavaScript remoting, the focus of the Force.com platform shifts to the back end. It serves the raw resources to power the user interface, both static files and dynamic data via controller method invocations. Once loaded, the user interface is rendered entirely in JavaScript within the browser, with callouts made to the Apex controller as needed for its data services.

Force.com with AngularJS

AngularJS is a popular open source Web development framework located at http://angularjs.org. It is a powerful tool for using the MVVM pattern, or Model-View-Whatever (MVW) as Google prefers it, in your Web application. For example, you can take advantage of its bidirectional data binding to tie the application's model to its view, making Angular responsible for keeping them in lockstep at all times. This type of tight data binding provides users an experience free of Refresh and Save buttons and confusing mismatches between the model and view.

The demonstration page shown in Figure 7.1 is adapted from steps 0 through 5 of the Angular tutorial available at http://docs.angularjs.org/tutorial. It retrieves a list of projects from the Force.com database and allows the user to order them by name or date created, and search the list by name.

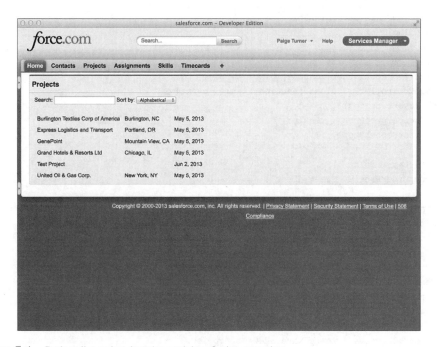

Figure 7.1   Project list using Angular and JavaScript remoting

An implementation of the Visualforce controller and page code for the Angular-powered project list can be found in Listings 7.19 and 7.20. The subsections that follow provide a code walk-through of the Angular-specific aspects of Listing 7.20.

Listing 7.19   **Visualforce Controller Using** `RemoteAction`

```
public with sharing class MyPageController7_20 {
  @RemoteAction
  public static List<Project__c> load() {
    return [SELECT Name, Location__c, CreatedDate
      FROM Project__c ];
  }
}
```

Listing 7.20   **Visualforce Page Using Angular**

```
<apex:page controller="MyPageController7_20">
<style>
.toolbar { margin-bottom: 20px; }
td { padding: 5px; }
</style>
<script>
function ProjectListCtrl($scope, $rootScope) {
  MyPageController7_20.load(function(result, event) {
    if (event.status) {
      $scope.projects = result;
      $rootScope.$apply();
    }
  }, { escape: false });
  $scope.orderProp = 'CreatedDate';
}
</script>
<apex:pageBlock tabStyle="Project__c" title="Projects">
<apex:outputPanel html-ng-app=""
  html-ng-controller="ProjectListCtrl">
  <div class="toolbar">
    Search: <input ng-model="query" />
    Sort by:
    <select ng-model="orderProp">
      <option value="Name">Alphabetical</option>
      <option value="CreatedDate">Newest</option>
    </select>
  </div>
  <table>
    <tr ng-repeat="project in projects
      | filter:query | orderBy:orderProp">
      <td>
        <apex:outputText value="{{project.Name}}" />
      </td>
      <td>
        <apex:outputText value="{{project.Location__c}}" />
```

```
    </td>
    <td>
      <apex:outputText value="{{project.CreatedDate
        | date}}" />
    </td>
  </tr>
  </table>
</apex:outputPanel>
</apex:pageBlock>
  <script src="//ajax.googleapis.com/ajax/
➥libs/angularjs/1.0.7/angular.min.js">
  </script>
</apex:page>
```

Angular Controller

The Angular controller is responsible for the business logic of a single view. In Listing 7.20, the Angular controller is named `ProjectListCtrl` and specified in an in-line `script` tag. It invokes the remote action `load` on the Visualforce controller with the option `escape: false`. This instructs it to forgo HTML entity encoding of the remote action's response. When the remote action is completed, the resulting array of projects is provided to Angular, and all its bound user interface elements are notified using the `$apply()` method.

Angular Template

Much like a Visualforce page, an Angular template brings the Angular controller and model together into a rendered Web page. It contains HTML, CSS, and Angular-specific markup.

Listing 7.20 contains a single Angular template within a Visualforce `outputPanel` component. Important aspects of the template are described in the following list:

- The `outputPanel` contains custom HTML attributes (prefaced with `html-` to make them acceptable to Visualforce) to specify the Angular controller and `ng-app` to register the DOM with Angular. In Visualforce, this sort of control over the HTML output is only possible in an `outputPanel`.

- The two HTML input fields are bound to the controller using the `ng-model` attribute.

- The table row is repeated for each element in the `projects` model, filtered by the input query and ordered by the drop-down selection.

- Markup (in double curly brace notation) is used to output elements of the model within `outputText` components.

- A standard HTML script tag includes version 1.0.7 of Angular from Google. This could just as well be loaded from a Force.com static resource or a Visualforce component with the script in-line.

Introduction to Force.com Sites

Sites is a feature of Force.com that enables public access to your Visualforce pages. A site is a collection of ordinary Visualforce pages and access control settings assigned to a unique base URL. You can define one or many sites within a Force.com organization. Sites can be individually brought up or down by your organization's system administrator.

This section divides the discussion of Force.com Sites into four parts, summarized next:

1. **Enabling and creating a site**—Turn on the Force.com Sites feature and create your first site.

2. **Security configuration**—Configure the privileges granted to the anonymous user of your site.

3. **Adding pages to a site**—Select Visualforce pages that are accessible within a site.

4. **Authenticating users**—Blend public and private pages by integrating a site with Customer Portal.

Enabling and Creating a Site

To enable Force.com Sites for the first time in your organization, go to the App Setup area and click Develop, Sites. You should see the screen shown in Figure 7.2.

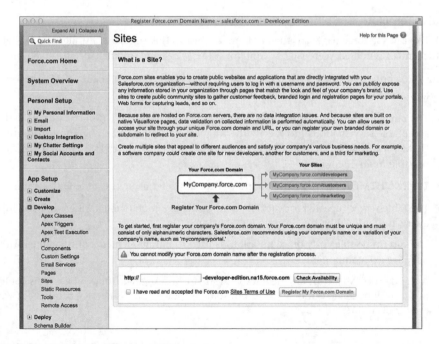

Figure 7.2   Enabling the Force.com Sites feature

You must pick a Force.com domain name to continue. A domain name provides a unique, root address for all of your sites. You can remap this address to your own brand-name address (not Force.com) by configuring a CNAME alias on your domain hosting provider.

Enter your domain name, select the box to indicate that you've read the terms of use, and click the Check Availability button. After your domain name has been accepted, you can define your first site. Adding a site also creates a number of sample components, pages, and controllers in your organization.

To create a site, go to the App Setup area; click Develop, Sites; then click the New button. You should see a page like Figure 7.3. Provide a label and name for the site, such as www. The label is shown in the list of sites and clicking on it allows you to edit the site's properties. Set the Active Site Home Page setting to UnderConstruction. This is a standard placeholder page provided with Force.com to let visitors know that the site is not available yet.

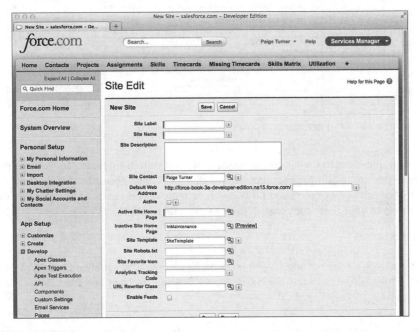

Figure 7.3   Creating a new site

After your first site is defined, the main Sites page should look as shown in Figure 7.4.

Security Configuration

When a new site is created, a corresponding profile is also created to manage the privileges of the guest user. The guest user is a special type of Salesforce.com license that represents the anonymous user of your site.

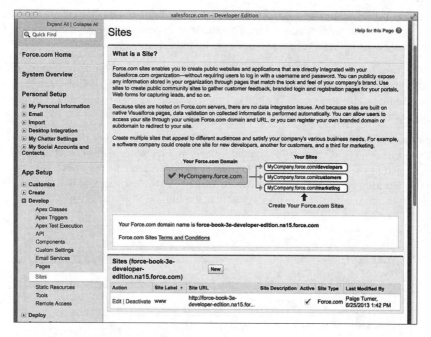

Figure 7.4   Sites main page

The guest profile for each site is configured using the native user interface. To view the profile, navigate to the Site Details page for the site and click the Public Access Settings button. Configure the privileges of the guest profile with extreme caution because mistakes can expose sensitive data in your Force.com organization to the entire world.

> **Note**
>
> The guest profile does not appear with other profiles in the Administration Setup area (Manage Users, Profiles). You must use the Public Access Settings button on the Sites Detail page to reach it.

If a page in a site uses static resources, make sure that they can be accessed from the guest profile. Go to each static resource and set its Cache Control to Public.

Adding Pages to a Site

A site starts off with a series of system-defined pages such as Exception and FileNotFound. These pages are shown to users in the event of errors in the site. You can redefine them by simply editing them.

You can also add your own custom pages to the site. To add pages, click the Edit button in the Site Visualforce Pages section. Select one or more pages from the list on the left and click the Add button to move them to the list of Enabled Visualforce Pages. Click Save when you're done.

The URL of your pages is the default Web address of the site followed by the name of the page. For example, in Figure 7.5, the default Web address is https://force-book-3e-developer-edition. na15.force.com. If a page named MyPage is added to the site, users can access it at https:// force-book-3e-developer-edition.na15.force.com/MyPage.

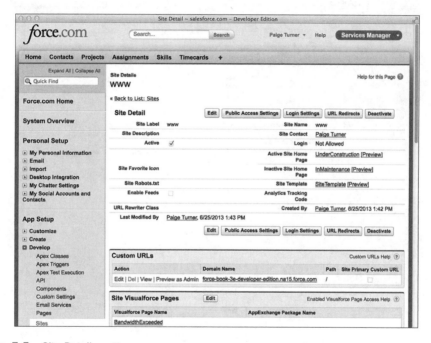

Figure 7.5   Site Details page

> **Note**
>
> A site must be activated before any pages in it are accessible. To activate a site, select its Active check box in the Site Details page or click the Activate link on the main Sites page.

Authenticating Users

Anonymous users can be converted to named, authenticated users through the Customer Portal, or portal for short. A portal allows you to extend Force.com to your partners and customers without requiring full user accounts for each of them. It is tightly integrated with Force.com Sites.

Enable portal integration by clicking the Login Settings button on the Site Details page. In the Login Settings section, click the Edit button and select an existing portal from the drop-down list, and then click the Save button. Figure 7.6 shows a site enabled to log in to the portal named Customer Portal.

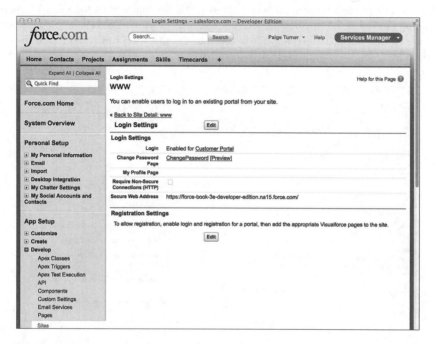

Figure 7.6   Login Settings page

> **Note**
>
> If no portals are listed, you must configure one that is login enabled. Go to the App Setup area and click Customize, Customer Portal, Settings. Setting up a portal is not within the scope of this book, so refer to the online documentation for more information.

Sample Application: Enhanced Skills Matrix

This section builds on the Services Manager's Skills Matrix feature developed in Chapter 6, "User Interfaces." Users of the Skills Matrix feature have requested the ability to compare a consultant's skills with those of other consultants without navigating to a new page. They would like to see the ratings of other consultants in the same skill visually layered atop the existing Skills Matrix user interface, as shown in Figure 7.7.

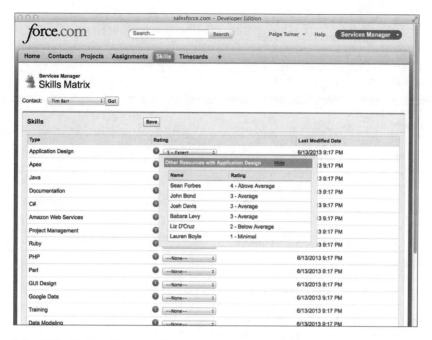

Figure 7.7   Skills Matrix with comparison overlay

The following technologies from this chapter are used in the development of the feature:

- **JavaScript integration**—jQuery UI (a free, open source JavaScript and CSS library for Web applications) is integrated to provide an easing effect, fading in and out the list of other resources and their skill ratings. jQuery UI is available at http://jqueryui.com.

- **Custom Visualforce components**—The overlay containing the other consultants' skills is encapsulated in its own custom Visualforce component and controller.

- **actionSupport component**—This component is used to show and hide the skills comparison overlay when the user hovers over an informational icon.

Begin by developing a custom component for retrieving and rendering a list of skill ratings and consultants. The input to this component is a skill type and a resource identifier of the currently selected consultant. The skill type is the name of a proficiency that consultants are measured on, a picklist value from Skill__c.Type__c, such as Java or Apex. The resource identifier is used to exclude the current consultant from the list because his or her skill ratings are already shown on the Skills Matrix user interface.

Listing 7.21 provides a sample implementation of the controller to support the requirements, and Listing 7.22 shows the custom component that uses it.

Listing 7.21 **CompareSkillsController**

```
public class CompareSkillsController {
  public String contact { get; set; }
  public String skill { get; set; }
  public List<Skill__c> getData() {
    return [ SELECT Contact__r.Name, Type__c, Rating__c
      FROM Skill__c
      WHERE Type__c = :skill
        AND Rating__c NOT IN ('', '0 - None') AND
        Contact__c != :contact
      ORDER BY Rating__c DESC ];
  }
}
```

Listing 7.22 **CompareSkillsComponent**

```
<apex:component controller="CompareSkillsController">
  <apex:attribute name="skillType" description="Type of skill"
    type="String" required="true" assignTo="{!skill}" />
  <apex:attribute name="contactId"
    description="Id of contact to compare with"
    type="String" required="true" assignTo="{!contact}" />
  <apex:pageBlock >
    <apex:pageBlockSection collapsible="false" columns="1">
      <apex:facet name="header">
        Other Resources with {!skillType}
        <span style="padding-left: 30px;">
          <a onclick="hideOverlay(); return false;"
          href="" style="text-decoration: underline;">Hide</a>
        </span>
      </apex:facet>
      <apex:pageBlockTable value="{!data}" var="item">
        <apex:column value="{!item.Contact__r.Name}" />
        <apex:column value="{!item.Rating__c}" />
      </apex:pageBlockTable>
    </apex:pageBlockSection>
  </apex:pageBlock>
</apex:component>
```

To incorporate this component into the Skills Matrix page, perform the following steps:

1. Add the code shown in Listing 7.23 to the bottom of the SkillsMatrixController class. The new method and property are used to refresh the skills comparison component.

Listing 7.23 **Adding Component Support to the Skills Matrix Controller**

```
public PageReference refreshCompareSkills() {
  return null;
}
public String selectedSkillType { get; set; }
```

2. Edit the Skills Matrix page to add `sidebar="false"` to the `apex:page` component. This frees up extra horizontal screen real estate that is used to display the skills comparison overlay. Also add the CSS in Listing 7.24 to the `style` tag.

Listing 7.24 **Adding Component CSS to the Skills Matrix Page**

```
.compare-skills {
  position: absolute;
  width: 400px; height: 250px;
  display: none;
}
```

3. Also on the Skills Matrix page, insert the code in Listing 7.25 after the closing tag of the form component. It adds an `outputPanel` containing the `CompareSkillsComponent`, rendered as an overlay with a fading effect from jQuery UI in the `showOverlay` JavaScript function.

Listing 7.25 **Adding `CompareSkillsComponent` to the Skills Matrix Page**

```
<apex:outputPanel id="compareSkills" styleClass="compare-skills">
  <c:CompareSkillsComponent skillType="{!selectedSkillType}"
    contactId="{!selectedContactId}" />
</apex:outputPanel>
<script src="//ajax.googleapis.com/ajax/libs
➥/jquery/1.10.1/jquery.min.js"></script>
<script src="//ajax.googleapis.com/ajax/libs
➥/jqueryui/1.10.3/jquery-ui.min.js"></script>
<script>
function showOverlay(e) {
  $('.compare-skills').css('top', e.layerY)
    .css('left', e.layerX).fadeIn();
}
function hideOverlay() {
  $('.compare-skills').fadeOut();
}
</script>
```

4. For the final step, insert the code given in Listing 7.26 to the Skills Matrix page, immediately following the opening tag of the column component containing the

skill rating (`headerValue="Rating"`). It adds an informational icon beside each skill. Hovering over this icon displays the overlay containing the skills comparison.

Listing 7.26   **Adding `actionSupport` to the Skills Matrix Page**

```
<apex:image value="/img/msg_icons/info16.png"
  style="margin-top: 2px; margin-right: 10px;">
  <apex:actionSupport event="onmouseover"
    action="{!refreshCompareSkills}" rerender="compareSkills"
    oncomplete="showOverlay(event);" onsubmit="hideOverlay();">
    <apex:param name="p1" value="{!skill.Type__c}"
    assignTo="{!selectedSkillType}" />
  </apex:actionSupport>
</apex:image>
```

Summary

In this chapter, you've seen some of the ways Visualforce can produce effective user interfaces, from action components that provide Ajax behavior to the integration of open source Web application technologies such as JQuery. Before switching gears in the next chapter, take a moment to review these key points:

- Stick with standard and custom Visualforce components wherever possible to keep your user interface running smoothly with the rest of Force.com today and in future releases.

- Strive to adopt the many features of Visualforce that foster modularity, such as composition and custom components, rather than copying and pasting code from page to page.

- You can use Visualforce to create public-facing Web pages through Force.com Sites. Sites are simply a series of configuration settings that enable a guest profile to access a set of pages, extending your existing investment in Visualforce.

8

Mobile User Interfaces

Mobile applications are subject to design constraints including processing power, reduced screen size, and limited or unreliable network connectivity. Addressing these constraints while still delivering functional applications is the goal of numerous technology platforms, development techniques, and dedicated technical books. There are endless methods for building mobile applications, all of them equally valid depending on the details of the device, application, and needs of the user.

Salesforce and the Force.com platform support the latest best practices and technology platforms used to develop mobile applications, extending them with dedicated toolkits and hooks in the Force.com platform. This chapter provides exposure to the common approaches to building mobile applications and dives deeper on one specific approach, the mobile Web (also referred to as HTML5) application. It is organized into the following sections:

- *Overview of Salesforce mobile technology—Get familiar with how Salesforce supports mobile devices in terms of its own applications and custom applications.*

- *Getting started with mobile Web applications—Walk through the technology components and choices for building mobile Web applications using Force.com.*

- *Sample application—Create a phone and tablet-friendly timecard entry feature for the Services Manager sample application.*

> Note
> The code listings in this chapter are available in a GitHub Gist at http://goo.gl/SVU7RT.

Overview of Salesforce Mobile Technology

Mobile devices are by definition always on the go, exposed to vagaries of battery life and network connectivity as well as the physical size constraints of displays and input devices. The formidable technical challenge of these problems and the huge demand for mobile devices have driven rapid innovation. From this innovation comes a proliferation of operating systems, user interface styles, development frameworks, and architectural techniques, all vying for developer attention.

Every significant technology vendor has framed mobile technology in its own terms. Salesforce is no exception. Salesforce offers its own mobile philosophy and supporting technologies, both in the application and platform space. These are discussed in this section, divided into two parts:

- **Salesforce applications**—There are three actively supported mobile applications from Salesforce, each with its own unique feature set.

- **Custom applications**—Salesforce advocates three distinct approaches to mobile application development, providing tools and frameworks to support them.

Salesforce Applications

Although it is possible to use Salesforce's standard Web user interface from a browser-equipped mobile device, it has significant drawbacks. The desktop-centric user interface is cumbersome on a smaller screen, requiring lots of zooming and panning to find and click anything. The performance is sluggish due to the large amount of information, media, and code on each page. And if network connectivity is lost, it can also mean the loss of functionality and work in progress.

To improve the experience for mobile users, Salesforce offers three applications specifically designed for mobile phones and tablets:

- **Salesforce Classic**—This is the original Salesforce mobile application. It is geared toward users who need offline access to data. Administrators can select data to synchronize with the mobile device by user or profile, and remotely delete the data at any point. By default, the standard Sales and Service Cloud application data is synchronized with the device, including contacts, accounts, and opportunities.

- **Salesforce Touch**—Salesforce Touch can be thought of as a reskinned subset of the Salesforce Web application, designed for devices that rely on touch input rather than a keyboard and mouse. All data remains on the Salesforce servers, not on the mobile device. Standard and custom object tabs are available, with limited record creation and editing functionality.

- **Chatter Mobile**—Chatter Mobile is focused on collaboration. You can post and comment on feeds, create and edit records, view and add files, participate in groups, and view dashboards and user profiles.

Many independent software vendors have released applications that address the Salesforce market. Some are tailored for a particular workflow, such as sales or service. Others are neutral, adopting the tabs and layouts from your Salesforce organization and providing generic data management in a mobile form factor. Run a search on your mobile device's application marketplace to learn more.

Custom Applications

There are many ways to develop custom mobile applications that leverage the Force.com platform. Salesforce has assembled tools and techniques for each of the three distinct approaches to mobile development, listed here:

- **Native applications**—Native applications have unrestricted access to all of the features of the mobile device. This power can be used to deliver the best possible user experience, but typically comes with a high development cost, especially if an application must be supported on multiple mobile vendors' devices.

- **Mobile Web applications**—On the opposite end of the spectrum, mobile Web applications run inside the mobile device's Web browser based on HTML5. They do not have access to the full set of device capabilities, but with this compromise comes advantages in terms of ease of development and distribution.

- **Hybrid applications**—Hybrid applications are mobile Web applications deployed inside a native application that serves as a "container." The most notable benefits are access to native device features and the ability to promote and distribute the application on device-specific marketplaces.

The Salesforce Mobile Software Development Kit (SDK) provides open source technology to aid in the development of all three types of custom mobile applications. Download it from the following location:

- **iOS**—https://github.com/forcedotcom/SalesforceMobileSDK-iOS

- **Android**—https://github.com/forcedotcom/SalesforceMobileSDK-Android

Note

The Salesforce Mobile SDK page at http://wiki.developerforce.com/page/Mobile_SDK is an excellent starting point for diving deeper into Salesforce's mobile development technology.

Native Applications

Native applications are purpose-built for each device platform. For example, a native mobile developer targets one or more mobile platforms such as iOS, Android, Windows Phone, and BlackBerry 10. Although there are vendors that promise shortcuts, strictly speaking each platform adds its own jargon, development tools and frameworks, and unique approach to mobile challenges such as user interface paradigm, hardware abstraction, and software deployment.

The advantages of native applications include usability, integration with hardware and native applications (such as those managing calendars and contacts), access to secure offline storage, and built-in application distribution. Disadvantages vary but typically involve the cost and complexity of supporting multiple devices and operating systems.

Salesforce Mobile SDK provides libraries and sample projects for developing native applications for iOS and Android. Specifically, it helps developers in four main areas:

- **Login**—The Mobile SDK simplifies the OAuth login process.

- **Offline data caching**—SmartStore is a component of the Mobile SDK that enables the secure storage of data for offline access.

- **REST**—The Force.com REST API is provided as a set of friendly infrastructure classes.

- **Application creation**—The Mobile SDK includes a tool called `forceios` that generates a sample native application to connect to a Salesforce organization and run a simple query. This can be a good starting point for your development.

Mobile Web Applications

Mobile Web applications rely on the mobile device's browser to function. Often they are ordinary Web pages designed to adapt their user interfaces from full-size monitors to tiny mobile screens. This usage of standard Web technology to deliver the same application to desktop and mobile users can be a huge time savings over native application development.

Another significant advantage to mobile Web applications is that they are served up from servers, not stored on the mobile device. This means developers can continually improve the application remotely, and users always see the latest version. Native and hybrid applications have a binary component that is downloaded and installed on the device. Although the binary can be updated after it is installed, that is an additional manual step for the user.

Unfortunately, mobile Web applications are rarely able to deliver the same level of user experience as a native application. Due to size and battery constraints, tablets and phones have a subset of the processing power of laptop and desktop computers. Their Web browser cannot render complex pages or execute code as quickly. Additionally, the standard user interface components that the user is familiar with from the mobile device are either Web-based approximations or entirely different, requiring the user to adapt to the new way of representing data and controls.

Salesforce Mobile SDK includes two libraries that are extremely helpful in building mobile Web applications integrated with Force.com, described next:

- **SmartSync**—SmartSync exposes Salesforce records as JavaScript objects, with query and CRUD access seamlessly supported. It extends a popular open source framework called Backbone.js to accomplish this.

- **`forcetk.js`**—This JavaScript library is a wrapper of the Salesforce REST API.

Hybrid Applications

Hybrid applications promise the best of both worlds, combining the flexibility of native with the ease of development of Web. In a hybrid application, some content is shipped in the binary like a normal native application, while some is left out and delivered through Web pages instead. Their distinguishing feature is a "container" that hosts the Web content and grants it access to native resources.

Being a mixture of native and Web, hybrid applications share the pros and cons of both. For example, if your hybrid application relies extensively on Web content, it will suffer the user experience limitations of mobile Web applications. In general, hybrid applications rely on the judgment of the developer to select the best way (native or Web) to implement functionality on a feature-by-feature basis.

This introduces a larger issue of complexity. Although developers have greater flexibility with hybrid applications, building them requires knowledge of both mobile Web and native technology, plus the "container" layer between them. The container in the Salesforce Mobile SDK is called Cordova (formerly PhoneGap).

> **Note**
>
> Due to their significant dependence of technology unrelated to Force.com, hybrid and native applications are outside the scope of this book. Refer to the Salesforce Mobile SDK home page at http://wiki.developerforce.com/page/Mobile_SDK for more information.

Getting Started with Mobile Web Applications

Out of all three types of custom mobile applications, Web applications are arguably those closest to and benefiting most from the Force.com platform, particularly if they are mobile versions of Visualforce pages. Mobile aside, Web applications can be challenging to build due to rapidly moving trends in usability, browser standards, and security practices. Mobile Force.com applications add a number of additional challenges that are addressed in this section.

At a high level, there are three major areas to examine when building mobile Web applications with Force.com:

- **Frameworks**—Web development frameworks typically adopt some design pattern such as MVC (Model-View-Controller) or MVVM (Model-View-View Model). These patterns separate logic from presentation and allow the construction of scalable, interactive Web applications. They usually bundle or recommend a templating and data access layer. Some frameworks are specifically tailored for mobile applications.

- **Data access**—Assuming that Force.com is the data layer for the mobile application, there are a few options for integrating it.

- **Deployment**—Deployment concerns how mobile users will find and start using your mobile application. This is more complex with mobile Web applications than native applications.

Frameworks

Web development frameworks can reduce and manage the complexity of building Web applications, particularly the Single Page Applications (SPAs) that are becoming commonplace. SPAs rely on the Web browser to execute the majority of the user interface code, such as fetching the model and using it to render views. This is in contrast to the original breed of Web applications, which performed these duties on the Web or application server.

Any Web framework could be relevant to mobile Web development, but this subsection divides them into two camps:

- **Mobile Components for Visualforce**—This Salesforce-provided open source library blends jQuery Mobile with Visualforce components to make mobile-ready Visualforce pages easier to create.

- **Web MVC frameworks**—Web frameworks such as Knockout, Backbone, Ember, and Angular are behind many popular, modern Web applications, including those from Salesforce. Any of these can be used to build mobile Force.com-enabled applications, and Salesforce provides sample applications to get you started.

Mobile Components for Visualforce

Mobile Components for Visualforce is a series of simple Visualforce components that generate HTML for mobile devices. They leverage jQuery Mobile framework, but wrap it to make it easier to use in Visualforce.

There are three types of components in Mobile Components for Visualforce, described here:

1. **Structural components**—These components help determine the layout of the page. The `App` component is the container for all other components. `SplitView` renders the traditional left-side navigation, right-side detail layout, and is typically used with the `SplitViewTemplate` in an `apex:composition` component. `Page` defines a dynamic content page as found in a Single Page Application. The `Header` and `Footer` components are children of `Page` and contain content to be placed at the top and bottom of the page. The `Content` component, also a child of `Page`, is the generic container for content.

2. **Data components**—The `List` component renders a list of records resulting from a SOQL query. The `Detail` component uses the page layout definition of an SObject to render its fields in proper position. Both of these components are read-only, meaning they do not allow the users to edit their data.

3. **Navigation component**—This component generates a navigation bar containing links to show content within the page or URLs outside of the page.

To install Mobile Components for Visualforce in your Salesforce organization, complete the following steps:

1. Download the source code by running `git clone https://github.com/forcedotcom/MobileComponents.git` or equivalent in a Git client application.

2. Zip the source code so that it can be deployed. For example: `cd MobileComponents/Visualforce; zip -r mobile_components.zip src/*`

3. Visit the Workbench home page at http://wiki.developerforce.com/page/Workbench. Click the Login to Workbench Now on Developerforce link or https://workbench.developerforce.com directly, authenticate to your organization by clicking the Login with Salesforce button, and select Deploy from the Migration menu. Check Rollback on Error and click the Choose File button in Google Chrome (the Browse button in Firefox) to locate your locally stored zip file. Proceed through the wizard to upload the file.

4. Test the deployment by visiting `/apex/MobilePage` in your Web browser.

Notes

The full documentation and source code for Mobile Components for Visualforce are available at http://wiki.developerforce.com/page/MobileComponents.

Web MVC Frameworks

Web MVC frameworks include jQuery Mobile, AngularJS, and Backbone.js. Although these frameworks can be used directly to build mobile Web applications with Force.com, Salesforce has put together open source projects called Salesforce Mobile Packs to make this process easier. There is one Mobile Pack for each of the supported frameworks. The Mobile Packs contain fully functional sample applications leveraging each of the frameworks with Force.com data.

Salesforce also provides Mobile Design Templates, which provide attractive and functional CSS and HTML for common Force.com data-rendering scenarios.

Note

Salesforce Mobile Packs can be found at http://www2.developerforce.com/mobile/services/mobile-packs. Mobile Design Templates are located at http://www2.developerforce.com/mobile/services/mobile-templates.

Data Access

Data access is one of the major design decisions involved in building a Force.com mobile Web application. There are a few different ways to use the Force.com REST API. This includes authenticating to Force.com and reading and writing its data.

There are two choices for authentication, described next:

- **OAuth**—In OAuth, the developer creates a Connected Application in Force.com and uses it when creating the application. For the user who has not yet authenticated, he or she is directed to a special Salesforce login page. After login, the user is prompted to share his or her information with the application. If granted access, the user is redirected back to the mobile Web application, which now has an access token that grants it permission to access Force.com on the user's behalf. Like a session with the Salesforce Web interface, the token eventually expires and must be refreshed by the application to obtain a valid one.

- **Session sharing**—If the mobile Web application is hosted inside Force.com or an application already authenticated to Force.com, a session identifier can be embedded in the page. This can be used to make requests to Force.com without asking the user to log in again.

These two authentication methods can also be combined in a single application, granting more flexibility in how the application is hosted.

When it comes to accessing Force.com data, the decisions depend on how you build your application. For example, some data access methods are available only for a specific Web MVC framework. Others only work when hosted within Visualforce pages. A few of the most common methods follow:

- **SmartSync**—SmartSync keeps your Web page's data model in sync with the Force.com data. As you retrieve or make changes to a collection or model in your Web application, SmartSync makes the necessary calls to Force.com to mirror them persistently in the Force.com database. SmartSync is an extension of the Backbone framework, so your application must be using Backbone to leverage it.

- **JavaScript remoting**—Available only to Visualforce pages, JavaScript remoting involves adding a `RemoteAction` annotation to a static controller method. This makes the method accessible to JavaScript without any of the overhead of the Visualforce view state. Keeping data access as lightweight as possible is critical for mobile applications, so JavaScript remoting is a best practice when building mobile applications in Visualforce.

- `actionFunction` **component**—This method of data access is only available to Visualforce pages. Like JavaScript remoting, it makes a call from the browser's JavaScript to the Visualforce controller. It requires less code than JavaScript remoting to call it, but performance is not as good due to its reliance on view state.

- **Force.com REST API**—The `forcetk.js` library wraps the Force.com REST API so that it is easier to use from JavaScript. Because your Web page will be served from a server other than the REST API endpoint, accessing the endpoint violates same-origin security policy in modern Web browsers. This policy states that a script on a page cannot access a host other than the one serving the page itself. To address this, a proxy is provided by Salesforce, called the AJAX Proxy. For more information, refer to the online documentation at http://www.salesforce.com/us/developer/docs/ajax/Content/ sforce_api_ajax_queryresultiterator.htm#ajax_proxy.

Deployment

Because mobile Web applications are just Web pages, deployment ultimately requires that the user simply visit your application's URL. If you've built your application to use OAuth for authentication, you can host its Web pages anywhere. If you're using session sharing, you need to host it in an application, referred to here as a container that the user has already used to authenticate to Salesforce.

The advantage of a container is that users don't need to authenticate to Salesforce again just to use your application. Additionally, they have all of the other features included in the container application. But don't be fooled. At the end of the day, the container is purely a Visualforce page viewer and bookmarker. To be successful, your Visualforce page has to be mobile ready.

The mobile applications that can serve as containers for Visualforce pages are Salesforce Classic and Salesforce Touch. To enable a Visualforce page to be shown in Salesforce Classic, follow these steps:

1. In the App Setup area, click Create, Tabs. Click the Visualforce tab you'd like to make available in Salesforce Classic, and check the Mobile Ready check box.

2. Create a configuration to make the Visualforce page visible. In the Administration Setup area, click Mobile Administration, Salesforce Classic, Configurations. Click the New Mobile Configuration button. Enter a name for the configuration, make it active, and select the users and profiles who will use this mobile configuration.

3. With your new configuration, you make tabs visible to the mobile device. Click the Customize Tabs button in the Mobile Tabs section of the configuration. Select a tab from the list of available tabs, click the Add button, and click the Save button.

> **Note**
>
> Refer to the Salesforce Classic Implementation Guide for more information, which can be found at http://www.salesforce.com/us/developer/docs/mobileImplGuide/index.htm.

The steps to add your Visualforce pages to Salesforce Touch are next:

1. In the Administration Setup area, click Mobile Administration, Salesforce Touch, Settings. Check the Enable Visualforce in Salesforce Touch check box. This step needs to be performed only once for an entire organization.

2. For each Visualforce page to be displayed in Touch, go to the App Setup area, click Develop, Pages. Click the Visualforce page, and check the Available in Touch check box. You also need a Visualforce tab for each page. To create one, go to the App Setup area; click Create, Tabs; and click the New button in the Visualforce Tabs section. Select the Visualforce page to be displayed in Touch, give your tab a label and name, pick a style, and click the Next button. On the following two pages, select the profiles that can access the tab and which custom applications include it. Then click Save to finish the Visualforce Tab Creation Wizard.

> **Note**
>
> Unless you plan to use your new Visualforce tabs with Salesforce Classic, there is no need to enable the Mobile Ready option. It has no effect on Salesforce Touch.

Sample Application: Mobile Timecard Entry

The goal of this section is to build a mobile-ready timecard entry interface for consultants. The requirements for this interface are as follows:

1. Users are already using Salesforce Touch. They do not want to install a new mobile application on their phones and tablets. They also don't want to authenticate to an additional application or page.

2. Allow hours to be entered on a project as quickly as possible, with minimal clicking around.

3. Timecards are precreated based on the current week and available assignments, so they are always valid. There is no need to know the assignment or look up any additional information.

4. Hours can be entered and saved, but do not need to be submitted right away. This allows the consultant to keep track of his or her hours on a daily basis rather than waiting until the end of a week.

5. Five of the most recent timecards can be displayed. Timecards in an Approved or Submitted status are locked and cannot be edited. Other timecards can be edited and saved or submitted.

The finished page is shown in Figure 8.1 on an iPhone and in Figure 8.2 on the Web. Upon viewing the page, the consultant is immediately able to see the timecards he or she is responsible for entering based on his or her assignments. The page is responsive, so in the mobile browser the list of timecards is shown at the top. With a wider screen, this navigation list is pulled to the left. Clicking on a timecard displays its hours, which are totaled dynamically as they are entered.

The mobile timecard entry page can be constructed in three steps, described next:

1. **List timecards**—Write a controller method that returns the five most recent timecards. If no timecards exist yet for the current week and projects that the consultant is assigned to, create and return them in the list of recent timecards. Render each timecard in a list that includes the week ending date, project name, and timecard status.

2. **Navigate to timecard**—Allow the user to navigate to a timecard by clicking it. This causes the panel described in the next step to be refreshed.

3. **View and edit timecard**—Display the hours (Monday through Friday only) and total hours for the currently selected timecard. If the timecard is not in an Approved or Submitted status, allow the hours to be edited. Provide a button to save changes made to the hours and another button to save changes and submit the timecard.

Figure 8.1   Mobile timecard entry page in iPhone

Figure 8.2   Mobile timecard entry page in Web browser

Listing 8.1 is the controller to implement the first step. It uses JavaScript remoting rather than ActionFunction to provide the best performance for the Visualforce page. The load method looks up the current user's Contact record and looks for Assignment records within the current week. For every Assignment record without a Timecard record, a Timecard record is created. Finally, the most recent five Timecard records by Week_Ending__c are returned.

Listing 8.1   **Visualforce Controller for Mobile Timecard**

```
public with sharing class MobileTimecardController {
  @RemoteAction
  public static List<Timecard__c> load() {
    Contact c = currentResource();
    if (c == null) {
      return null;
    }
    Date currentWeekEnding =
      Date.today().toStartOfWeek().addDays(6);
    // Create a current week's timecard for each assignment
    for (Assignment__c a : [ SELECT Project__c
      FROM Assignment__c WHERE Contact__c = :c.Id
      AND Status__c = 'Scheduled'
      AND Start_Date__c < :currentWeekEnding
      AND End_Date__c >= :currentWeekEnding
      ]) {
      if ([ SELECT Id FROM Timecard__c
        WHERE Contact__c = :c.Id
        AND Week_Ending__c = :currentWeekEnding
        AND Project__c = :a.Project__c
        LIMIT 1].size() == 0) {
        insert new Timecard__c(Project__c = a.Project__c,
          Week_Ending__c = currentWeekEnding,
          Contact__c = c.Id);
      }
    }
    List<Timecard__c> timecards = [ SELECT Project__r.Name,
      Week_Ending__c, Status__c,
      Monday_Hours__c, Tuesday_Hours__c, Wednesday_Hours__c,
      Thursday_Hours__c, Friday_Hours__c
      FROM Timecard__c
      WHERE Contact__c = :c.Id
      ORDER BY Week_Ending__c DESC
      LIMIT 5 ];
    return timecards;
  }
  private static Contact currentResource() {
    List<Contact> contacts =
      [ SELECT Id, Name FROM Contact
        WHERE User__c = :UserInfo.getUserId() ];
    if (contacts != null && contacts.size() == 1) {
      return contacts.get(0);
    }
    return null;
  }
}
```

Listing 8.2 is a Visualforce page that provides the timecard list functionality for the first step. It does not include the Visualforce header, sidebar, or standard stylesheets to improve load performance. It uses Twitter Bootstrap for simple styling and responsive grid system, and AngularJS to dynamically bind data from the Visualforce controller to and from the HTML elements. The AngularJS aspects of the page are important to examine closely:

- MobileTimecardCtrl is the name of the AngularJS controller. MobileTimecardController is the Visualforce controller, which is referenced when RemoteAction methods are called. Note the usage of its load method. This sets a scope variable called timecards, which is bound to the HTML list items using the ng-repeat attribute.

- Ignore the use of the ng-click attribute and the navClass callout in the list items for now. Those are part of the second step, for navigation.

- Bootstrap is an open source project consisting of CSS and JavaScript to help produce clean, consistent, responsive Web applications for desktop and mobile browsers. For more information, see https://github.com/twbs/bootstrap. In this page, the important parts of Bootstrap are the grid. The row-fluid CSS class sets up a row in the visual grid system that positions the elements in your page. The span family of CSS classes (span1 through span12) makes up the columns of your page. A single row can consist of a single span12, or 12 span1 elements, and everything in between. In the mobile timecard page, the navigation bar on the left is a span3, and the detail area, shown when a timecard is clicked, is span9.

Listing 8.2   **Visualforce Page for Mobile Timecard**

```
<apex:page showHeader="false" standardStylesheets="false"
  sidebar="false"
  controller="MobileTimecardController">
<head>
  <meta name="viewport"
    content="width=device-width,initial-scale=1.0,
    maximum-scale=1.0,user-scalable=0"/>
<link
href="https://netdna.bootstrapcdn.com/twitter-bootstrap/2.3.1/css/
➥bootstrap.css"
rel="stylesheet" />
<style>
input[type="number"] { width: 30px; }
</style>
</head>
<body>
<script>
function MobileTimecardCtrl($scope, $rootScope, $location) {
  MobileTimecardController.load(function(result, event) {
    if (event.status) {
```

```
        $scope.timecards = result;
        $rootScope.$apply();
      }
    }, { escape: false });
  }
</script>
<apex:outputPanel html-ng-app=""
  html-ng-controller="MobileTimecardCtrl" styleClass="container-fluid">
<div class="row-fluid">
  <div class="span3">
    <div class="well sidebar-nav">
      <ul class="nav nav-list">
        <li ng-class="navClass('{{timecard.Id}}')"
          ng-repeat="timecard in timecards">
          <a ng-click="nav('{{timecard.Id}}')">
{{timecard.Project__r.Name}}:
{{timecard.Week_Ending__c | date:'M/d/yyyy'}}
              <br /><span class="label">{{timecard.Status__c}}</span>
          </a></li>
      </ul>
    </div>
  </div>
  <div class="span9">
  </div>
</div>
</apex:outputPanel>
<script
src="//ajax.googleapis.com/ajax/libs/angularjs/1.2.0rc1/
➥angular.min.js">
</script>
</body>
</apex:page>
```

Listing 8.3 implements the second step, in-page navigation, with the addition of two functions for the `MobileTimecardCtrl` AngularJS controller. Insert it after the `load` function in the first `script` tag.

For a simple page like this, creating many Visualforce pages, one for each view, adds unnecessary overhead. An alternative is to allow the user to navigate but stay within the page, providing the page with the logic and visual templates necessary to encompass all of the user interactions. Clicks on anchors change the "route" understood by the Web framework, but it is handled entirely by the Web framework. The browser does not load a new Web page. This type of dynamic navigation within a page is typical of a Single Page Application, described in Chapter 7, "Advanced User Interfaces."

The `navClass` method returns the HTML class needed to display highlighting around the "active" (selected) timecard by comparing the list element's route to the current path reported by the browser. With every timecard displayed in the list, this method is called to determine its style class.

The `nav` method is called when the user clicks a timecard. Rather than using the standard `href` attribute, the `ng-click` attribute allows the navigation to stay within AngularJS. The method first finds the selected timecard in the model, the list of timecards previously retrieved using the Visualforce controller's `load` method. It then sets that timecard to the `edit` variable so that it can be bound to the detail region of the page, to be added in the third step. It also checks to see if the timecard is in an editable state, setting a `readOnly` variable accordingly.

Listing 8.3   **Angular Controller Addition for Navigation**

```
$scope.navClass = function(page) {
    var currentRoute = $location.path().substring(1) || '';
    return page === currentRoute ? 'active' : '';
}
$scope.nav = function(timecardId) {
  $location.path(timecardId);
  for (var idx in $scope.timecards) {
    if ($scope.timecards[idx].Id == timecardId) {
      $scope.edit = $scope.timecards[idx];
      $scope.readOnly = $scope.edit.Status__c == 'Submitted' ||
        $scope.edit.Status__c == 'Approved';
      return;
    }
  }
  $scope.edit = null;
}
```

Listings 8.4, 8.5, and 8.6 implement the changes needed to allow timecards to be viewed and edited. Listing 8.4 adds a new method to simply save the timecard. The AngularJS code in the browser maintains edits made to the timecard data and passes it into the Visualforce controller where it is updated in the Force.com database.

Listing 8.4   **Visualforce Controller Addition to Edit Timecard**

```
@RemoteAction
public static void save(Timecard__c timecard) {
  update timecard;
}
```

Insert the code in Listing 8.5 into the `div` element with class `span9`. This is the right side of the page and will contain the detail of the selected timecard. There are two portions of HTML, but only one is visible at any given moment. They are displayed conditionally using the `ng-show` attribute. If there is a currently selected timecard, the `edit` variable will contain it; otherwise, it is null. The timecard fields are rendered using `input` elements, and they are disabled if the timecard is not editable. The bidirectional data binding of AngularJS is demonstrated with the dynamic calculation of total hours in the timecard from the user input fields.

Listing 8.5   **Visualforce Page Addition to Edit Timecard**

```
    <div class="row-fluid">
      <div class="span12" ng-show="edit != null">
<form><fieldset>
  <legend>Timecard for {{edit.Project__r.Name}},
  Week Ending {{edit.Week_Ending__c | date:'M/d/yyyy'}}
  </legend>
  <div class="control-group">
    <div class="controls">
      <input type="number" ng-model="edit.Monday_Hours__c"
        placeholder="M" ng-readonly="readOnly"></input>
      <input type="number" ng-model="edit.Tuesday_Hours__c"
        placeholder="T" ng-readonly="readOnly"></input>
      <input type="number" ng-model="edit.Wednesday_Hours__c"
        placeholder="W" ng-readonly="readOnly"></input>
      <input type="number" ng-model="edit.Thursday_Hours__c"
        placeholder="Th" ng-readonly="readOnly"></input>
      <input type="number" ng-model="edit.Friday_Hours__c"
        placeholder="F" ng-readonly="readOnly"></input>
  <label>Total Hours: {{edit.Monday_Hours__c + edit.Tuesday_Hours__c +
  edit.Wednesday_Hours__c + edit.Thursday_Hours__c +
  edit.Friday_Hours__c}}</label>
      <div ng-hide="readOnly">
        <button ng-click="save('Saved')" type="submit"
          class="btn">Save</button>
        <button ng-click="save('Submitted')" type="submit"
          class="btn">Submit</button>
      </div>
    </div>
  </div>
</fieldset>
</form>
      </div>
      <div class="span12" ng-show="edit == null">
      Please select a timecard to edit it.
      </div>
    </div>
```

Listing 8.6 is the final piece to the timecard entry page. Insert it into the AngularJS controller. It adds a `save` method, which is wired up to the Save and Submit buttons in Listing 8.5. It sets the status of the timecard and calls the Visualforce controller's `save` action to save it. It then resets the page so that no timecard is selected.

Listing 8.6   **Angular Controller Addition to Edit Timecard**

```
$scope.save = function(status) {
  $scope.edit.Status__c = status;
  MobileTimecardController.save($scope.edit,
    function(result, event) {
      if (event.status) {
        $location.path('/');
        $scope.edit = null;
        $rootScope.$apply();
      }
    }, { escape: false });
}
```

To test this feature, install Salesforce Touch on your mobile device and perform the following steps:

1. Enable the page for Touch access. Go to the App Setup area and click Develop, Pages. Click the Visualforce page, click the Edit button, check the Available in Touch check box, and click the Save button.

2. Add a Visualforce tab for your new page. In the App Setup area, click Create, Tabs. Click the New button in the Visualforce Tabs section. Select the MobileTimecard Visualforce page, give the tab a label and name that you'd like to see on your mobile device. Select a tab style, profiles, and application visibility, and save the tab.

3. Launch Salesforce Touch on your mobile device and log in.

4. Click the List icon in the upper-left corner to overlay the list of accessible pages. You should see your Mobile Timecard page as an option. Select it to start using the mobile timecard entry feature.

Summary

Mobile development with Force.com is a rapidly changing subject, with an active open source community around it. There are a wealth of options for building mobile applications, some directly baked into Salesforce products, some born within Salesforce but supported by the community, and many other general-purpose technologies that can be helpful.

Before moving on to the next chapter, take a moment to review a few highlights related to mobile development:

- Salesforce provides three mobile applications that are ready to download and use for Android and iOS devices: Salesforce Classic, Salesforce Touch, and Chatter Mobile. Of the three, the first two are the most interesting to mobile developers because they can be extended with custom Visualforce pages.

- There are three major types of custom mobile applications: native, Web, and hybrid. Native is the closest to the mobile device's hardware and therefore offers the best performance and depth of features. Web runs within the mobile device's Web browser, and offers the least control to the developer but can be easier to develop and deploy. Hybrid strives to be the best of both approaches, a mix and match of native and Web. Pick the option that makes the most sense for your application, users, and development skill set.

- Although Visualforce is a good starting point for mobile Web applications, your Visualforce controllers and pages need to be optimized for this purpose. Visually they should be responsive, adapting to the screen resolution of the device. In terms of data, they should be frugal, requesting data only as needed and avoiding page navigation. Using Visualforce as the container for a Single Page Application is a helpful pattern. A number of open source projects are available to help with Web applications, from data management to responsive design.

9

Batch Processing

You've learned two ways you can process database records within the Force.com platform: triggers and Visualforce controllers. Each has its own set of platform-imposed limitations, such as how many records can be created at one time. As you accumulate tens of thousands of records or more in your database, you might need to process more records than permitted by the governor limits applying to triggers and controllers.

Although Salesforce has simplified and incrementally relaxed governor limits in recent Force.com releases, triggers and Visualforce controllers are fundamentally not suited to processing large amounts of data in a multitenant environment. They are driven by user interaction, and must be limited to provide good performance to all users. The Force.com platform carefully controls its resources to maintain high performance for all, so resource-intensive tasks such as processing millions of records must be planned and executed over time, balanced with the demands of other customers.

Batch processing makes this possible, and Batch Apex is the Force.com feature that enables batch processing on the platform. With Batch Apex, data-intensive tasks are taken offline, detached from user interactions, the exact timing of their execution determined by Salesforce itself. In return for relinquishing some control, you, the developer, receive the ability to process orders of magnitude more records than you can in triggers and controllers.

In this chapter, you will learn how to use Batch Apex to create, update, and delete millions of records at a time. It is divided into five sections:

- **Introduction to Batch Apex**—Learn the concepts and terminology of Batch Apex, what it can do, and when you should and should not use it.

- **Getting started with Batch Apex**—Walk through a simple example of Batch Apex. Develop the code, run it, and monitor its execution.

- **Testing Batch Apex**—Like any other Apex code, proper test coverage is required. Learn how to kick off Batch Apex jobs within test code.

- **Scheduling Batch Apex**—Although Salesforce has the final say on when Batch Apex is run, you can schedule jobs to run using a built-in scheduler. Learn how to use the scheduling user interface and achieve finer-grained control in Apex code.

- **Sample application**—Enhance the Services Manager application by creating a scheduled batch process to identify missing timecards.

> **Note**
>
> The code listings in this chapter are available in a GitHub Gist at http://goo.gl/lw8XT.

Introduction to Batch Apex

Prior to the availability of Batch Apex, the only options for processing data exceeding the governor limits of triggers and controllers were tricky workarounds to shift work off the platform. For example, you might have hundreds of thousands of records spanning multiple Lookup relationships to be summarized, deduplicated, cleansed, or otherwise modified en masse algorithmically. You could use the Web Services API to interact with the Force.com data from outside of Force.com itself, or you could use JavaScript to process batches of data inside the Web browser. These approaches are usually slow and brittle, requiring lots of code and exposing you to data quality problems over time due to gaps in error handling and recovery. Batch Apex allows you to keep the large, data-intensive processing tasks within the platform, taking advantage of its close proximity to the data and transactional integrity to create secure, reliable processes without the limits of normal, interactive Apex code. This section introduces you to concepts and guidelines for using Batch Apex to prepare you for hands-on work.

Batch Apex Concepts

Batch Apex is an execution framework that splits a large data set into subsets and provides them to ordinary Apex programs that you develop, which continue to operate within their usual governor limits. This means with some minor rework to make your code operate as Batch Apex, you can process data volumes that would otherwise be prohibited within the platform. By helping Salesforce break up your processing task, you are permitted to run it within its platform.

A few key concepts in Batch Apex are used throughout this chapter:

- **Scope**—The scope is the set of records that a Batch Apex process operates on. It can consist of 1 record or up to 50 million records. Scope is usually expressed as a SOQL statement, which is contained in a Query Locator, a system object that is blessedly exempt from the normal governor limits on SOQL. If your scope is too complex to be specified in a single SOQL statement, then writing Apex code to generate the scope (called an iterable scope) programmatically is also possible. Unfortunately, using Apex code dramatically reduces the number of records that can be processed because it is subject to the standard governor limit on records returned by a SOQL statement.

- **Batch job**—A batch job is a Batch Apex program that has been submitted for execution. It is the runtime manifestation of your code, running asynchronously within the Force.com platform. Because batch jobs run in the background and can take many hours to complete their work, Salesforce provides a user interface for listing batch jobs and their statuses, and to allow individual jobs to be canceled. This job information is also available as a standard object in the database. Although the batch job is not the atomic unit of work within Batch Apex, it is the only platform-provided level at which you have control over a batch process.

- **Transaction**—Each batch job consists of transactions, which are the governor limit-friendly units of work you're familiar with from triggers and Visualforce controllers. By default, a transaction is up to 2,000 records (with no limit for an iterable scope), but you can adjust this downward in code. When a batch job starts, the scope is split into a series of transactions. Each transaction is then processed by your Apex code and committed to the database independently. Although the same block of your code is being called upon to process potentially thousands of transactions, the transactions themselves are normally stateless. None of the variables within it are saved between invocations unless you explicitly designate your Batch Apex code as stateful when it is developed. Salesforce doesn't provide information on whether your transactions are run in parallel or serially, nor how they are ordered. Observationally, transactions seem to run serially, in order based on scope.

In the remainder of this section, these concepts are applied to take you one step closer to writing your own Batch Apex.

Understanding the `Batchable` Interface

To make your Apex code run as a batch, you must sign a contract with the platform. This contract takes the form of an interface called `Batchable` that must be implemented by your code. It requires that you structure your processing logic into the following three methods:

- **start**—The `start` method is concerned with the scope of work, the raw set of records to be processed in the batch. When a batch is submitted to Salesforce for processing, the first thing it does is invoke your `start` method. Your job here is to return a `QueryLocator` or an `Iterable` that describes the scope of the batch job.

- **execute**—After calling the `start` method, Force.com has the means to access all the records you've requested that it operate on. It then splits these records into sets of up to 200 records and invokes your `execute` method repeatedly, once for each set of records. At this point, your code can perform the substance of the batch operation, typically inserting, updating, or deleting records. Each invocation of `execute` is a separate transaction. If an uncaught exception is in a transaction, no further transactions are processed and the entire batch job is stopped.

> **Caution**
>
> Transactions that complete successfully are never rolled back. So, an error in a transaction stops the batch, but transactions executed up to that point remain in the database. Thinking of an overall Batch Apex job as transactional is dangerous, because this is not its default behavior. Additionally, you cannot use savepoints to achieve a single pseudotransaction across the entire batch job. If you must achieve jobwide rollback, this can be implemented in the form of a compensating batch job that reverses the actions of the failed job.

- **finish**—The `finish` method is invoked once at the end of a batch job. The job ends when all transactions in the scope have been processed successfully, or if processing has failed. Regardless of success or failure, `finish` is called. There is no requirement to do anything special in the method. You can leave the method body empty if no postprocessing is needed. It simply provides an opportunity for you to receive a notification that processing is complete. You could use this information to clean up any working state or notify the user via email that the batch job is complete.

With this initial walk-through of the `Batchable` interface, you can begin to apply it to your own trigger or Visualforce controller code. If you find a process that is a candidate to run as a batch, think about how it can be restructured to conform to this interface and thus take advantage of Batch Apex.

Applications of Batch Apex

Like any feature of Force.com, Batch Apex works best when you apply it to an appropriate use case that meshes well with its unique capabilities. The following list provides some guidelines when evaluating Batch Apex for your project:

- **Single database object**—Batch Apex is optimized to source its data from a single, "tall" (containing many records) database object. It cannot read data from other sources, such as callouts to Web services. If the records you need to process span many database objects that cannot be reached via parent-child or child-parent relationships from a single database object, you should proceed carefully. You will need to develop separate Batch Apex code for every database object. Although this is doable and you can share code between them, it creates maintenance headaches and quickly exposes you to the limitation of five active batch jobs per organization.

- **Simple scope of work**—Although Batch Apex allows the use of custom code to provide it with the records to process, it is most powerful when the scope of work is expressed in a single SOQL statement. Do some work up front to ensure that the source of data for your batch can be summed up in that single SOQL statement.

- **Minimal shared state**—The best design for a Batch Apex process is one where every unit of work is independent, meaning it does not require information to be shared with other units of work. Although creating stateful Batch Apex is possible, it is a less mature feature and more difficult to debug than its stateless counterpart. If you need shared state to be maintained across units of work, try to use the database itself rather than variables in your Apex class.

- **Limited transactionality**—If your batch process is a single, all-or-nothing transaction, Batch Apex is only going to get you halfway there. You will need to write extra code to compensate for failures and roll back the database to its original state.

- **Not time-critical**—Salesforce provides no hard guarantees about when Batch Apex is executed or its performance. If you have an application that has time-based requirements such that users will be prevented from doing their jobs if a batch does not run or complete by a specific time, Batch Apex might not be a good fit. A better fit is a process that must run within a time window on the order of hours rather than minutes.

These guidelines might seem stifling at first glance, but Batch Apex actually enables an impressive breadth of interesting applications to be developed that were previously impossible with other forms of Apex.

Getting Started with Batch Apex

You don't need an elaborate use case or huge data volumes to get started with Batch Apex. This section walks you through the development of a simple Batch Apex class that writes debug log entries as it runs. The class is submitted for execution using the Force.com IDE and monitored in the administrative Web user interface. Two more versions of the Batch Apex class are developed: one to demonstrate stateful processing and the other an iterable scope. The section concludes with a description of important Batch Apex limits.

Developing a Batch Apex Class

Although the class in Listing 9.1 performs no useful work, it leaves a trail of its activity in the debug log. This is helpful in understanding how Force.com handles your batch-enabled code. It also illustrates the basic elements of a Batch Apex class, listed next:

- The class must implement the `Database.Batchable` interface. This is a parameterized interface, so you also need to provide a type name. Use SObject for batches with a `QueryLocator` scope, or any database object type for an `Iterable` scope.

- The class must be global. This is a requirement of Batch Apex classes.

Listing 9.1 **Sample Batch Apex Code**

```
global class Listing9_1 implements Database.Batchable<SObject> {
  global Database.QueryLocator start(Database.BatchableContext context) {
    System.debug('start');
    return Database.getQueryLocator(
      [SELECT Name FROM Project__c ORDER BY Name]);
  }
  global void execute(Database.BatchableContext context,
    List<SObject> scope) {
    System.debug('execute');
    for(SObject rec : scope) {
      Project__c p = (Project__c)rec;
      System.debug('Project: ' + p.Name);
    }
  }
  global void finish(Database.BatchableContext context) {
    System.debug('finish');
  }
}
```

Before actually running the code in the next subsection, review these implementation details:

- The `start` method defines the scope by returning a `QueryLocator` object constructed from an in-line SOQL statement. The SOQL statement returns all Project records in ascending order by the Name field. The SOQL statement can use parameters (prefaced with a colon) like any in-line SOQL in Apex code. Relationship queries are acceptable, but aggregate queries are not allowed. You can also pass a SOQL string into the `getQueryLocator` method, which allows the scope of the batch to be specified with dynamic SOQL.

- The `execute` method is called once per transaction with a unique group of up to 2,000 records from the scope. The records are provided in the `scope` argument.

- The `finish` method is called when all transactions have completed processing, or the batch job has been interrupted for any reason.

- The `BatchableContext` object argument in all three methods contains a method for obtaining the unique identifier of the current batch job, `getJobID`. This identifier can be used to look up additional information about the batch job in the standard database object AsyncApexJob. You can also pass this identifier to the `System.abortJob` method to stop processing of the batch job.

Working with Batch Apex Jobs

Batch Apex can be executed from a Visualforce page, scheduled to run automatically at specific times, or kicked off from within a trigger. But the easiest way to experiment with it is in the Execute Anonymous view in the Force.com IDE.

First, enable debug logging for your user in the Administration Setup area; select Monitoring, Debug Logs; and add your user to the list of monitored users by clicking the New button. This is no different than debugging any Apex class. Using the Execute Anonymous view, enter the code in Listing 9.2 and execute it. The batch is submitted and its unique job identifier displayed in the results box.

Listing 9.2   **Running Sample Batch Apex Code**

```
Listing9_1 batch = new Listing9_1();
Id jobId = Database.executeBatch(batch);
System.debug('Started Batch Apex job: ' + jobId);
```

The `executeBatch` method of the `Database` class does the work here. It queues the batch job for processing when Force.com is ready to do so. This could be in seconds or minutes; it is not specified. The `Listing9_1` sample class is very simple, but in many cases you would need to pass arguments, either in the constructor or via setter methods, to adjust the behavior of a batch process. This is no different from any Apex class.

To start a batch in response to a button click or other user interface action, apply the code shown in Listing 9.2 within a Visualforce custom controller or controller extension class. Now that you have submitted your batch job, it's time to monitor its progress. In your Web browser, go to the Administration Setup area and select Monitoring, Apex Jobs. This page, shown in Figure 9.1, allows you to manage all the batch jobs in your Force.com organization.

Figure 9.1   Apex Jobs user interface

The single `Listing9_1` job you executed should be visible. By this time, it is most likely in the Completed status, having few records to process. If Force.com is very busy, you might see a status of Queued. This means the job has not been started yet. A status value of Processing indicates the job is currently being executed by the platform. If a user interrupts the job by clicking the Abort link on this page, the job status becomes Aborted. A job with a Failed status means an uncaught exception was thrown during its execution. If you scroll to the right, you can also see the Apex Job Id, which should match the one returned by the `Database.executeBatch` method.

Take a closer look at the values in the Total Batches and Batches Processed columns. To avoid confusion, disregard the word *Batches* here. Total Batches is the number of transactions needed to complete the batch job. It is equal to the scope (which defaults to 200) divided into the number of records returned by the `start` method. The Batches Processed column contains the number of times the `execute` method of your Batch Apex class was invoked so far. As the processing proceeds, you should see it increment until it is equal to the Total Batches value.

For example, if you have fewer than 200 Project records in your database, you should see a 1 in both columns when the batch is complete. If you have between 201 and 400 records, you should see 2 instead. If you have 1,500 records and the system is processing the 300th record, you should see a value of 8 in Total Batches and 1 in Processed Batches. All the information on the page is also accessible programmatically, contained in the standard object named AsyncApexJob.

You have seen the batch job run its course. Proceed back to the Debug Logs page. Here you can review the job's execution in detail, thanks to the `System.debug` statements throughout the code. Figure 9.2 is an example of what you might see there.

Figure 9.2   Debug logs from sample Batch Apex code

Four separate logs each cover a different aspect of the batch execution. Each is described next in the order they are executed, although this might not be the order shown on the Debug Logs page:

1. Results of evaluating the code in the Execute Anonymous view.

2. Invocation of the `start` method to prepare the data set for the batch.

3. Results of running the `execute` method, where the batch job performs its work on the subsets of the data.

4. All the transactions have been processed, so the `finish` method is called to allow postprocessing to occur.

These results are somewhat interesting, but appreciating what the batch is doing is hard without more data. You could add 200 more Project records, or you can simply adjust the scope to process fewer records per transaction. Listing 9.3 is an example of doing just that, passing the number 2 in as the scope, the second argument of the `Database.executeBatch` method. This indicates to Force.com that you want a maximum of two records per transaction in the batch job.

Listing 9.3   **Running Sample Batch Apex Code with Scope Argument**

```
Listing9_1 batch = new Listing9_1();
Id jobId = Database.executeBatch(batch, 2);
System.debug('Started Batch Apex job: ' + jobId);
```

After running this code in the Execute Anonymous view, return to the debug logs. You should now see two additional logs in the `execute` phase, for a total of three transactions of two records each. The three transactions are needed to process the six Project records.

Using Stateful Batch Apex

Batch Apex is stateless by default. That means for each execution of your `execute` method, you receive a fresh copy of your object. All fields of the class are initialized, static and instance. If your batch process needs information that is shared across transactions, one approach is to make the Batch Apex class itself stateful by implementing the `Stateful` interface. This instructs Force.com to preserve the values of your static and instance variables between transactions.

To try a simple example of stateful Batch Apex, create a new Apex class with the code in Listing 9.4.

Listing 9.4   **Stateful Batch Apex Sample**

```
global class Listing9_4
  implements Database.Batchable<SObject>, Database.Stateful {
  Integer count = 0;
  global Database.QueryLocator start(Database.BatchableContext context) {
    System.debug('start: ' + count);
    return Database.getQueryLocator(
      [SELECT Name FROM Project__c ORDER BY Name]);
  }
  global void execute(Database.BatchableContext context,
    List<SObject> scope) {
    System.debug('execute: ' + count);
    for(SObject rec : scope) {
      Project__c p = (Project__c)rec;
      System.debug('Project ' + count + ': ' + p.Name);
      count++;
```

```
    }
  }
  global void finish(Database.BatchableContext context) {
    System.debug('finish: ' + count);
  }
}
```

Take a moment to examine the differences between this class and the original, stateless version. Implementing the interface `Database.Stateful` is the primary change. The other changes are simply to provide proof in the debug log that the value of the `count` variable is indeed preserved between transactions.

Run the modified class with a scope of two records and examine the debug log. Although the log entries might not be ordered in any discernible way, you can see all the Project records have been visited by the batch process. Assuming you have six Project records in your database, you should see a total of six new debug log entries: one to begin the batch, one for the `start` method, three entries' worth of transactions (of two records each), and one for the `finish` method.

Notice the value of the `count` variable throughout the debug output. It begins at 0 in the first transaction, increments by two as Project records are processed, and begins at 2 in the second transaction. Without implementing `Database.Stateful`, the `count` variable would remain between 0 and 2 for every transaction. The value of the `count` variable is 6 when the `finish` method is reached.

Using an Iterable Batch Scope

All of the sample code so far has used a `QueryLocator` object to define the scope of its batch. This enables up to 50 million records to be processed by the batch job, but requires that the scope be defined entirely using a single SOQL statement. This can be too limiting for some batch processing tasks, so the iterable batch scope is offered as an alternative.

The iterable scope allows custom Apex code to determine which records are processed in the batch. For example, you could use an iterable scope to filter the records using criteria that are too complex to be expressed in SOQL. The downside of the iterable approach is that standard SOQL limits apply. This means you can process a maximum of 50,000 records in your batch job, a dramatic reduction from the 50 million record limit of a `QueryLocator` object.

To develop a batch with iterable scope, you must first write code to provide data to the batch. There are two parts to this task:

- **Implement the `Iterator` interface**—The `Iterator` is a class for navigating a collection of elements. It navigates in a single direction, from beginning to end. It requires that you implement two methods: `hasNext` and `next`. The `hasNext` method returns `true` if additional elements are left to navigate to, `false` when the end of the collection has been reached. The `next` method returns the next element in the collection. `Iterator` classes must be global.

- **Implement the `Iterable` interface**—Think of this class as a wrapper or locator object that directs the caller to an `Iterator`. It requires a single global method to be implemented, called `Iterator`, which returns an `Iterable` object. Like `Iterator`, classes implementing `Iterable` must be global.

You could write two separate classes, one to implement each interface. Or you can implement both interfaces in a single class, the approach taken in the code in Listing 9.5.

Listing 9.5   **Project Iterator**

```
global class ProjectIterable
  implements Iterator<Project__c>, Iterable<Project__c> {
  List<Project__c> projects { get; set; }
  Integer i;
  public ProjectIterable() {
    projects = [SELECT Name FROM Project__c ORDER BY Name ];
    i = 0;
  }
  global Boolean hasNext() {
    if (i >= projects.size()) {
      return false;
    } else {
      return true;
    }
  }
  global Project__c next() {
    i++;
    return projects[i-1];
  }
  global Iterator<Project__c> Iterator() {
    return this;
  }
}
```

With the implementation of the `Iterable` class ready for use, examine the code in Listing 9.6. It is very similar to the first Batch Apex example. The only notable differences are that the parameterized type has been changed from `SObject` to `Project__c`, and the `start` method now returns the `Iterable` class developed in Listing 9.5.

Listing 9.6   **Iterable Batch Apex Sample**

```
global class Listing9_6
  implements Database.Batchable<Project__c> {
  global Iterable<Project__c> start(Database.BatchableContext context) {
    System.debug('start');
    return new ProjectIterable();
```

```
  }
  global void execute(Database.BatchableContext context,
    List<Project__c> scope) {
    System.debug('execute');
    for(Project__c rec : scope) {
      System.debug('Project: ' + rec.Name);
    }
  }
  global void finish(Database.BatchableContext context) {
    System.debug('finish');
  }
}
```

Turn on the debug log for your user and run the `Listing9_6` job. Examine the logs and see for yourself that you've accomplished the same work as the `Listing9_1` code using an iterable scope instead of a `QueryLocator` object.

Limits of Batch Apex

You must keep in mind several important limits of Batch Apex:

- Future methods are not allowed anywhere in Batch Apex.

- Batch jobs are always run as the system user, so they have permission to read and write all data in the organization.

- The maximum heap size in Batch Apex is 12MB.

- Calling out to external systems using the `HTTP` object or `webservice` methods is limited to one for each invocation of `start`, `execute`, and `finish`. To enable your batch process to call out, make sure the code implements the `Database.AllowsCallouts` interface in addition to the standard `Database.Batchable` interface.

- Transactions (the `execute` method) run under the same governor limits as any Apex code. If you have intensive work to do in your `execute` method and worry about exceeding the governor limits when presented with the default 200 records per transaction, reduce the number of records using the optional `scope` parameter of the `Database.executeBatch` method.

- The maximum number of queued or active batch jobs within an entire Salesforce organization is five. Attempting to run another job beyond the five raises a runtime error. For this reason, you should tightly control the number of batch jobs that are submitted. For example, submitting a batch from a trigger is generally a bad idea if you can avoid it. In a trigger, you can quickly exceed the maximum number of batch jobs.

Testing Batch Apex

Batch Apex can be tested like any Apex code, although you are limited to a single transaction's worth of data (one invocation of the `execute` method). A batch job started within a test runs synchronously, and does not count against the organization's limit of five batch jobs.

The class in Listing 9.7 tests the Batch Apex example from Listing 9.1 and achieves 100% test coverage. The annotation `IsTest(SeeAllData=true)` allows the test to access the data in the organization rather than requiring it to create its own test data. Alternatively, you could modify the code to omit the annotation and insert a few Project records to serve as test data.

Listing 9.7 **Batch Apex Test**

```
@IsTest(SeeAllData=true)
public with sharing class Listing9_7 {
  public static testmethod void testBatch() {
    Test.startTest();
    Listing9_1 batch = new Listing9_1();
    ID jobId = Database.executeBatch(batch);
    Test.stopTest();
  }
}
```

The test method simply executes the batch with the same syntax as you have used in the Execute Anonymous view. The batch execution is bookended with the `startTest` and `stopTest` methods. This ensures that the batch job is run synchronously and is finished at the `stopTest` method. This enables you to make assertions (`System.assert`) to verify that the batch performed the correct operations on your data.

Scheduling Batch Apex

Along with Batch Apex, Salesforce added a scheduler to the Force.com platform. This enables any Apex code, not just Batch Apex, to be scheduled to run asynchronously at regular time intervals. Prior to the introduction of this feature, developers had to resort to off-platform workarounds, such as invoking a Force.com Web service from an external system capable of scheduling jobs.

This section describes how to prepare your code for scheduling and how to schedule it from Apex and the administrative user interface.

Developing Schedulable Code

An Apex class that can be scheduled by Force.com must implement the `Schedulable` interface. The interface requires no methods to be implemented; it simply indicates to the platform that your class can be scheduled. Code that is executed by the scheduler runs as the system user, so sharing rules or other access controls are not enforced. At most, ten classes can be scheduled at one time.

The class in Listing 9.8 enables the Batch Apex example from Listing 9.1 to be schedulable. It does this by implementing the `Schedulable` interface, which has a single method: `execute`. Although you could implement this interface directly on your batch class, the best practice recommended by Salesforce is to create a separate `Schedulable` class.

Listing 9.8   **Schedulable Batch Apex**

```
global class Listing9_8 implements Schedulable {
  global void execute(SchedulableContext sc) {
    Listing9_1 batch = new Listing9_1();
    Database.executeBatch(batch);
  }
}
```

Scheduling Batch Apex Jobs

To schedule a job using the user interface, go to the App Setup area and click Develop, Apex Classes. Click the Schedule Apex button. In Figure 9.3, the `Listing9_8` class has been configured to run Saturday mornings at 11:00 a.m. between 7/10/2013 and 8/10/2013.

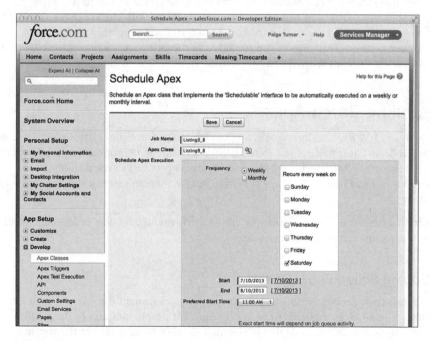

Figure 9.3   Schedule Apex user interface

To view and cancel scheduled jobs, go to the Administration Setup area and click Monitoring, Scheduled Jobs. This is shown in Figure 9.4 with the previously scheduled job. At this point, you can click Manage to edit the schedule, or Del to cancel it.

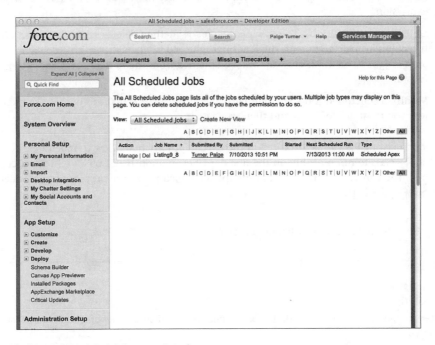

Figure 9.4   All Scheduled Jobs user interface

The same management of scheduled jobs available in the user interface can be automated using Apex code, as described next:

- **Create a scheduled job**—Use the System.schedule method to schedule a new job. This method requires three arguments: the name of the job, the schedule expression, and an instance of class to schedule. The schedule expression is a string in crontab-like format. This format is a space-delimited list of the following arguments: seconds, minutes, hours, day of month, month, day of week, and year (optional). Each argument is a value specifying when the job is to run in the relevant units. All arguments except seconds and minutes permit multiple values, ranges, wildcards, and increments. For example, the schedule expression 0 0 8 ? * MON-FRI schedules the job for weekdays at 8:00 a.m. The 8 indicates the eighth hour, the question mark leaves day of month unspecified, the asterisk indicates all months, and the day of week is Monday through Friday. The time zone of the user scheduling the job is used to calculate the schedule.

Note

For a full reference to schedule expressions, refer to the Force.com Apex Code Developer's Guide section on the subject, available at http://www.salesforce.com/us/developer/docs/apexcode/index_Left.htm#StartTopic=Content/apex_scheduler.htm.

- **View a scheduled job**—To get attributes about a scheduled job, such as when it will be executed next, query the standard object `CronTrigger`. It includes useful fields such as `NextFireTime`, `PreviousFireTime`, as well as `StartTime` and `EndTime`, calculated from the time the scheduled job was created to the last occurrence as specified by the schedule expression.

- **Delete a scheduled job**—The `System.abortJob` method deletes scheduled jobs. It requires a single argument, the identifier returned by the `SchedulableContext` `getTriggerID` method. This can also be obtained from the Id field of a `CronTrigger` record.

- **Modify a scheduled job**—The standard object `CronTrigger` is read-only, so to modify a job, you must delete it first and then re-create it.

The code in Listing 9.9 can be executed in the Execute Anonymous view to schedule the `Listing9_8` class to run monthly on the first day of every month at 1:00 a.m. in the user's time zone. You can verify this by examining the scheduled job in the user interface or querying the `CronTrigger` object.

Listing 9.9   **Sample Code to Schedule Batch Apex**

```
System.schedule('Scheduled Test', '0 0 1 * * ?', new Listing9_8());
```

> **Caution**
>
> After an Apex class is scheduled, its code cannot be modified until all of its scheduled jobs are deleted.

Sample Application: Missing Timecard Report

A common application of Batch Apex is to distill a large number of records down to a smaller, more digestible set of records that contain actionable information. In the Services Manager sample application, consultants enter timecards against assignments, specifying their daily hours for a weekly period. When consultants fail to enter their timecards in a timely manner, this can impact the business in many ways: Customers cannot be invoiced, and the budget of billable hours can be overrun without warning. With a large number of timecards, consultants, and projects, manually searching the database to identify missing timecards isn't feasible. This information needs to be extracted from the raw data.

The management users of the Services Manager have requested a tool that enables them to proactively identify missing timecards. They would like to see a list of the time periods and the assignments that have no timecard so that they can work with the consultants to get their time reported. This information could later be used as the basis of a custom user interface, report or dashboard component, or automated email notifications to the consultants.

This section walks through the implementation of the missing timecard report. It consists of the following steps:

1. Create a custom object to store the list of missing timecards.

2. Develop a Batch Apex class to calculate the missing timecard information.

3. Run through a simple test case to make sure the code works as expected.

Creating the Custom Object

Your Services Manager users in supervisory positions have asked to see missing timecards of their consultants. Specifically they want the dates of missing timecards, the offending consultants, and their assigned projects. There are two fields necessary to provide the requested information: the assignment, which automatically includes the resource and project as references, and the week ending date that lacks a timecard for the assignment.

Create a new custom object to store this information, naming it Missing Timecard. Add a lookup field to Assignment and a Date field named Week_Ending__c to mirror the field of the same name in the Timecard object. Create a custom tab for this object as well. When you're done, the Missing Timecard object definition should resemble Figure 9.5.

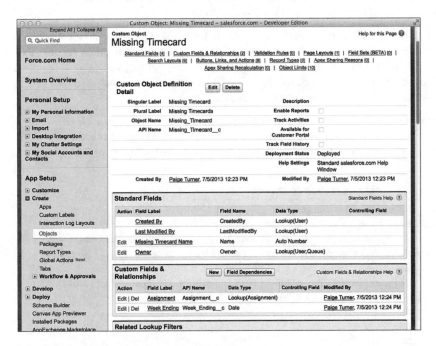

Figure 9.5   Missing timecard custom object definition

Developing the Batch Apex Class

A good design approach for Batch Apex is to consider the input schema, output schema, and the most direct algorithm to transform input to output. You've already designed the output schema based on what the users want to see: the Missing Timecard object. That leaves the input and the algorithm to be designed.

Consider the algorithm first, which drives the input. The algorithm loops through assignments that are not in Tentative or Closed status. It builds a list of Week Ending dates of valid time-cards (in Submitted or Approved status) in the same project as the assignment. It then cycles through the weeks between the start and end dates of the assignment, up to the current day. If a week ending date is not found in the list of timecard Week Ending dates, it is considered missing and its assignment and date are added to the Missing Timecards object.

With the algorithm nailed down, move on to the input. The key to a concise, maintainable Batch Apex class is formulating the right SOQL query to provide the input records. Most of the effort is in finding the optimal SObject to base the query on. If you pick the wrong SObject, you could be forced to augment the input in your `execute` method, resulting in more queries, this time subject to SOQL governor limits.

It is clear from the algorithm that the batch input must include Assignment records and corresponding Timecard records. But Assignment and Timecard are two separate many-to-many relationships with no direct relationship with each other.

Although basing the query on the Assignment or Timecard objects might be tempting, this leads to a weak design. For example, if you query the assignments in the `start` method and then augment this with Timecard records in the `execute` method, you need to build dynamic SOQL to optimize the second query given the input Assignment records. This is a sure sign that you should continue to iterate on the design.

When you switch tracks and design the batch around the Project object, life becomes easier. From Project, you have access to Timecard and Assignment records at the same time. The code in Listing 9.10 implements the missing timecard feature with a query on Project as the input.

Listing 9.10 **MissingTimecardBatch**

```
global class MissingTimecardBatch
  implements Database.Batchable<SObject> {
  global Database.QueryLocator start(Database.BatchableContext context) {
    return Database.getQueryLocator([ SELECT Name, Type__c,
      (SELECT Name, Start_Date__c, End_Date__c
        FROM Assignments__r WHERE Status__c NOT IN ('Tentative', 'Closed')),
      (SELECT Status__c, Week_Ending__c
        FROM Timecards__r
        WHERE Status__c IN ('Submitted', 'Approved'))
      FROM Project__c
    ]);
  }
  global void execute(Database.BatchableContext context,
    List<SObject> scope) {
```

```
    List<Missing_Timecard__c> missing = new List<Missing_Timecard__c>();
    for (SObject rec : scope) {
      Project__c proj = (Project__c)rec;
      Set<Date> timecards = new Set<Date>();
      if (proj.Assignments__r != null) {
        for (Assignment__c assign : proj.Assignments__r) {
          if (proj.Timecards__r != null) {
            for (Timecard__c timecard : proj.Timecards__r) {
              timecards.add(timecard.Week_Ending__c);
            }
          }
        }
/** Timecards are logged weekly, so the Week_Ending__c field is always
 * a Saturday. We need to convert an assignment, which can contain an
 * arbitrary start and end date, into a start and end period expressed
 * only in terms of Saturdays. To do this, we use the toStartOfWeek
 * method on the Date object, and then add 6 days to reach a Saturday.
 */
        Date startWeekEnding =
          assign.Start_Date__c.toStartOfWeek().addDays(6);
        Date endWeekEnding =
          assign.End_Date__c.toStartOfWeek().addDays(6);
        Integer weeks = 0;
        while (startWeekEnding.addDays(weeks * 7) < endWeekEnding) {
          Date d = startWeekEnding.addDays(weeks * 7);
          if (d >= Date.today()) {
            break;
          }
          if (!timecards.contains(d)) {
            missing.add(new Missing_Timecard__c(
              Assignment__c = assign.Id,
              Week_Ending__c = d));
          }
          weeks++;
        }
      }
    }
  }
  insert missing;
}
global void finish(Database.BatchableContext context) {
}
}
```

Testing the Missing Timecard Feature

To achieve adequate test coverage, add unit tests to the Batch Apex class that create assignments and timecards in various combinations, kick off the batch, and then query the Missing Timecard object and verify the presence of the correct data.

You can also test informally from the user interface and the Execute Anonymous view in the Force.com IDE. For example, create an Assignment record for the GenePoint project, starting 4/1/2015 and ending 4/30/2015 for Rose Gonzalez, and set its status to Scheduled. Enter a timecard for her for week ending 4/11/2015 on the GenePoint project, and set its status to Approved. Now run the `MissingTimecardBatch` from Force.com using the code in Listing 9.11.

Listing 9.11   **Running `MissingTimecardBatch`**

```
Database.executeBatch(new MissingTimecardBatch());
```

Check the Apex Jobs to monitor the progress of your batch job. When it's done, visit the Missing Timecard tab. You should see three Missing Timecard records for the GenePoint assignment, with the dates 4/4/2015, 4/18/2015, and 4/25/2015. The 4/11/2015 date is not included because a valid Timecard record exists for it.

To try some more test scenarios, first clear the Missing Timecard records so you don't have to sift through duplicates. The code in Listing 9.12 is an easy way to do so, and you can run it from the Execute Anonymous view.

Listing 9.12   **Reset Results of `MissingTimecardBatch`**

```
delete [ SELECT Id FROM Missing_Timecard__c ];
```

Summary

Batch processing in Force.com enables you to query and modify data in volumes that would otherwise be prohibited by governor limits. In this chapter, you've learned how to develop, test, and schedule batch jobs, and applied batch processing to the real-world problem of identifying missing database records.

When using Batch Apex in your own applications, consider these key points:

- Batch Apex is optimized for tasks with inputs that can be expressed in a single SOQL statement and that do not require all-or-nothing transactional behavior.

- With its limit of five active batch jobs per organization, one input data set per job, and a lack of precise control over actual execution time, Batch Apex is the nuclear option of Force.com data processing: powerful, but challenging to build and subject to proliferation problems. Use it sparingly, when all other options are exhausted. If triggers or Visualforce controllers can do the same job given expected data volumes, consider them first.

- You can implement the `Schedulable` interface to run any Apex code at regular time intervals, not just Batch Apex. Schedules can be managed via the administrative user interface and in Apex code.

10

Integration with Force.com

The Force.com platform offers various features to integrate its data and processes with those of other applications. These features are leveraged by independent software vendors as part of stand-alone integration products and also exposed to developers and system administrators of Force.com. This chapter describes the integration features that can bridge Force.com with other applications.

Force.com integration features leverage the Web standards of REST and SOAP to send and receive data over HTTP. REST stands for Representational State Transfer, a common form of Web-accessible API. SOAP is an acronym for Simple Object Access Protocol. These standards can be used to communicate with Force.com bidirectionally, meaning you can call into and out of Force.com with them.

This chapter is divided into the following sections:

- **Apex callouts**—Initiate requests to systems on the Web via REST and SOAP directly from inside your Apex code.

- **Calling into Force.com using REST**—With the Force.com REST API, you can access Force.com data and logic using a REST-style interface.

- **Calling into Force.com using SOAP**—Learn how to use the Enterprise API to make the data objects and Apex code in your organization available outside of Force.com.

- **Sample application**—Walk through an integration scenario with the Services Manager sample application, extending it to calculate and transmit corporate performance metrics to a fictional industry-benchmarking organization.

> **Note**
> The code listings in this chapter are available in a GitHub Gist at http://goo.gl/GBXT6.

Apex Callouts

A callout is a request made to a system outside of Force.com from within the platform. There are many Web APIs, free and premium, that can be quickly integrated into your Apex code using Apex callouts. This section describes how to work with the two different styles of callouts in Force.com:

1. **Calling RESTful services from Apex**—Force.com includes classes for issuing HTTP and HTTPS requests, encoding and decoding URLs and Base64 content, and performing cryptographic signing and hashing often needed to comply with the security requirements of external services.

2. **Calling SOAP services from Apex**—Apex code can be generated directly from WSDL, producing methods for invoking an external Web service and representing the input and output data in native Apex data structures rather than SOAP.

> ### Caution
>
> Force.com tightly controls outbound requests from its platform. Understanding the limits before jumping into development of integrations is important. These limitations apply to both Web service callouts and HTTP requests.
>
> Request and response messages cannot exceed the maximum Apex heap size, normally 6MB. Apex code can make a maximum of ten HTTP requests in a single transaction. By default, a single request cannot run longer than 10 seconds. If a transaction contains more than one request, the total time of all requests cannot exceed 120 seconds.

Calling RESTful Services from Apex

Twitter, Facebook, Yahoo!, Google, and countless others provide REST APIs for their services. REST is designed for lightweight clients, those running inside Web browsers or other scripting environments. Rather than generating static language bindings from a metadata description, as found with WSDL in the Web services world, the REST approach is dynamic. Its emphasis is on a concise syntax for URLs that represent resources and the use of HTTP methods to describe actions on those resources.

REST services usually return data in XML or JSON format, with the format specified by the caller of the service. JSON stands for JavaScript Object Notation, a standard format for representing JavaScript objects as strings. Like XML, it's widely used for communication between programs.

To invoke REST-style services, Apex can make HTTP requests from the Force.com platform to external servers on the Internet, as well as parse their JSON and XML responses. The core Apex classes that allow you to work with HTTP are described here:

- **HttpRequest**—This class contains the parameters for making an HTTP request. It includes methods for working with the request body, HTTP headers, the HTTP method type, client certificates, HTTP compression, and timeouts.

- **HttpResponse**—When an HTTP request is sent, an instance of the `HttpResponse` class is returned. Methods are available for getting the raw response body, HTTP status code, and HTTP headers.

- **Http**—This class is used to perform the HTTP operation. It contains a single method called `send` to initiate the operation, which accepts an instance of `HttpRequest` and returns an `HttpResponse`.

In addition to these three classes, here are two other useful classes for working with HTTP in Apex:

1. **EncodingUtil**—This class contains methods for URL and Base64 encoding and decoding.

2. **Crypto**—Use the `Crypto` class to compute cryptographic hashes and signatures commonly required to authenticate to HTTP services. It includes the methods `generateDigest` to generate a one-way hash digest for a message, `generateMac` to generate a message authentication code given a private key, and `sign` to produce a digital signature for a message using a private key.

To get started with HTTP in Apex, try writing a method to invoke a RESTful service. The service used in the following example is provided by Yahoo!. It's a geocoding service, returning latitude and longitude given a street, city, and state. The service is documented at http://developer.yahoo.com/boss/geo. Listing 10.1 is a sample of the result of invoking the service.

Listing 10.1   **Sample JSON Response from Yahoo! Geocoding REST Service**

```
cbfunc({
 "query": {
  "count": 1,
  "created": "2013-07-21T05:03:20Z",
  "lang": "en-US",
  "results": {
   "place": {
   "centroid": {
    "latitude": "37.547031",
    "longitude": "-122.314827"
    }
   }
  }
 }
});
```

In the code sample in Listing 10.2, the geocoding service is called and its response parsed using the JSON API provided by Force.com.

Listing 10.2   **Integrating the Yahoo! Geocoding Service**

```
public class Listing10_2 {
  private static String APP_ID = 'B1tiUc7k';
  public static Result geocode(String location) {
    HttpRequest req = new HttpRequest();
    String query = 'select centroid from geo.places where text="'
      + location + '"';
    String url = 'http://query.yahooapis.com/v1/public/yql?appid='
      + APP_ID + '&q=' + EncodingUtil.urlEncode(query, 'UTF-8')
```

```
      + '&format=json';
    req.setEndpoint(url);
    req.setMethod('GET');
    Http http = new Http();
    HTTPResponse res = http.send(req);
    JSONParser parser = JSON.createParser(res.getBody());
    while (parser.nextToken() != null) {
      if ((parser.getCurrentToken() == JSONToken.FIELD_NAME) &&
        (parser.getText() == 'centroid')) {
          parser.nextToken();
          return (Result)parser.readValueAs(Result.class);
      }
    }
    return null;
  }
  public class Result {
    public String latitude;
    public String longitude;
    public String asString() {
      return latitude + ', ' + longitude;
    }
  }
}
```

> **Tip**
>
> The `Listing10_2` class will not work without a Remote Site Setting authorizing Force.com to call out to the Yahoo! service. To add this setting, go to the Administration Setup area and click Security Controls, Remote Site Settings. Click the New Remote Site button and enter a name to remember the site (no spaces allowed) and the root of the URL (http://query.yahooapis.com).

To test the code, open the Execute Anonymous view in the Force.com IDE and execute the statements given in Listing 10.3. The result (contained in the debug log) should be a single line containing the latitude and longitude of the input address.

Listing 10.3   **Testing the Yahoo! Geocoding Integration**

```
Listing10_2.Result r = Listing10_2.geocode
  ('1 market st san francisco ca');
System.debug(r.toString());
```

Calling SOAP Services from Apex

Force.com provides a code generation tool in its native user interface for creating Apex-friendly classes and methods from SOAP Web service definitions found in WSDL files. Like most code generation tools, using it is a hit-or-miss experience. When it works on your WSDL, it can save considerable effort over the alternative of manually constructing and parsing SOAP messages. But be prepared for cryptic error messages when code cannot be generated due to the imped-ance mismatch between WSDL, SOAP, and Apex.

If you're able to use your WSDL wholesale or slim it down to successfully generate Apex code, most of your work is done. Invoking the remote SOAP Web service becomes a relatively simple matter of preparing the right input via Apex classes, invoking a method, and using the result-ing Apex classes in your program. No interaction with HTTP or XML is necessary because these details are hidden by the generated Apex code.

> **Caution**
>
> For integrations that require a series of Web service calls strung together with cookies to main-tain state between them, you cannot use the Apex code generated from WSDL. Additionally, generated code does not support HTTP-level authentication.
>
> In general, no developer-modifiable options exist in the generated code, which uses an internal, undocumented API to perform the actual Web service callout. If your Web service call requires control over the SOAP message content or HTTP headers, you must write code to make the request from scratch using HTTPRequest, as described in the next subsection.

Here are the steps needed to generate Apex from WSDL:

1. Save the WSDL file on your local machine.

2. Go to the App Setup area and click Develop, Apex Classes.

3. Click the Generate from WSDL button.

4. Click the Browse button and locate the WSDL in your file system and then click the Parse WSDL button. The WSDL must describe a document-style service because Remote Procedure Call (RPC) is not supported.

5. Each WSDL namespace can be mapped to an Apex class name to be generated. You can map multiple namespaces to the same class. Force.com suggests an Apex class name based on the WSDL, but you can override this suggestion. When you're done naming the classes, click the Generate Apex Code button.

6. If you refresh your Force.com IDE by right-clicking the project and selecting Force.com, Refresh from Server, you should see the new Apex class. If not, make sure that it was generated successfully and that you've subscribed to new Apex classes by right-clicking the Force.com project and selecting Force.com, Add/Remove Metadata Components.

> **Caution**
>
> Due to the complexity of WSDL, conflicts between its naming conventions and Apex syntax rules, and the limit on Apex class size, the WSDL to Apex feature might not work as expected in all cases. Investigate these issues further in the Force.com online help. As a best practice, keep your WSDL as simple as possible. Manually edit it to strip out extraneous services and ports.

Before you can run this code, you must authorize Force.com to make an outbound call to the endpoint of the Web service. Go to the Administration Setup area, click Security Controls, Remote Site Settings, and then add the host.

Calling into Force.com Using REST

Force.com provides a REST form of its core data access API to query and modify standard and custom objects. It also allows Apex developers to turn custom classes into REST Web services. This section provides an introduction to using REST to call into Force.com in three parts:

- **Getting started with Force.com REST API**—Learn how Force.com functionality is exposed in the REST style and how to authenticate to it.

- **Force.com REST API walk-through**—Using your computer's command line, you can take an interactive tour of the Force.com REST API.

- **Creating custom Apex REST Web services**—With a few simple modifications, an Apex class can be serving REST-style requests from the Web.

> **Note**
>
> Because REST requests and responses are typically so concise, you can practice using them directly from your computer's command line using standard OS-level tools to make Web requests. The examples in this section rely on the tool named cURL, available free for every platform at http://curl.haxx.se.

Getting Started with Force.com REST API

Data access concepts in Force.com translate naturally into the REST style of API. SObjects and rows within them become URLs, and HTTP actions express DML operations: GET for read-only requests for basic information, POST to create records, PATCH to update records, and DELETE to delete them. Because not all HTTP clients support the full range of methods, Force.com also allows a special URL parameter (_HttpMethod) to specify the action. By default, REST API calls return JSON-encoded responses, but you can override this by appending .xml to the end of URLs, or by sending the standard HTTP Accept header with the desired content type.

Almost every REST API call requires authentication to Force.com. This is done using OAuth. OAuth is an industry-standard way of negotiating access to a system without requiring users to share their login credentials. OAuth operates using tokens instead. Tokens have advantages over the typical username/password credentials. They can be audited and revoked by the user. They also typically provide limited access to the system. In the case of Force.com, OAuth access tokens grant bearers the ability to make API calls only. They cannot log in to the Salesforce Web user interface.

> **Note**
>
> OAuth is a complex subject well beyond the scope of this book. The Force.com REST API Developer's Guide, found at www.salesforce.com/us/developer/docs/api_rest/index.htm, provides some introductory information on using OAuth to authenticate to Force.com.

If you are calling the REST API on behalf of another user, OAuth is the recommended approach for authentication because you do not need to store others' usernames and passwords. But when you're learning and experimenting with simple REST API examples, OAuth can present a significant hurdle.

A shortcut is to use the username-password OAuth flow, which still accepts username and password directly. Listing 10.4 provides a sample request and response.

Listing 10.4   Sample Password Authentication Request and Response

```
curl https://login.salesforce.com/services/oauth2/token
  -d "grant_type=password" -d "client_id=$CLIENT_ID"
  -d "client_secret=$CLIENT_SECRET"
  -d "username=$USERNAME" -d "password=$PASSWORD"
{
    "id": "https://login.salesforce.com/id/...",
    "issued_at": "1374386510993",
    "instance_url": "https://na15.salesforce.com",
    "signature": "...",
    "access_token": "..."
}
```

The value in the response's `access_token` field is needed to run all of the examples in this section. To get one yourself, set the `$USERNAME` environment variable to your Salesforce username, `$PASSWORD` to your Salesforce password with security token appended. The variables `$CLIENT_ID` and `$CLIENT_SECRET` are your OAuth Consumer Key and Consumer Secret. These come from a Connected App, which you can create using the following steps:

1. In the App Setup area, click Create, Apps.

2. Click the New button in the Connected Apps section.

3. Fill out Connected App Name, API Name, and Contact Email.

4. Check Enable OAuth Settings.

5. Set the Callback URL to http://localhost.

6. In Available OAuth Scopes, select Access and Manage Your Data (api).

The resulting Connected App is shown in Figure 10.1.

Figure 10.1   Connected App configuration

Force.com REST API Walk-Through

Now that you have obtained an OAuth access token, you are ready to try the Force.com REST API. Set the access token as the environment variable $TOKEN. Also, be sure to replace na15 in the following examples with your own instance of Force.com. To identify your instance, look at the instance_url field of the OAuth username-password flow, or the URL in your Web browser when you log in to Force.com.

> **Note**
>
> This section is not a complete reference to the REST API. Consult the Force.com REST API Developer's Guide, found at www.salesforce.com/us/developer/docs/api_rest/index.htm, for the latest and most detailed information on the REST API, which Salesforce continuously improves in each major release of the platform.

Listing 10.5 is an example of one of the simplest REST API calls. It returns the services available via REST in the specified version and instance of the Force.com platform. Here, the result indicates four services. In subsequent examples, you'll try all the services, except recent. The recent service returns the same data as you see in the Recent Items box in the Web user interface.

Listing 10.5 **Services Available Request and Response**

```
curl https://na15.salesforce.com/services/data/v28.0\
  -H "Authorization: OAuth "$TOKEN -H "X-PrettyPrint:1"
{
  "sobjects" : "/services/data/v28.0/sobjects",
  "identity" : "https://login.salesforce.com/id/... ",
  "connect" : "/services/data/v28.0/connect",
  "search" : "/services/data/v28.0/search",
  "quickActions" : "/services/data/v28.0/quickActions",
  "query" : "/services/data/v28.0/query",
  "tooling" : "/services/data/v28.0/tooling",
  "chatter" : "/services/data/v28.0/chatter",
  "recent" : "/services/data/v28.0/recent"
}
```

> **Tip**
>
> The backslash (\) character found at the end of the first line in Listing 10.5 and other listings in this chapter is a line-continuation character for UNIX shells. Translate it as appropriate to your own command-line environment.

To retrieve basic information on an SObject, use the `sobjects` service, as demonstrated in Listing 10.6. You can also omit the object name (`/Project__c`) to get a list of all SObjects, or append `/describe` to the end of the URL to obtain the full, detailed list of fields on the SObject. If an error occurs in processing this request or any REST request, the response contains `message` and `errorCode` keys to communicate the error message and code.

Listing 10.6 **Basic Information Request for an SObject**

```
curl https://na15.salesforce.com/services/data/v28.0/sobjects/Project__c\
  -H "Authorization: OAuth "$TOKEN -H "X-PrettyPrint:1"
```

Another usage of the `sobjects` service is shown in Listing 10.7. Here an individual record is returned, identified by its unique identifier. The `fields` parameter specifies a subset of fields to return. You can omit this parameter to retrieve all fields. If your record is a binary object such as a Document, append `/body` to the URL to retrieve the binary content.

Listing 10.7 **Record Retrieval by Unique Identifier Request and Response**

```
curl https://na15.salesforce.com/services/data/v28.0\
/sobjects/Project__c/a01i0000000rMq1?fields=Name,Status__c\
  -H "Authorization: OAuth "$TOKEN -H "X-PrettyPrint:1"
{
  "attributes" : {
    "type" : "Project__c",
    "url" : "/services/data/v20.0/sobjects/Proj__c/a01i0000000rMq1AAE"
```

```
  },
  "Name" : "GenePoint",
  "Status__c" : "Green",
  "Id" : "a01i0000000rMq1AAE"
}
```

Listing 10.8 demonstrates record retrieval by external identifier. The record with a `Project_` `ID__c` value of `Project-00001` on the `Project__c` SObject is returned.

Listing 10.8 Request for Retrieval of Record by External Identifier

```
curl https://na15.salesforce.com/services/data/v28.0\
/sobjects/Project__c/Project_ID__c/Project-00001\
 -H "Authorization: OAuth "$TOKEN -H "X-PrettyPrint:1"
```

A simple SOQL query is shown in Listing 10.9. To run a SOSL query, use `search` instead of `query` in the URL.

Listing 10.9 SOQL Query Request

```
curl https://na15.salesforce.com/services/data/v28.0\
/query?q=SELECT+Name+FROM+Project__c\
 -H "Authorization: OAuth "$TOKEN -H "X-PrettyPrint:1"
```

To create a record, make a `POST` request with the SObject type in the URL and a JSON or XML request body containing the record's field values. Listing 10.10 creates a new `Project__c` record named Test Project. A successful response provides the new record's unique identifier.

Listing 10.10 Create Record Request and Response

```
echo '{ "Name": "Test Project" }' |\
  curl -X POST -H 'Content-type: application/json'\
  -H "Authorization: OAuth "$TOKEN -H "X-PrettyPrint:1" -d @-\
  https://na15.salesforce.com/services/data/v28.0/sobjects/Project__c
{
  "id" : "a01i0000003aFzrAAE",
  "success" : true,
  "errors" : [ ]
}
```

> **Tip**
>
> To adapt the command in Listing 10.10 to run in Windows Command Prompt, remove the single quotation mark characters (`'`) in the `echo` statement, replace the single quotation mark characters around the `Content-type` header with double quotation mark characters (`"`), remove the backslash (`\`) line-continuation characters and concatenate the lines into a single line, and replace `$TOKEN` with `%TOKEN%`.

Updating a record follows a similar process to creating a record. Make a PATCH request with the URL containing the SObject type and unique identifier, and a request body with the field values to update. In Listing 10.11, the record created in Listing 10.10 gets its name updated.

Listing 10.11   **Update Record Request**

```
echo '{ "Name": "Updated Test Project" }' |\
  curl -X PATCH -H 'Content-type: application/json'\
  -H 'Authorization: OAuth '$TOKEN -H "X-PrettyPrint:1" -d @-\
  https://na15.salesforce.com/services/data/v28.0\
/sobjects/Project__c/a01i0000003aFzrAAE
```

The only difference between an upsert and update request is that upsert uses an external identifier rather than the unique identifier. If the external identifier value is not found, the request creates the record and its unique identifier is returned. Otherwise, the record is updated, and nothing is returned upon success. Listing 10.12 demonstrates an upsert of a Project__c record.

> **Note**
>
> Listing 10.12 will return an INVALID_FIELD_FOR_INSERT_UPDATE error unless you change the Project_ID__c field type from Auto Number to Text first because Auto Number fields are read-only.

Listing 10.12   **Upsert Record Request and Response**

```
echo '{ "Name": "Upserted Project" }' |\
  curl -X PATCH -H 'Content-type: application/json'\
  -H "Authorization: OAuth "$TOKEN -H "X-PrettyPrint:1" -d @-\
  https://na15.salesforce.com/services/data/v28.0\
/sobjects/Project__c/Project_ID__c/Project-11111
```

Deleting a record by its unique identifier is shown in Listing 10.13. You can also delete a record by its external identifier. In both cases, nothing is returned by a successful request.

Listing 10.13   **Delete Record Request**

```
curl -X DELETE\
  -H 'Authorization: OAuth '$TOKEN -H "X-PrettyPrint:1"\
  https://na15.salesforce.com/services/data/v28.0\
/sobjects/Project__c/a01i0000003aFzrAAE
```

Creating Custom Apex REST Web Services

Force.com REST API is a powerful but generic way to access data. For some application-specific data access scenarios, such as those involving transactions that span multiple database objects, a custom API is helpful. You can expose your Apex classes as REST services, making simple atomic units of work accessible to callers outside of Force.com, and hiding the implementation details from them. Requests to custom Apex REST services are made via HTTP in JSON or XML format, dictated by the Content-Type header, with JSON the default.

For an Apex class to become a REST Web service, it must follow different rules than ordinary Apex classes. The most significant rules are listed here:

- **Global class access modifier**—A class that contains any REST services must use the global access modifier. This means the class is visible to all programs running in the Force.com organization.

- **URL mapping annotation**—A class containing REST services must be mapped to a URL so that it can be invoked. Define the URL mapping using the @RestResource annotation.

- **HTTP verb annotation**—Each method accessible via REST must be annotated with a corresponding HTTP verb. The verbs are @HttpDelete, @HttpGet, @HttpPatch, @HttpPost, and @HttpPut, and the same verb can't be assigned to more than one method. These methods must also be global and static.

- **Method parameters**—The REST request body is automatically mapped into the parameters of the method. Method parameters are not supported for the @HttpDelete and @HttpGet verbs. The REST request URL is never automatically mapped to method parameters and requires code to extract its values.

- **Data types**—Data types supported in REST methods are primitive types (except Blob and sObject), sObjects, List and Map (String keys only) containing primitives or sObjects, and user-defined classes.

- **Security**—REST methods run as a system administrator, without regard for object-, field-, or record-level sharing rules. To enforce record sharing rules, define the class with the with sharing keyword. To enforce object- and field-level security, use the results of the getDescribe method (Schema.DescribeSObjectResult and Schema.DescribeFieldResult) to check the user's permission to the data.

- **Supporting classes**—User-defined Apex classes, inner or outer, that are arguments or return values for a REST service method must be defined as global.

Additionally, custom Apex REST Web services are subject to standard Apex governor limits. A subset of these governor limits is listed in Table 10.1.

Table 10.1   Subset of Apex REST Service Governor Limits

Resource Type	Governor Limit
SOQL	100 queries
Records from SOQL	50,000 records
DML	150 DML statements
Records in DML	10,000 records
Stack depth	16
Heap	6,000,000 bytes
Apex code	200,000 lines of code executed

Listing 10.14 defines a simple Apex REST service that returns a record in the Project custom object given its unique identifier.

Listing 10.14   Custom Apex REST Web Service

```
@RestResource(urlMapping='/Listing10_14/*')
global with sharing class Listing10_14 {
  @HttpGet
  global static Project__c doGet() {
    RestRequest req = RestContext.request;
    String projectId = req.requestURI.substring(
      req.requestURI.lastIndexOf('/')+1);
    Project__c result = [SELECT Id, Name, Status__c, Owner.Name
      FROM Project__c WHERE Id = :projectId];
    return result;
  }
}
```

In Listing 10.15, the custom REST Web service is invoked and returns fields from the Project record with unique identifier a01i0000000rMq1.

Listing 10.15   Custom Apex REST Web Service Request and Response

```
curl -H 'Authorization: OAuth '$TOKEN -H "X-PrettyPrint:1"\
 "https://na15.salesforce.com/services/apexrest/Listing10_14/a01i0000000rMq1"
{
  "attributes" : {
    "type" : "Project__c",
    "url" : "/services/data/v27.0/sobjects/Project__c/a01i0000000rMq1AAE"
  },
  "Name" : "GenePoint",
```

```
  "Owner" : {
    "attributes" : {
      "type" : "Name",
      "url" : "/services/data/v27.0/sobjects/User/005i0000000LUJsAAO"
    },
    "Name" : "Tim Barr",
    "Id" : "005i0000000LUJsAAO"
  },
  "OwnerId" : "005i0000000LUJsAAO",
  "Id" : "a01i0000000rMq1AAE",
  "Status__c" : "Green"
}
```

Calling into Force.com Using SOAP

Force.com provides many SOAP APIs, each focused on a different area of platform functionality. For example, you can query and modify standard and custom objects using SOAP. You can also make custom classes into SOAP Web services. This section provides an introduction to using SOAP to call into Force.com in three parts:

1. **Understanding Force.com SOAP API**—This section describes high-level concepts common to all the subsequent sections, including how to invoke SOAP Web services from Java and the handling of data types and errors.

2. **Using the Enterprise API**—The Enterprise API is a set of SOAP Web services that allow fine-grained, strongly typed access to the data in your Force.com database, including execution of SOQL and SOSL queries and full read and write capabilities on the records of all objects.

3. **Creating custom Apex SOAP Web services**—Although Force.com provides a built-in SOAP API to access your data, you can also define your own custom SOAP API using Apex code. Custom Apex SOAP Web services are typically written to optimize for application-specific usage patterns; for example, combining what would be many SOAP API calls into a single, robust method executed entirely on the Force.com platform.

Understanding Force.com SOAP API

Force.com SOAP API allows data, logic, and metadata to be accessed from outside the Force.com platform by any program that can communicate using SOAP messages over HTTP. With a strongly typed language like Java or C#.NET, stub code is generated from the Force.com SOAP API's WSDL. The program must log in to Force.com to establish a session and can then invoke the SOAP API methods.

This section describes concepts that can be applied to using any Force.com SOAP API method. It consists of the following parts:

- **Basics of Force.com SOAP API**—Learn about the two different styles of Force.com SOAP API methods, how they are secured, and limits placed on their use.

- **Generating stub code**—Walk through the process for generating Java code from Force. com SOAP API WSDL.

- **Logging in**—The first SOAP API call typically establishes a session with Force.com by logging in. This session is used to make subsequent SOAP API calls until it is invalidated explicitly or it expires.

- **Force.com data types in SOAP**—Understand how data types in Force.com objects are expressed in the SOAP API.

- **Error handling**—Force.com SOAP API signals errors in a few ways, depending on where the errors originate.

Basics of Force.com SOAP API

The Force.com SOAP API comes in two forms, Enterprise and Partner. Both APIs have the same core set of calls, such as `query` to execute a SOQL query. The difference between the APIs is how database objects are represented in your code.

The Enterprise API provides a strongly typed representation of the objects in your Force.com database. This allows your code to operate naturally with Force.com data, using the field names and data types as you would in Apex code. When you redefine an object or add a new object, the Enterprise WSDL is automatically updated to reflect the changes. You need to manually regenerate the client code from the latest WSDL, but this is a small price to pay for concise, maintainable code.

The Partner API is designed for independent software vendors who write applications that must interoperate with many different Force.com organizations. They cannot rely on a single, static representation of standard and custom objects because all customers of Force.com are free to create their own database schemas. With the Partner API, you can write generic code to access any object in any Force.com organization. It's more verbose to work with than the Enterprise API, but more flexible as well.

> **Note**
>
> This book does not cover the Partner API. For more information about it, consult the Force.com SOAP API Developer's Guide, available at www.salesforce.com/us/developer/docs/api/index.htm.

Versions

With each major release of the Force.com platform, new versions of its WSDL are also released. To take advantage of new features, your code must be updated to use the latest WSDL.

If the new features are not needed, no action is required. Your code will continue to work without modification. This is because each WSDL has an endpoint URL in it that includes its version.

> **Note**
>
> In its documentation, Salesforce commits to maintaining Web service versions for a minimum of three years. It also states that one year of notice will be provided for discontinued Web service versions.

Security

Force.com uses Secure Sockets Layer (SSL) v3 and Transport Layer Security (TLS) to protect the communications between your client application and the Force.com platform.

After your client program has logged in, all the API calls respect the full set of data security features in Force.com at the object, field, and record level. For this reason, configuring a Force.com profile and user account dedicated solely to integration is a good practice. It might have elevated privileges compared with other, Web-based users. You can configure this profile to accept logins only from the API address of your corporate integration server using the Login IP Ranges on the profile or logins at specific times that your integration is scheduled to run using the Login Hours section.

API Limits

Salesforce limits the number of API calls that can be executed during a 24-hour period. Every call into Force.com is counted against this limit, including calls made by the Force.com IDE. The exact limit depends on the edition of Force.com you have licensed.

To view your API limit and current consumption, go to the Administration Setup area and click Company Profile, Company Information. You can configure Force.com to email you when your organization is close to its API call limit. Go to the Administration Setup area and click Monitoring, API Usage Notifications. Click the New button to define a new notification, specifying the user to receive the notification, the usage threshold that triggers notifications, and how often they are sent.

Generating Stub Code

If you're using a strongly typed language like C#.NET or Java to integrate with Force.com, your first step is to generate stub code from a Force.com WSDL. All standard Force.com WSDLs are available in the App Setup area; to access them, click Develop, API. Click each WSDL link and save the resulting document on your local file system.

Each language and development tool typically provides a facility for parsing WSDL and generating stub code that can be incorporated into your program. The steps for generating Java stub code from WSDL are described next.

> **Note**
>
> Salesforce advises that you use the Force.com Web Service Connector (WSC) with its SOAP API. Download it from https://github.com/forcedotcom/wsc. Download the source code from https://github.com/forcedotcom/wsc. Follow the instructions there to compile the source code into a WSC JAR file, which requires Maven (http://maven.apache.org/). If you would rather download a WSC JAR file than build it, find one at http://code.google.com/p/sfdc-wsc/downloads/list.

Follow these steps to create Java stub code using WSC and the Eclipse IDE:

1. Create a new Java project. In this example, the project is named `Chapter10`.

2. Copy the WSC jar and `enterprise.wsdl` files into the top level of your Java project.

3. Create a new Run Configuration to execute the stub generator. Figure 10.2 shows the Run Configuration.

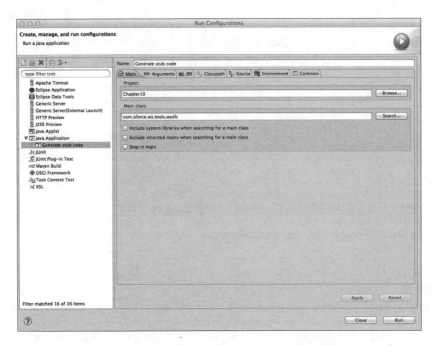

Figure 10.2   Eclipse Run Configuration to generate stub code using WSC

4. Click the Arguments tab and enter **enterprise.wsdl.xml ./enterprise.jar** in the Program Arguments text box. These arguments tell the program to generate the stub code for the `enterprise.xml.wsdl` file into a jar named `enterprise.jar`.

5. Click the Run button on the Run Configuration and refresh your project. It should contain the stub code for the Force.com Enterprise API, as depicted in Figure 10.3.

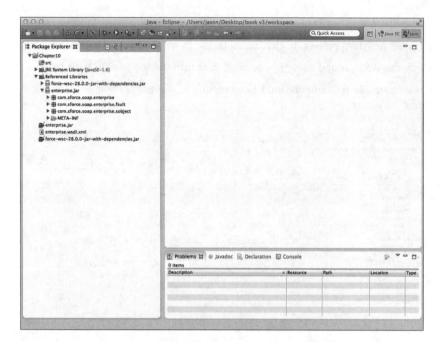

Figure 10.3   Java project with stub code generated

Logging In

Logging in to Force.com from a program begins with the user credentials of username and password, the same as logging in to the native user interface using a Web browser. This subsection describes four additional details to be aware of to successfully log in, summarized here:

- **API Enabled permission**—The user logging in must have the API Enabled permission on his or her profile.

- **Security token or white-listed IP address**—Force.com requires either a security token appended to the password or API calls to be issued from a white-listed IP address.

- **Login call**—When successful, the login method returns two items of information needed in subsequent calls: a URL to the Salesforce server and the user's session identifier.

- **Troubleshooting login problems**—Force.com includes a Login History report that can be helpful in identifying problems.

API Enabled Permission

The user logging in via API must have the API Enabled permission set on his or her profile. This permission is found in the Administrative Permissions section. A profile with the API Enabled permission is shown in Figure 10.4.

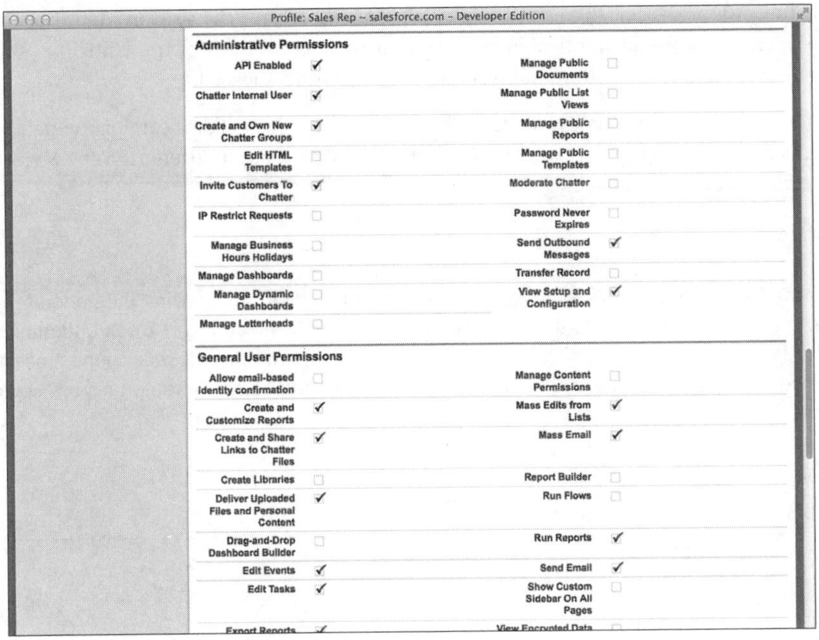

Profile: Sales Rep ~ salesforce.com – Developer Edition

Administrative Permissions

API Enabled	✓	Manage Public Documents	☐
Chatter Internal User	✓	Manage Public List Views	☐
Create and Own New Chatter Groups	✓	Manage Public Reports	☐
Edit HTML Templates	☐	Manage Public Templates	☐
Invite Customers To Chatter	✓	Moderate Chatter	☐
IP Restrict Requests	☐	Password Never Expires	☐
Manage Business Hours Holidays	☐	Send Outbound Messages	✓
Manage Dashboards	☐	Transfer Record	☐
Manage Dynamic Dashboards	☐	View Setup and Configuration	✓
Manage Letterheads	☐		

General User Permissions

Allow email-based identity confirmation	☐	Manage Content Permissions	☐
Create and Customize Reports	✓	Mass Edits from Lists	✓
Create and Share Links to Chatter Files	✓	Mass Email	✓
Create Libraries	☐	Report Builder	☐
Deliver Uploaded Files and Personal Content	✓	Run Flows	☐
Drag-and-Drop Dashboard Builder	☐	Run Reports	✓
Edit Events	✓	Send Email	✓
Edit Tasks	✓	Show Custom Sidebar On All Pages	☐
Export Reports	✓	View Encrypted Data	☐

Figure 10.4   Profile with the API Enabled permission

> **Caution**
>
> A few editions of Force.com don't allow API access. If you don't see the API Enabled permission on the profile page or cannot enable it, contact Salesforce support.

Security Token or White-Listed IP Address

The security token is a string of characters appended to the end of a user's password. It allows a user to log in to Force.com from any IP address, assuming that IP address restrictions are not configured on his or her profile. To obtain a security token, visit the Personal Setup area and click My Personal Information, Reset My Security Token. A new security token is generated and emailed to the address associated with the user.

An alternative to security tokens is IP white-listing. White-listing instructs Force.com to accept requests from a specific IP address. To white-list an IP address, go to the Administration Setup area and click Security Controls, Network Access. Click the New button, enter the IP address in the Start IP Address and End IP Address fields, and then click the Save button.

The Login Call

To log in, invoke the `login` method with a username and password. If the login is successful, a `LoginResult` object is returned; otherwise, an exception is raised. The `LoginResult` object contains the URL of the server to send SOAP API requests to and the session identifier that uniquely identifies your authenticated session with Force.com. Both of these attributes must be sent in the HTTP headers of subsequent requests for them to succeed.

Listing 10.16 contains sample Java code to log in. Note that WSC takes care of the details described earlier for logging in, but this is not the case if you use a different Web service stack, such as Apache Axis.

> **Note**
>
> The code in Listing 10.16 doesn't include exception handling or importing the generated stub code. It also doesn't factor in the use of corporate proxies, which might block outbound HTTPS traffic. Java can be configured to pass connections through a proxy. If your connections to Force.com are failing, check with your network administrator to see whether a proxy could be the cause.

Listing 10.16   **Java Fragment to Log In**

```
ConnectorConfig config = new ConnectorConfig();
config.setUsername(user);
config.setPassword(pass);
EnterpriseConnection connection = Connector.newConnection(config);
```

When you're done with a session, you can invoke the logout API call. It causes the session to become invalid, ensuring that it is not used accidentally elsewhere by your program.

By default, sessions expire after two hours, but you can change this in the Administration Setup area by clicking Security Controls, Session Settings. Web service calls that use an expired or invalid session throw an exception with an INVALID_SESSION_ID exception code.

Troubleshooting Login Problems

All logins to Force.com create an entry in the login history, shown in Figure 10.5. To view it, go to the Administration Setup area and click Manage Users, Login History.

The login history can be helpful for troubleshooting login problems. If you see your program's login attempt listed but failed, the login request has successfully reached Force.com's servers but is being rejected. If the request is not listed at all, you need to investigate the connection between your server and Force.com.

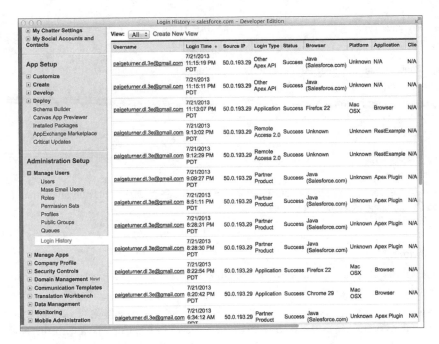

Figure 10.5   Login history page

Force.com Data Types in SOAP

Table 10.2 lists the Force.com data types and their mapping to SOAP data types.

Table 10.2   Mapping of Force.com Data Types to SOAP Types

Force.com Data Type	SOAP Type
Auto Number	String.
Formula	Depends on the data type of the formula. Can be Double, String, Date.
Roll-Up Summary	Double.
Lookup Relationship, Master-Detail Relationship	ID.
Checkbox	Boolean.
Currency	Double.
Date, Datetime	Date. Always UTC, convert to local time zone. If time portion isn't present, midnight is returned.
Number	Integer (numbers with no fractional component); otherwise Double.

Force.com Data Type	SOAP Type
Percent	Double.
Email, Phone, Picklist, Picklist (Multi-Select), Text, Text Area, Text (Long), URL	String.
Binary (Attachment, Document)	Base64-encoded string.

> **Note**
>
> Refer to the documentation for your programming language or SOAP utility library to map SOAP types to language-specific data types.

Error Handling

Three categories of errors are raised by Force.com SOAP API, described here from lowest to highest level of abstraction:

1. **System exceptions**—System exceptions are language-specific and indicate lower-level problems occurring in the Web services stack. For example, using Java with the WSC, the `ConnectionException` contains nested exceptions to indicate specific problems, such as a `java.net.SocketException`.

2. **API faults**—API faults are caused by malformed SOAP messages, authentication failures, or query-related problems. They are SOAP-level errors that contain an exception code and a message. For example, in Java, a `LoginFault` class extends `ApiFault` and indicates that the login to Force.com failed. A general API fault with an exception code of `INSUFFICIENT_ACCESS` indicates that the user does not have sufficient access to perform the operation.

3. **Application errors**—These are language-neutral, Force.com-specific errors that vary based on the Web services involved. For example, services that modify one or more records return an `Error` object upon failure. The `Error` object contains a status code, a message, and an array of fields impacted by the error. As a concrete example, if your record modification violates the referential integrity of the Force.com database, an `Error` object containing `FIELD_INTEGRITY_EXCEPTION` as its status code is returned.

Using the Enterprise API

At the highest level, the Enterprise API consists of core services that allow query and modification of Force.com data, plus a set of types reflecting the standard and custom objects defined in your Force.com organization. Using these core services and types is a fairly straightforward exercise after your code has established a session with Force.com.

This section divides the Enterprise API into four functional groups, described here:

1. **Retrieving records**—Retrieve records using SOQL or SOSL queries, by unique identifier, or based on their modification or deletion time stamp.

2. **Writing records**—Learn how to create and update records using the Enterprise API.

3. **Deleting and undeleting records**—By deleting records, you send them to the recycling bin, where they can later be undeleted if necessary.

4. **Modifications in bulk**—Modifications can be performed on up to 200 records at a time to conserve API calls and improve performance.

Retrieving Records

The most common way to retrieve records is via SOQL. This is accomplished with the `query` service. A SOQL statement is passed as input, and a `QueryResult` object is returned. This object contains an array of records returned by the query.

The number of records returned by the `query` service is a function of the batch size. The default batch size in Java using WSC is 2,000 records, 500 for Axis and other Web service clients. If a query result contains more records than the batch size, use the `queryMore` service to retrieve additional batches of records.

The code in Listing 10.17 demonstrates the `query` and `queryMore` services in Java to build a list of Project records.

Listing 10.17   **Java Fragment to Execute SOQL Query**

```java
List<Project__c> projects = new ArrayList<Project__c>();
QueryResult qr = connection.query("SELECT Id, Name FROM Project__c");
boolean done = false;
if (qr.getSize() > 0) {
  while (!done) {
    SObject[] records = qr.getRecords();
    if (records != null) {
      for (SObject record : records) {
        projects.add((Project__c)record);
      }
      if (qr.isDone()) {
        done = true;
      } else {
        qr = connection.queryMore(qr.getQueryLocator());
      }
    }
  }
}
```

You can set a custom batch size (up to 2,000 records) by providing a `QueryOptions` header. This is demonstrated in Java in Listing 10.18.

Listing 10.18 **Java Fragment for Setting Query Batch Size**

```
connection.setQueryOptions(2000);
```

There's no guarantee Force.com will return the requested number of records in a batch. For example, if a SOQL statement selects two or more custom fields of type long text, the batch size will never be more than 200 records. Queries on binary data always return a single record at a time.

Other Ways to Retrieve Records

A few other approaches are available for retrieving records, described next:

- **Using SOSL**—The `search` service executes a SOSL statement and returns a `Search Result` object, which contains an array of `SearchRecord` objects. Each `SearchRecord` contains an SObject instance representing a matching record. Because SOSL can return many object types, each `SearchRecord` object can contain a different type of SObject.

- **By unique identifier**—If you know the unique identifier of an object, you can retrieve it by using the `retrieve` service. Its inputs are a string containing a comma-separated list of field names to retrieve, the type of object as a string, and an array of up to 2,000 record unique identifiers. It returns an array of SObject instances.

- **By time stamp**—The `getUpdated` and `getDeleted` services return the unique identifiers of records updated or deleted between a range of dates.

Writing Records

The basic services for writing records closely resemble their counterparts in Apex code. Services exist for creating, updating, upserting, deleting, and undeleting records. These services can accept one record at a time or up to 200 records in a single invocation.

Creating Records

To create one or more records, invoke the `create` service, passing in an array of SObjects. Each SObject must contain at a minimum the values for the required fields defined on the object. The service returns an array of `SaveResult` objects. Each `SaveResult` indicates success or failure of an individual record. In the case of failure, the `SaveResult` also contains an array of `Error` objects indicating the error reason.

The code in Listing 10.19 demonstrates the `create` service in Java. It creates a Contact record from the values of `firstName` and `lastName`.

Listing 10.19   **Java Fragment to Create Record**

```
Contact contact = new Contact();
contact.setFirstName(firstName);
contact.setLastName(lastName);
SaveResult[] result = connection.create(
  new SObject[] { contact });
if (result != null && result.length == 1) {
  if (result[0].isSuccess()) {
    System.out.println("Created contact with Id: "
      + result[0].getId());
} else {
    System.out.println("Failed to create contact: " +
      result[0].getErrors()[0].getMessage());
  }
}
```

Updating Records

To modify existing records, use the update service. Its arguments and return value are identical to those of the create method. The major difference is that the SObjects must contain a value for the Id field. This value is the unique identifier of the record to be updated.

Use the upsert service when you want to create records that don't exist and update them if they do exist. To determine whether a record exists, the upsert service examines a field containing unique identifiers. This field can be the internal Id field or a custom field designated as an external identifier. The first argument to the upsert service is the name of the unique identifier field, and the second is an array of SObjects. The service returns an array of UpsertResult objects. Like the SaveResult object, it contains a success or failure indicator and an array of errors upon failure.

Note

You must perform an additional step to set fields to null during an update or upsert. Each object instance has a special array field called fieldsToNull. To set a field to null, add the name of the field to this list.

Deleting and Undeleting Records

To delete records, call the delete service and pass in an array of record unique identifiers to delete. Unlike the other DML operations, delete accepts different types of objects in a single call. The service returns an array of DeleteResult objects indicating the success or failure of each deletion, as well as any error messages.

The undelete service restores deleted records from the Recycle Bin. Its input is a list of record unique identifiers, and it returns an array of UndeleteResult objects for use in tracking the outcome of each undeletion.

Modifications in Bulk

Bulk modifications involve more than one record. You can create, update, upsert, delete, or undelete a maximum of 200 records in a single call. By default, Force.com allows partial failure, meaning some records can fail while others succeed. To override this behavior, add the AllOrNoneHeader to the call and set it to true. This causes Force.com to roll back all modifications made by the call unless all records are successfully processed.

The ability to process multiple object types in a single call is a powerful feature of bulk modifications. This is supported on create, update, delete, and undelete operations, but not upsert. For example, you can create a Resource and Skill in one round-trip to Force.com. This requires that the Skill record references its parent Resource using an external identifier rather than an Id because an Id for the record doesn't exist yet.

There are several important limitations of bulk create and update calls that involve multiple object types:

- Up to ten unique object types are allowed per call.

- You can't reference a new record of the same type in a single call. For example, if two Contact records were related to each other, you would need to create the parent first and then create the child and relate it to the parent in a separate call.

- If there are related records in the call, parent records must be located ahead of child records in the request.

- You cannot modify records of multiple object types if they participate in the Salesforce Setup menu. This limitation includes custom settings objects, GroupMember, Group, and User.

Creating Custom Apex SOAP Web Services

With SOAP Web services, you can create higher-level APIs of your own directly in the Force.com platform and invoke them from your own programs outside of Force. Your custom SOAP services can bundle a series of related queries or updates into a single call, providing an atomic unit of work and reducing network traffic and API call consumption.

> **Caution**
>
> Custom SOAP services run with administrative rights by default, granting your Apex code access to all data in the organization.

One way to understand the value of Apex SOAP Web services is to first examine limitations in the Enterprise API. The Enterprise API is a direct representation of the objects in your database as SOAP message types, with methods to query and modify them per record or in batches. This low-level access to the Force.com database through standard protocols and messages opens your Force.com applications to the outside world but isn't perfect for every integration scenario. The following list points out some areas in which the Enterprise API can fall short:

- **Transactions**—There is limited support in the Enterprise API for transactions that span multiple objects. If an external program must modify many objects in an atomic operation, it needs to detect failure for each call and apply a compensating action to reverse prior successes.

- **Integrated security**—The Enterprise API always applies object-, field-, and record-level sharing rules of the currently logged-in user. This cannot be disabled by an external program calling into Force.com. If greater rights are needed, an administrator must alter the user's profile or the program must log in with the credentials of a more privileged user. This can complicate integration programs by requiring many logins of varying privileges or put the organization at risk by running integration programs with administrative rights.

- **Performance**—As your integration programs get more complex, they can become chatty, making many calls to Force.com to fetch different types of records and postprocess them off-platform. This consumes more of the API calls toward the organization's daily limit and reduces performance by putting more data on the wire.

The definition of a custom SOAP service is slightly different from that of a regular Apex class. The differences are listed here:

- **Global class access modifier**—A class that contains any SOAP services must use the `global` access modifier. This means the class is visible to all programs running in the Force.com organization.

- **SOAP methods**—Each method accessible via SOAP must be defined with the `webservice` keyword. These methods must also be static.

- **Security**—SOAP methods run as a system administrator, without regard for object-, field-, or record-level sharing rules. To enforce record sharing rules, define the class with the `with sharing` keyword. To enforce object- and field-level security, use the results of the `getDescribe` method (`Schema.DescribeSObjectResult` and `Schema.DescribeFieldResult`) to check the user's permission to the data.

- **Supporting classes**—User-defined Apex classes, inner or outer, that are arguments or return values for a SOAP service method must be defined as `global`. Member variables of these classes must be defined using the `webservice` keyword.

- **No overloading**—SOAP service methods cannot be overloaded. Overloaded methods result in a compile error.

- **Prohibited types**—The Map, Set, Pattern, Matcher, Exception, and Enum types are not allowed in the arguments or return types of Apex SOAP services.

Additionally, SOAP services written in Apex must abide by its governor limits. A subset of these governor limits is listed in Table 10.3.

Table 10.3 **Subset of Apex SOAP Service Governor Limits**

Resource Type	Governor Limit
SOQL	100 queries
Records from SOQL	50,000 records
DML	150 DML statements
Records in DML	10,000 records
Stack depth	16
Heap	6,000,000 bytes
Apex code	200,000 lines of code executed

Listing 10.20 defines a simple Apex SOAP service that creates a record in the Project custom object given a name.

Listing 10.20 **Sample Apex Code for Custom SOAP Service**

```
global class Listing10_20 {
  webservice static ID createProject(String name) {
    Project__c proj = new Project__c(Name = name);
    insert proj;
    return proj.Id;
  }
}
```

Calling an Apex SOAP Service

To call an Apex SOAP service from client code, follow these steps:

1. In the App Setup area, click Develop, Apex Classes.

2. Locate the class containing the Apex SOAP service and click the WSDL link.

3. Save the WSDL on your local file system. You'll need this plus the Enterprise WSDL in order to call the custom Apex SOAP service.

4. Generate stub code from the custom WSDL and add it to your project.

5. Authenticate using the Enterprise WSDL by passing a `ConnectorConfig` to `Connector.newConnection` method; then change the service endpoint to the one from the custom WSDL.

6. Create a new `SoapConnection` from the `ConnectorConfig`, and invoke the custom Apex SOAP service method.

Listing 10.21 demonstrates the invocation of the custom `createProject` service in Java using the WSC, with the stub code generated to a `.jar` file named `Listing10_20`.

Listing 10.21 Java Fragment for Invoking Custom Apex SOAP Service

```
ConnectorConfig config = new ConnectorConfig();
config.setUsername(user);
config.setPassword(pass);
Connector.newConnection(config);
config.setServiceEndpoint(com.sforce.soap.Listing10_20.Connector.END_POINT);
SoapConnection sconn = new SoapConnection(config);
String projectId = sconn.createProject("Test Project");
```

Sample Application: Anonymous Benchmarking

In a services organization, utilization is a valuable metric for managing the business. A simple definition of utilization is the number of hours worked, typically hours billable to the client, divided by the total number of hours in a time period, expressed as a percentage.

In this section, the Services Manager sample application is extended with a Visualforce page that performs a basic utilization calculation between two dates. To calculate billable hours worked, it queries the Timecard custom object. For available hours, it uses a built-in Apex function for date arithmetic to compute the number of working hours between the two dates.

Integration comes into the picture with the addition of anonymous benchmarking. Imagine an independent organization that collects and analyzes the performance data of services companies. Companies submit their anonymized metrics and compare their performance with that of other companies in their industry. For the Services Manager sample application, you have access to a fictional benchmarking organization reachable through a SOAP Web service call.

The remainder of the section describes the design and implementation of the utilization page, controller, and integration to the anonymous benchmarking SOAP Web service. It is divided into the following subsections:

- **Visualforce page design**—Build a simple Visualforce page to capture the start and end dates of the utilization calculation, and display the results.

- **Visualforce controller design**—Develop a controller to retrieve the billable hours worked and the available hours, and perform the utilization calculation.

- **Integrating the SOAP Web service**—Add code to the controller to call out to the anonymous benchmarking SOAP Web service to share the results of the utilization calculation.

- **Sample implementation**—Examine sample code for the utilization page and controller. Try this code in its entirety, copy portions of it, or contrast it with your own implementation.

Visualforce Page Design

The goal of this section is a Visualforce page resembling what's shown in Figure 10.6. A user has entered start and end dates to compute utilization, selected the Share Anonymously check box to indicate that she would like the results sent out over the Web to the benchmarking service, and clicked the Calculate button. This populated the lower three rows with the utilization results. The results include the total hours worked in the time period (from the Timecard object), the total number of consulting resources in the system (from the Contact object), and the utilization as a percentage.

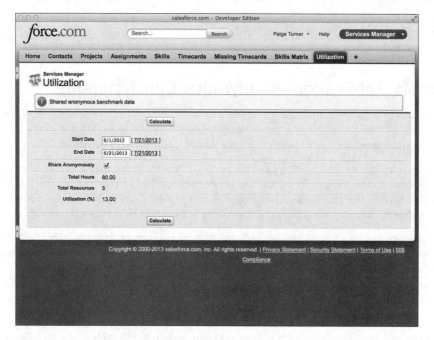

Figure 10.6   Utilization Visualforce page

The page is styled to look like part of the native Force.com native user interface. The `sectionHeader` component is used to render the heading bar. This is followed by the `pageMessages` component to show errors and information to the user. The Calculate button is a `commandButton`, enclosed in a `pageBlockButtons` component. The Start and End date fields are both `inputField` components with their `value` attributes set to SObject Date fields in the controller, providing a calendar picker user interface when focus is received. The styling of each row is accomplished by `pageBlockSectionItem` components, each with two child components. For example, the `pageBlockSectionItem` to render the row for Start Date contains an `outputLabel` and an `inputField`.

Begin by prototyping this page, focusing on the appearance, layout, and user interaction. Create a custom controller class, adding a placeholder action method to calculate the utilization. Create member variables for the start and end dates, binding them to any Date field in a standard or custom object. This binding means you can use the `inputField` component to render the start and end date fields, making them calendar input controls rather than plain text fields. Add a Boolean member variable for the Share Anonymously option, bound to an `input-Checkbox` component.

You're ready to move on to build out the controller to compute utilization and integrate the benchmarking SOAP Web service.

Visualforce Controller Design

The job of the controller is to take the user input and calculate utilization, optionally sending the results to the Web service. Real-world calculations of utilization can be complex. For example, some organizations subtract paid time off from the total hours available. Or with a large or diverse pool of resources, utilization might be calculated separately per business unit or geographic region.

In the Services Manager sample application, the utilization calculation is intentionally kept simple. One minor complication is in defining the available working hours, the denominator in the utilization formula. Rather than assuming that all consultants are billable 24 hours a day, use Force.com to store the company's business hours.

To manage business hours, go to the Administration Setup area and click Company Profile, Business Hours. Force.com comes preconfigured with business hours that run for 24 hours per day, 7 days a week. Because you don't expect your consultants to work 168-hour weeks, click the Edit link and update the default business hours to something more reasonable. To designate a day off, leave the start and end time blank. Figure 10.7 shows the business hours configuration for a 45-hour workweek, working 8:00 a.m. to 5:00 p.m. weekdays with Saturdays and Sundays off.

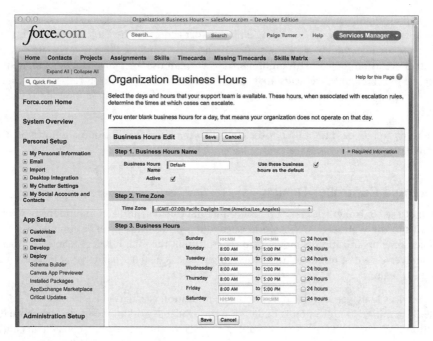

Figure 10.7   Configuring business hours

With business hours configured, you're ready to compute utilization. The following list outlines the steps:

1. Write a SOQL query to select the `Total_Hours__c` field from all timecards that are billable and between the start and end dates entered by the user.

2. Add up all the values of the `Total_Hours__c` field. This is the numerator in the utilization calculation.

3. Assume that the `Week_Ending__c` field of timecards is always a Saturday. If the start or end date entered by the user is not a Saturday, adjust it accordingly. If you do not take this simplifying step, you'll have to compensate for non-Saturday time ranges by subtracting the hours of individual days from the total.

4. The number of hours available must account for the business hours of the organization. The business hours you configured in the Force.com native user interface are stored in a standard object named `BusinessHours`, queryable from SOQL. Write SOQL to obtain the unique identifier of the default `BusinessHours` record. Call the static `diff` method on the `BusinessHours` class, passing the unique identifier and the adjusted start and end dates. This returns a long value with the number of milliseconds elapsed between the two dates during which the organization was open for business.

Integrating the SOAP Web Service

The fictional anonymous benchmarking service provides a URL to the WSDL for its Web service. The Web service allows companies to submit their utilization calculations anonymously for contribution in a database. Companies are differentiated by industry only, using a standard industry classification system called the North American Industry Classification System (NAICS), developed by the United States Census Bureau. NAICS codes are six-digit numbers. The list of NAICS codes is available at www.census.gov/eos/www/naics/reference_files_tools/2007/naics07_6.txt. For example, 541511 is the code for companies providing Custom Computer Programming Services.

To integrate the Web service, begin by generating an Apex class from the WSDL. The WSDL is available at http://force-book-developer-edition.na6.force.com/AnonymousBenchmarkWsdl. Download it to your local machine and then follow these steps:

1. In the App Setup area, click Develop, Apex Classes and click the Generate from WSDL button.

2. Click the Browse button, locate the WSDL file in your file system, and click the Parse WSDL button.

3. You should see the screen shown in Figure 10.8, which is prompting for an Apex class name to receive the generated code. You can name your class anything you want, but this example uses the name BenchmarkWS. Then click the Generate Apex Code button.

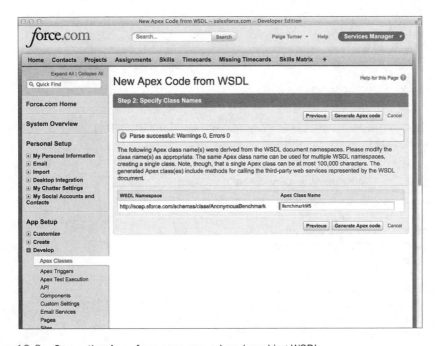

Figure 10.8   Generating Apex from anonymous benchmarking WSDL

You should now have a new Apex class called `BenchmarkWS`. Before you can test it out, enable the endpoint URL in Remote Site Settings. In the Administration Setup area, click Security Controls, Remote Site Settings. Click the New Remote Site button and enter a name for the site and its URL (https://force-book-developer-edition.na6.force.com). Figure 10.9 shows the result of adding the remote site.

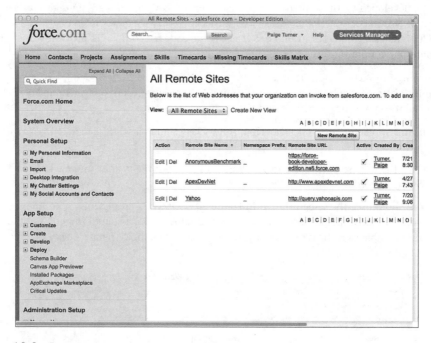

Figure 10.9   Remote site settings

Finally, test the generated Apex class using the code given in Listing 10.22. You can execute this code directly from the Execute Anonymous view.

Listing 10.22   **Testing the Web Service Call from Apex**

```
BenchmarkWS.AnonymousBenchmark service =
  new BenchmarkWS.AnonymousBenchmark();
BenchmarkWS.UtilizationEntry ue =
  new BenchmarkWS.UtilizationEntry();
ue.naicsCode = '541511';
ue.startDate = Date.parse('7/1/2013');
ue.endDate = Date.parse('7/31/2013');
ue.totalHours = 35;
ue.totalResources = 1;
ue.utilization = 88;
```

```
BenchmarkWS.SubmissionStatus[] results =
  service.submitUtilizationData(
    new BenchmarkWS.UtilizationEntry[] { ue });
if (results != null) {
  for (BenchmarkWS.SubmissionStatus result : results) {
    if (!result.success) {
      System.debug(result.errorMessage);
    }
  }
}
```

Sample Implementation

Listing 10.23 contains the controller code for the utilization Visualforce page, and Listing 10.24 contains the page itself. This implementation brings together the three elements discussed in this section: the user interface to calculate utilization, the utilization computation itself, and the Web service callout.

Listing 10.23 **Sample Code for Utilization Controller**

```
public class UtilizationController {
  public Timecard__c card1 { get; private set; }
  public Timecard__c card2 { get; private set; }
  public Boolean shared { get; set; }
  public Decimal utilization { get; private set; }
  public Decimal totalHours { get; private set; }
  public Integer totalResources { get; private set; }
  public UtilizationController() {
    card1 = new Timecard__c();
    card2 = new Timecard__c();
  }
  public PageReference calculate() {
    Date startDate = card1.Week_Ending__c;
    Date endDate = card2.Week_Ending__c;
    // assumes all active resources are billable
    List<Contact> contacts = [ SELECT Id FROM Contact
      WHERE Active__c = TRUE AND Start_Date__c < :startDate ];
    List<Timecard__c> timecards = [ SELECT Week_Ending__c,
      Total_Hours__c FROM Timecard__c
      WHERE Billable__c = true AND
        Week_Ending__c >= :startDate AND
        Week_Ending__c <= :endDate
      ORDER BY Week_Ending__c ];
    totalHours = 0;
    if (timecards.size() == 0) {
```

```
    return null;
  }
  for (Timecard__c timecard : timecards) {
    totalHours += timecard.Total_Hours__c;
  }
  // adjust start and end dates to match timecard week endings
  Timecard__c firstTimecard = timecards.get(0);
  Timecard__c lastTimecard = timecards.get(timecards.size() - 1);
  if (startDate < firstTimecard.Week_Ending__c) {
    startDate = firstTimecard.Week_Ending__c.addDays(-6);
    card1.Week_Ending__c = startDate;
  }
  if (endDate > lastTimecard.Week_Ending__c) {
    endDate = lastTimecard.Week_Ending__c;
    card2.Week_Ending__c = endDate;
  }
  totalResources = contacts.size();
  Long availableHours = totalResources *
    calculateAvailableHours(startDate, endDate);
  utilization = 100 * totalHours.divide(availableHours, 2);
  if (shared) {
    shareUtilization();
  }
  return null;
}
public static Long calculateAvailableHours(
  Date startDate, Date endDate) {
  BusinessHours bh = [ SELECT id FROM BusinessHours
    WHERE IsDefault = true ];
  DateTime startTime = DateTime.newInstance(
    startDate.year(), startDate.month(), startDate.day(),
    0, 0, 0);
  DateTime endTime = DateTime.newInstance(
    endDate.year(), endDate.month(), endDate.day(),
    0, 0, 0);
  Decimal diff = Decimal.valueOf(
    BusinessHours.diff(bh.id, startTime, endTime));
  return diff.divide(3600000, 0).round();
}
private void shareUtilization() {
  BenchmarkWS.AnonymousBenchmark service =
    new BenchmarkWS.AnonymousBenchmark();
  BenchmarkWS.UtilizationEntry ue =
    new BenchmarkWS.UtilizationEntry();
  ue.naicsCode = '541511';
  ue.startDate = card1.Week_Ending__c;
  ue.endDate = card2.Week_Ending__c;
```

```
      ue.totalHours = totalHours;
      ue.totalResources = totalResources;
      ue.utilization = utilization;
      BenchmarkWS.SubmissionStatus[] results =
        service.submitUtilizationData(
          new BenchmarkWS.UtilizationEntry[] { ue });
      if (results != null) {
        for (BenchmarkWS.SubmissionStatus result : results) {
          if (!result.success) {
            ApexPages.addMessage(new ApexPages.Message(
              ApexPages.Severity.ERROR, result.errorMessage));
          } else {
            ApexPages.addMessage(new ApexPages.Message(
              ApexPages.Severity.INFO,
              'Shared anonymous benchmark data'));
          }
        }
      }
    }
  }
}
```

Listing 10.24 Sample Code for Utilization Visualforce Page

```
<apex:page controller="UtilizationController">
<apex:sectionHeader title="Services Manager"
  subtitle="Utilization" />
<apex:form>
<apex:pageMessages id="msgs" />
<apex:pageBlock id="util">
<apex:pageBlockButtons>
  <apex:commandButton action="{!calculate}"
    value="Calculate" rerender="msgs, util" />
</apex:pageBlockButtons>
<apex:pageBlockSection columns="1">
  <apex:pageBlockSectionItem>
    <apex:outputLabel value="Start Date" />
    <apex:inputField value="{!card1.Week_Ending__c}" />
  </apex:pageBlockSectionItem>
<apex:pageBlockSectionItem>
  <apex:outputLabel value="End Date" />
  <apex:inputField value="{!card2.Week_Ending__c}" />
</apex:pageBlockSectionItem>
<apex:pageBlockSectionItem>
  <apex:outputLabel value="Share Anonymously" />
  <apex:inputCheckbox value="{!shared}" />
</apex:pageBlockSectionItem>
```

```
<apex:pageBlockSectionItem>
  <apex:outputLabel value="Total Hours" />
  <apex:outputText value="{!totalHours}" />
</apex:pageBlockSectionItem>
<apex:pageBlockSectionItem>
  <apex:outputLabel value="Total Resources" />
  <apex:outputText value="{!totalResources}" />
</apex:pageBlockSectionItem>
<apex:pageBlockSectionItem>
  <apex:outputLabel value="Utilization (%)" />
  <apex:outputText value="{!utilization}" />
</apex:pageBlockSectionItem>
</apex:pageBlockSection>
</apex:pageBlock>
</apex:form>
</apex:page>
```

Summary

With its integration features, the Force.com platform is open for interoperability with other applications and systems running on Force.com, elsewhere on the Internet, and behind your corporate firewall. The capability to call the platform bidirectionally using Web standards helps to break down the functional silos of Force.com and other applications.

Chapter 11, "Advanced Integration," covers additional integration features, such as the ability to securely embed other applications within the user interface, build custom developer tools, and provide external applications with a real-time stream of updated data. Before jumping in, take a minute to review the following points from this chapter:

- You can call out to SOAP and REST Web services from Apex using its built-in support for HTTP, XML, and JSON, as well as the WSDL to Apex tool.

- OAuth is a Web standard for authentication, configured in Force.com using Connected Apps.

- With code annotations and tools to map Apex to SOAP and REST, your Apex code can become Web services, ready for incorporation into programs running outside of Force.com.

11

Advanced Integration

This chapter focuses on Force.com integration features that are highly specialized and not typically essential for everyday application development. They are features often used by independent software vendors to extend the Force.com platform at a low level to add new capabilities.

Due to their specialized nature and complexity, the APIs covered here each have their own dedicated reference guides at http://developer.force.com. The intent of this chapter is to provide a brief introduction to the APIs and sample code that can serve as a way to get started with them.

This chapter is divided into sections that each address a different integration feature:

- **Introduction to the Force.com Streaming API**—The Streaming API provides near-real-time notifications about the creation and modification of database records.

- **Working with the Force.com Bulk API**—The Bulk API is a way to get mass quantities of database records in and out of Force.com.

- **Getting started with Force.com Canvas**—Canvas provides a secure mechanism to embed user interfaces, hosted outside Force.com, into Chatter and Visualforce pages.

- **Introduction to the Force.com Tooling API**—The Tooling API is used by the Force.com IDE and other tools to maintain code artifacts and access debugging functionality.

- **Understanding the Force.com Metadata API**—The Metadata API enables you to write code to perform development and configuration management tasks such as database object maintenance and application migration. It is the same API used by the Force.com IDE.

- **Sample application**—In an integration scenario for the Services Manager sample application, a Java program is developed to update Force.com with information from a human resources database.

> **Note**
>
> The code listings in this chapter are available in a GitHub Gist at http://goo.gl/7kuTFT.

Introduction to the Force.com Streaming API

The Force.com Streaming API delivers notifications to your program when records in the Force.com database are created or modified. This can be useful for user interfaces that have a real-time data requirement or to keep an external database in sync with Force.com. Streaming API is a scalable alternative to polling Force.com for changes or writing triggers with callouts.

This section provides an introduction to Force.com Streaming API in two parts, described here:

1. **Overview**—Learn the key concepts involved in the Streaming API.

2. **Getting started with Force.com Streaming API**—Construct a working example that uses the Streaming API within a Visualforce page.

> **Note**
>
> For more information about the Streaming API, consult the Force.com Streaming API Developer's Guide, found at http://www.salesforce.com/us/developer/docs/api_streaming/index.htm.

Overview

Streaming notifications in Force.com are best understood in terms of publishers and subscribers. Force.com can be configured to publish notifications when something interesting happens with a database object. This publishing configuration is expressed through a PushTopic. The PushTopic defines the database object to monitor, a public name that subscribers can reference called a Channel, and guidance on what conditions in the database object must be satisfied to create a notification. The subscriber is a program inside or outside of Force.com that uses the Bayeux protocol (CometD implementation) to register interest in and receive the streaming notifications.

PushTopics are ordinary Force.com database records, but contain four components that are critical to properly configuring your streaming notifications, described in the following list:

1. **Channel name**—This is the name that client applications will use to subscribe to the streaming notifications on this PushTopic. It must be 25 characters or fewer and be unique in your organization.

2. **SOQL query**—The SOQL query defines the database object and fields that you are monitoring for changes, plus optionally the criteria used to determine whether a change is worthy of a notification. To receive notifications, the subscriber must have at least read access to the object, field-level security to the fields in the WHERE clause, and visibility to the records causing the notifications via sharing rules.

3. **NotifyForOperations**—By default, notifications are sent on the Channel when matching records are created or updated (`All`). Use this field to limit notifications to only creation (`Create`) or only modification (`Update`) of records.

4. **NotifyForFields**—This setting instructs the Channel on what fields in the SOQL query are considered changes and trigger a notification. Any filters in a `WHERE` clause are always evaluated first. By default, it is set to `Referenced`, which means all fields in the query are factored into the decision. Other valid values are `All` (all fields in the object, even those not in `SELECT` or `WHERE`), `Select` (fields in a `SELECT` clause only), and `Where` (fields in a `WHERE` clause only).

As soon as a PushTopic is created, it is instantly available to subscribers. Likewise, when it is modified, the new definition takes effect immediately. You can delete a PushTopic record to stop its notifications, or set `IsActive` to `false` to disable it temporarily.

Each Force.com organization has a limit of 20 PushTopics. There are also per-edition limits on subscribers per topic and notifications per day. There are also a number of limitations on the SOQL query used in PushTopics, described next:

- **Subset of objects**—All custom objects are supported, but only a handful of standard objects: Account, Campaign, Case, Contact, Lead, Opportunity, and Task.
- **Subset of query features**—Aggregate queries, semi-join and anti-joins, count, limit, relationship fields, order by, group by, and formula fields are not supported.
- **Required fields**—The query must include the `Id` field.
- **Maximum length**—The query cannot exceed 1,300 characters.

Getting Started with Force.com Streaming API

A simple way to experiment with the Streaming API is to create a Visualforce page to serve as the subscriber. You can then visually see notifications as they arrive. Figure 11.1 shows a sample Visualforce page to do this. The button on the top starts and stops notifications by creating and deleting a PushTopic record. The table below it displays notifications as they arrive from Force.com, in response to the creation and modification of Timecard records.

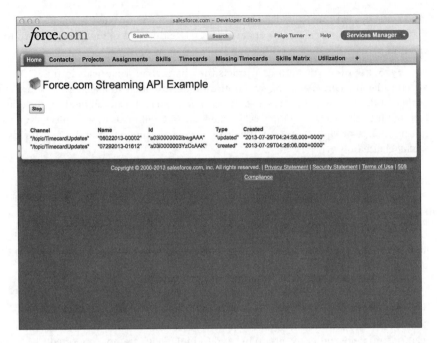

Figure 11.1   Streaming API example

To try this example in your own Salesforce organization, create the controller class in Listing 11.1. Then download the CometD library at http://download.cometd.org/cometd-2.2.0-distribution.tar.gz. Uncompress it and extract the following files:

- `cometd-2.2.0/cometd-javascript/common/target/org/Cometd.js`

- `cometd-2.2.0/cometd-javascript/jquery/src/main/webapp/jquery/jquery-1.5.1.js`

- `cometd-2.2.0/cometd-javascript/jquery/src/main/webapp/jquery/json2.js`

- `cometd-2.2.0/cometd-javascript/jquery/src/main/webapp/jquery/jquery.cometd.js`

Place them into a zip file and upload it as a static resource named `cometd`. Now you can create the Visualforce page given in Listing 11.2.

Listing 11.1   **Visualforce Controller for Streaming API Example**

```
public with sharing class MyPageController11_1 {
  public Boolean started { get; set; }
  private static final String TOPIC_NAME = 'TimecardUpdates';
  public MyPageController11_1() {
```

```
  started = 1 == [ SELECT count() FROM PushTopic
    WHERE Name = :TOPIC_NAME ];
}
public PageReference stop() {
  PushTopic p = [ SELECT Id from PushTopic
    WHERE Name = :TOPIC_NAME LIMIT 1];
  if (p != null) {
    delete p;
  }
  started = false;
  return null;
}
public PageReference start() {
  PushTopic p = new PushTopic();
  p.Name = TOPIC_NAME;
  p.Query = 'SELECT Id, Name, Status__c FROM Timecard__c';
  p.ApiVersion = 28.0;
  p.NotifyForOperations = 'All';
  p.NotifyForFields = 'Referenced';
  insert p;
  started = true;
  return null;
}
}
```

Listing 11.2 **Visualforce Page for Streaming API Example**

```
<apex:page controller="MyPageController11_1">
  <apex:form id="form">
    <apex:includeScript value="{!URLFOR($Resource.cometd,
      'Cometd.js')}"/>
    <apex:includeScript value="{!URLFOR($Resource.cometd,
      'jquery-1.5.1.js')}"/>
    <apex:includeScript value="{!URLFOR($Resource.cometd,
      'jquery.cometd.js')}"/>
    <apex:includeScript value="{!URLFOR($Resource.cometd,
      'json2.js')}"/>
    <apex:sectionHeader title="Force.com Streaming API Example" />
    <br />
    <apex:commandButton action="{!start}" value="Start"
      rerender="form" rendered="{!NOT started}" />
    <apex:commandButton action="{!stop}" value="Stop"
      rendered="{!started}" />
    <apex:outputPanel id="comet" rendered="{!started}">
      <script type="text/javascript">
(function($) {
```

```
$(document).ready(function() {
  $.cometd.init({
    url: window.location.protocol + '//' + window.location.hostname +
      '/cometd/28.0/',
    requestHeaders: { Authorization: 'OAuth {!$Api.Session_ID}'}
  });
  $.cometd.subscribe('/topic/TimecardUpdates', function(message) {
    $('#content').append(
    '<tr><td>' + JSON.stringify(message.channel) + '</td>' +
    '<td>' + JSON.stringify(message.data.sobject.Name) + '</td>' +
    '<td>' + JSON.stringify(message.data.sobject.Id) + '</td>' +
    '<td>' + JSON.stringify(message.data.event.type) + '</td>' +
    '<td>' + JSON.stringify(message.data.event.createdDate) + '</td>' +
    '</tr>');
    });
  });
}) (jQuery)
    </script>
  </apex:outputPanel>
  <p />
  <table id="content" width="80%"><tr><th>Channel</th><th>Name</th>
    <th>Id</th><th>Type</th><th>Created</th></tr>
  </table>
  </apex:form>
</apex:page>
```

Working with the Force.com Bulk API

The Force.com Bulk API allows the import or export of large quantities of records, split into units of work called batches. Up to 20 million records per 24-hour period can be imported into Force.com. Both REST and SOAP versions of the API are provided.

This section focuses on hands-on examples with the REST flavor of the Bulk API. The examples require a tool named cURL, available free for every platform at http://curl.haxx.se.

This section provides an introduction to Force.com Bulk API in three parts, described here:

1. **Overview**—Get to know the terminology and workflow of the Bulk API, and prepare to use it by authenticating using OAuth.

2. **Importing records**—Walk through API usage examples of creating a job to import records and verify its successful completion.

3. **Exporting records**—In a series of API calls, submit a SOQL query for a bulk export and retrieve the results.

> **Note**
>
> For a comprehensive look at the Bulk API, refer to the Force.com Bulk API Developer's Guide, found at http://www.salesforce.com/us/developer/docs/api_asynch/index.htm.

Overview

Bulk API operates in terms of a two-tier system of containers to track units of data movement work. Each tier is described here:

- **Batch**—A batch is a set of records to be imported. The records are represented in CSV or XML format. For import jobs, a batch cannot exceed 10,000 records. Batches are not applicable to export jobs, which use result files that cannot exceed 1GB.

- **Job**—A job is a list of batches. The job specifies the type of operation that will be performed in the batches, such as insert or query.

Authentication

Bulk REST API calls require authentication to Force.com. Use the username-password OAuth flow, which accepts username and password, to establish an authenticated session. Listing 11.3 provides a sample request and response.

Listing 11.3   Sample Password Authentication Request and Response

```
curl https://login.salesforce.com/services/oauth2/token
  -d "grant_type=password" -d "client_id=$CLIENT_ID"
  -d "client_secret=$CLIENT_SECRET"
  -d "username=$USERNAME" -d "password=$PASSWORD"
{
    "id": "https://login.salesforce.com/id/...",
    "issued_at": "1374386510993",
    "instance_url": "https://na15.salesforce.com",
    "signature": "...",
    "access_token": "..."
}
```

The value in the response's `access_token` field is needed to run all of the examples in this section. To get one yourself, set the `$USERNAME` environment variable to your Salesforce username, `$PASSWORD` to your Salesforce password with security token appended. The variables `$CLIENT_ID` and `$CLIENT_SECRET` are your OAuth Consumer Key and Consumer Secret. These come from a Connected App, which you can reuse from Chapter 10, "Integration with Force.com."

Now that you have obtained an OAuth access token, you are ready to try the Bulk API examples. Set the access token as the environment variable `$TOKEN`. Also, be sure to replace `na15` in the following examples with your own instance of Force.com. To identify your instance, look at the `instance_url` field of the OAuth username-password flow, or the URL in your Web browser when you log in to Force.com.

Importing Records

To import records, an authenticated user creates an import job, adds batches of data to it, closes the job, checks for completion, and then retrieves the results. The results are provided per batch and indicate the status of each imported record. Examples of each step in this process are provided in the remainder of this subsection.

Listing 11.4 creates a bulk import job. It specifies that the records in the job are to be inserted into the Project custom object from a CSV file.

Listing 11.4 **Creating a Bulk Import Job**

```
echo '<?xml version="1.0" encoding="UTF-8"?>
  <jobInfo xmlns="http://www.force.com/2009/06/asyncapi/dataload">
  <operation>insert</operation>
  <object>Project__c</object>
  <contentType>CSV</contentType></jobInfo>' |\
  curl -X POST -H 'Content-type: application/xml' \
  -H "X-SFDC-Session: "$TOKEN -d @-\
  https://na15.salesforce.com/services/async/28.0/job
```

> **Tip**
>
> To adapt the command in Listing 11.4 and other listings in this chapter to run in Windows Command Prompt, remove the single quotation mark characters (') in the `echo` statement, replace the single quotation mark characters around the `Content-type` header with double quotation mark characters ("), remove the backslash (\) line-continuation characters and concatenate the lines into a single line, and replace `$TOKEN` with `%TOKEN%`.

Make a note of the job identifier, in the `id` field of the XML response. It is used in all of the requests that follow. In Listing 11.5, `JOB_ID` is a placeholder for the job identifier returned from the import creation request. Replace it with your own. The records in the batch are sent in the body of the request, composed of three Project records with unique names.

Listing 11.5 **Adding Records to Bulk Import Job**

```
echo 'Name
  Project1
  Project2
  Project3' |\
  curl -X POST -H 'Content-type: text/csv' \
  -H "X-SFDC-Session: "$TOKEN --data-binary @-\
  https://na15.salesforce.com/services/async/28.0/job/JOB_ID/batch
```

Save the batch identifier that is returned. You will need it to check for the results of the batch.

You can add more batches to the job by repeating the request. When you're done adding batches, send the request in Listing 11.6 to close the job, again setting the job identifier to your own. Closing the job signals to Force.com that it can begin processing the job.

Listing 11.6   **Closing the Bulk Import Job**

```
echo '<?xml version="1.0" encoding="UTF-8"?>
  <jobInfo xmlns="http://www.force.com/2009/06/asyncapi/dataload">
  <state>Closed</state></jobInfo>' |\
  curl -X POST -H 'Content-type: application/xml' \
  -H "X-SFDC-Session: "$TOKEN -d @-\
  https://na15.salesforce.com/services/async/28.0/job/JOB_ID
```

Job processing is asynchronous, so requests complete immediately but processing continues in the background. To check for the status of the job, send the request in Listing 11.7 with your job identifier.

Listing 11.7   **Checking the Status of the Bulk Import Job**

```
curl https://na15.salesforce.com/services/async/28.0/job/JOB_ID \
  -H "X-SFDC-Session: "$TOKEN
```

When the job is complete, you can retrieve the results of its batches. Each batch result indicates the success or failure of every record within the batch. Listing 11.8 shows a sample request to retrieve the batch status. Replace the job identifier and batch identifier (BATCH_ID) with your own.

Listing 11.8   **Retrieving Results of the Bulk Import Job**

```
curl https://na15.salesforce.com/services/async/28.0/\
job/JOB_ID/batch/BATCH_ID/result \
  -H "X-SFDC-Session: "$TOKEN
```

Exporting Records

The Bulk API can also be used to query Force.com to export large numbers of records in a CSV or XML file format. First a bulk export job is created; then a batch is added to the job containing a SOQL statement. The SOQL cannot contain relationship fields; nested queries; or the aggregate functions COUNT, ROLLUP, SUM, or GROUP BY CUBE. Next, the status of the job is checked, and, finally, the results retrieved in files, each up to 1GB in size.

To begin, create a bulk export job using the request in Listing 11.9.

Listing 11.9   **Creating the Bulk Export Job**

```
echo '<?xml version="1.0" encoding="UTF-8"?>
  <jobInfo xmlns="http://www.force.com/2009/06/asyncapi/dataload">
  <operation>query</operation>
  <object>Project__c</object>
  <contentType>CSV</contentType></jobInfo>' |\
  curl -X POST -H 'Content-type: application/xml' \
  -H "X-SFDC-Session: "$TOKEN -d @-\
  https://na15.salesforce.com/services/async/28.0/job
```

Keep track of the job identifier returned in the response. Create a batch within the job, specifying the SOQL statement. In Listing 11.10, the names and identifiers of the Project records will be exported. Replace JOB_ID with your job identifier.

Listing 11.10   **Creating the Bulk Export Batch**

```
echo 'SELECT Id, Name FROM Project__c' |\
  curl -X POST -H 'Content-type: text/csv' \
  -H "X-SFDC-Session: "$TOKEN --data-binary @-\
  https://na15.salesforce.com/services/async/28.0/job/JOB_ID/batch
```

Make a note of the batch identifier. Use the request in Listing 11.11 to check the status of your export job.

Listing 11.11   **Checking the Status of the Bulk Export Job**

```
curl https://na15.salesforce.com/services/async/28.0/job/JOB_ID\
  -H "X-SFDC-Session: "$TOKEN
```

When the job is complete, the results are ready to retrieve. This is a two-step process. First, retrieve the list of result identifiers. Then, for each result identifier, make a request to retrieve the actual results. Listing 11.12 is an example of the first step. Be sure to replace the JOB_ID and BATCH_ID placeholders with your own values.

Listing 11.12   **Retrieving Result Identifiers of the Bulk Export Job**

```
curl https://na15.salesforce.com/services/async/28.0/\
job/JOB_ID/batch/BATCH_ID/result \
  -H "X-SFDC-Session: "$TOKEN
```

The last step in the process is shown in Listing 11.13. In addition to job and batch identifiers, replace RESULT_ID with one of the result identifiers from the prior request.

Listing 11.13   **Retrieving Results of the Bulk Export Job**

```
curl https://na15.salesforce.com/services/async/28.0/\
job/JOB_ID/batch/BATCH_ID/result/RESULT_ID \
  -H "X-SFDC-Session: "$TOKEN
```

Getting Started with Force.com Canvas

The Force.com Canvas allows you to integrate Force.com with custom applications, located outside of Force.com, at the user interface level. It consists of a flexible content "container" located in Force.com and code libraries (JavaScript and Java) to augment your custom application to take advantage of the Force.com Canvas. The libraries provide functionality around security, sizing of the content container, and communication between Canvas applications and the container.

This section provides an introduction to Force.com Canvas in two parts, described here:

1. **Overview**—Learn the basic components of the Canvas and how they work.

2. **Getting started with the Force.com Canvas**—Walk through an example of a Canvas application hosted on your local computer.

> **Note**
>
> The Force.com Canvas is a complex and relatively new area of Force.com with many ways to implement it. Consult the Force.com Canvas Developer's Guide, found at http://www.salesforce.com/us/developer/docs/platform_connect/index.htm, for the most current and complete information on this feature.

Overview

Canvas integrates applications at the user interface level, through the Web browser. The typical scenario for an integrated user interface is mashing up Force.com data with data from an external system. In this scenario, the external system can maintain its own database and processes, but leverage Force.com data opportunistically from the currently logged-in user. The alternative is typically heavier-weight integration whereby the servers of the external application attempt to stay synchronized with data from Force.com.

The two most important features of the Canvas are authentication and cross-domain XMLHttpRequest (XHR). These are described in the following list:

- **Authentication**—Authentication enables your external Web application to verify that it is truly hosted inside a Force.com organization, with an authenticated Force.com user at the helm. It does this in one of two ways: by allowing the Web user to OAuth to Force.com or via Signed Request. OAuth is no different from OAuth in other contexts. Signed

Request is a method whereby the Force.com platform digitally signs a request to your application's Web server. The request includes the identity and session information of the authenticated Force.com user. If the request is decrypted and the signature verified, you can trust that it originated from Force.com and can use the session to make subsequent requests to Force.com. Canvas Java SDK provides code for verifying data sent by the Signed Request authentication method.

- **Cross-domain XHR**—Because your Web application is being served inside an IFRAME, it is subject to cross-domain scripting limitations enforced by the standard security policies of Web browsers. This means JavaScript in your Web pages cannot call out to servers other than the one serving the parent Web page. Because a common scenario with mashups is to include data from Force.com, Canvas JavaScript SDK provides API calls to proxy your requests back to Salesforce.

Getting Started with Force.com Canvas

Because so much of a Canvas application resides outside of Force.com by definition, it is a challenge to provide a generic, widely accessible example without pulling in many other technologies. This section walks through an example that leverages a local Web server and two static HTML pages to demonstrate OAuth authentication and cross-domain XHR requests.

The purpose of the example is to highlight the most common features of Canvas, and to do so without requiring an application server. In a more realistic application of Canvas, the OAuth process would originate on the Web server so the authorizations can be stored and managed securely rather than forcing the user to authenticate every time the page is rendered. Alternatively, Signed Request could be used to provide a transparent single sign-on process for the user, whereby the Force.com session is shared securely with the external Web application.

Figure 11.2 shows the sample application running within the Canvas App Previewer. The Login link has been clicked, prompting the user with an OAuth authorization pop-up. When authorization is complete, a callback Web page closes the pop-up and refreshes the parent window. The access token obtained during this process is displayed. The user can then click the My Chatter Profile link, which makes a cross-domain XHR request using the Canvas JavaScript SDK to the Chatter REST endpoint to get the current user's Chatter profile and display the raw JSON response.

Figure 11.2   Canvas App in Canvas App Previewer

The following steps describe the process for getting the example up and running:

1. **Create Connected App**—In the App Setup area, go to Create, Apps and create a new Connected App. Set the Name, API Name, and Contact Email fields. Check Enable OAuth Settings. Provide a Callback URL, and add "Access and Manage Your Data (api)" to the Selected OAuth Scopes list. In the Supported App Types section, check Force.com Canvas. For the Canvas App URL, provide the URL to your local Web server and the path you are using to host the Canvas App pages. For Access Method, select OAuth Webflow (GET). For Locations, select Chatter Tab and Visualforce Page, and then click the Save button. Figure 11.3 shows an example of this configuration.

Figure 11.3   Connected App configuration

2. **Set up local Web server with SSL**—Get a Web server running on your machine to host the Canvas App. Make sure you have enabled SSL, using a self-signed certificate if necessary. Test the SSL configuration with your browser before proceeding. If there are any untrusted or invalid certificate errors, the Canvas App will fail to load or function properly.

3. **Add Canvas App pages**—Create the two pages in Listing 11.14 and Listing 11.15 within a directory on your Web server, naming them `index.html` and `callback.html`, respectively. In the examples here, they are located in a directory called `chapter11`, but you can put them anywhere as long as they match the settings in your Connected App.

4. **Configure Canvas App pages**—In your version of Listing 11.14, replace `REDIRECT_URI` and `CLIENT_ID` with the Callback URL and Consumer Key, respectively, from your Connected App configuration. Also update the instance URL in the `SCRIPT` tag used to load the Canvas Javascript API to match your organization.

5. **Preview the Canvas App**—You should now be able to see the Canvas App in the App Setup area, Canvas App Previewer. You can also see it in the Chatter tab. If there are issues, use your Web browser's debugging facility to troubleshoot.

Listing 11.14   Main HTML Page for Canvas Example

```html
<html>
  <head>
  <script type="text/javascript"
    src="https://na15.salesforce.com/canvas/sdk/js/28.0/canvas-all.js">
  </script>
  </head>
  <body>
    <script>
function profileHandler(e) {
  var profileUrl = Sfdc.canvas.oauth.instance() +
    "/services/data/v28.0/chatter/users/me";
  Sfdc.canvas.client.ajax(profileUrl, {
    client: Sfdc.canvas.oauth.client(),
    failure: function(data) {
      alert(data);
    },
    success: function(data) {
    if (data.status === 200) {
      Sfdc.canvas.byId("chatter_profile").innerHTML =
        JSON.stringify(data.payload);
     }
    }
  });
}
function loginHandler(e) {
  var uri;
  if (!Sfdc.canvas.oauth.loggedin()) {
    uri = Sfdc.canvas.oauth.loginUrl();
    Sfdc.canvas.oauth.login({
      uri: uri,
      params: {
        response_type : "token",
        client_id : "CLIENT_ID",
        redirect_uri : encodeURIComponent("REDIRECT_URI")
      }
    });
  }
  return false;
}
Sfdc.canvas(function() {
  var login = Sfdc.canvas.byId("login");
  var loggedIn = Sfdc.canvas.oauth.loggedin();
  if (loggedIn) {
    Sfdc.canvas.byId("oauth").innerHTML = Sfdc.canvas.oauth.token();
    var profile = Sfdc.canvas.byId("profile");
    profile.onclick = profileHandler;
```

```
    }
  login.onclick = loginHandler;
});
</script>
    <h1>Force.com Canvas Example</h1>
    <div>access_token</div>
    <textarea id="oauth" rows="2" cols="80" disabled="true"></textarea>
    <div>
      <a id="login" href="#">Login</a><br/>
      <a id="profile" href="#">My Chatter Profile</a><br />
    </div>
    <textarea id="chatter_profile" rows="20" cols="80"></textarea>
  </body>
</html>
```

Listing 11.15 **Callback HTML Page for Canvas Example**

```
<html xmlns="http://www.w3.org/1999/xhtml" lang="en">
<head>
<script type="text/javascript">
try {
  window.opener.Sfdc.canvas.oauth.childWindowUnloadNotification(
    self.location.hash);
} catch (ignore) {}
self.close();
</script>
</head>
<body>
</body>
</html>
```

Introduction to the Force.com Tooling API

The Force.com Tooling API enables the creation of developer productivity tools for the Force.com platform. With the Tooling API, features of tools such as the Force.com IDE are accessible to your own programs. This includes the ability to compile code, perform code completion in an editor, set breakpoints for debugging, and retrieve trace log results.

This section provides an introduction to Force.com Tooling API in two parts, described here:

1. **Overview**—Examine the high-level features of the Tooling API.

2. **Getting started with the Force.com Tooling API**—Build a working example of the Tooling API that allows you to edit and compile an Apex class within a Visualforce page.

> **Note**
>
> Consult the Force.com Tooling API Developer's Guide, found at http://www.salesforce.com/us/
> developer/docs/api_tooling/index.htm.

Overview

The Tooling API is available in both REST and SOAP forms. This section focuses on Apex class deployment; however, the Tooling API also provides the following services:

- **Code**—Check the syntax of Apex classes, triggers, Visualforce pages, and Visualforce components.

- **Deployment**—Commit code changes to your organization.

- **Debugging**—Set heap dump markers and overlay Apex code or SOQL statements on an Apex execution. Set checkpoints to generate log files. Access debug log and heap dump files.

- **Custom fields**—Manage custom fields on custom objects.

Getting Started with Force.com Tooling API

The power of the Tooling API can be demonstrated using a basic Visualforce page that calls to the Tooling API's REST endpoint from the Apex controller. Figure 11.4 shows the sample user interface. On the left side are the Apex classes available in the organization, accessible with an ordinary SOQL query on `ApexClass`. On the upper-right side is the body of the selected Apex class. Below it is a Save button, which deploys changes to the class body.

The process for deploying Apex code or other types of Force.com logic is to create a `MetadataContainer`, add to it the wrapper object corresponding to the type of artifact to be deployed (in this case, `ApexClassMember`), create a `ContainerAsyncRequest`, and track the progress of the request using a specialized Tooling API query service.

Below the Save button are two fields that illustrate the internal state of the deployment: the ContainerId and RequestId. These are maintained both to check the status of the deployment (via the Refresh Status button), and to properly clean up (by deleting the `MetadataContainer`) when the user clicks the Start Over button.

To use the example, click Edit beside the class you'd like to edit. Make a change to the class body and click Save. You should see two successful JSON responses concatenated in the log output box, and the other buttons in the user interface should become enabled.

Figure 11.5 shows the results of clicking the Refresh Status button. According to the JSON response, the deployment is complete and without compiler errors. Click the Start Over button. You should see your changes to the selected Apex class reflected in the user interface and anywhere that Apex code is visible.

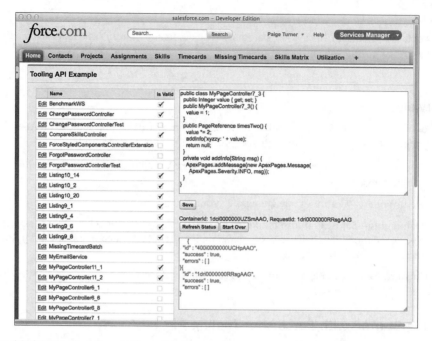

Figure 11.4 Result of Save button click

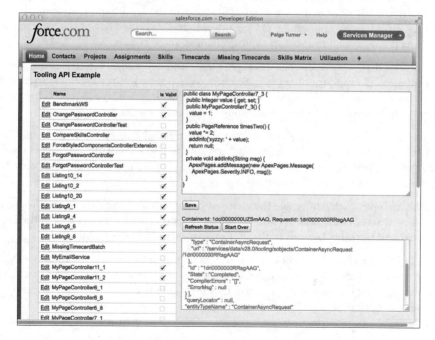

Figure 11.5 Result of Refresh Status button click

The code in Listing 11.16 and Listing 11.17 provides an implementation of the controller and page for the Tooling API example. The controller makes extensive use of HTTP callouts and the built-in JSON parsing support.

> **Note**
>
> For the sample code to work, you must add a Remote Site setting to allow requests to the Tooling API endpoint. The endpoint is the root of your instance URL, for example, https://na15. salesforce.com.

Listing 11.16   **Visualforce Controller for Tooling API Example**

```
public class MyPageController11_16 {
  public String editBody { get; set; }
  public String editClassId { get; set; }
  public String containerId { get; set; }
  public String requestId { get; set; }
  public String log { get; set; }
  public List<ApexClass> getClasses() {
    return [ SELECT Id, Name, IsValid FROM ApexClass
      ORDER BY Name ];
  }
  public PageReference edit() {
    editBody = [ SELECT Body FROM ApexClass
      WHERE Id = :editClassId LIMIT 1 ][0].Body;
    return null;
  }
  public PageReference save() {
    log = '';
    // Create MetadataContainer
    HttpRequest req = newRequest('/sobjects/MetadataContainer',
      'POST');
    Map<String, Object> args = new Map<String, Object>();
    args.put('Name', 'ClassContainer');
    String result = sendRequest(req, args);
    containerId = null;
    try {
      containerId = getResultId(result);
    } catch (Exception e) {
      log += result;
      return null;
    }
    // Create ApexClassMember
    req = newRequest('/sobjects/ApexClassMember',
      'POST');
    args = new Map<String, Object>();
    args.put('ContentEntityId', editClassId);
```

```
            args.put('Body', editBody);
            args.put('MetadataContainerId', containerId);
            log += sendRequest(req, args);
            // Create ContainerAsyncRequest
            req = newRequest('/sobjects/ContainerAsyncRequest', 'POST');
            args = new Map<String, Object>();
            args.put('IsCheckOnly', 'false');
            args.put('MetadataContainerId', containerId);
            result = sendRequest(req, args);
            log += result;
            requestId = getResultId(result);
            return null;
        }
        public PageReference reset() {
            cleanup(containerId);
            editClassId = '';
            requestId = '';
            containerId = '';
            log = '';
            editBody = '';
            return null;
        }
        public PageReference refresh() {
            String soql = 'SELECT Id, State, CompilerErrors, ErrorMsg FROM ' +
                'ContainerAsyncRequest where id = \'' + requestId + '\'';
            HttpRequest req = newRequest('/query/?q=' +
                EncodingUtil.urlEncode(soql, 'UTF-8'),
                'GET');
            log = sendRequest(req, null);
            return null;
        }
        public static void cleanup(String containerId) {
            sendRequest(newRequest('/sobjects/MetadataContainer/' + containerId,
                'DELETE'), null);
        }
        private static HttpRequest newRequest(String toolingPath,
            String method) {
            HttpRequest req = new HttpRequest();
            req.setHeader('Authorization',
                'Bearer ' + UserInfo.getSessionID());
            req.setHeader('Content-Type', 'application/json');
            req.setHeader('X-PrettyPrint' , '1');
            req.setEndpoint(getInstanceUrl() +
                '/services/data/v28.0/tooling' + toolingPath);
            req.setMethod(method);
            return req;
        }
```

```
  private static String sendRequest(HttpRequest req,
    Map<String, Object> args) {
    Http h = new Http();
    if (args != null) {
      req.setBody(Json.serialize(args));
    }
    HttpResponse res = h.send(req);
    return res.getBody();
  }
  private static String getInstanceUrl() {
    String url = System.URL.getSalesforceBaseUrl()
      .toExternalForm();
    url = url.replace('visual.force', 'salesforce');
    url = url.replace('c.', '');
    return url;
  }
  private static Id getResultId(String body) {
    Map<String, Object> result = (Map<String, Object>)
      JSON.deserializeUntyped(body);
    return (Id)result.get('id');
  }
}
```

Listing 11.17   Visualforce Page for Tooling API Example

```
<apex:page controller="MyPageController11_16">
  <apex:form id="form">
  <apex:pageBlock title="Force.com Tooling API Example">
  <apex:pageBlockSection columns="2">
  <apex:pageBlockTable value="{!classes}" var="c">
    <apex:column >
      <apex:commandLink value="Edit" action="{!edit}"
        rerender="editor">
        <apex:param name="editClassId"
          assignTo="{!editClassId}" value="{!c.Id}" />
      </apex:commandLink>
    </apex:column>
    <apex:column value="{!c.Name}" />
    <apex:column value="{!c.IsValid}" />
  </apex:pageBlockTable>
  <apex:outputPanel id="editor">
    <apex:inputTextArea id="editBody" rows="15" cols="90"
      value="{!editBody}" disabled="{!editClassId == NULL}" />
    <p/><apex:commandButton value="Save" action="{!save}"
      disabled="{!editClassId == NULL}" rerender="editor" />
    <p/>
    ContainerId: {!containerId},
```

```
    RequestId: {!requestId}<br />
    <apex:commandButton value="Refresh Status" action="{!refresh}"
        disabled="{!requestId == NULL}" rerender="editor" />
    <apex:commandButton value="Start Over" action="{!reset}"
        disabled="{!containerId == NULL}" />
    <p/>
    <textarea disabled="true" rows="10" cols="90">
        {!log}
    </textarea>
    </apex:outputPanel>
    </apex:pageBlockSection>
    </apex:pageBlock>
    </apex:form>
</apex:page>
```

Understanding the Force.com Metadata API

The Metadata API allows the direct manipulation of objects, page layouts, tabs, and most of the other configurable features in Force.com. By using the Metadata API, you can automate many of the click-intensive tasks commonly performed in the Force.com IDE or in the native Web user interface, such as the creation of database objects and fields.

This section provides an introduction to the Metadata API in two parts, described here:

1. **Overview**—The Metadata API is different from the Enterprise API in two major ways. First, it can operate on objects in memory or using zip files containing many objects represented as XML files. Second, its operations are asynchronous, returning immediately with a result identifier to use for follow-up calls to check the status.

2. **Getting started with the Metadata API**—Walk through a sample of calling the Metadata API to create a new object using Java.

Note

The details of how the Metadata API operates on each type of metadata in Force.com are outside the scope of this book. Consult the Force.com Metadata API Developer's Guide, found at www.salesforce.com/us/developer/docs/api_meta/index.htm, for the latest information and detailed descriptions of all the available methods of the Metadata API. Salesforce continues to expand the reach of the Metadata API in every release.

Overview

The Metadata API consists of two types of services: file-based and object-based. These service types are summarized next:

- **File-based services**—The file-based services are `deploy` and `retrieve`. The `deploy` service takes a Base64-encoded zip file containing the components to deploy into the Force.com organization. The zip file must contain a manifest file named `package.xml` at its root to describe the contents of the zip. The `retrieve` service downloads metadata from Force.com and returns it as a zip file complete with `package.xml` as manifest. Its input is a `RetrieveRequest` object to specify the types of metadata to download. Both services can operate on up to 1,500 metadata objects per call.

- **Object-based services**—The object-based services are `create`, `update`, and `delete`. To invoke `create` or `delete`, pass an array of `Metadata` objects. The `Metadata` object is the superclass of a wide array of objects that contain metadata for specific features of Force.com. For example, the `CustomObject` class represents a custom database object, and `Layout` represents a page layout. Unlike data records in which a unique identifier (`Id`) field is the key, metadata uniqueness comes from a combination of its type and `fullName` field. The `update` service takes an array of `UpdateMetadata` objects, which each contain a `Metadata` object and the current name of the object to replace.

> **Note**
>
> Force.com's documentation uses the term *declarative* to describe its file-based services, and *CRUD* (for create, read, update, and delete) to describe its object-based services.

All Metadata API services are asynchronous, returning immediately with an `AsyncResult` object. This object contains a unique identifier for tracking the status of the asynchronous operation. For object-based services, the service to check status is called `checkStatus`. For the file-based service `deploy`, the status service is `checkDeployStatus`, and for `retrieve`, it's `checkRetrieveStatus`.

Getting Started with the Metadata API

To get started with the Metadata API, follow these steps:

1. In the App Setup area, click Develop, API.

2. Right-click the Download Metadata WSDL link and save it on your local file system. You'll need this plus the Enterprise WSDL in order to call the Metadata API.

3. Generate stub code from the WSDL (for example, by using WSC as described in Chapter 10) and add it to your project.

Listing 11.18 demonstrates usage of the Metadata API in Java by creating a new database object given a name and its plural name. The code assumes the existence of a member variable called `sessionId`, previously populated from the `login` call's `LoginResult`. It prepares the minimum set of metadata required to call the `create` service, which is a custom object name, full name, label, deployment status, sharing model, and name field. After invoking the asynchronous `create` service, it loops to check the status using the `checkStatus` service until the invocation is complete.

Listing 11.18   **Java Fragment for Creating Object**

```java
public void createObject(String name, String pluralName) {
  try {
    ConnectorConfig config = new ConnectorConfig();
    config.setUsername(user);
    config.setPassword(pass);
    com.sforce.soap.enterprise.Connector.newConnection(config);
    config.setServiceEndpoint(Connector.END_POINT);
    MetadataConnection connection = new MetadataConnection(config);
    CustomObject obj = new CustomObject();
    obj.setFullName(name + "__c");
    obj.setLabel(name);
    obj.setPluralLabel(pluralName);
    obj.setDeploymentStatus(DeploymentStatus.Deployed);
    obj.setSharingModel(SharingModel.ReadWrite);
    CustomField nameField = new CustomField();
    nameField.setType(FieldType.AutoNumber);
    nameField.setLabel("Name");
    obj.setNameField(nameField);
    AsyncResult[] result = connection.create(
      new Metadata[] { obj });
    if (result == null) {
      System.out.println("create failed");
      return;
    }
    boolean done = false;
    AsyncResult[] status = null;
    long waitTime = 1000;
    while (!done) {
      status = connection.checkStatus(
        new String[] { result[0].getId() });
      if (status != null) {
        done = status[0].isDone();
        if (status[0].getStatusCode() != null) {
          System.out.println("Error: " +
            status[0].getStatusCode() + ": " +
            status[0].getMessage());
        }
        Thread.sleep(waitTime);
        waitTime *= 2;
        System.out.println("Current state: " +
          status[0].getState());
      }
    }
    System.out.println("Created object: " +
```

```
    status[0].getId());
  } catch (Throwable t) {
    t.printStackTrace();
  }
}
```

Sample Application: Database Integration

This section explores a common integration scenario using the Services Manager sample application. It describes the scenario and the implementation strategy and ends with sample code.

Integration Scenario

Force.com applications often require the use of data that is stored in other enterprise systems. This information can initially be pushed to Force.com through Data Loader or another data migration tool. But when Force.com is not the system of record for this information and updates occur, Force.com is left with stale data.

Updated data could be reloaded into Force.com through data migration tools, scheduled to run at regular time intervals, but this approach can quickly become impractical. This is especially true where there are requirements for real-time updates, integration to multiple systems, intricate data mappings, or complex business rules governing the updates.

Imagine that the company using your Services Manager application has a human resources system containing the names, addresses, and other core information about employees. This employee information is duplicated in Force.com in the Contact standard object. Because Force.com is not the system of record for these fields, they should be set to read-only on their page layouts to maintain data integrity between Force.com and the human resources system. But when the human resources system is updated, Force.com must also be updated. This is the goal of the integration.

Implementation Strategy

To retrieve changes from the human resources system, you could call out from Force.com using HTTP or a REST Web service call, as described in Chapter 10. But when you would do this is not clear because Force.com does not receive notifications when the human resource system is updated. Polling the system for changes would be inefficient and quickly hit governor limits on Web service callouts.

Instead, use the Enterprise API to connect to Force.com and upsert the modified records. Begin by updating a single field called `Active__c`, indicating whether the employee is active. After you get this field working, move on to support additional fields such as the address and phone fields of the Contact record.

The first problem is finding a common key to employees in both systems. Assume that the human resources system cannot be changed and focus on adapting Force.com to maintain the mapping between the two systems. Create a new field named Resource ID (API name of `Resource_ID__c`) on the Contact object to store employee identifiers used by the human resources system. For this example, make it a Number type, six digits in length, required, unique, and an external ID.

> **Caution**
>
> Remember that you need to regenerate the client code from Enterprise WSDL after you add this new field; otherwise, it will not be available to your program.

Sample Implementation

The code in Listing 11.19 is a sample Java implementation of the integration. It assumes that you've already generated the Java stub code from Enterprise WSDL using the WSC. It expects a file named `import.json` to be located in the working directory. This is a JSON-encoded file containing an array of Contact records to update. Listing 11.20 is an example of the file format expected by the program.

> **Note**
>
> The sample implementation uses a JSON library available at www.json.org/java.

Listing 11.19   **Sample Java Implementation of Integration Scenario**

```
import java.io.BufferedReader;
import java.io.FileReader;
import java.io.IOException;
import java.util.ArrayList;
import java.util.List;
import org.json.JSONArray;
import org.json.JSONException;
import org.json.JSONObject;
import com.sforce.soap.enterprise.Connector;
import com.sforce.soap.enterprise.EnterpriseConnection;
import com.sforce.soap.enterprise.UpsertResult;
import com.sforce.soap.enterprise.sobject.Contact;
import com.sforce.soap.enterprise.sobject.SObject;
import com.sforce.ws.ConnectionException;
import com.sforce.ws.ConnectorConfig;
public class Listing11_19 {
  EnterpriseConnection connection;
  public void login(String user, String pass, String securityToken) {
    ConnectorConfig config = new ConnectorConfig();
```

```
  config.setUsername(user);
  config.setPassword(pass + securityToken);
  try {
    connection = Connector.newConnection(config);
  } catch (ConnectionException e) {
    e.printStackTrace();
  }
}
public void processImportFile(String jsonFile) {
  List<SObject> changes = new ArrayList<SObject>();
  try {
    String json = readFileAsString(jsonFile);
    JSONArray array = new JSONArray(json);
    for (int i=0; i<array.length(); i++) {
      changes.add(importResource(array.getJSONObject(i)));
    }
    if (changes.size() > 0) {
      UpsertResult[] results = connection.upsert("Resource_ID__c",
        changes.toArray(new SObject[changes.size()]));
      int line = 0;
      for (UpsertResult result : results) {
        System.out.print(line + ": ");
        if (!result.isSuccess()) {
          for (com.sforce.soap.enterprise.Error e
            : result.getErrors()) {
            System.out.println(e.getStatusCode() + ": " +
              e.getMessage());
          }
        } else {
          System.out.println("success");
        }
        line++;
      }
    }
  } catch (Throwable t) {
    t.printStackTrace();
  }
}
private Contact importResource(JSONObject rec)
  throws JSONException {
  Contact result = new Contact();
  result.setResource_ID__c(Double.valueOf(
    rec.getInt("ResourceID")));
  result.setActive__c(rec.getBoolean("Active"));
  return result;
}
private static String readFileAsString(String filePath)
```

```
    throws IOException {
    StringBuffer fileData = new StringBuffer(1000);
    BufferedReader reader = new BufferedReader(
      new FileReader(filePath));
    char[] buf = new char[2048];
    int numRead = 0;
    while((numRead = reader.read(buf)) != -1) {
      fileData.append(buf, 0, numRead);
    }
    reader.close();
    return fileData.toString();
  }
  public static void main(String[] args) {
    Listing11_19 demo = new Listing11_19();
    demo.login("USERNAME", "PASSWORD", "SECURITYTOKEN");
    demo.processImportFile("import.json");
  }
}
```

Listing 11.20   **Sample JSON Input File**

```
[
  {
    "ResourceID": 100000,
    "Active": false
  },
  {
    "ResourceID": 100001,
    "Active": false
  }
]
```

Before running the program, change the Resource ID values in the file to match your contacts, and the arguments of the login method to your user credentials.

Note that the only field updated by the sample implementation is `Active__c`. As a challenge, enhance the program to support updates to additional fields of the Contact object, or related objects like User.

Summary

This chapter has provided the basics of Force.com's Streaming, Bulk, Canvas, Tooling, and Metadata APIs. Consider the following points for review as you move on to the next chapter:

- The Streaming API allows you to get extremely granular and timely notifications about your data, at the level of changes to individual fields. On the other end of the spectrum, the Bulk API is optimized to move millions of records at a time in and out of the platform.

- Canvas is a container technology for displaying your Web user interface within Force.com and providing integration of security context and other services that go well beyond what is possible with a raw IFRAME.

- With the Metadata and Tooling APIs, you can build tools that automate development tasks, such as creating and modifying database objects and code. You can also use it to back up your entire organization's configuration or replicate it to a new Force.com account.

12

Social Applications

This chapter introduces Chatter, a layer of functionality that spans all Salesforce applications and the Force.com platform. Chatter provides the means for users to communicate with each other in the context of the applications and data central to their work, privately and entirely internal to their company. It is delivered securely to their Web browsers and most mobile devices. In adopting Chatter, Salesforce customers, partners, and application developers gain the best features of consumer services such as Facebook that form a social glue that makes interacting at work a compelling, relevant, and professional experience.

Chatter is a collection of collaboration features, including user profiles, forums, polls, questions and answers, file sharing, and private messaging. This chapter focuses on the integration of the most basic Chatter features into custom applications. Brief descriptions of its sections follow:

- **Overview of the Chatter data model**—The heart of Chatter is the data model, standard objects in the Force.com database that allow any application to participate in the conversation and automate Chatter interactions. Once you have an understanding of its data model, incorporating Chatter into your Apex programs is straightforward.

- **Using Chatter in Apex**—Although the Chatter data model is available, it's the lowest-level way to access Chatter features. Chatter in Apex is a built-in library that provides Chatter features as first-class Apex classes.

- **Introduction to the Chatter REST API**—The Chatter REST API is valuable for integrating Chatter into applications residing outside of the Force.com platform. Like Chatter in Apex, it hides implementation details of Chatter that would otherwise be exposed by direct access to the data model.

- **Working with Chatter Visualforce components**—Learn how to add Chatter functionality to your custom user interfaces with minimal effort using standard Visualforce components.

- **Sample application**—Modify the Services Manager sample application to make staying in touch with resources on a project team using Chatter easy.

> **Note**
>
> The code listings in this chapter are available in a GitHub Gist at http://goo.gl/FfsbSo.

Overview of the Chatter Data Model

Chatter posts, comments, and the list of records followed in Chatter are stored in standard database objects, accessible in SOQL, SOSL, Apex code, the Web Services API, and generally anywhere you need them. With this developer-friendly approach, you can build any number of interesting Chatter-aware programs. You can automatically follow a set of records based on user actions, batch process posts and comments to identify patterns, build an alternative user interface for Chatter, and even extend Chatter outside of your organization by integrating it with external applications.

After you have a good grasp of the data model, all of these scenarios are trivial to implement on the platform. But compared with the standard platform objects such as Contacts and Accounts, Chatter has a slightly more complex data model, including objects with some distinctive qualities, summarized here:

- **Dynamic**—The objects in the Chatter schema can appear and disappear based on the Chatter configuration. For example, when Chatter is disabled in an organization, the Chatter objects are completely hidden, as if they never existed. Also, objects containing Chatter posts are dynamically created when Chatter is enabled for a custom object.

- **Relationship-rich**—The whole purpose of Chatter is to link social and business data, so Chatter objects consist primarily of foreign keys to other objects.

- **Designed for high volume**—Chatter objects usually do not allow records to be updated. Some objects can't even be queried directly and must be referenced indirectly from a parent object.

This section introduces you to the Chatter data model by exploring these four areas:

- **Chatter posts**—Learn how to query, create, and delete the three main types of Chatter posts, based on the parent record's object type.

- **Feed-tracked changes**—Feed-tracked change records are created automatically by Force. com to provide an audit trail of database activity. They can be queried but never directly created, updated, or deleted.

- **Chatter comments**—You can query, create, and delete Chatter comments, given a parent post.

- **Followed records**—Get a list of followers for a record, and follow and unfollow records by creating and deleting simple Chatter configuration records.

Chatter Posts

Chatter posts are stored using a series of relationships that follow a common pattern, illustrated in Figure 12.1. Starting from the right of the diagram, a Feed object, suffixed with the word *Feed*, contains Chatter posts. Feed objects exist for each Chatter-enabled parent object type. The parent object is on the left, and the line between them indicates that a single parent record can have zero to many posts.

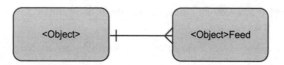

Figure 12.1   Chatter post schema pattern

> **Note**
>
> Feed objects are unusual for Force.com in that they are read-only. To insert or delete Chatter posts, you must use the generic `FeedItem` object, discussed later in this chapter.

The Feed objects appear and disappear based on the Chatter configuration. For example, if Chatter is enabled on the `Project__c` custom object, then an object named `Project__Feed` exists, the object used to store posts related to Projects. If Chatter is later disabled for `Project__c`, the `Project__Feed` object is removed from the Force.com database.

The five types of post content, indicated by the `Type` field of the Feed objects, are described here:

- **Text (`TextPost`)**—This is the default type of Chatter post. It contains plaintext, with no HTML markup or rich formatting allowed. The text is contained in the `Body` field. The sample code in this chapter focuses on the text post type because the other post types behave almost identically, differing only on the fields used to store data.

- **URL (`LinkPost`)**—The Chatter user interface allows you to attach a single URL to a post, which appears immediately below the post text. The URL value is stored in the `LinkUrl` field, with the URL label in `Title`.

- **File (`ContentPost`)**—From the Chatter user interface, you can select a file to attach to a post. The file can be a reference to another Chatter-attached file or uploaded from your local computer. The file content is base-64 encoded and placed in the `ContentData` field. Several additional file-related metadata fields are also stored with the file: `ContentFileName` and `ContentDescription` (input by the user during upload), `ContentType` (file MIME type), and `ContentSize` (file size in bytes).

- **Field change (`TrackedChange`)**—This post type is relevant only to feed-tracked changes. It is generated by Force.com itself and cannot be created by users or programs.

- **Status update (`UserStatus`)**—Chatter users can change their status from their profile page or any Chatter user interface. This action triggers Force.com to insert a status update Chatter post, with the `Body` field set to the new status.

The remainder of this subsection contains SOQL queries and Apex code snippets to demonstrate how to work with posts and their parent feed objects. They are organized into the following four scenarios:

- **Standard object feeds**—When Chatter is enabled for an organization, most standard objects have corresponding Chatter feeds.

- **Custom object feeds**—Every custom object that is Chatter-enabled by the administrator has its own feed.

- **User feeds**—Separate feeds exist for the Chatter user profile as well as the standard User object.

- **Home tab feed**—The Home tab has its own feed, called NewsFeed. This contains a collection of all the activity in followed records.

> **Caution**
>
> Understanding posts and feeds is critical because the rest of the section builds upon this knowledge.

Standard Object Feeds

When Chatter is enabled for an organization, feed objects exist for every standard object that supports Chatter. Listing 12.1 is an example of retrieving the ten most recent Chatter posts on the Contact object using the `ContactFeed` object.

Listing 12.1 **Chatter Query on Standard Object**

```
SELECT ParentId, Body, Type, CreatedBy.Name, CreatedDate
  FROM ContactFeed
  ORDER BY CreatedDate DESC LIMIT 10
```

To create a post on the `Contact` object, you need the Id of a Contact record to serve as the parent of the post. This Id becomes the `ParentId` column in `FeedItem`. Force.com takes care of determining which feeds the post belongs to based on the type of object referenced by the `ParentId`. This means you can use the same code to create posts regardless of the type of object you're posting about.

The sample code in Listing 12.2 contains a method for creating a Chatter post. Pass it the Id of a Contact record in the `recordId` argument, and the text of the post body in the `text` argument. Make a note of the return value because it is used later to remove the post.

Listing 12.2 **Creating a Chatter Post**

```
public Id post(Id recordId, String text) {
  FeedItem post = new FeedItem(ParentId = recordId, Body = text);
  insert post;
  return post.Id;
}
```

Tip

You can quickly test the method in Listing 12.2 using the Execute Anonymous feature in the Developer Console or the Force.com IDE. For example: `Id i = post([SELECT Id FROM Contact LIMIT 1].Id, 'test');`

Unlike creating posts, the code to delete posts is object-specific, not generic. It requires the specific feed object containing the post to be known. For example, if you created a post with a Contact record as the `ParentId`, delete the post from the `ContactFeed` object, as shown in Listing 12.3.

Listing 12.3   **Deleting a Chatter Post**

```
public void deleteContactPost(Id postId) {
  ContactFeed post = [ SELECT Id FROM ContactFeed
    WHERE Id = :postId ];
  delete post;
}
```

Custom Object Feeds

Chatter posts on custom objects behave identically to standard objects, with two exceptions. The naming scheme for the feed objects is slightly different, and a feed object does not exist until Chatter is enabled on the custom object. For example, if you enable Chatter on the `Project__c` object, the `Project__Feed` Chatter object becomes available.

Listing 12.4 demonstrates a query for posts on the `Project__c` object. As you can see, the columns are identical to that of the standard feed, but the FROM clause refers to the `Project__c`-specific feed object. To get any feed object's name, strip the `__c` from the end of your custom object's API name and then add the `__Feed` suffix. You can follow this pattern to access the posts of any custom object.

Listing 12.4   **Chatter Query on Custom Object**

```
SELECT ParentId, Body, Type, CreatedBy.Name, CreatedDate
  FROM Project__Feed
```

Note

The procedure for creating and deleting Chatter posts in custom objects is identical to that of standard objects.

User Feeds

Two feeds contain user-related Chatter posts:

- **UserFeed**—UserFeed contains feed-tracked changes for fields on your User object, as well as posts by other users on your profile. You cannot query another user's UserFeed unless you log in to Force.com as that user.

- **UserProfileFeed**—The UserProfileFeed is a superset of the UserFeed. It includes Chatter from other objects followed by the user, such as groups. It requires the use of the Chatter REST API to query it, described later in this chapter.

The SOQL in Listing 12.5 returns the Chatter posts for the current user, the user logged in to Force.com and executing the query.

Listing 12.5   **Chatter Query on UserFeed**

```
SELECT ParentId, Id, Type, CreatedById, CreatedDate
  FROM UserFeed
```

> **Note**
>
> The procedure for creating and deleting Chatter posts in UserFeed is identical to that of standard objects.

News Feed

If you've experimented with Chatter in the Force.com user interface, you might have noticed that the Home tab aggregates all the posts and comments you follow in one place. The Chatter appearing on the Home tab is accessible only via the Chatter REST API.

Chatter Comments

The handling of Chatter comments is slightly different from that of other Chatter data. Comment data is stored in a single, large object called `FeedComment` that cannot be queried directly. The Feed object becomes a junction object, associating Chatter posts to the subject of the post and zero or more comments. This three-way relationship is shown in Figure 12.2, with the left side the parent of the post and the right side the list of comments.

Figure 12.2   Chatter comment schema pattern

The relationship between the Feed junction object and the `FeedComment` object is called `FeedComments`. Listing 12.6 provides an example of querying it. The result is all the posts in the `Project__c` custom object feed and all of the comments for each post.

Listing 12.6   **Chatter Query for Comments**

```
SELECT ParentId, Type, CreatedById, CreatedDate, Body,
  (SELECT CommentBody, CreatedById, CreatedDate FROM FeedComments)
  FROM Project__Feed
```

To create a comment, insert a record into the `FeedComment` object. Listing 12.7 provides a sample method for doing this. To test it, you need the Id value of a record in a Feed object. For example, if you want to add a comment to an Account post, get the Id of the post to comment on from the `AccountFeed` object. This Id value is then passed into the method as the first argument, `postId`. The second argument is the text of the comment to create. Save the `postId` and the value returned by this method, as these are needed to delete the comment.

Listing 12.7   **Creating a Chatter Comment**

```
public Id comment(Id postId, String text) {
  FeedComment comment = new FeedComment(
    FeedItemId = postId, CommentBody = text);
  insert comment;
  return comment.Id;
}
```

You cannot update a FeedComment record, but you can delete it. Like with deleting posts, deleting comments is tricky because you cannot directly query the `FeedComment` object to retrieve the record to delete. If your program creates or queries FeedComment records and can keep them around in a cache, that is ideal. If this is not possible, you must query the `FeedComment` object in order to delete it.

Listing 12.8 shows a sample method for deleting a comment by querying it first via its parent post. To use it, you must pass the `FeedItemId` of the parent post in the `Project__Feed` object as the `postId`, and the Id of the FeedComment record as `commentId`, returned by the comment sample method. Although this example operates on comments in `Project__Feed` only, the same pattern can be applied to comments in all feeds.

Listing 12.8   **Deleting a Chatter Comment**

```
public void deleteComment(Id postId, Id commentId) {
  Project__Feed post = [ SELECT Id,
    (SELECT Id from FeedComments WHERE Id = :commentId)
    FROM Project__Feed WHERE Id = :postId ];
  delete post.FeedComments[0];
}
```

Feed-Tracked Changes

Feed-tracked changes provide an audit trail of modifications to a set of fields. For each record in an object that has feed-tracked changes enabled, there can be many corresponding feed-tracked change records. Each change record captures the original field value, the new field value, the field name, and the new and old currencies if multicurrency is enabled in the organization and the field is a currency type.

The change records for all objects in an organization with feed-tracked changes enabled are stored in a single object called FeedTrackedChange. The schema pattern for this object is illustrated in Figure 12.3.

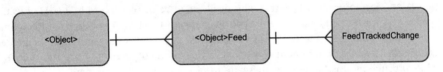

Figure 12.3   Chatter feed-tracked changes schema pattern

FeedTrackedChange cannot be queried or modified in any way by any user, even an administrator. Like Chatter comments, it must be queried indirectly via its junction object. Listing 12.9 shows an example of querying all posts on Contact records and their corresponding FeedTrackedChange records.

Listing 12.9   **Querying Chatter Feed-Tracked Changes**

```
SELECT ParentId, Type, CreatedById, CreatedDate,
   (SELECT FeedItemId, FieldName, OldValue, NewValue
    FROM FeedTrackedChanges)
   FROM ContactFeed
```

To see the query in action, enable feed-tracked changes on the Contact Phone field; then change the Phone value on a record and run the query. You should see a new record with a Type value of TrackedChange containing a nested FeedTrackedChange record. The nested record has the old and new Phone values along with the full field name, Contact.Phone. Had you changed two feed-tracked change fields within the same transaction, you would see two nested FeedTrackedChange records instead of one.

Followed Records

Users register interest in the Chatter activity of a record by clicking Follow icons in the Force.com user interface or by automatically following owned records. Users can follow other users as well as records in standard and custom objects. The information about followers is prominently displayed throughout the standard user interface, and used to email digests and notifications to users if Chatter is configured to do so.

All of this functionality hinges upon a single, simple object, called `EntitySubscription`. Its two important fields are `ParentId`, the record being followed, and `SubscriberId`, the Id of the user doing the following. For every record-to-user relationship in the organization, a unique record in `EntitySubscription` exists to express it.

With simple queries on the `EntitySubscription` object, you can retrieve a list of records followed by a user, or the users following a specific record. Less useful might be a query for the full set of following relationships in the entire organization, as shown in Listing 12.10.

Listing 12.10   **Querying Chatter Following Relationships**

```
SELECT ParentId, SubscriberId, CreatedById, CreatedDate
  FROM EntitySubscription
```

To follow a record programmatically, insert a new `ParentId` and `SubscriberId` pair into the `EntitySubscription` object. Listing 12.11 provides a sample method to do this. Test it by passing in the Id of a record to follow and the Id of a User record to follow it.

Listing 12.11   **Method for Following a Record**

```
public Id follow(Id recordId, Id userId) {
  EntitySubscription e = new EntitySubscription(
    ParentId = recordId, SubscriberId = userId);
  insert e;
  return e.Id;
}
```

For example, call it with the Id of an Account record and your user's Id value; then refresh the Account's view page to see yourself instantly listed as a follower. Make a note of the Id value returned by the method. This is used later to unfollow the record.

> **Note**
>
> Each EntitySubscription record uniquely identifies a relationship between parent record and User record, so a runtime error is thrown if a new record matches an existing record's `ParentId` and `SubscriberId`.

Unfollowing a record involves deleting the appropriate row in the `EntitySubscription` object that relates the record to the user. Listing 12.12 provides a sample method for doing just that. To use the method, pass the EntitySubscription record identifier returned by the `follow` sample method in Listing 12.11.

Listing 12.12   **Method for Unfollowing a Record**

```
public void unfollow(Id subscriptionId) {
  delete [ SELECT Id FROM EntitySubscription
    WHERE Id = :subscriptionId ];
}
```

Although this simple example can work, it's unlikely that your program would possess the unique identifier of the EntitySubscription record. You could just as easily delete records on more readily available information, such as the EntitySubscription's `ParentId` or `SubscriberId`.

Using Chatter in Apex

Although Chatter data is accessible in Apex using SOQL queries, Chatter in Apex provides a simpler solution. It consists of a series of Apex classes called `ConnectApi` that expose Chatter features in a simpler way, as an API rather than a data model. With Chatter in Apex, Chatter data is preformatted for display, and many features can be accessed with a single method call. Using the data model is typically not as easy or concise.

> **Note**
>
> For more information about Chatter in Apex, visit the online documentation at http://www.
> salesforce.com/us/developer/docs/apexcode/Content/apex_classes_connect_api.htm.

Listing 12.13 and Listing 12.14 are the Visualforce controller and page to display the current user's feed items and comments. The Chatter in Apex `getFeedItemsFromFeed` method returns the posts and comments for the current user (the `'me'` argument), and these are iterated over in the Visualforce page using nested `repeat` components.

Listing 12.13   **Visualforce Controller for Chatter Example**

```
public with sharing class MyPageController12_13 {
  public List<ConnectApi.FeedItem> getFeedItems() {
    return ConnectApi.ChatterFeeds.getFeedItemsFromFeed(null,
      ConnectApi.FeedType.Record, 'me').items;
  }
}
```

Listing 12.14   **Visualforce Page for Chatter Example**

```
<apex:page controller="MyPageController12_14">
<style>
img { margin: 4px; width: 25px; }
.actor { font-weight: bold; }
```

```
.comments { margin-left: 40px; }
</style>
<apex:repeat value="{!feedItems}" var="feedItem">
<div>
  <apex:image url="{!feedItem.photoUrl}"/>
  <span class="actor">{!feedItem.actor.name}</span>:
  <span class="text">{!feedItem.body.text}</span>
  <apex:outputPanel >
    <apex:repeat value="{!feedItem.comments.comments}"
     var="comment">
      <div class="comments">
        <apex:image url="{!comment.user.photo.smallPhotoUrl}"/>
        <span class="actor">{!comment.user.name}</span>:
        <span class="text">{!comment.body.text}</span>
      </div>
    </apex:repeat>
  </apex:outputPanel>
</div>
</apex:repeat>
</apex:page>
```

Introduction to the Chatter REST API

The Chatter REST API provides access to Chatter functionality, including feeds, users, groups, followers, and files. Being a REST API, it can be integrated in Web, mobile, and desktop applications built in any technology that is capable of making HTTP requests. It is a valuable alternative to using the Chatter data model directly, hiding the details of how Chatter data is represented and offering a high-level API instead.

> **Note**
>
> For more information about the Chatter REST API, consult the Chatter REST API Developer's Guide, found at http://www.salesforce.com/us/developer/docs/chatterapi/index.htm.

To get started with Chatter REST API, examine some examples of REST requests for common Chatter functionality. Like other REST examples in the book, the following three listings can be run from the command line. They assume you have an authorization token set in the TOKEN environment variable, and that you replace the instance na15 with your own Salesforce instance.

Listing 12.15 requests the News Feed of the current user, which is the Chatter feed found on the Home tab. To request a different user's News Feed, replace me with the user record's unique identifier.

Listing 12.15   **Sample Request for News Feed**

```
curl https://na15.salesforce.com/services/data/v28.0\
/chatter/feeds/news/me/feed-items\
 -H "Authorization: OAuth "$TOKEN -H "X-PrettyPrint:1"
```

Listing 12.16 returns a list of all of the records followed by the current user.

Listing 12.16   **Sample Request for Followed Records**

```
curl https://na15.salesforce.com/services/data/v28.0\
/chatter/users/me/following\
 -H "Authorization: OAuth "$TOKEN -H "X-PrettyPrint:1"
```

To create a simple text-type feed post, follow the sample found in Listing 12.17.

Listing 12.17   **Sample Request for Posting a Feed Item**

```
echo '{ "body" : { "messageSegments" :\
 [ { "type": "Text", "text" : "Hello world" } ] } }' |\
  curl -X POST -H 'Content-type: application/json'\
  -H "Authorization: OAuth "$TOKEN -H "X-PrettyPrint:1" -d @-\
  https://na15.salesforce.com/services/data/v28.0\
/chatter/feeds/news/me/feed-items
```

> **Tip**
>
> To adapt the command in Listing 12.17 and other listings in this chapter to run in Windows
> Command Prompt, remove the single quotation mark characters (') in the `echo` statement,
> replace the single quotation mark characters around the `Content-type` header with double
> quotation mark characters ("), remove the backslash (\) line-continuation characters and con-
> catenate the lines into a single line, and replace $TOKEN with %TOKEN%.

Working with Chatter Visualforce Components

When Chatter is enabled on an object, users viewing a record of that object see a rich user
interface to manage posts and comments, followers, and their interest in following the record.
This same native user interface functionality is also available to Visualforce developers. Using
Chatter components, you can embed the same Chatter toolbar, in its entirety or in pieces,
within your custom user interfaces.

Chatter is supported in Visualforce through eight dedicated components in the `chatter` namespace, and an additional Chatter-specific attribute on the generic `detail` component, as described here:

- **feed**—This component renders a list of Chatter posts and comments for the selected record. It also provides a text box at the top for creating new posts. The selected record is specified using the `entityId` attribute.

- **feedWithFollowers**—This component embeds the full Chatter toolbar. It includes the functionality of the `feed` component, and adds the list of followers to the right side, the Show/Hide Chatter buttons, and the Follow/Unfollow buttons.

- **feedWithFollowers**—This component embeds the full Chatter toolbar. It includes the functionality of the `feed` component, and adds the list of followers to the right side, the Show/Hide Chatter buttons, and the Follow/Unfollow buttons.

- **newsFeed**—Use this component to render the News Feed for the current user, the same feed data shown on the Home tab.

- **follow**—Including this component on a page renders a Follow button if the user is not following the record and an Unfollow button otherwise.

- **followers**—The `followers` component simply displays a list of users following the current record. Users are represented as thumbnail photos, which can be clicked to drill into their profiles.

- **showChatter**—This attribute of the `detail` component, if set to `true`, includes the full Chatter toolbar at the top of the detail page.

- **userPhotoUpload**—This component allows you to upload a photo for the current user's Chatter profile.

To try one of the Chatter components, create a new Visualforce page that uses a standard controller. Pick an object that you know has Chatter enabled. Listing 12.18 shows a custom `Project__c` page that includes the `feedWithFollowers` component, and Figure 12.4 is the result of visiting the custom page. There are no posts, comments, or followers of the `Project__c` record, but the `feedWithFollowers` component has made creating and viewing all of these items using the standard Force.com-styled user interface possible.

Listing 12.18 **Visualforce Page with Chatter Component**

```
<apex:page standardController="Project__c">
  <apex:sectionHeader title="Project"
    subtitle="{!record.Id}" />
  <apex:pageBlock title="Chatter Components">
    <chatter:feedWithFollowers entityId="{!record.Id}" />
  </apex:pageBlock>
</apex:page>
```

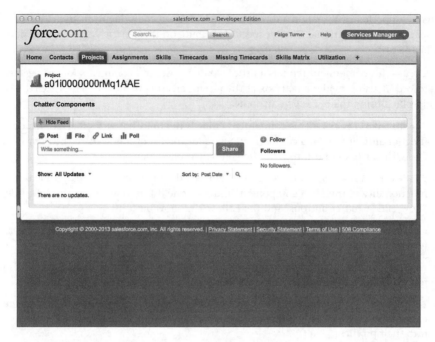

Figure 12.4   Output of Visualforce page with Chatter component

You should be aware of a few gotchas with Visualforce Chatter components as you begin using them:

- A Visualforce page cannot contain more than one of the five Chatter components at one time. If you attempt to use more than one, the page cannot be saved.

- Chatter components cannot be added to a Visualforce page unless the API version of the page is at least 20.0. If the API version is set incorrectly, an Unknown Component error will prevent the page from being saved.

- You cannot use Chatter components with Visualforce Sites. The Chatter components will be invisible to Sites users.

Sample Application: Follow Project Team

One of the initial challenges with using Chatter is building up a relevant set of records to follow. Salesforce's automatic following of owned records is a good start. But users of your Services Manager sample application would like a quick-and-easy way to follow all the resources assigned to a consulting project.

This section walks through a sample implementation of a custom button called Follow Team, added to the Project object's layout. The button launches a Visualforce page that uses the standard `Project__c` controller and a controller extension. Because the page is shown when the user clicks the button, the `action` attribute of the page invokes the custom controller code to perform the following logic immediately, without additional user action. The results of the following logic are displayed in a page message.

Following records in Chatter using Apex code involves adding records to the `EntitySubscription` object. The sample code in Listing 12.19 is the full controller extension implementation.

Listing 12.19 **Controller Extension Code**

```
public with sharing class FollowProjectControllerExtension {
  private ApexPages.StandardController controller;
  public FollowProjectControllerExtension(
    ApexPages.StandardController stdController) {
    this.controller = stdController;
  }
  public PageReference followProject() {
    Id currentUserId = UserInfo.getUserId();
    Set<Id> userIds = new Set<Id>();
    for (List<Assignment__c> assignments :
      [ SELECT Contact__r.User__c FROM Assignment__c WHERE
          Project__c = :controller.getRecord().Id ]) {
      for (Assignment__c assignment : assignments) {
        Id uid = assignment.Contact__r.User__c;
        if (currentUserId != uid && uid != null) {
          userIds.add(uid);
        }
      }
    }
    if (userIds.size() == 0) {
      error('Project has no assignments.');
      return null;
    }
    Set<String> subs = new Set<String>();
    for (List<EntitySubscription> recs :
      [ SELECT ParentId FROM EntitySubscription
        WHERE SubscriberId = :currentUserId
        AND ParentId IN :userIds ]) {
      for (EntitySubscription rec : recs) {
        subs.add(rec.ParentId);
      }
    }
    Integer followCount = 0;
    List<EntitySubscription> adds = new List<EntitySubscription>();
    for (Id userId : userIds) {
      if (!subs.contains(userId)) {
```

```
        adds.add(new EntitySubscription(
          ParentId = userId, SubscriberId = currentUserId));
        followCount++;
      }
    }
    insert adds;
    info(followCount + ' users followed');
    return null;
  }
  private static void info(String text) {
    ApexPages.Message msg = new ApexPages.Message(
      ApexPages.Severity.INFO, text);
    ApexPages.addMessage(msg);
  }
  private static void error(String text) {
    ApexPages.Message msg = new ApexPages.Message(
      ApexPages.Severity.ERROR, text);
    ApexPages.addMessage(msg);
  }
}
```

Two tricky areas of the implementation are as follows:

- Duplicate records cannot be added, so existing EntitySubscription records on the assigned users must be checked first. This is done by building a set of record identifiers that are already followed, storing them in the subs variable, and consulting them before creating a new EntitySubscription.

- Retrieving the users to follow from a project is somewhat indirect. Start with the list of Assignment records for the Project record. Each Assignment record contains a Contact that is assigned to the project. Each Contact includes a User__c field, which optionally contains a reference to a Salesforce User record. The User record identifier becomes the ParentId, the record to follow.

The Visualforce page behind the custom Follow Team button is provided in Listing 12.20. Key points in the page are the action attribute to invoke the following logic when the page is shown, and the pageMessages component to provide feedback to the user about the newly followed records, if any.

Listing 12.20 **Visualforce Page for Custom Button**

```
<apex:page standardController="Project__c"
  extensions="FollowProjectControllerExtension"
  action="{!followProject}">
  <apex:pageMessages />
</apex:page>
```

> **Caution**
>
> Invoking a controller method upon Visualforce page load is bad practice for security reasons, as it can be exploited in a Cross Site Request Forgery (CSRF) attack. Visualforce pages are normally protected from CSRF using hidden variables that prevent a hijacker from redirecting the browser to a simple URL. To protect a page like the one in Listing 12.20, you could add a token that is checked in the controller before executing the logic. For more information, examine the security-related documents available at wiki.developerforce.com/index.php/Security.

After you have created the controller extension class and the page, add a custom button on the `Project` custom object called Follow Team. Figure 12.5 shows the button configuration.

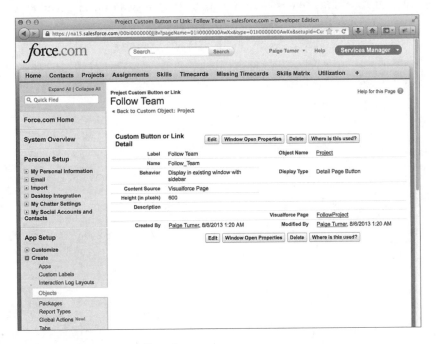

Figure 12.5   Custom button configuration

To test the new feature, add the button to the Project's page layout. Then visit a Project record that has at least one Assignment and where the Assignment has a Contact with a non-null `User__c` field. Note that if a project has assignments but none of the contacts assigned have an associated user record, you will receive the "Project has no assignments" error message. Click the Follow Team button. Refresh the current user's profile to verify that the assigned user is followed.

Summary

Chatter provides the building blocks for developers to create socially aware applications inside and outside the Force.com platform. As you review the key integration features of Chatter, consider the potential it brings to drive new applications and interactions in your organization:

- Chatter is itself a platform, consisting of a public data model, user interface components, and tight integration with the greater Force.com platform. This provides flexibility for any application to exercise and extend Chatter functionality.

- With Chatter in Apex, you can access Chatter data and metadata from your Apex code without the overhead and complexity of dealing with the raw database records. The Chatter REST API offers the same advantages but can be used with any technology.

Index

Symbols

+ (addition) operator, 110
& (AND) operator, 110
&& (AND) operator, 110
- (arithmetic negation) operator, 110
= (assignment) operator, 110
\ (backslash), UNIX line-continuation character, 309
/ (division) operator, 110
== (equality) operator, 110
=== (exact equality) operator, 110
!== (exact inequality) operator, 110
> (greater than) operator, 110
>= (greater than or equal to) operator, 110
( ) (grouping operators), 110
? : (if/then/else expression shortcut), 110
< (less than) operator, 110
<= (less than or equal to) operator, 110
! (logical negation) operator, 110
* (multiplication) operator, 110
!= (not equal to) operator, 110
| (OR) operator, 110
|| (OR) operator, 110
<< (signed shift left) operator, 110
>> (signed shift right) operator, 110
+ (string concatenation) operator, 110
- (subtraction) operator, 110
– (unary decrement) operator, 110
++ (unary increment) operator, 110
>>> (unsigned shift right) operator, 110
^ (XOR) operator, 110
4GL developer contributions, 12

A

abortJob method, 296
Accept button, 213
accessibility (fields), 78-79, 89-90
accessing data
    mobile Web applications
        actionFunction component, 270
        authentication, 269-270
        JavaScript remoting, 270
        REST API, 270
        SmartSync, 270
    REST API, 306
AccessLevel field, 163
access modifiers, 118
accounts receivable profile, 18, 86
actionFunction component, 235-236
    mobile Web application data access, 270
    Visualforce
        controller, 236
        page code, 236
actionPoller component, 237
actions, 203-204
    asynchronous
        as JavaScript events, 237-238
        as JavaScript functions, 235-236
        partial page refreshes, 234-235
        status messages, 238-240
        as timed events, 237
    container components, 205
    custom controllers, 195-197
        custom logic, invoking, 195
        trigger page navigation, 195
        view state preservation, 195
        wrapper pattern, 195-196
    expressions
        standard controllers, 192
        standard set controllers, 193
actionStatus component, 238-240
actionSupport component, 237-238, 262
addError method, 225
addFields method, 246
addInfo method, 225
addition (+) operator, 110

administrative permissions, 75
aggregate functions, 144-145
  AVG, 144
  COUNT, 144-145
  COUNT_DISTINCT, 144
  governor limits, 145
  MAX, 144
  MIN, 144
  records, grouping, 146
  SUM, 144-145
AggregateResult object, 145
aggregate SOQL queries, 144
  aggregate functions, 144-145
    AVG, 144
    COUNT, 144-145
    COUNT_DISTINCT, 144
    governor limits, 145
    MAX, 144
    MIN, 144
    records, grouping, 146
    SUM, 144-145
  grouping records, 145-146
    with aggregate functions, 146
    filtering grouped, 146
    without aggregate functions, 145-146
  grouping records with subtotals, 147-148
    debug log excerpt, 147
    GROUP BY CUBE clause, 147-148
    GROUP BY ROLLUP clause, 147
Ajax (Asynchronous JavaScript and XML)
  actions, 234
    as JavaScript events, 237-238
    as JavaScript functions, 235-236
    partial page refreshes, 234-235
    status messages, 238-240
    as timed events, 237
    Visualforce support, 234
  Proxy, 270
Amazon Web Services, 2-3
AND (&) operator, 110
AND (&&) operator, 110
AngularJS, 251-253
  controllers
    ProjectListCtrl, 253
    timecard editing, 279
    Visualforce, implementing, 252

  demonstration page, 251
  templates, 253
  timecard entry in-page navigation
    controller, 277
  tutorial Web site, 251
  Visualforce page code, 252-253
  Web site, 251
**anonymous benchmarking SOAP Web
service, 333-335**
anti-joins
  overview, 152
  restrictions, 153
Apex, 7
  AggregateResult object, 145
  aggregate SOQL queries, 144
    aggregate functions, 144-145
    grouping records, 145-146
    grouping records with subtotals,
      147-148
  arrays
    creating, 111
    initializing, 111-112
    sorting, 112
  Batch
    Batchable interface, 283-284
    batch jobs, 282, 286-289
    classes, creating, 285-286
    iterable scope, 290-292
    limitations, 292
    missing timecard class,
      developing, 298-299
    project evaluation guidelines,
      284-285
    scheduling, 293-296
    scope, 282
    stateful, 289-290
    testing, 293
    transactions, 283
  callouts, 301-302
    REST services, 302-304
    SOAP services, 305-306
  Chatter, 378-379
    Visualforce controller, 378
    Visualforce page, 378
    Web site, 378

classes
    ConnectApi, 378
    custom Apex REST services, creating,
        312-314
    custom Apex SOAP Web services
        rules, 327
        HTTP, 302-303
code deployment in Tooling API, 355
Code Developer's Guide Web site, 108
code execution
    asynchronous, 116
    conditional statements, 113
    Execute Anonymous View, 104-105
    exception statements, 114-115
    governor limits, 120
    loops, 114
    recursion, 115
collections
    clearing, 109
    cloning, 109
    emptiness, 109
    size, 109
custom Apex REST Web services,
    312-314
    Apex class rules, 312
    creating, 313
    governor limits, 312
    invoking, 313-314
custom settings, 180-181
    creating, 180
    deleting, 180
    governor limits, 180
    hierarchy type, 181
    updating, 180
    values, retrieving, 180
custom SOAP Web services, 326
    Apex class rules, compared, 327
    calling, 328
    creating records example, 328
    governor limits, 327
    invoking, 329
    limitations, 326-327
    Services Manager anonymous
        benchmarking, 333-335
database integration
    data integrity, 122
    DML statements. See DML,
        statements

objects, referencing, 121-122
    overview, 120-121
    queries. See queries
    security, 133
data types, 106
    Blob, 106
    Boolean, 106
    converting, 107-108
    Date, 106
    date to string conversions, 109
    Datetime, 106
    Decimal, 106
    Double, 106
    ID, 106
    Integer, 106
    Long, 106
    Object, 106
    String, 106
    string to date conversions, 109
    Time, 106
debugging, 133
    checkpoints, 133-135
    execution logs, 134
dynamic, 174
    instances, creating, 179
    schema metadata, 177-179
    SOQL queries, 175-176
    SOSL queries, 176
governor limits, 100, 120
    Apex code, 120
    databases, 120
    heaps, 120
    namespaces, 120
lists
    creating, 111
    initializing, 111-112
    nesting, 111
    overview, 111
    sorting, 112
managed sharing, 162
    organization-wide sharing defaults,
        changing, 163
    rules, creating, 163-167
    sharing objects, 162-163
maps, 112-113
object-oriented principles, 117
    encapsulation, 117-118
    information-hiding notation, 118

inheritance, 119
modularity, 119
polymorphism, 119
operators, 109
  AND (&&), 110
  addition (+), 110
  arithmetic negation (-), 110
  assignment (=), 110
  bitwise, 110
  division (/), 110
  equality (==), 110
  exact equality (===), 110
  exact inequality (!==), 110
  greater than (>), 110
  greater than or equal to (>=), 110
  grouping, 110
  if/then/else expression (? :), 110
  less than (<), 110
  less than or equal to (<=), 110
  logical negation (!), 110
  multiplication (*), 110
  not equal to (!=), 110
  OR (||), 110
  signed shift left (<<), 110
  signed shift right (>>), 110
  string concatenation (+), 110
  subtraction (-), 110
  unary decrement (--), 110
  unary increment (++), 110
  unsigned shift right (>>>), 110
ORM code snippet, 30
overview, 100-101
receiving email, 172-173
  class, creating, 173-174
  governor limits, 173
  personalizing based on sender
    identity, 173
  services, configuring, 174-175
  uncaught exceptions, 173
sending email, 168
  attachments, 172
  blind-carbon-copies, 171
  carbon copies, 171
  mass emails, 170-171
  notifications, 181-182
  organization-wide email address
    unique identifiers, 172
  reply-to addresses, 171

  sendEmail method, 171
  sender display names, 171
  signatures, 172
  SingleEmailMessage object, 168-169
  templates, 169-170
  tracking, 172
sets, 112
SOQL queries, 126-128
SOSL, 155-157
Test Runner View (IDE), 103
transaction processing
  DML database methods, 157-158
  record locking, 161
  savepoints, 159-160
triggers, 130-131
  batching, 132
  bulkifying, 132
  definitions, 131-132
  error handling, 132-133
  names, 131
  timecard validation, creating,
    138-139
unit tests, 136
  results, viewing, 137
  running, 137
  test data, 137
  test methods, 136
  Test Runner View, 103
  TimecardManager class, 140-141
variables, 105
  access modifiers, 118
  checkpoints, 133-135
  classes, 117
  constants, 107
  declaring, 105-106
  enums, 107
  names, 105-106
  rounding, 108

APIs
Bulk, 344
  authentication, 345-346
  exporting records, 347-349
  importing records, 346-347
  two-tier system, 345
  Web site, 345
Canvas, 349
  authentication, 349-350
  cross-domain XHR, 350

example application, 350-354
Web site, 349
Metadata, 360
object creation example, 361-363
services, 360-361
Web site, 360
REST
authentication, 306-307
Chatter, 379-380
Connected Apps, creating, 307
creating record requests, 310
data access, 306
data integration, 31
deleting record requests, 311
Force.com REST API Developer's
Guide Web site, 308
mobile Web application data
access, 270
record retrieval by external
identifiers, 310
record retrieval by unique
identifiers, 309
services available call, 308-309
SObject basic information
request, 309
SOQL query request, 310
updating record requests, 311
upserting record requests, 311
SOAP
data integration, 31
enabled permissions, 318-319
Enterprise. *See* Enterprise API
error handling, 321
Force.com data types, 321
IP white-listing, 319
limits, 316
logging in/out, 318-320
login call, 320
login problems, troubleshooting, 320
Partner, 315
security, 316
security tokens, 319
stub code, generating, 316-317
Web Service Connector (WSC), 316
WSDL versions, 315-316
Streaming
example, 341-344
PushTopcis, 340-341
Web site, 340

Tooling, 354
Apex code, deploying, 355
internal state of deployment, 355
overview, 355
query service, 355
status, refreshing, 355
user interface, 356
Visualforce controller example,
357-359
Visualforce page example, 359-360
Web site, 355
App Builder Tools, 33
App Engine, 3
AppExchange, 16
applications
AppExchange, 16
Connected Apps, creating, 351
custom, creating, 58
LDV deployments, 22
mobile
Chatter Mobile, 264
containers, 271
hybrid, 265, 267
native, 265-266
Salesforce Classic, 264
Salesforce Mobile SDK, 265
Salesforce Touch, 264
timecard entry page. *See* mobile
timecard entry page
Web. *See* mobile applications, Web
services, 6
Services Manager. *See* Services Manager
application
single-page, 250
AngularJS, 251-253
JavaScript remoting, 250
social. *See* Chatter
architectures
application services, 6
declarative metadata, 7
multilenancy, 4-6
programming languages, 7
relational databases, 6
security, 71
Visualforce, 186-187

arithmetic negation (-) operator, 110
arrays
   creating, 111
   initializing, 111-112
   sorting, 112
Assignment object
   fields, 54
   overview, 53
assignment (=) operator, 110
asynchronous actions
   as JavaScript events, 237-238
   as JavaScript functions, 235-236
   partial page refreshes, 234-235
   status messages, 238-240
      actionStatus component, 238-240
      dynamic, 239
      images/stylized messages, 239
   as timed events, 237
asynchronous code execution, 116
Asynchronous JavaScript and XML. *See* Ajax
asyncMethod, 116
attachments (email), 172
attributes
   page components, 200
   reRender, 234
   showChatter, 381
   view components, 199
authentication
   Bulk API, 345-346
   Canvas, 349-350
   mobile Web applications, 269-270
   REST APIs, 306-307
   sites users, 258
auto numbers, 40-41, 322
availability (PushTopics), 341
AVG aggregate function, 144

B

backslash (\), UNIX line-continuation
  character, 309
Batchable interface, 283-284
Batch Apex, 116
   Batchable interface, 283-284
   batch jobs, 282
      executing, 286
      execution detail, viewing, 288
      progress, monitoring, 287-288
      scope, 289

classes, creating, 285-286
   iterable scope, 290-292
   limitations, 292
   missing timecard class, developing,
     298-299
   project evaluation guidelines, 284-285
   scheduled jobs
      creating, 295
      editing, 296
      viewing, 296
   scheduling, 293-296
      Apex user interface, 294-295
      sample code, 296
      schedulable code development, 294
   scope, 282
   stateful, 289-290
   testing, 293
   transactions, 283
batch jobs, 282
   bulk export
      batches, creating, 348
      creating, 347-348
      results, retrieving, 348-349
      status, checking, 348
   bulk import
      closing, 347
      creating, 346
      records, adding, 346-347
      results, retrieving, 347
      status, checking, 347
   executing, 286
   execution detail, viewing, 288
   limitations, 292
   progress, monitoring, 287-288
   scheduled
      creating, 295
      deleting, 296
      editing, 296
   scheduling, 293-296
      Apex user interface, 294-295
      schedulable code development, 294
   scope, 289
   triggers, 132
BenchmarkWS class, 334
binary data types, 322
bitwise operators, 110
blind-carbon-copies (email), 171
blobs, 106

Boolean data type, **106**
break keyword (loops), **114**
browsing data, **42-44**
Bulk API, **344**
 authentication, 345-346
 records
  exporting, 347-349
  importing, 346-347
 two-tier system, 345
 Web site, 345
bulk jobs
 export
  batches, creating, 348
  creating, 347-348
  results, retrieving, 348-349
  status, checking, 348
 import
  closing, 347
  creating, 346
  records, adding, 346-347
  results, retrieving, 347
  status, checking, 347
bulk modifications (records), 326
business analyst contributions, 11
business units
 collaboration, testing, 97-98
 security, 85-88
buttons
 custom
  custom objects, creating, 38
  Visualforce pages, 215
 native user interface, 213
 standard, 37

C

callouts (Apex), 301-302
 REST services, 302-304
  formats, 302
  HTTP classes, 302-303
  integrating, 303-304
  invoking, 303
  testing, 304
 SOAP services, 305-306
Canvas, 349
 authentication, 349-350
 cross-domain XHR, 350

example application
 adding pages, 352
 callback HTML page, 354
 configuring pages, 352
 Connected App, creating, 351
 local Web servers, configuring, 352
 main HTML page, 353-354
 previewing, 352
 running in App Previewer, 350
 Web site, 349
carbon copies (email), 171
catch keyword (exceptions), 115
channel names, 340
Chatter
 Apex, 378-379
  Visualforce controller example, 378
  Visualforce page, 378
  Web site, 378
 comments, 374-375
  creating, 375
  deleting, 375
  query, 375
  schema pattern, 374
 feed-tracked changes, 376
 following records, 376-378
  following relationships, 377
  method, 377
  unfollowing, 377-378
 Mobile, 264
 objects
  dynamic, 370
  high-volume design, 370
  relationship-rich, 370
 posts, 370-372
  content, 371
  creating, 372-373
  custom object feeds, 373
  deleting, 373
  Feed objects, 370-371
  news feeds, 374
  schema pattern, 370
  standard object feeds, 372-373
  user feeds, 374
 REST API, 379-380
  followed records request, 380
  news feed request, 379-380
  post request, 380
  Web site, 379

Services Manager Follow Team button, 382-385
  configuring, 385
  controller extension code, 383-384
  testing, 385
  Visualforce page, 384-385
Visualforce components, 380-382
  feed, 381
  feedWithFollowers, 381
  follow, 381
  followers, 381
  limitations, 382
  newsFeed, 381
  showChatter attribute, 381
  userPhotoUpload, 381
  Visualforce page, creating, 381

checkboxes
  defined, 38
  SOAP type, mapping, 322

checkpoints, 133-135

child relationships
  child-to-parent, 125-126
  metadata, 178
  semi-joins
    child-to-child, 153
    child-to-parent, 153

classes
  access modifiers, 118
  Apex
    ConnectApi, 378
    custom Apex REST services, creating, 312-314
    custom Apex SOAP Web services rules, 327
    HTTP, 302-303
  Batch Apex, creating, 285-286
  BenchmarkWS, 334
  constructors, 118
  defining, 118
  information-hiding notation, 118
  inheritance, 119
  initializers, 118
  inner, 118
  Iterable, 291
  Iterator, 290
  methods, 117

MissingTimecardBatch
  creating, 298-299
  reset results, 300
  running, 300
MyEmailService, 173-174
properties, 117
TimecardManager
  creating, 138-139
  unit tests, 140-141
variables, 117

clear method (collections), 109
Clone button, 213
clone method (collections), 109
closing bulk import jobs, 347
cloud computing
  benefits, 2
  overview, 2
  PaaS, 2
    Amazon Web Services, 2-3
    Force.com, 3-4
    Google Cloud Platform, 3
    Windows Azure, 3

Cloudforce conference, 17
code execution (Apex)
  asynchronous, 116
  conditional statements, 113
  exception statements, 114-115
    examples, 115
    handling, 115
    raising, 115
  governor limits, 120
  loops, 114
  recursion, 115

Code Share, 16
collections
  arrays
    creating, 111
    initializing, 111
    sorting, 112
  clearing, 109
  cloning, 109
  emptiness, 109
  lists
    creating, 111
    initializing, 111
    nesting, 111
    sorting, 112

maps, 112-113
sets, 112
size, 109
ComeD library, 342
commandButton component, 203
commandLink component, 203
comments (Chatter), 374-375
    creating, 375
    deleting, 375
    query, 375
    schema pattern, 374
communication errors, 220-221
CompareSkillsComponent
    creating, 259-260
    support, adding, 261
CompareSkillsController, 260
composition (modular Visualforce
    pages), 243-244
conditional statements, 113
condition expressions, 194
configuration management, 14
configuring
    Canvas App pages, 352
    email services, 174-175
    field accessibility, 89-90
    Follow Team button, 385
    IDE, 138
    local Web servers, 352
    sharing rules, 92-93
ConnectApi classes, 378
Connected Apps, creating
    Canvas, 351
    REST API, 307
constants, 107
constructors, 118
Consultant profile
    permissions, 86
    Services Manager application, 18
    testing, 96
ContactFeed object, 372
Contact object
    CSV import file, 69
    fields, 51
    overview, 51
ContainerId field, 355

containers
    dynamicComponent elements, 248
    mobile applications, 271
    static resources, 241-242
continue keyword (loops), 114
controlled by parent records, 81
controller attribute (pages), 200
controllers, 186-187
    actionFunction component, 236
    actions
        as JavaScript events, 237-238
        timed events, 237
    AngularJS, 253
        mobile timecards, editing, 279
        project list example, 252
        timecard entry in-page
            navigation, 277
    Chatter example, 378
    custom, 193-197
        actions, 195-197
        exposing data, 193-194
    dynamic field reference, 247
    extensions, 197
    governor limits, 221
    mobile timecards
        editing, 277
        list functionality, 274
    partial page refresh, 235
    Services Manager
        business hours, configuring, 331
        Follow Team button extension code,
            383-384
        Skills Matrix, 225-227, 229-231
        utilization calculation, 332
        utilization code, 335-337
    standard, 191-193
        multiple records, 192-193
        single records, 191-192
    Streaming API example, 342
    Tooling API example, 357-359
    unit tests, 222
conversion methods, 108
converting data types, 107-108
    conversion methods, 108
    dates to strings, 109
    exceptions, 114
    implicit conversion, 107-108
    strings to dates, 109

COUNT aggregate function, **144-145**
COUNT_DISTINCT aggregate function, **144**
Create Lookup Field dialog box, **61**
Create New Object dialog box, **59**
create permission, **75**
createProject service, **329**
create service, **324**
cross-domain XHR, **350**
CRUD (create, read, update, delete)
  operations, **31**
Crypto class, **303**
CSRF (Cross Site Request Forgery)
  attacks, **385**
CSS (components), adding, **261**
CSV files
  Contact import, 69
  exporting, 64-65
  Project import, 65
cURL, **306**
currency
  fields, 38
  SOAP data type, mapping, 322
custom Apex Web services
  REST, 312-314
    Apex class rules, 312
    creating, 313
    governor limits, 312
    invoking, 313-314
  SOAP, 326
    Apex class rules, compared, 327
    calling, 328
    creating records example, 328
    governor limits, 327
    invoking, 329
    limitations, 326-327
    Services Manager anonymous
      benchmarking, 333-335
custom applications, creating, **58**
custom buttons
  custom objects, creating, 38
  Visualforce pages, 215
custom components
  creating, 259-260
  CSS, adding, 261
  defining, 244-245

Google Map example, 245-246
support, adding, 259-260
custom controllers, **193-197**
  actions, 195-197
    custom logic, invoking, 195
    trigger page navigation, 195
    view state preservation, 195
    wrapper pattern, 195-196
  exposing data, 193-194
custom fields. *See* fields, creating
custom links
  custom objects, creating, 38
  Visualforce pages, 215
custom objects, **22**
  creating, 35, 59-60
    activities, allowing, 36
    custom buttons/links, 38
    custom fields, 37
    definition, 35-36
    deployment status, 36
    descriptions, 36
    field history tracking, 36
    help settings, 36
    labels, 35
    names, 35
    page layouts, 37
    record name label, 36
    reports, allowing, 36
    search layouts, 37
    standard buttons/links, 37
    standard fields, 36
    triggers, 37
    validation rules, 37
  missing timecards, creating, 297
  tabs, creating, 63
  tools, 33-34
    App Builder Tools, 33
    data, 34
    Force.com IDE, 34
    metadata, 33
    Schema Builder, 34
custom settings, **180-181**
  defined, 47
  governor limits, 180
  hierarchy, 49, 181
  list, 48

records
    creating, 180
    deleting, 180
    updating, 180
storage limits, 49
types, 47-48
values, retrieving, 180
custom tabs, 215

D

data
batch processing. *See* Batch Apex
browsing, 42-44
entering, 41-42
exposing (custom controllers), 193-194
expressions
    standard controllers, 192
    standard set controllers, 193
importing, 64
    import process, 66
    preparations, 64-66
    verification, 67-69
integration, 29
    metadata XML, 30-31
    native user interface, 31
    object-relational mapping, 30
    REST APIs, 31
    SOAP APIs, 31
integrity, 122
mobile Web applications access, 269-270
    actionFunction component, 270
    authentication, 269-270
    JavaScript remoting, 270
    REST API, 270
    SmartSync, 270
modeler contributions, 11
relationships
    explicitly defined, 26
    integrity enforced, 26
    records, creating, 121
    Services Manager application, 55-58
    SOQL, 26-27
    SOQL versus SQL, 27-28
    SOSL, 29
    viewing, 121
REST API access, 306

security
    architecture, 71
    field accessibility, 73
    object-level. *See* object-level security
    overview, 71-74
    permission sets, 72
    profiles, 72
    record-level, 72
    sharing model, 73
    sharing reasons, 74
Services Manager application integration
    implementation strategy, 363-364
    sample implementation, 364-366
    scenario, 363
storage custom settings
    defined, 47
    governor limits, 180
    hierarchy, 49, 181
    list, 48
    records, 180
    storage limits, 49
    types, 47-48
    values, retrieving, 180
tools, 34
    Data Loader, 34
    Excel Connector, 34
    Import Wizard, 34
Database.com, 4
databases
administrator contributions, 12
Apex integration
    DML statements. *See* DML,
        statements
    integrity, 122
    objects, referencing, 121-122
    overview, 120-121
    queries. *See* queries
    security, 133
change exceptions, 114
custom settings, 47-48
    defined, 47
    hierarchy, 49
    list, 48
    storage limits, 49
    types, 47-48
data. *See* data
developer contributions, 12
fields. *See* fields

governor limits, 120
integration, 29
  logical, 13
  metadata XML, 30-31
  native user interface, 31
  object-relational mapping, 30
  REST APIs, 31
  SOAP APIs, 31
objects. *See* objects
queries. *See* queries
records. *See* records
relational, 6
relationships. *See* relationships
security
  Apex, 133
  architecture, 71
  field accessibility, 73
  object-level. *See* object-level security
  object permissions, 73
  overview, 71-74
  permission sets, 72
  profiles, 72
  record-level, 72
  sharing model, 73
  sharing reasons, 74
services, 7
tables. *See* objects
triggers, 130-131
  batching, 132
  bulkifying, 132
  custom objects, creating, 37
  definitions, 131-132
  email notifications, 181-182
  error handling, 132-133
  names, 131
  page navigation, 195
  timecard validation, creating,
    138-139
data components, 200-203
  metadata-aware, 200-201
    inputField, 201
    outputField, 201
  Mobile Components for Visualforce, 268
  primitive, 201-202
    inputCheckbox, 202
    inputFile, 202
    inputHidden, 202
    inputSecret, 202

    inputText, 202
    inputTextArea, 202
    outputLabel, 202
    selectCheckboxes, 202
    selectList, 202
    selectRadio, 202
  repeating, 201-203
dataList component, 203
Data Loader tool, 34
  data preparation, 64-66
    Contact CSV import file, 69
    exporting CSV files, 64-65
    Project CSV import file, 65
  data verification, 67-69
  importing data, 66
Data Manipulation Records. *See* DML
data model (Services Manager)
  design goals
    Developer Edition, optimization, 50
    standard objects, leveraging, 50
  implementing
    custom application, creating, 58
    custom objects, creating, 59-60
    custom object tabs, creating, 63
    field visibility, 64
    Lookup relationship, creating, 60
    Master-Detail relationships,
      creating, 60-62
    validation rules, creating, 63
  specification, 50
    assignments, 53-54
    contacts, 51
    data relationships, 55-58
    projects, 52
    skills, 53
    timecards, 53-56
dataTable component, 203
data types
  Apex, 106
    blob, 106
    Boolean, 106
    converting, 107-108
    converting dates to strings, 109
    converting strings to dates, 109
    date, 106
    datetime, 106
    decimal, 106
    double, 106

ID, 106
Integer, 106
long, 106
object, 106
string, 106
time, 106
arrays
    creating, 111
    initializing, 111-112
    sorting, 112
collections
    clearing, 109
    cloning, 109
    emptiness, 109
    size, 109
converting, 114
fields, selecting, 38
lists
    creating, 111
    initializing, 111-112
    nesting, 111
    overview, 111
    sorting, 112
maps, 112-113
rich, 25
sets, 112
SOAP types, mapping, 321
dates, 38
    converting to strings, 109
    defined, 106
    SOAP type, mapping, 322
    String conversions, 109
datetime data type
    converting to strings, 109
    defined, 106
    SimpleDateFormat pattern, 109
    SOAP type, mapping, 322
    string conversions, 109
DE accounts
    logging in, 32
    orgs, 32
    registration, 32
debugging
    Apex, 133
        checkpoints, 133-135
        execution logs, 134
    batch jobs execution details,
        viewing, 288

Visualforce
    component identifier problems, 240
    user interfaces, 216
decimals
    defined, 106
    rounding, 108
declarative metadata, 7
declaring
    future methods, 116
    variables, 105-106
delegated administration sharing reason, 82
Delete button, 213
delete permission, 76
delete service, 325
Delete statement, 130
deleting
    Chatter comments, 375
    custom setting records, 180
    PushTopics, 341
    record requests, 311
    records, 130, 325
    scheduled batch jobs, 296
dependent fields, 46
deploying mobile Web applications, 271-272
deployment status, 36
detail component, 209
Developer Console
    Apex, debugging, 133-134
    unit test results, viewing, 137
    Visualforce user interfaces, debugging,
        216-218
Developer Force Web site, 16
development
    Batch Apex schedulable code, 294
    discussion boards, 16
    environments, 32
    lifecycle, 12
        configuration management, 14
        end of life, 15
        integrated logical databases, 13
        integrated unit testing, 14-15
        interoperability, 15
        MVC pattern, 15
        native user interfaces, 14
    mobile applications
        hybrid, 265, 267
        native, 265-266
        Salesforce Mobile SDK, 265
        Web. *See* mobile applications, Web

Visualforce
  process, 188
  tools, 188-190
dialog boxes
  Create Lookup Field, 61
  Create New Object, 59
  Open Perspective, 101
dirty writes, 161
division (/) operator, 110
DML (Data Manipulation Language), 128
  database methods, 157-158
    insert example, 158
    opt_allOrNone parameter, 158
  statements
    Delete, 130
    Insert, 129
    Undelete, 130
    Update, 129
    Upsert, 129-130
DmlException exception, 114
domain names (sites), 255
double data type
  defined, 106
  rounding, 108
Do-While loops, 114
Dreamforce conference, 17
dynamic Apex, 174
  instances, creating, 179
  queries
    governor limits, 176
    SOQL, 175-176
    SOSL, 176
  schema metadata, 177
    child relationship, 178
    field, 177-178
    limits, 177
    object, 177
    picklist, 178
    record type, 179
dynamic Chatter objects, 370
dynamicComponent elements, 248
dynamic field references, 246-248
dynamic status messages, 239
dynamic Visualforce, 246
  component generation, 248-249
  dynamic field references, 246-248

E

EC2 (Elastic Compute Cloud), 2-3
editing
  mobile timecards, 277-279
  scheduled batch jobs, 296
edit page, 211
edit permission, 75
Elastic Beanstalk, 2
email
  fields, 38
  integration, 9
  receiving, 172-173
    class, creating, 173-174
    governor limits, 173
    personalizing based on sender
      identity, 173
    services, configuring, 174-175
    uncaught exceptions, 173
  sending, 168
    attachments, 172
    blind-carbon-copies, 171
    carbon copies, 171
    mass emails, 170-171
    notifications (Services Manager
      application), 181-182
    organization-wide email address
      unique identifiers, 172
    reply-to addresses, 171
    sendEmail method, 171
    sender display names, 171
    signatures, 172
    SingleEmailMessage object, 168-169
    templates, 169-170
    tracking, 172
  SOAP data type, mapping, 322
enabled permissions (SOAP API), 318-319
encapsulation, 117-118
EncodingUtil class, 303
end of life, 15
enhancedList component, 209
Enhanced Profile List Views, 74
Enhanced Profile User Interface, 74
Enterprise API
  overview, 315
  records
    bulk modifications, 326
    creating, 324-325

deleting/undeleting, 325
retrieving, 323-324
updating, 325
upserting, 325
writing, 324
EntitySubscription object, 377
enums, 107
environments, 32
equality (==) operator, 110
error handling
SOAP API, 321
triggers, 132-133
Visualforce, 220-221
communication, 220-221
uncaught exceptions, 220
errors
communication, 220-221
data type conversions, 108
events
JavaScript, 237-238
timed, 237
exact equality (===) operator, 110
exact inequality (!==) operator, 110
Excel Connector, 34
exceptions
incoming email, 173
statements, 114-115
examples, 115
handling, 115
raising, 115
uncaught, 220
EXCLUDES keyword (multi-select picklists), 154
Execute Anonymous view (IDE)
batch jobs, running, 286
missing timecard report, testing, 300
REST services integration, testing, 304
executeBatch method, 286
execute method (Batchable interface), 283
execution logs, 134
exporting
CSV files, 64-65
records, 347-349
batches, creating, 348
creating bulk export jobs, 347-348
results, retrieving, 348-349
status, checking, 348

expressions
combining, 194
condition, 194
if/then/else, 110
scheduling, 295
standard controllers
actions, 192
data, 192
navigation, 192
standard set controllers
action, 193
data, 193
filters, 193
navigation, 193
pagination, 193
extensions (controller), 197
extensions attribute (pages), 200
external IDs, 39

F

facets, 239
FeedComments relationship, 375
feed component, 381
Feed objects, 370-371
custom objects, 373
news, 374
standard objects, 372-373
users, 374
FeedTrackedChange object, 376
feed-tracked changes (Chatter), 376
feedWithFollowers component, 381
Field change Chatter posts, 371
fields, 23
accessibility, 73, 78-79, 89-90
Assignment object, 54
auto number, 41
categories, 23
checkboxes, 38
Contact object, 51
ContainerId, 355
creating, 37
default values, 39
descriptions, 39
external IDs, 39
help text, 39
labels, 39
names, 39

required, 39
types, selecting, 38
unique, 39
date/time, 38
dependent, 46
dynamic references, 246-248
email/phone/URL, 38
field sets, 247-248
fieldsToNull, 325
formula, 24-25, 41
history tracking, 25, 36
logical, 23
metadata, 177-178
multi-select picklists, 154
NotifyForFields, 341
NotifyForOperations, 341
numbers/percent/currency/
  geolocation, 38
picklists, 38
    metadata, 178
    multi-select, 154
    SOAP type, mapping, 322
Project object, 52
query results, sorting, 125
relationships. *See* relationships
RequestId, 355
rich data types, 25
roll-up summary, 41, 45
security, 77
    field accessibility, 78-79, 89-90
    profiles, 78
sharing objects, 162-163
Skill object, 54
standard, 36
text, 38
Timecard object, 56
unique identifiers, 24
validation rules, 24
visibility, 64
fieldsToNull field, 325
fields variable, 247
file-based services, 361
File Chatter posts, 371
files (CSV)
Contact import, 69
exporting, 64-65
Project import, 65

filtering
multi-select picklists, 154
records
    grouped, 146
    SOQL, 124-125
standard set controllers, 193
finally keyword (exceptions), 115
finish method (Batchable interface), 284
follow component, 381
followers component, 381
following records (Chatter), 376-378
following relationships, 377
method, 377
relationships, 377
request, 380
unfollowing, 377-378
Follow Team button, 382-385
configuring, 385
controller extension code, 383-384
testing, 385
Visualforce page, 384-385
Force.com
architecture
    application services, 6
    declarative metadata, 7
    multilenancy, 4-6
    programming languages, 7
    relational databases, 6
Database.com, 4
developers, 3
perspective, 101
Project, 103
services, 7
    business logic, 8
    database, 7
    integration, 8-9
    user interface, 8
technology integrations, 4
Force.com-styled components, 204-205
action containers, 205
notifications, 205
page structure, 205
paging, 205
samples
    controller, 206
    page, 207
table, 205

forcetk.js library, 266
For loops, 114, 127
formatting
    datetime data types, 109
    REST services, 302
    SimpleDateFormat pattern, 109
    strings for dates, 109
formulas, 24-25, 41, 322
frameworks (mobile Web applications),
    268-269
    Mobile Components for Visualforce,
        268-269
    Web MVC, 269
functions (aggregate), 144-145
    AVG, 144
    COUNT, 144-145
    COUNT_DISTINCT, 144
    governor limits, 145
    MAX, 144
    MIN, 144
    records, grouping, 146
    SUM, 144-145
future methods, 116
    declaring, 116
    limitations, 116

G

geolocation fields, 38
getCurrentUserContact method, 225
getDescribe method, 177
getInstance method, 181
getSObject method, 176
Google Cloud Platform, 3
governor limits, 120
    aggregate functions, 145
    Apex code, 120
    custom Apex Web services
        REST, 312
        SOAP, 327
    custom settings, 180
    databases, 120
    dynamic queries, 176
    Force.com Apex Code Developer's Guide
        Web site, 100
    heaps, 120
    inbound email, 173
    namespaces, 120

overview, 100
    Visualforce, 221
greater than (>) operator, 110
greater than or equal to (>=) operator, 110
GROUP BY clause (record groupings), 145
GROUP BY CUBE clause, 147-148
GROUP BY ROLLUP clause, 147
groups
    operators, 110
    records, 145-146
        with aggregate functions, 146
        filtering, 146
        subtotals, 147-148
        without aggregate functions, 145-146
    users, 80
        public, 80
        roles, 80

H

The Hammer, 6
handleInboundEmail method, 172
handling
    errors
        SOAP API, 321
        triggers, 132-133
        Visualforce, 220-221
    exceptions, 115
HAVING keyword (grouped records,
    filtering), 146
heap governor limits, 120
Hello World
    code example, 105
    Visualforce example, 189-191
help
    settings (custom objects), 36
    text, 39
hierarchy custom settings, 49, 181
high volume objects, 370
history tracking
    custom objects, 36
    fields, 25
HTTP Apex classes, 302-303
Http class, 302
HttpRequest class, 302
HttpResponse class, 302
hybrid applications, 265, 267

I

IaaS. *See* PaaS
id attribute (view components), 199
IDE
    Execute Anonymous view
        batch jobs, running, 286
        missing timecard report, testing, 300
        REST services integration, testing, 304
    installation, 101
    perspective, 101
    Project, 103
    Schema Explorer, 103
    Services Manager application
      configuration, 138
    Views
        Apex Test Runner, 103
        Execute Anonymous, 104-105
        Problems, 103
    Visualforce page editor, 189
Ideas Web site, 16
IDs
    defined, 106
    external, 39
    string conversion, 108
iframe component, 204
if/then/else expression shortcut (? :), 110
image component, 204
implicit conversions (data types), 107-108
importing
    data, 64
        import process, 66
        preparations, 64-66
        Contact CSV import file, 69
        exporting CSV files, 64-65
        Project CSV import file, 65
        verification, 67-69
    records, 346-347
        adding records to bulk import jobs,
        346-347
        closing bulk import jobs, 347
        creating bulk import jobs, 346
        results, retrieving, 347
        status, checking, 347
Import Wizard, 34
InboundEmailHandler interface, 172
inbound email. *See* receiving email
include component, 242

includeScript component, 205
INCLUDES keyword (multi-select
    picklists), 154
inclusion (modular Visualforce), 242
information-hiding notation, 118
Infrastructure as a Service. *See* PaaS
inheritance (Apex), 119
initializers, 118
inner classes, 118
inner joins, 149-150
inputCheckbox component, 202
inputField component, 201
inputFile component, 202
inputHidden component, 202
inputSecret component, 202
inputTextArea component, 202
inputText component, 202
insert database method, 158
Insert statement, 129
installing
    IDE, 101
    Mobile Components for Visualforce,
      268-269
instances, creating, 179
Integers, 106
integration, 29
    Apex callouts, 301-304
    databases in Apex, 120-121
        DML statements. *See* DML,
          statements
        integrity, 122
        objects, referencing, 121-122
        queries. *See* queries
        security, 133
    logical databases, 13
    metadata XML, 30-31
    native user interface, 31
    object-relational mapping, 30
    REST APIs, 31
    services, 8-9
    Services Manager application
        implementation strategy, 363-364
        sample implementation, 364-366
        scenario, 363
    SOAP APIs, 31
    specialist contributions, 12

Visualforce and native user interface, 209-210
custom buttons/links, 215
custom tabs, 215
page layouts, 213
standard buttons, 213
standard pages, 210-211
interfaces
Batchable, 283-284
InboundEmailHandler, 172
Schedulable, 294
Stateful, 290
interoperability, 15
IP white-listing, 319
isEmpty method, 109
@isTest, 136
iterable batch scope, 290-292
Iterable class, 291
Iterator class, 290

J

Java
createProject service, 329
create service, 324
Metadata API object creation example, 361-363
query batch sizes, setting, 324
SOQL queries, executing, 323
stub code, generating, 317
JavaScript
dynamic action status messages, 239
events, 237-238
forcetk.js library, 266
JQuery UI, 259
Object Notation (JSON), 302, 364-366
remoting, 250, 270
Skills Matrix comparison overlay, 261
Visualforce components, referencing, 240
job function security, 85-86
jobs
bulk export
batches, creating, 348
creating, 347-348
results, retrieving, 348-349
status, checking, 348

bulk import
closing, 347
creating, 346
records, adding, 346-347
results, retrieving, 347
status, checking, 347
joins
anti-joins
overview, 152
restrictions, 153
inner, 149-150
outer, 148-149
semi-joins
child-to-child, 153
child-to-parent, 153
parent-to-child, 151
restrictions, 153
jQuery UI, 259
JSON (JavaScript Object Notation), 302, 364-366

K

keywords
break, 114
catch, 115
continue, 114
EXCLUDES, 154
finally, 115
HAVING, 146
INCLUDES, 154
LIMIT, 125
throw, 115
try, 115

L

labels
custom objects, 35
fields, 39
layouts
page, 37
search, 37
LDV (Large Data Volume) deployments, 22
less than (<) operator, 110
less than or equal to (<=) operator, 110
licensing
orgs, 32
profiles, 76

lifecycles (development), 12
   configuration management, 14
   end of life, 15
   integrated logical databases, 13
   integrated unit testing, 14-15
   interoperability, 15
   MVC pattern, 15
   native user interfaces, 14
LIMIT keyword (records), 125
links
   custom
      custom objects, creating, 38
      Visualforce pages, 215
   standard, 37
listings
   actionFunction component (Visualforce)
      controllers, 236
      pages, 236
   actionPoller component, 237
   actionStatus component, 238
      with facets, 239
      JavaScript functions, 239
   actionSupport component, 237-238
   aggregate functions
      COUNT, 145
      SUM, 145
   AngularJS project list example
   (Visualforce)
      controller, 252
      page code, 252-253
   Apex ORM code snippet, 30
   arrays
      creating, 111
      initializing, 112
   Batch Apex
      class, 285
      execution scope, 289
      iterable batch example, 291
      project iterator, 291
      running batch jobs, 286
      schedulable code, 294
      scheduling example, 296
      stateful example, 289
      test, 293
   Bulk API password authentication, 345
   bulk export jobs
      creating, 348
      results, retrieving, 348-349
      status, checking, 348

bulk import jobs
   closing, 347
   creating, 346
   records, adding, 346
   results, retrieving, 347
   status, checking, 347
Canvas App
   callback HTML page, 354
   main HTML page, 353-354
Chatter
   feed-tracked changes, 376
   following records, 377
   following relationships, 377
   unfollowing records, 378
   Visualforce component page, 381
   Visualforce controller example, 378
   Visualforce page example, 378
Chatter comments
   creating, 375
   deleting, 375
   query, 375
Chatter posts
   creating, 372
   custom object query, 373
   deleting, 373
   standard object query, 372
   user feed query, 374
Chatter REST API requests
   followed records, 380
   news feed, 380
   posts, 380
class definitions, 118
commandButton component, 203
conditional statements, 113
constants, defining, 107
Contact CSV import file, 69
custom Apex REST Web services
   creating, 313
   invoking, 313
custom Apex SOAP Web services
   creating record example, 328
   invoking, 329
custom controllers
   extensions, 197
   read-only access to Project
      record, 194
   wrapper patterns, 195-196

custom settings
    creating custom setting records, 180
    deleting, 181
    updating, 180
    values, retrieving, 180
data integrity, 122
data type conversions
    conversion methods, 108
    errors, 108
    ID and string, 108
    implicit conversion, 107
    strings to dates, 109
datetime data types, formatting, 109
dynamic queries
    SOQL, 175
    SOSL, 176
Enterprise API
    creating records, 325
    query batch sizes, 324
    record retrieval SOQL query, 323
enums, defining, 107
error-severity message, 221
exception statements, 115
Force.com-styled components
    controller, 206
    page, 207
formula field example, 24-25
future method declaration, 116
Hello World, 105
include component, 242
inputField component, 201
insert DML database method, 158
instances, creating, 179
lists
    creating, 111
    initializing, 112
    nesting, 111
maps, 113
Metadata API object creation, 362-363
metadata XML example, 31
MissingTimecardBatch class
    creating, 298-299
    reset results, 300
    running, 300
mobile timecard entry page
    editing timecards, 277-279
    listing timecards controller, 274

listing timecards Visualforce
    page, 275
    navigation, AngularJS controller, 277
outputField component, 201
Project CSV import file, 65
receiving email, 173
records
    creating, 121
    deleting, 130
    inserting, 129
    locking, 161
    relationships, creating, 121
    undeleting, 130
    updating, 129
    upserting, 130
records, grouping
    with aggregate functions, 146
    debug log excerpt, 147
    filtering grouped, 146
    GROUP BY CUBE clause, 147-148
    GROUP BY ROLLUP clause, 147
    without aggregate functions, 146
recursion, 115
repeat component, 203
REST API
    authentication, 307
    creating record requests, 310
    deleting record requests, 311
    record retrieval by external
        identifiers, 310
    record retrieval by unique
        identifiers, 309
    services available call, 309
    SObject basic information
        request, 309
    SOQL query request, 310
    updating record requests, 311
    upserting record requests, 311
rounding operations, 108
savepoints, 160
schema metadata
    child relationship, 178
    field, 177
    object, 177
    picklist, 178
    record type, 179

sending email
    mass email, 171
    SingleEmailMessage object, 168
    template, 170
Services Manager application
    anonymous benchmark Web service,
        testing, 334
    email notifications, 182
    integration implementation example,
        364-366
    utilization controller, 335-337
    Utilization page code, 337-338
Services Manager Follow Team button
    controller extension code, 383
    Visualforce page, 384
Services Manager Skills Matrix
    controller, 226-227
    unit test, 229-231
    Visualforce page, 228
Services Manager Skills Matrix
  comparison overlay
    actionSupport, adding, 262
    CompareSkillsComponent, 260
    CompareSkillsController, 260
    component CSS, adding, 261
    component support, adding, 261
    JavaScript integration, 261
sets, 112
sharing rules, inserting, 167
Skill type field error condition
  formula, 63
SOAP API, logging in, 320
SOQL
    child-to-child semi-join, 153
    child-to-parent relationships, 126
    child-to-parent semi-join, 153
    filter conditions, 124
    Group Object query, 166
    inner join, 150
    multi-select picklists, 154
    outer join, 148
    parent-to-child query, 151
    parent-to-child relationships, 126
    Project Share Object query, 165
    query in Apex, 127
    query in Apex with For loop, 127
    record limits, 125
    relationship query, 28

semi-join, 152
sort fields, 125
statement, 124
SOSL
    Apex, 156
    query, 29
SQL relationship query, 27
standard controllers
    multiple records, 192
    single records, 191
Streaming API Visualforce
  controller, 342
test methods, 136
TimecardManager class
    creating, 139
    unit tests, 140-141
Tooling API example (Visualforce)
    controller, 357-359
    page, 359-360
triggers
    batching, 132
    definition, 131
validateTimecard trigger, 138
validation rule example, 24
variables
    declaring, 105
    name case insensitivity, 106
view components syntax, 199
Visualforce
    controller partial page refresh, 235
    controller unit test, 222
    dynamic components, 248-249
    dynamic field references, 247
    Hello World example, 190
    pages as templates, 243
    partial page refresh, 235
    record-level security, 219
    view components, 244, 246
Yahoo! geocoding REST service
    integrating, 303
    invoking, 303
    testing, 304
lists
  creating, 111
  custom settings, 48
  initializing, 111-112
  nesting, 111

overview, 111

pages, 211

sorting, 112

List/Set Iteration For loops, 114

listViews component, 208

local Web servers, configuring, 352

locking records, 161

logging in

DE accounts, 32

SOAP API, 318-320

enabled permissions, 318-319

IP white-listing, 327

logging out, 320

login call, 320

problems, troubleshooting, 320

security tokens, 319

logical databases integration, 13

logical negation (!) operator, 110

login method, 320

LoginResult object, 320

logs

debug, 288

execution, 134

long data type, 106

Lookup relationships

creating, 60

defined, 39

Master-Detail relationships, compared, 40

Services Manager application, 55

SOAP type, mapping, 322

loops, 114, 127

M

managed sharing (Apex), 162

organization-wide sharing defaults, changing, 163

restrictions, 163

sharing objects, 162-163

sharing rules, creating, 163-167

inserting, 167

Project object, 164

SOQL queries, 165-166

viewing, 163, 167

manual sharing reason, 82

maps, 112-113

mashups, 9

MassEmailMessage object, 170-171

mass emails, sending, 170-171

Master-Detail relationships

creating, 60-62

defined, 40

Lookup relationships, compared, 40

Services Manager application, 55-57

SOAP type, mapping, 322

MAX aggregate function, 144

messages component, 220-221

metadata

declarative, 7

schema, 177

child relationship, 178

field, 177-178

limits, 177

object, 177

picklist, 178

record type, 179

tools, 33

XML, 30-31

Metadata API, 360

object creation example, 361-363

services, 360-361

Web site, 360

metadata-aware components, 200-201

inputField, 201

outputField, 201

methods

abortJob, 296

access modifiers, 118

action, 195-197

addError, 225

addFields, 246

addInfo, 225

Apex test, 136

clear, 109

clone, 109

defined, 117

DML database, 157-158

insert example, 158

opt_allOrNone parameter, 158

execute, 283

executeBatch, 286

finish, 284

future, 116

declaring, 116

limitations, 116

getCurrentUserContact, 225
getDescribe, 177
getInstance, 181
getSObject, 176
handleInboundEmail, 172
isEmpty, 109
login, 320
nav, 277
navClass, 277
overloading, 119
query
    SOQL, 175
    SOSL, 176
rollback, 159
schedule, 295
sendEmail, 171
setBccSender, 171
setCcAddresses, 171
setDocumentAttachments, 172
setFileAttachments, 172
setOrgWideEmailAddressId, 172
setReplyTo, 171
setSaveAsActivity, 172
setSavePoint, 159
setSenderDisplayName, 171
setUseSignature, 172
size, 109
start, 283
testAsUser, 231
testNoContactForUser, 231
testNoContactSelected, 231
testNoSkills, 231
testSave, 231
testWithSkills, 231
valueOf
    date to string conversions, 109
    string to date conversions, 109
MIN aggregate function, **144**
MissingTimecardBatch class
creating, 298-299
reset results, 300
running, 300
missing timecard reports, **296-297**
missing timecards information,
    calculating, 298-299
missing timecards list custom object,
    creating, 297
testing, 299-300

mobile applications
Chatter Mobile, 264
containers, 271
hybrid, 265, 267
native, 265-266
Salesforce
    Classic, 264
    Mobile SDK, 265
    Touch, 264
timecard entry page
    editing timecards, 277-279
    in-page navigation, 276-277
    listing timecards, 273-276
    requirements, 272
    testing, 279
    viewing in Web browsers, 273
    viewing on iPhones, 273
Web, 265
    data access, 269-270
    deployment, 271-272
    frameworks, 268-269
    overview, 266
    Salesforce SDK libraries, 266
Mobile Components for Visualforce, 268-269
documentation/source code Web
    site, 269
installing, 268-269
types, 268
Mobile Design templates, 269
Mobile Packs, 269
mobile timecard entry pages
in-page navigation, 276-277
requirements, 272
testing, 279
timecards
    editing, 277-279
    listing, 273-276
viewing
    iPhones, 273
    Web browsers, 273
Model-View-Controller (MVC) pattern, 15
Modify All permission, 76
modularity (Apex), 119
modular Visualforce pages, 241
composition, 243-244
custom components, 244-246
    defining, 244-245
    Google Map example, 245-246
inclusion, 242
static resources, 241-242

monitoring batch jobs, 287-288
multilenancy, 4-6
multiplication (*) operator, 110
multi-select picklists, 154
MVC (Model-View-Controller) pattern, 15
MyEmailService class, 173-174

N

NAICS (North American Industry Classification
  System) codes, 333
names
  channel, 340
  custom objects, 35
  fields, 39
  sender display (email), 171
  sites domain names, 255
  triggers, 131
  variables, 105-106
  view components, 199
namespaces, 120
native applications, 265-266
native user interfaces
  CRUD (create, read, update, delete)
    operations, 31
  data integration, 31
  development lifecycle, 14
  new features, enabling, 41
  view components, 208-209
    detail, 209
    enhancedList, 209
    listViews, 208
    relatedList, 209
  Visualforce development tool, 189
  Visualforce integration, 209-210
    custom buttons/links, 215
    custom tabs, 215
    page layouts, 213
    standard buttons, 213
    standard pages, 210-211
navClass method, 277
navigation
  expressions
    standard controllers, 192
    standard set controllers, 193
  Mobile Components for Visualforce, 268
  mobile timecard entry page, 276-277
nav method, 277
nesting lists, 111

New button, 213
New Custom Field Wizard
  default values, 39
  descriptions, 39
  external IDs, 39
  help text, 39
  labels, 39
  names, 39
  required fields, 39
  types, selecting, 38
  unique fields, 39
New Custom Object Tab Wizard, 63
news feeds
  defined, 381
  requests, 379-380
North American Industry Classification System
  (NAICS) codes, 333
not equal to (!=) operator, 110
notifications, 205
  action status
    actionStatus component, 238-240
    dynamic, 239
    images/stylized messages, 239
  Streaming API
    PushTopics, 340-341
    Web site, 340
NotifyForFields field, 341
NotifyForOperations field, 341
NullPointerException exception, 114
number data type, 38, 322

O

OAuth, 270, 306-307
object-level security, 72, 74
  field-level security, 77
    field accessibility, 78-79
    profiles, 78
  permission sets, 76-77
  profiles, 74
    administrative permissions, 75
    Enhanced Profile List Views, 74
    Enhanced Profile User Interface, 74
    field-level security, 78
    licenses, 76
    object permissions, 75-76
    Services Manager, creating, 89-90
    Services Manager, listing, 85-86
    types, 74

object-oriented programming, 117
  analysis and design specialist
    contributions, 12
  encapsulation, 117-118
  information-hiding notation, 118
  inheritance, 119
  modularity, 119
  polymorphism, 119
Object-Relational Mapping (ORM), 30
objects, 22, 106
  AggregateResult, 145
  Assignment
    fields, 53
    overview, 53
  Chatter
    dynamic, 370
    high-volume design, 370
    relationship-rich, 370
  Contact
    CSV import file, 69
    fields, 51
    overview, 51
  ContactFeed, 372
  creating, 35, 59-60
    activities, allowing, 36
    custom buttons/links, 38
    custom fields, 37
    definition, 35-36
    deployment status, 36
    descriptions, 36
    field history tracking, 36
    help settings, 36
    labels, 35
    with Metadata API, 361-363
    names, 35
    page layouts, 37
    record name label, 36
    reports, allowing, 36
    search layouts, 37
    standard buttons/links, 37
    standard fields, 36
    triggers, 37
    validation rules, 37
  EntitySubscription, 377
  Feed, 370-371
    custom objects, 373
    news, 374
    standard objects, 372-373
    users, 374

  FeedTrackedChange, 376
  logical, 22
  LoginResult, 320
  MassEmailMessage, 170-171
  metadata, 177
  operational tasks, 22
  permissions, 73, 75-76
  Project
    CSV import file, 65
    custom object tab, creating, 63
    fields, 52
    overview, 52
    sharing rules, 164
  records
    creating, 42, 121
    relationships, creating, 121
    types, 47
  referencing in Apex, 121-122
  SaveResult, 324
  security, 218
  services, 361
  sharing, 162-163
    fields, 162-163
    restrictions, 163
  SingleEmailMessage, 168-169
  Skill
    fields, 54
    overview, 54
    validation rule, creating, 63
  SOQL relationships, 125-126
    child-to-parent, 125-126
    parent-to-child, 126
  standard, 22
  tabs, creating, 41
  Timecard
    fields, 56
    overview, 53
  undelete support, 23
  Views, 43-44
Open Perspective dialog box, 101
operations specialist contributions, 12
operators, 109
  & (AND) operator, 110
  AND (&&), 110
  addition (+), 110
  arithmetic negation (-), 110
  assignment (=), 110
  bitwise, 110

division (/), 110
equality (==), 110
exact equality (===), 110
exact inequality (!==), 110
greater than (>), 110
greater than or equal to (>=), 110
grouping, 110
if/then/else expression (? :), 110
less than (<), 110
less than or equal to (<=), 110
logical negation (!), 110
multiplication (*), 110
not equal to (!=), 110
OR (||), 110
signed shift left (<<), 110
signed shift right (>>), 110
string concatenation (+), 110
subtraction (-), 110
unary decrement (--), 110
unary increment (++), 110
unsigned shift right (>>>), 110
opt_allOrNone parameter (DML database
   methods), 158
organization-wide
   email address unique identifiers, 172
   security defaults
      overview, 80-82
      Services Manager application, 91
orgs, 32
ORM (Object-Relational Mapping), 30
OR (|) operator, 110
OR (||) operator, 110
outbound email. See sending email
outer joins, 148-149
outputField component, 201
outputLabel component, 202
outputLink component, 204
outputPanel component, 204
outputText component, 204
overloading methods, 119
overriding
   standard buttons, 213
   standard pages, 210-211
ownership (records), 79-80

P

PaaS (Platform as a Service), 2
   Amazon Web Services, 2-3
   Force.com, 3-4
   Google Cloud Platform, 3
   Windows Azure, 3
pageBlockButtons component, 228
pageBlock component, 228
pageBlockTable component, 228
pageMessages component, 220-221
pages
   adding to sites, 256-257
   Canvas App
      adding, 352
      configuring, 352
   components, 200
   layouts
      custom objects, creating, 37
      Visualforce pages, adding, 213
   security, 219
   standard native user interface
      edit, 211
      list, 211
      overriding, 211
      tab, 210
      view, 211
   structure components, 205
   view state, preserving, 195
   Visualforce, 187
      actionFunction component, 236
      adding to page layouts, 213
      adding to Salesforce Touch, 271
      AngularJS example code, 252-253
      asynchronous actions. See
         asynchronous actions
      Chatter components, 381
      Chatter example, 378
      dynamic, 246-249
      JavaScript events, 237-238
      mobile timecards, 275-276, 278
      modular, 241-246
      native user interface buttons/links
         navigation, 215
      as native user interface tabs, 215
      partial refreshes, 234-235

performance tuning, 217-218
public access. *See* sites
security, 218-220
Services Manager Follow Team
   button, 384-385
Services Manager Skills Matrix,
   228-229
Services Manager Utilization, 337-338
Services Manager Utilization page,
   creating, 330-331
standard pages, overriding, 210-211
Streaming API example, 343
timed events, 237
Tooling API example, 359-360
viewing from native user interface
   buttons, 213
viewing in Salesforce Classic, 271
pagination expressions, 193
paging components, 205
ParentId field, 162
parent-to-child relationships, 126
   queries, 151
   semi-join, 151
partial page refreshes, 234-235
Partner SOAP API, 315
percent data type, 38, 322
performance
   custom Apex SOAP Web services, 327
   Visualforce pages, tuning, 217-218
permissions
   administrative, 75
   enabled (SOAP API), 318-319
   object, 73, 75-76
   Services Manager profiles, 85-86
   sets, 72, 76-77
perspectives, 101
phone data type, 322
phone fields, 38
picklists, 38
   metadata, 178
   multi-select, 154
   SOAP type, mapping, 322
Platform as a Service. *See* PaaS
platform documentation, 16
polymorphism, 119
posts (Chatter), 370-372
   content, 371
   creating, 372-373
   deleting, 373

Feed objects, 370-371
   custom object, 373
   news, 374
   standard objects, 372-373
   user, 374
schema pattern, 370
primitive components, 204-205
primitive data components, 201-202
   inputCheckbox, 202
   inputFile, 202
   inputHidden, 202
   inputSecret, 202
   inputText, 202
   inputTextArea, 202
   outputLabel, 202
   selectCheckboxes, 202
   selectList, 202
   selectRadio, 202
private records, 81
Problems View (IDE), 103
procedural sharing reasons, 82
profiles, 74
   administrative permissions, 75
   defined, 72
   Enhanced Profile List Views, 74
   Enhanced Profile User Interface, 74
   field-level security, 78
   licenses, 76
   object permissions, 75-76
   Services Manager application, 18, 91-92
      accounts receivable, 18
      consultants, 18
      creating, 89-90
      listing, 85-86
      project managers, 18
      sales representatives, 18
      staffing coordinators, 18
      Vice President, 18
   types, 74
   user groups, 80
programming languages, 7
ProjectListCtrl controller, 253
project manager profile
   permissions, 86
   Services Manager application, 18
projects, 103
   CSV import file, 65
   custom object tab, creating, 63

development lifecycle, 12
  configuration management, 14
  end of life, 15
  integrated logical databases, 13
  integrated unit testing, 14-15
  interoperability, 15
  MVC pattern, 15
  native user interfaces, 14
  fields, 52
  overview, 52
  selecting, 10-11
  sharing rules, 164
  team selection, 11-12
  tools/resources
    AppExchange, 16
    Code Share, 16
    developer discussion boards, 16
    Developer Force Web site, 16
    Dreamforce/Cloudforce
      conferences, 17
    Ideas site, 16
    platform documentation, 16
    systems integrators, 17
    technical support, 17
  Visualforce, 188
properties, 117
public groups, 80
public read-only records, 81
public read/write records, 81
PushTopics, 340-341
  availability, 341
  components, 340-341
  deleting, 341
  limitations, 341

Q

quality assurance engineer contributions, 12
queries
  batch sizes, setting, 324
  dirty writes, 161
  exceptions, 114
  joins
    anti-joins, 152-153
    inner, 149-150
    outer, 148-149
    semi-joins. *See* semi-joins
  parent-to-child, 151
  SOQL. *See* SOQL queries

SOSL, 29
  Apex, 155-157
  dynamic, 176
  record retrieval, 324
  syntax, 155
QueryException exception, 114
query method
  SOQL, 175
  SOSL, 176
queryMore service, 323
query service, 323

R

raising exceptions, 115
RCED (read, create, edit, delete)
  operations, 31
Read permission, 75
receiving email, 172-173
  class, creating, 173-174
  governor limits, 173
  personalizing based on sender
    identity, 173
  services, configuring, 174-175
  uncaught exceptions, 173
records
  adding to bulk import jobs, 346-347
  batch processing. *See* Batch Apex
  controlled by parent option, 81
  counts, returning, 145
  creating, 42, 121
  custom setting
    creating, 180
    deleting, 180
    updating, 180
  deleting, 130
  Enterprise API
    bulk modifications, 326
    creating, 324-325
    deleting/undeleting, 325
    retrieving, 323-324
    updating, 325
    upserting, 325
    writing, 324
  exporting, 347-349
    batches, creating, 348
    creating bulk export jobs, 347-348
    results retrieving, 348-349
    status, checking, 348

feed-tracked changes (Chatter), 376
filtering, 124-125
following
    method, 377
    relationships, querying, 377
    request, 380
grouping, 145-146
    with aggregate functions, 146
    filtering grouped, 146
    without aggregate functions, 145-146
grouping with subtotals, 147-148
    debug log excerpt, 147
    GROUP BY CUBE clause, 147-148
    GROUP BY ROLLUP clause, 147
importing, 346-347
    adding records to bulk import jobs,
        346-347
    closing bulk import jobs, 347
    creating bulk import jobs, 346
    results, retrieving, 347
    status, checking, 347
inserting, 129
limits, 125
locking, 161
ownership, 79-80
private, 81
public read-only, 81
public read/write, 81
PushTopics, 340-341
    availability, 341
    components, 340-341
    deleting, 341
    limitations, 341
relationships, creating, 121
requests
    creating, 310
    deleting, 311
    updating, 311
    upserting, 311
retrieving
    external identifiers, 310
    unique identifiers, 309
security, 72, 79
    record ownership, 79-80
    user groups, 80
    Visualforce user interfaces, 219
sharing, 80-82
    organization-wide defaults,
        80-82, 163

Services Manager application, 87-88
    restrictions, 163
    sharing objects, 162-163
    sharing reasons, 82
sharing rules
    inserting, 167
    Project object, 164
    SOQL queries, 165-166
    viewing, 163, 167
type metadata, 179
types, 46-47
undeleting, 130
unfollowing, 377-378
updating, 129
upserting, 129-130
viewing, 42
recursion, 115
registration, 32
relatedList component, 209
relational databases, 6
relationship-rich Chatter objects, 370
relationships
    child metadata, 178
    comparison, 40
    creating, 39-40
    data, 25
        explicitly defined, 26
        integrity enforced, 26
        SOQL, 26-27
        SOQL versus SQL, 27-28
        SOSL, 29
        viewing, 121
    FeedComments, 375
    fields, 38
        comparison, 40
        creating, 39-40
        Lookup, 39
        Master-Detail, 40
    following, 377
    Lookup, 39
        creating, 60
        Services Manager application, 55
        SOAP type, mapping, 322
    Master-Detail, 40
        creating, 60-62
        Services Manager application, 55-57
        SOAP type, mapping, 322
    parent-to-child queries, 151
    records, creating, 121

Services Manager application, 55-58

SOQL, 125-126

  child-to-parent, 125-126

  parent-to-child, 126

  viewing, 121

repeat component, 203

repeating components, 201-203

reply-to addresses (email), 171

reports

  custom objects, allowing, 36

  missing timecard, 296-297

    missing timecards information, calculating, 298-299

    missing timecards list custom object, creating, 297

    testing, 299-300

Representational State Transfer. *See* REST

RequestId field, 355

requests

  Chatter posts, 380

  followed records, 380

  news feed, 379-380

  password authentication, 307

  records

    creating, 310

    deleting, 311

    retrieving, 309-310

    updating, 311

    upserting, 311

  services available, 308

  SObject basic information, 309

  SOQL query, 310

reRender attribute, 234

resources

  Apex Code Developer's Guide Web site, 108

  AppExchange, 16

  Code share, 16

  developer discussion boards, 16

  Developer Force Web site, 16

  Dreamforce/Cloudforce conferences, 17

  Ideas Web site, 16

  platform documentation, 16

  REST API, 308

  security Web site, 385

  systems integrators, 17

  technical support, 17

REST (Representational State Transfer), 301

API

  authentication, 306-307

  Chatter, 379-380

  Connected Apps, creating, 307

  creating record requests, 310

  data access, 306

  deleting record requests, 311

  Developer's Guide Web site, 308

  mobile Web application data access, 270

  record retrieval by external identifiers, 310

  record retrieval by unique identifiers, 309

  services available call, 308-309

  SObject basic information request, 309

  SOQL query request, 310

  updating record requests, 311

  upserting record requests, 311

custom Apex REST Web services, 312-314

  Apex class rules, 312

  creating, 313

  governor limits, 312

  invoking, 313-314

integration, 9

services, calling from Apex, 302-304

  formats, 302

  HTTP classes, 302-303

  integrating, 303-304

  invoking, 303

  testing, 304

rich data types, 25

roles. *See* profiles

rollback method, 159

roll-up summaries

  fields, 41, 45

  SOAP type, mapping, 322

rounding, 108

RowCause field, 163

rules

  Apex Web services classes

    REST, 312

    SOAP, 327

  governor limits, 120

    aggregate functions, 145

    Apex code, 120

custom Apex REST Web services, 312
custom Apex SOAP Web services, 327
custom settings, 180
databases, 120
dynamic queries, 176
Force.com Apex Code Developer's
    Guide Web site, 100
heaps, 120
inbound email, 173
namespaces, 120
overview, 100
Visualforce, 221
managed sharing, 153
    creating, 163-167
    organization-wide sharing defaults,
        changing, 163
    restrictions, 163
    sharing objects, 162-163
sharing, 82
    inserting, 167
    Services Manager application, 92-93
    viewing, 163, 167
validation
    fields, 24
    Skill object creating, 63

S

S2S (Salesforce-to-Salesforce), 9
SaaS. *See* **PaaS**
Salesforce
    Classic, 264
        implementation guide, 271
        Visualforce pages, viewing, 271
    Mobile Packs, 269
    Mobile SDK
        download Web sites, 265
        home page, 267
        libraries, 266
    Object Query Language. *See* SOQL
    Object Search Language. *See* SOSL
    Touch, 264
        mobile timecard entry page,
            testing, 279
        Visualforce pages, viewing, 271
Salesforce-to-Salesforce (S2S), 9
sales representatives profile
    permissions, 86
    Services Manager application, 18

sample application. *See* **Services Manager**
    application
savepoints, 159-160
    example, 159-160
    limitations, 159
    restoring to, 159
    setting, 159
SaveResult objects, 324
Schedulable interface, 294
schedule method, 295
scheduling Batch Apex, 293-296
    Apex user interface, 294-295
    sample code, 296
    schedulable code development, 294
    scheduled jobs
        creating, 295
        deleting, 296
        editing, 296
Schema Builder, 34
    custom objects, creating, 59-60
    Lookup relationships, creating, 60
    Master-Detail relationships,
        creating, 60-62
Schema Explorer, 103
    relationships, viewing, 121
    SOQL queries, running, 123
scope
    Batch Apex, 282
    batch jobs
        adjusting, 289
        iterable batch, 290-292
search layouts, 37
sectionHeader component, 228
Secure Coding Guideline document Web
    site, 218
security
    Apex, 133
    architecture, 71
    authentication
        Bulk API, 345-346
        Canvas, 349-350
        mobile Web applications, 269-270
        REST APIs, 306-307
        sites users, 258
    Cross Site Request Forgery attacks, 385
    custom Apex SOAP Web services, 327
    fields, 77
        accessibility, 73, 78-79, 89-90
        profiles, 78

object-level. *See* object-level security
objects, 218
overview, 71-74
permission sets, 72, 76-77
profiles, 72, 74
   administrative permissions, 75
   Enhanced Profile List Views, 74
   Enhanced Profile User Interface, 74
   field-level security, 78
   licenses, 76
   object permissions, 75-76
   Services Manager, creating, 89-90
   Services Manager, listing, 85-86
   types, 74
records, 72, 79
   record ownership, 79-80
   sharing model, 80-82
   user groups, 80
   Visualforce user interfaces, 219
resources Web site, 385
Secure Coding Guideline document Web
   site, 218
Services Manager application
   business units, 85-88
   designing, 85
   field accessibility, 89-90
   implementing, 88-89
   job functions, 85-86
   organization-wide defaults, 91
   profiles, 89-92
   sharing rules, 92-93
   Skills Matrix, 224-225
   testing, 94-98
sharing model, 73
sharing reasons, 74
sites, 255-256
SOAP API
   IP white-listing, 319
   overview, 316
   tokens, 319
Visualforce user interfaces, 218
   object-level, 218
   page-level, 219
   record-level, 219
selectCheckboxes component, 202
selectedContactId variable, 225

selecting
   field types, 38
   projects, 10-11
   teams, 11-12
selectList component, 202
selectRadio component, 202
semi-joins
   child-to-child, 153
   child-to-parent, 153
   parent-to-child, 151
   restrictions, 153
sendEmail method, 171
sender display names (email), 171
sending email, 168
   attachments, 172
   blind-carbon-copies, 171
   carbon copies, 171
   mass emails, 170-171
   notifications (Services Manager
      application), 181-182
   organization-wide email address unique
      identifiers, 172
   reply-to addresses, 171
   sendEmail method, 171
   sender display names, 171
   signatures, 172
   SingleEmailMessage object, 168-169
   templates, 169-170
   tracking, 172
services, 7
   application, 6
   business logic, 8
   create, 324
   createProject, 329
   custom Apex REST Web, 312-314
      Apex class rules, 312
      creating, 313
      governor limits, 312
      invoking, 313-314
   custom Apex SOAP Web, 326
      Apex class rules, compared, 327
      calling, 328
      creating records example, 328
      governor limits, 327
      invoking, 329
      limitations, 326-327
      Services Manager anonymous
         benchmarking, 333-335

database, 7
delete, 325
email, configuring, 174-175
integration, 8-9
Metadata API, 360-361
query, 323
queryMore, 323
REST, calling from Apex, 302-304
    formats, 302
    HTTP classes, 302-303
    integrating, 303-304
    invoking, 303
    testing, 304
SOAP, calling from Apex, 305-306
sobjects
    record retrieval by external
        identifiers, 310
    record retrieval by unique
        identifiers, 309
    SObject basic information
        request, 309
update, 325
upsert, 325
user interface, 8
Web, integration, 9
Services Manager application
anonymous benchmarking service,
    333-335
background, 17-18
business hours, configuring, 331
database integration
    implementation strategy, 363-364
    sample implementation, 364-366
    scenario, 363
data model design goals, 49-50
    Developer Edition optimization, 50
    standard objects, leveraging, 50
data model implementation
    custom application, creating, 58
    custom objects, creating, 59-60
    custom object tabs, creating, 63
    field visibility, 64
    Lookup relationship, creating, 60
    Master-Detail relationships,
        creating, 60-62
    validation rules, creating, 63
data model specification, 50
    assignments, 53-54

contacts, 51
data relationships, 55-58
projects, 52
skills, 53
timecards, 53-56
email notifications, 181-182
Follow Team button, 382-385
    configuring, 385
    controller extension code, 383-384
    testing, 385
    Visualforce page, 384-385
hours utilization calculation, 332
IDE configuration, 138
importing data, 64
    data preparation, 64-66
    import process, 66
    verification, 67-69
missing timecard report, 296-297
    missing information, calculating,
        298-299
    missing timecards list custom object,
        creating, 297
    testing, 299-300
mobile timecard entry page
    editing timecards, 277-279
    in-page navigation, 276-277
    listing timecards, 273-276
    requirements, 272
    testing, 279
    viewing in Web browsers, 273
    viewing on iPhones, 273
security
    business units, 85-88
    designing, 85
    field accessibility, 89-90
    implementing, 88-89
    job functions, 85-86
    organization-wide defaults, 91
    profiles, creating, 89-90
    roles, 91-92
    sharing rules, 92-93
    testing, 94-98
Skills Matrix
    complete list of skill types,
        creating, 224
    contacts drop-down list, creating, 224
    controller, creating, 225-227
    controller tests, 229-231
    data security, 224-225

page, creating, 224
requirements, 223
sample implementation, 223
skills list, creating, 224
Visualforce page, 228-229
Skills Matrix comparison overlay, 259-262
actionSupport, adding, 262
component CSS, adding, 261
component support, adding, 261
custom components, creating, 259-260
JavaScript integration, 261
TimecardManager class, creating, 138-139
timecard validation
trigger, creating, 138-139
unit testing, 140-141
user roles, 18
accounts receivable, 18
consultants, 18
project managers, 18
sales representatives, 18
staffing coordinators, 18
Vice President, 18
utilization
controller code, 335-337
page code, 337-338
Visualforce page, creating, 330-331
session sharing, 270
setBccSender method, 171
setCcAddresses method, 171
setDocumentAttachments method, 172
setFileAttachments method, 172
setOrgWideEmailAddressId method, 172
setReplyTo method, 171
sets, 112
setSaveAsActivity method, 172
setSavepoint method, 159
setSenderDisplayName method, 171
setUseSignature method, 172
sharing
reasons, 74
delegated administration, 82
manual, 82
procedural, 82
records, 82
sharing rules, 82

records, 73, 80-82
organization-wide defaults, 80-82, 163
procedural, 82
restrictions, 163
Services Manager application, 87-88
sharing reasons, 82
rules, 82, 92-93
inserting, 167
Services Manager application, 92-93
viewing, 163, 167
sharing objects, 162-163
fields, 162-163
restrictions, 163
showChatter attribute, 381
signatures (email), 172
signed shift left (<<) operator, 110
signed shift right (>>) operator, 110
SimpleDateFormat pattern, 109
Simple Object Access Protocol. See SOAP
SingleEmailMessage object, 168-169
single-page applications, 250
AngularJS, 251-253
controllers, 253
demonstration page, 251
templates, 253
tutorial Web site, 251
Visualforce controller, implementing, 252
Visualforce page code, 252-253
Web site, 251
JavaScript remoting, 250
sites
creating, 255
domain name, 255
enabling, 254
main page, 255
pages, adding, 256-257
security, 255-256
user authentication, 258
size
collections, 109
query batches, 324
static resources, 241
size method (collections), 109
Skill object
fields, 54
overview, 54
validation rule, creating, 63

Skills Matrix
comparison overlay, 259-262
actionSupport, adding, 262
component CSS, adding, 261
component support, adding, 261
custom component, creating,
259-260
JavaScript integration, 261
complete list of skill types, creating, 224
contacts drop-down list, creating, 224
controllers
creating, 225-227
tests, 229-231
data security, 224-225
page, creating, 224
requirements, 223
sample implementation, 223
skills list, creating, 224
Visualforce page, 228-229
SmartSync
library, 266
mobile Web applications data
access, 270
SOAP (Simple Object Access Protocol), 301
API, 31
enabled permissions, 318-319
Enterprise. *See* Enterprise API
error handling, 322
Force.com data types, 321
IP white-listing, 319
limits, 316
logging in/out, 318-320
login call, 320
login problems, troubleshooting, 320
Partner, 315
security, 316
security tokens, 319
stub code, generating, 316-317
Web Service Connector (WSC), 316
WSDL versions, 315-316
custom Apex SOAP Web services, 326
Apex class rules, compared, 327
calling, 328
creating records example, 328
governor limits, 327
invoking, 329
limitations, 326-327

Services Manager anonymous
benchmarking, 333-335
services, calling from Apex, 305-306
sobjects service
record retrieval
external identifiers, 310
unique identifiers, 309
SObject basic information request, 309
social applications. *See* **Chatter**
Software as Service. *See* **PaaS**
SOQL (Salesforce Object Query
Language), 26-27
aggregate queries, 144
aggregate functions, 144-145
grouping records, 145-146
grouping records with subtotals,
147-148
Chatter queries
comments, 375
custom object, 373
feed-tracked changes, 376
following relationships, 377
standard object, 372
user feed, 374
dirty writes, 161
joins
anti-joins, 152-153
inner, 149-150
outer, 148-149
semi-joins. *See* semi-joins
multi-select picklists, 154
queries
Apex, 126-128
child-to-parent, 125-126
dynamic, 175-176
example, 26-27
parent-to-child, 126, 151
PushTopics, 340
record retrieval, 323
record sharing, 165-166
relationships, 125-126
REST API request, 310
results, sorting, 125
Schema Explorer, 123
records
filter conditions, 124-125
limits, 125

SQL, compared, 27-28
    column list functions, 28
    governor limits, 28
    implicit joins, 27
    nested resultsets, 27-29
    statements, 124
        filter conditions, 124
        record limits, 125
        sort fields, 125
sorting
    lists/arrays, 112
    query results, 125
SOSL (Salesforce Object Search Language), 29
    Apex, 155-157
    dirty writes, 161
    queries
        dynamic, 176
        example, 29
    record retrieval, 324
    syntax, 155
        column list functions, 28
        governor limits, 28
        implicit joins, 27
        nested resultsets, 27-29
SQL versus SOQL, 27-28
Staffing Coordinator profile
    permissions, 86
    Services Manager application, 18
    testing, 96-97
standard buttons
    custom objects, creating, 37
    listing of, 213
    overriding, 213
standardController attribute, 200
standard controllers, 191-193
    multiple records, 192-193
    single records, 191-192
standard fields
    custom objects, creating, 36
    defined, 23
standard links, 37
standard objects, 22
standard pages
    edit, 211
    list, 211
    overriding, 210-211
    tab, 210
    view, 211

standard set controllers, 192-193
start method (Batchable interface), 283
stateful Batch Apex, 289-290
Stateful interface, 290
statements
    conditional, 113
    Delete, 130
    DML. *See* DML, statements
    exception, 114-115
        examples, 115
        handling, 115
        raising, 115
    Insert, 129
    loops, 114
    SOQL, 124
        filter conditions, 124
        record limits, 125
        sort fields, 125
    Undelete, 130
    Update, 129
    Upsert, 129-130
static resources, 241-242
status
    bulk export jobs, 348
    bulk import jobs, 347
    messages, displaying, 238
        dynamic, 239
        images/stylized, 239
Status update Chatter posts, 371
storage custom settings, 47-48
    defined, 47
    hierarchy, 49
    limits, 49
    list, 48
    types, 47-48
Streaming API
    example, 341-344
        CometD library, 342
        Visualforce controller, 342
        Visualforce page, 343
    PushTopics, 340-341
        availability, 341
        components, 340-341
        deleting, 341
        limitations, 341
    Web site, 340
strings
    concatenation (+) operator, 110
    converting to dates, 109

date conversions, 109
defined, 106
ID conversion, 108
structural components (Mobile Components for Visualforce), 268
stub code, generating, 316-317
stylesheet component, 205
subtraction (-) operator, 110
SUM aggregate function, 144-145
systems integrators, 17

T

table components, 205
tables. *See* objects
tabs
    creating, 41, 63, 215
    page, 210
targetObjectIds unique identifiers
    email templates, 169
    MassEmailMessage object, 170
teams, selecting, 11-12
technical support, 17
technology integrations, 4
templateIds unique identifiers, 170
templates
    AngularJS, 253
    Mobile Design, 269
    sending email, 169-170
    Visualforce pages as, 243-244
testAsUser method, 231
testing
    anonymous benchmarking Web
        service, 334
    Batch Apex, 293
    REST services integration, 304
    Services Manager application, 97-98
        Follow Team button, 385
        mobile timecard entry page, 279
    Services Manager security, 94-98
        additional users, creating, 94-95
        Consultant profile, 96
        data preparation, 95-96
        Staffing Coordinator profile, 96-97
        Vice President profile, 97
    unit tests
        Apex. *See* Apex, unit tests
        integrated, 14-15
        missing timecard report, 299-300

Skills Matrix controllers, 229-231
    TimecardManager class, 140-141
    Visualforce controllers, 222
test methods (Apex), 136
testNoContactForUser method, 231
testNoContactSelected method, 231
testNoSkills method, 231
testSave method, 231
testWithSkills method, 231
text
    Chatter posts, 371
    fields, 38
    SOAP data type, mapping, 322
Text Area data type, 322
throw keyword (exceptions), 115
time data type, 38, 106
TimecardManager class
    creating, 138-139
    unit tests, 140-141
Timecard object
    fields, 56
    overview, 53
timed events, 237
Tooling API, 354
    Apex code, deploying, 355
    internal state of deployment, 355
    overview, 355
    query service, 355
    status, refreshing, 355
    user interface, 356
    Visualforce examples
        controller, 357-359
        page, 359-360
    Web site, 355
tools
    cURL, 306
    custom objects, 33-34
        App Builder Tools, 33
        data, 34
        Force.com IDE, 34
        metadata, 33
        Schema Builder, 34
    data, 34
        Data Loader, 34
        Excel Connector, 34
        Import Wizard, 34
    Data Loader
        data preparation, 64-66
        data verification, 67-69
        importing data, 66

Schema Builder
  custom objects, creating, 59-60
  Lookup relationships, creating, 60
  Master-Detail relationships, creating, 60-62
  Visualforce development, 188-190
  Web Service Connector, 316
tracking email, **172**
transaction processing
  DML database methods, 157-158
    insert example, 158
    opt_allOrNone parameter, 158
  record locking, 161
  savepoints, 159-160
    example, 159-160
    limitations, 159
    restoring to, 159
    setting, 159
transactions
  Batch Apex, 283
  custom Apex SOAP Web services, 327
triggers, **130-131**
  batching, 132
  bulkifying, 132
  custom objects, creating, 37
  definitions, 131-132
  email notifications, 181-182
  error handling, 132-133
  names, 131
  page navigation, 195
  timecard validation, creating, 138-139
troubleshooting SOAP API login problems, **320**
try keyword (exceptions), **115**
tuning Visualforce user interfaces, **217-218**
TypeException exception, **114**

U

unary decrement (–) operator, **110**
unary increment (++) operator, **110**
uncaught exceptions, **220**
undelete service, **325**
Undelete statement, **130**
undeleting records, **130**, **325**
unfollowing records, **377-378**
unique identifiers
  email templates, 169
  fields, 24

mass emails, 170
organization-wide email addresses, 172
record retrieval, 309, 324
unit tests
  Apex, 136
    results, viewing, 137
    running, 137
    test data, 137
    test methods, 136
    Test Runner View, 103
  integrated, 14-15
  missing timecard report, 299-300
  Skills Matrix controllers, 229-231
  TimecardManager class, 140-141
  Visualforce controllers, 222
UNIX line-continuation character (\), **309**
unsigned shift right (>>>) operator, **110**
update service, **325**
Update statement, **129**
updating
  custom setting records, 180
  records, 129
    Enterprise API, 325
    requests, 311
upserting records
  Enterprise API, 325
  requests, 311
upsert service, **325**
Upsert statement, **129-130**
URLs
  Chatter posts, 371
  fields, 38
  SOAP data type, mapping, 322
user feeds (Chatter posts), **374**
user interfaces
  Apex Test Runner View, 103
  custom, creating. *See* Visualforce
  designer contributions, 12
  Enhanced Profile, 74
  jQuery, 259
  modularity, 119
  native. *See* native user interface
  services, 8
  Tooling API example, 356
UserOrGroupId field, **162**
userPhotoUpload component, **381**
users
  authentication
    Bulk API, 345-346

Canvas, 349-350

mobile Web applications, 269-270

REST APIs, 306-307

sites, 258

creating, 94-95

groups, 80

public, 80

roles, 80

permission sets, 72

profiles, 74

administrative permissions, 75

defined, 72

Enhanced Profile List Views, 74

Enhanced Profile User Interface, 74

field-level security, 78

licenses, 76

object permissions, 75-76

Services Manager, 85-86, 89-90

types, 74

roles (Services Manager application), 18, 91-92

accounts receivable, 18

consultants, 18

project managers, 18

sales representatives, 18

staffing coordinators, 18

Vice President, 18

V

validateTimecard trigger, 131

validation rules

custom objects, 37

fields, 24

Skill object, creating, 63

valueOf method

date to string conversions, 109

string to date conversions, 109

variables, 105

access modifiers, 118

checkpoints, 133-135

classes, 117

constants, 107

data types, 106

blob, 106

Boolean, 106

converting, 107-108

converting dates to strings, 109

converting strings to dates, 109

date, 106

datetime, 106

decimal, 106

double, 106

ID, 106

Integer, 106

long, 106

object, 106

string, 106

time, 106

declaring, 105-106

enums, 107

fields, 247

names, 105-106

rounding, 108

selectedContactId, 225

verifying data imports, 67-69

Vice President profile

permissions, 86

Services Manager application, 18

testing, 97

View All permission, 76

view components (Visualforce), 198

action, 203-204

attributes, 199

Chatter support, 380-382

feed, 381

feedWithFollowers, 381

follow, 381

followers, 381

limitations, 382

newsFeed, 381

userPhotoUpload, 381

component body, 199

custom, 244-246

CompareSkillsComponent, creating, 259-260

CSS, adding, 261

defining, 244-245

Google Map example, 245-246

support, adding, 261

data, 200-203

metadata-aware, 200-201

primitive, 201-202

repeating, 201-203

facets, 239

Force.com-styled, 204-205
    action containers, 205
    notifications, 205
    page structure, 205
    paging, 205
    sample controller, 206
    sample page, 207
    table, 205
identifier problems, debugging, 240
Mobile Components for Visualforce,
    268-269
    documentation/source code Web site,
        269
    installing, 268-269
    types, 268
names, 199
native user interface, 208-209
    detail, 209
    enhancedList, 209
    listViews, 208
    relatedList, 209
page, 200
primitive, 204-205
referencing from JavaScript, 240
syntax, 198-199
visibility, 200
viewing
    batch jobs execution detail, 288
    fields, 64
    mobile timecard entry pages
        iPhones, 273
        Web browsers, 273
    relationships, 121
    scheduled batch jobs, 296
    sharing rules, 163, 167
    unit test results, 137
    Visualforce pages
        native user interface buttons, 213
        Salesforce Classic, 271
        Salesforce Touch, 271
view page, 211
Views, browsing data, 43-44
    Apex Test Runner, 103
    Execute Anonymous, 104-105
    Problems, 103
view state, preserving, 195
Visualforce
    architecture, 186-187

asynchronous actions
    Ajax support, 234
    as JavaScript events, 237-238
    as JavaScript functions, 235-236
    partial page refreshes, 234-235
    status messages, 238-240
    as timed events, 237
Chatter components, 380-382
    feed, 381
    feedWithFollowers, 381
    follow, 381
    followers, 381
    limitations, 382
    newsFeed, 381
    userPhotoUpload, 381
controllers, 186-187
    actionFunction component, 236
    AngularJS project list example, 252
    Chatter example, 378
    custom, 193-197
    dynamic field reference, 247
    editing mobile timecards, 277
    extensions, 197
    governor limits, 221
    mobile timecard list
        functionality, 274
    partial page refresh, 235
    Services Manager Follow Team
        button extension code, 383-384
    Services Manager Skills Matrix,
        225-227, 229-231
    standard, 191-193
    Streaming API example, 342
    unit tests, 222
debugging, 216
development
    process, 188
    tools, 188-190
dynamic, 246
    component generation, 248-249
    dynamic field references, 246-248
error handling, 220-221
    communication, 220-221
    uncaught exceptions, 220
Hello World example, 189-191
Mobile Components, 268-269
    documentation/source code Web
        site, 269

installing, 268-269
types, 268
modular, 241
    composition, 243-244
    custom components, 244-246
    inclusion, 242
    static resources, 241-242
native user interface integration,
    209-210
    custom buttons/links, 215
    custom tabs, 215
    page layouts, 213
    standard buttons, 213
    standard pages, 210-211
overview, 186
pages, 187
    actionFunction component, 236
    adding to page layouts, 213
    adding to Salesforce Touch, 271
    AngularJS example code, 252-253
    Chatter components, 381
    Chatter example, 378
    dynamic, 246-249
    JavaScript events, 237-238
    mobile timecards, 275-276, 278
    native user interface buttons/links
        navigation, 215
    as native user interface tabs, 215
    performance tuning, 217-218
    security, 218-220
    Services Manager Follow Team
        button, 384-385
    Services Manager Skills Matrix,
        228-229
    Services Manager Utilization, 337-338
    Services Manager Utilization page,
        creating, 330-331
    standard pages, overriding, 210-211
    Streaming API example, 343
    timed events, 237
    Tooling API example, 359-360
    viewing from native user interface
        buttons, 213
    viewing in Salesforce Classic, 271
performance, tuning, 217-218
public access. *See* sites

security, 218
    object-level, 218
    page-level, 219
    record-level, 219
Services Manager application
    business hours, configuring, 331
    hours utilization calculation, 332
    utilization controller code, 335-337
    Utilization page, 330-331, 337-338
Streaming API page, 343
Tooling API example
    controller, 357-359
    page, 359-360
view components, 198
    action, 203-204
    attributes, 199
    component body, 199
    custom. *See* custom components
    data, 200-203
    facets, 239
    Force.com-styled, 205-208
    identifier problems, debugging, 240
    names, 199
    native user interface, 208-209
    page, 200
    primitive, 204-205
    referencing from JavaScript, 240
    syntax, 198-199
    visibility, 200

W

web developer contributions, 12
Web development frameworks, 268-269
    Mobile Components for Visualforce,
        268-269
        documentation/source code Web
            site, 269
        installing, 268-269
        types, 268
    Web MVC, 269
Web servers, configuring, 352
Web services
    Connector (WSC), 316
    Description Language. *See* WSDL
    integration, 9

Web sites
AJAX Proxy, 270
AngularJS, 251
anonymous benchmark WSDL, 333
Apex Code Developer's Guide, 100, 108
AppExchange, 16
Bulk API, 345
Canvas, 349
Chatter
   Apex, 378
   REST API, 379
Code Share, 16
CometD library, 342
cURL, 306
Data Loader Mac OS X version, 34
DE account registration, 32
developer discussion boards, 16
Developer Force, 16
Dreamforce/Cloudforce conferences, 17
Excel Connector, 34
expressions, scheduling, 295
Force.com IDE, 34
Ideas, 16
IDE installation, 101
jQuery UI, 259
Large Data Volume (LDV)
  deployments, 22
Metadata API, 360
Mobile Components for Visualforce, 269
Mobile Packs, 269
multilenancy whitepaper, 5
NAICS codes, 333
OAuth, 307
REST API Developer's Guide, 308
Salesforce
  Classic implementation guide, 271
  Mobile SDK, 265, 267
Secure Coding Guideline document, 218
security resources, 385
SimpleDateFormat pattern, 109
SOAP Partner API, 315
Streaming API, 340
systems integrators, 17
Tooling API, 355
Visualforce pages, performance
  tuning, 218
Web Service Connector, 316
Yahoo! geocoding REST service, 303

whatIds unique identifiers
email templates, 169
MassEmailMessage object, 170
While loops, 114
Windows Azure, 3
wizards
Import, 34
New Custom Field
  default values, 39
  descriptions, 39
  external IDs, 39
  help text, 39
  labels, 39
  names, 39
  required fields, 39
  types, selecting, 38
  unique fields, 39
New Custom Object Tab, 63
wrapper patterns, 195-196
write locks, 161
WSC (Web Service Connector), 316
WSDL (Web Services Description Language)
Services Manager anonymous
  benchmark, 333
stub code, generating, 316-317
versions, 315-316

X

XML metadata, 30-31
XOR (^) operator, 110

Y

Yahoo! geocoding REST service
integrating, 303
invoking, 303
testing, 304

Third Edition

Jason Ouellette

Development with the Force.com Platform

Building Business Applications in the Cloud

Developer's Library

FREE
Online Edition

Safari
Books Online

Your purchase of ***Development with the Force.com Platform*** includes access to a free online edition for 45 days through the **Safari Books Online** subscription service. Nearly every Addison-Wesley Professional book is available online through **Safari Books Online**, along with over thousands of books and videos from publishers such as Cisco Press, Exam Cram, IBM Press, O'Reilly Media, Prentice Hall, Que, Sams, and VMware Press.

Safari Books Online is a digital library providing searchable, on-demand access to thousands of technology, digital media, and professional development books and videos from leading publishers. With one monthly or yearly subscription price, you get unlimited access to learning tools and information on topics including mobile app and software development, tips and tricks on using your favorite gadgets, networking, project management, graphic design, and much more.

Activate your FREE Online Edition at
informit.com/safarifree

STEP 1: Enter the coupon code: LYUVHFH.

STEP 2: New Safari users, complete the brief registration form.
Safari subscribers, just log in.

If you have difficulty registering on Safari or accessing the online edition,
please e-mail customer-service@safaribooksonline.com